PRAISE FOR WILLIAM KUHN'S

Reading Jackie

"William Kuhn reveals the Jackie I knew as a person and professional: serious, smart, intuitive about ideas and aesthetics, but also down to earth in the sense of understanding the potential audience for a book. In *Reading Jackie* I learned so much about her I didn't know, and Kuhn tells the story with such flowing grace of phrase and structure. A splendid work."
— Bill Moyers

"Unexpectedly and intelligently dishy. . . . Quite a fascinating portrait of a complex woman, who had the interests and enthusiasms of her class and was allowed to indulge those passions with singular force and focus."   —*The Boston Globe*

"It is enlightening to see [Jackie] not simply as the stylish wife of two powerful men, but also as a career woman who oversaw the publication of close to 100 books in her two decades at Viking and Doubleday, and to know she was greatly admired by both her peers and the authors she edited."
— *The Star-Ledger* (Newark)

"Absorbing. . . . Fascinating. . . . A treat for bibliophiles and Jackiephiles—and especially for those whom those interests overlap."   —*Richmond Times-Dispatch*

"Enlightening and surprising. . . . Impeccably researched. . . . Provides insights that would never have been available to outsiders."   —*Buffalo News*

"What's clear from [*Reading Jackie*] is that Jackie was a remarkably perceptive and sensitive editor with a regard for writing and a sense of what makes writing good—far more than just a socialite in an office with a drop-dead Rolodex."
                                          —*Los Angeles Times*

"Embedded in the book is a fascinating look at the vanities of New York publishing in the late twentieth century: how books got acquired, edited, and sold; how the tastes of a few individuals shaped reading habits of the masses."
                                          —*San Francisco Chronicle*

"*Reading Jackie* illuminates a literary life. . . . The portrait that emerges is of a highly cultured, witty woman who loved ballet, art and history and developed a deep knowledge of many topics."   —*Fort Worth Star-Telegram*

"[Kuhn] makes the compelling argument that Onassis was much more intellectual and thoughtful than many portrayals in the media suggested."   —*Town and Country*

WILLIAM KUHN

Reading Jackie

William Kuhn is a biographer and historian. He is the author of three previous books, including, most recently, a controversial biography, *The Politics of Pleasure: A Portrait of Benjamin Disraeli*. His *Henry and Mary Ponsonby: Life at the Court of Queen Victoria* was a BBC Radio Four Book of the Week, read by actor Geoffrey Palmer.

www.williamkuhn.com

Reading Jackie

ALSO BY WILLIAM KUHN

Democratic Royalism:
The Transformation of the British
Monarchy, 1861–1914

Henry and Mary Ponsonby:
Life at the Court of Queen Victoria

The Politics of Pleasure:
A Portrait of Benjamin Disraeli

Reading Jackie

HER AUTOBIOGRAPHY IN BOOKS

William Kuhn

ANCHOR BOOKS

A DIVISION OF RANDOM HOUSE, INC.

NEW YORK

FIRST ANCHOR BOOKS EDITION, NOVEMBER 2011

Copyright © 2010 by William Kuhn

Grateful acknowledgment is made to the following for
permission to reprint previously published material:

Estate of C.P. Cavafy: Excerpt from "Ithaka" by C.P. Cavafy, copyright © by C.P. Cavafy.
Reprinted by permission of the Estate of C.P. Cavafy
c/o Rogers, Coleridge & White Ltd., 20 Powis Mews, London W11 1JN.

The Groton School: Excerpt from "Growing Up with Jackie, My Memories 1941–1953"
by Hugh D. Auchincloss III (*Groton School Quarterly*, vol. LX, no. 2, May 1998).
Reprinted by permission of The Groton School.

Ms. Magazine: Excerpt from "On Jacqueline Kennedy Onassis" by Gloria Steinem
(*Ms.*, March 1979). Reprinted by permission of *Ms.* Magazine.

The Library of Congress has cataloged the Nan A. Talese / Doubleday edition as follows:
Kuhn, William M.
Reading Jackie : her autobiography in books / William Kuhn. — 1st ed.
p. cm.
1. Onassis, Jacqueline Kennedy, 1929–1994. 2. Book editors—United States—Biography.
3. Editors—United States—Biography. 4. Presidents' spouses—United States—
Biography.
I. Title.
PN149.9.O53K84 2010
070.5'09492—dc22
[B] 2010032689

Anchor ISBN: 978-0-307-74465-4

Author photograph © Gregory L. Gaymont
Book design by Robert Bull
Frontispiece image © Paul Adao/New York News Services

www.anchorbooks.com

Printed in the United States of America
10 9 8 7 6 5 4 3 2 1

for Emma Riva

and

for Maria Carrig

Contents

Author's Note

I considered calling her Mrs. Kennedy or Mrs. Onassis, the names she might have preferred herself. I also wanted to avoid the inequality of the old convention whereby women were called by their first names and men by their last names. However, as this book explores what she did on her own, after both her husbands died, it didn't seem quite right to refer to her by their names. Although aware of its limitations and of an implication of familiarity I don't intend, I've called her Jackie, not only for clarity but because it's the way most people know her, because it's simpler, and because it's the way we speak now.

Reading Jackie

prologue

In the end the diagnosis came as something of a relief. She had been feeling unwell for so long and didn't know what it was. She had had flu symptoms ever since the previous summer, when she and her companion Maurice Tempelsman had traveled in southern France. They went not to the beaches and shops along the Riviera where everyone imagined she liked to go, but along the Rhône, to the Roman towns at Arles and Avignon. She wrote a postcard to one of her authors, Peter Sís, saying she'd been to Roussillon, where they made a famous paint out of local clay and ochre-colored pigment. Sís was also a painter and an illustrator, and she loved talking to him about art. She didn't tell him that she hadn't felt quite right. She expected all that to clear up. Then, during the fall, when she didn't improve, and in the Caribbean around Christmas, when she was worse, she knew she needed some help. When the doctors told her in January 1994 that she had non-Hodgkin's lymphoma, it wasn't the end of the world. Yes, it was cancer. But they thought they'd found it early enough to treat it and make her well. At least she knew what she was dealing with. She could read about it in a book. The doctors recommended chemotherapy, and even that wasn't too bad. She told Arthur Schlesinger, once Jack Kennedy's special assistant, now a distinguished historian and her old friend, that she could take a book along and read as the drugs dripped into her arm. The woman who had taught a nation what it was like to have courage had an instinct not to overdramatize things, to play it low-key, to stay upbeat. She lost her hair. Well, she would wear a wig. She sometimes didn't feel like going into her office at Doubleday. Well, she could telephone her authors from home.

In the spring of 1994, Steve Rubin, the head of Doubleday, called in Jackie, who was now a senior editor, to say that he'd give her a sabbatical until she felt better. She saw her old friend Nancy Tuckerman and asked her, "Nancy, what's a sabbatical?" The two women had known each other since fifth grade at the Chapin School in New York. They'd also been roommates at Miss Porter's School in Farmington, Connecticut. Tuckerman had served as White House social secretary and worked for Aristotle Onassis at Olympic Airways, where she helped to found the first New York City Marathon with the airline's sponsorship, and now her office was right next to Jackie's at Doubleday. Tuckerman was used to Jackie's innocent way of asking a question in order to raise a laugh. She had seen her do this to the teachers at school and be sent to the principal's office. So now, faced with the question "What's a sabbatical?" she replied, "Jackie, I've worked partly for you for years, and you've never given *me* a sabbatical, so how should I know what a sabbatical is?"

There were scenes at the hospital. Jackie suffered from side effects of the chemotherapy. She had to go back to New York Hospital–Cornell Medical Center, where she was being treated for an ulcer. There they discovered that the cancer had spread and more invasive methods of administering chemotherapy had to be tried. During one of her hospital stays, former president Nixon, now living in retirement part of the year in New Jersey, had a stroke and was sent to the same hospital. Tuckerman, as Jackie's spokesperson, fielded calls from the press. A young voice from a tabloid called to ask, "Could Mrs. Onassis and President Nixon be photographed together?" The suggestion that two seriously ill people should be wheeled into a common room for a photo op was grotesque, and also a little funny. Jackie had never been able to stand Dick Nixon, and once when he called her because he wanted her permission to publish a photograph of them together in his memoirs, she refused to return his phone calls until one day, by mistake, she picked up the phone and there he was. "Hel-*lo,* President Nixon . . ."

As Jackie's condition worsened, the press grew more impatient for news. Jackie's attitude to reporters had always been that they should be told as little as possible. As far back as the White House, her formula had been to give them minimum information with maximum politeness. Tuckerman knew that Jackie wouldn't want them to know that her illness was developing complications and becoming more serious, so her press bulletins remained opaque and featureless. This irritated the head of the hospital. He didn't want Jacqueline Onassis dying in his hospital to the surprise of the whole world. So he called Tuckerman in to upbraid her. Why, the hospital head asked her, was she telling the press that Jackie was doing "as well as can be expected" when she knew, in fact, that Jackie was dying?

Nancy Tuckerman defended herself as best she could. She was also under pressure from Jackie's family to divulge as little as possible about her health. Caroline and John had had trouble getting through the front doors of the hospital because of the gathered reporters and photographers. The family didn't want to encourage more crowds or speculation. Tuckerman fell back on the only human defense she could think of before the big man across the desk from her: "She's my friend. And I'm not going to say she's dying when I have not been told so."

Shortly afterward Jackie's cancer spread to areas of her body where it refused to respond to chemotherapy. The doctors had to tell her that there was nothing more they could do.

Maurice Tempelsman was called aside to speak with one of the oncologists. Tuckerman was left alone standing by Jackie's hospital bed.

"What's going to happen, Nancy?" Jackie asked her.

"You're going home, Jackie."

. . .

In her last days Jackie had enough energy to do a short walk through Central Park on Tempelsman's arm, placidly and unconcernedly allowing photographers to snap her picture while she was wearing a headscarf and a trench coat in the May sunshine. After a while she went to bed. Some of her friends recall reading to her from three of her favorite books: the Danish writer Isak Dinesen's *Out of Africa;* the French novelist and memoirist Colette's *Chéri,* whose hero was an effeminate man wearing pearls with his silk pajamas; and Jean Rhys's famous *Wide Sargasso Sea,* about an heiress who loved, in spite of herself, a domineering, unsuitable man. As Jackie grew weaker, however, she grew less able to resist the take-over Kennedys' coming in and taking over. She'd learned to keep her distance from that family. She intended to be buried in Arlington Cemetery next to JFK, but his surviving brother and sisters had never been her best friends. They were brash, overbearing, and abrasive, everything she wasn't. One of Jackie's close friends remembered cutting short a journey to Italy and flying back to be at her bedside. As Jackie slipped into a coma, one of the Kennedy sisters posted herself in the bedroom to be a kind of public address system for Jackie's intimates, who were slipping in to kneel by the bed. "As her friends visited her, whispering their last goodbyes, pressing religious medals into her hands, the sister narrated in a loud voice: '_____ says she loves you, Jackie!' " Jackie had a bright scarf tied around her head. Her eyes were closed and her hands were calmly folded in front of her. In the last moments when she had consciousness and energy to think about it, she might well have laughed to herself at Jack's clueless sister hitting exactly the wrong note.

Her son, John F. Kennedy, Jr., on the other hand, spoke lines that she certainly would have loved had she been there to hear them. When he came downstairs at 1040 Fifth Avenue to tell the assembled reporters that his mother's life had ended the previous evening, on May 19, 1994, the one unusual thing, the most *personal* thing, he mentioned was his mother's books. She was "surrounded," John told the crowd, "by her friends and her family and her books and the people and the things that she loved. She did it in her own way and on her own terms, and we all feel lucky for that." A few days later, in his eulogy at her memorial service, he said that one of his mother's essential characteristics had been "her love of words." If who we are finally is the record of whom and what and how we have loved, then John managed to strike exactly the right note, because it is those twin loves—of books and of words—that help to define who his mother was.

.   .   .

Jacqueline Bouvier Kennedy Onassis was one of the most private women in the world, yet when she went to work as an editor in the last two decades of her life, she revealed herself as she did nowhere else. In the books she selected for publication she built on a lifetime of spending time by herself as a reader and left a record of the growth of her mind. Her books tell us what she cared about, whom she believed in, and what ideas she wished to endorse in print. Her books are the autobiography she never wrote. Not only do the books show what interested her when she worked first at Viking and then at Doubleday, they also recall the themes and events of her entire life. "I drop everything for a book on ballet," she had written when she was barely out of her teens. In her thirties she asked choreographers such as George Balanchine and dancers such as Rudolf Nureyev to the White House. As an editor she brought out a book of recollections by Balanchine's friends, commissioned autobiographies from dancers Martha Graham and Judith Jamison, and asked Nureyev to write an introduction to fairy tales by Alexander Pushkin. A biography of Fred Astaire and Michael Jackson's *Moonwalk* were both on her list. The woman who riveted a nation with her poise at her husband's funeral showed in her final decades that the question of how to move elegantly through space was something she had dwelled on for a lifetime. She edited nearly a hundred books in a publishing career of almost twenty years. What these books show is that Jackie's journey, which might seem a record of interrupted marriages, child rearing in different locations, and constant travel, actually had an enviable coherence. To read her books, and to learn the story of how she helped them to publication, is to travel with her on that road, to revisit the memories that meant the most to her, to see what made her tick, to find out where she wanted to go next, and to learn what she wanted to leave behind.

The Jackie we think we know is linked to the men she married. She was the woman in Oleg Cassini suits who was JFK's wife. Or she was his widow, the woman who launched the idea of Camelot as the way he and his White House ought to be remembered. Or she was the woman who married a Greek billionaire, who went on spending sprees at his expense, who suffered from his humiliations when he was alive and from his attempt to shut her out of his fortune when he died. But the more interesting Jackie is one who made her own way, independent of men, when her children were busy with school and after both her husbands had died. This was a Jackie who was able to declare on her own terms what mattered to her.

This was a Jackie who, through her books, told us what she was thinking, what she was learning, and what, as she reflected on an extraordinary life, was worth remembering.

In one of the only autobiographical reflections she ever wrote, Jackie described herself as a small girl, sent upstairs to take a nap and secretly reading books from her mother's library, books that were "far too old for me." Then, at the end of an hour, she carefully wiped the soles of her bare feet so the nanny would not discover that she had been out of bed. Similarly, Jackie's one-time assistant in the White House Mary Barelli Gallagher wrote that while most people imagined Jackie was off living a high life with the jet set, she was usually by herself in her room, reading a book. In the weeks before she died, she was at home with the manuscript of a British writer, Antony Beevor, who had written about postwar Paris, a city she knew well. He'd struggled with the conclusion and it wasn't right. He knew she wasn't feeling well, so he remembers being shocked to receive a fax from her saying she had read it and had a suggestion for how to fix it.

Something else that few people know about the real Jackie is that she was a talented writer. English teachers at school early on recognized this ability, but as Nancy Tuckerman remarked, Jackie hid her talent and kept it secret. The last thing she wanted was to be known as "a brain." For most of the twentieth century it was not cool for an American girl to be smart. Just as Jackie was finishing college, she applied for *Vogue*'s Prix de Paris, a competition in which the prize was a stint interning at the magazine's offices in Paris and New York. It says a lot about her talent that although there were hundreds of applicants from colleges and universities all over America, she was the winner. The *Vogue* editorial staff who read Jackie's essay thought she wrote marvelously and had already grasped the magazine's editorial point of view. Her mother, afraid that she would lose her daughter to Paris for good, made her turn down the prize, but Jackie never ceased to admire writers. Nor did she entirely stop writing herself: an anonymous piece she published in *The New Yorker* was key to her decision to start work at Viking. Her silky voice on the page is as distinct as if she were still alive. When one of her letters turns up, it nowadays commands a high price at auction, but few people know that pages and pages of her writing and books that bear her distinctive editorial mark are freely available in public libraries—if you know where to look. Jackie as a writer is the second of three identities that appealed to her sense of who she was, or might be.

Above all, this is a book about what Jackie did when she was an editor. It's the first book published by the company where she spent most of her publishing career but which for the most part kept her role under wraps to protect her privacy. As Steve Rubin wrote in a small, privately circulated book at Doubleday after she died, "There was an unwritten law among all of us at Doubleday—that we would never publicly discuss Jackie. The genesis of this posture was nothing more than a desire to shield her, but the flip side of this protective gesture was the fact that few people understood how committed and talented she was at the work she chose to do." Now that more than a decade has passed, it is no longer a question of not hurting the feelings of a living friend or of wheeling skeletons out of her closet, but of showing how a middle-aged woman remade her life in the years after she moved out from the shadow cast by her husbands. That woman is Everywoman, and this book is about her rather than about the icon staring down from Andy Warhol canvases. This book celebrates the accomplishments of a woman whose editorial talents have never been sung.

In two different letters to famous writers whom Jackie

counted among her friends, she used a nearly identical phrase to say why books and writing meant so much to her. To Truman Capote, who had written a letter to say how sorry and sad he was that she had lost her baby Patrick in 1963, she wrote gratefully, marveling how "all the things you write move people." Later in life she became good friends with the Irish writer Edna O'Brien. When O'Brien's novel *Time and Tide* came out in 1992, Jackie told her why she couldn't put the book down: "You have the power to move more than anyone I know." The power to move was the magic Jackie found in her favorite writers and books. The shy woman with the whispery voice also had the ambition to move us through the books she published, and this is her story as well.

Jackie's library, her personal selection of books she decided to keep, to read, to commission, was not just a row of books standing on the shelf. It was her self-portrait. Partly at her insistence before she died, John and Caroline Kennedy decided to auction Jackie's book collection in 1996. She had recognized long before, however, how revealing a collection of books might be. She loved eighteenth-century France and admired one of its great patrons of the arts, Madame de Pompadour. Nancy Mitford wrote a lighthearted biography of Pompadour which had a serious point to make about Pompadour's library: "The books of somebody who reads are an infallible guide to the owner's mentality."

Oscar Wilde had been one of Jackie's favorite writers ever since she was a young woman. When this became known early in JFK's presidency, a group of midwestern ladies chose Wilde's work for their reading group and were shocked to discover that he had been gay. Jackie felt an affinity with Wilde. Like her, Wilde loved style for style's sake, he loved a well-tailored jacket, and he loved books. His most recent biographer puts it this way: Wilde "regarded books as his 'friends,' and his collection as both a record of his life and an emblem of his personality." Wilde described "the volumes that most affected and charmed him as his 'golden books.' These were the books that revolutionized his conception of the world, the books in which he recognized an aspect of himself for the first time. As events in his biography, these readerly encounters were as significant as his first meetings with friends and lovers."

A library represents the possibility of human understanding and is one way of keeping the world's chaos at bay. In her lifetime Jackie put together several libraries. There was not only her own personal collection of books, but also a collection of books for the White House, an endowed presidential library for research in Boston, and the nearly one hundred books she brought out at two different publishers. Jane Hitchcock, a young friend of Jackie's later years, a novelist and playwright, wrote two best-selling thrillers at Jackie's house on Martha's Vineyard. Jackie's children acknowledged her close friendship with their mother by asking her to speak at Jackie's memorial service at St. Ignatius Loyola on Park Avenue. When Jackie's book collection was auctioned at Sotheby's, Hitchcock said, "I think it's too bad because in another time Edith Wharton's library was so well documented." Whole books have been written on Edith Wharton's library because it was so central to understanding an important writer's mind. "People's libraries in Wharton's day," Hitchcock continued, "were like their clothes. You wrapped yourself not just in beautiful dresses but in beautiful books. People's tastes were formed and defined by what they read." Their choice of books was a key that unlocked their most intimate selves.

Jackie was not a snob when it came to books. She loved Edith Wharton, but she liked reading about witchcraft too. Jackie even told one of her authors, Jonathan Cott, as he worked on the story of an eccentric Englishwoman who lived most of her life in Egypt, that he had to be less reserved in his writing. Jackie wrote in the margin of Cott's manuscript, "Say that she was a witch. Dottiness was her cover up. Say all witches cackle or seem eccentric." She wanted him to let go, to get behind his heroine's apparent nuttiness and capture her inner witch. This slightly offbeat Jackie, her beautiful hair smelling not only of perfume but also of the cigarettes she sometimes liked to smoke when she was working, scribbling in the white space along the edge of a manuscript, is the Jackie we know when we understand that first and foremost she was a reader.

chapter 1

SSH! I'M READING.

— *Jackie to her roommate, Nancy Tuckerman,*
at Miss Porter's School

Miss Porter's School is a college prep school for girls arranged in a dozen historic houses on either side of a two-lane highway running through Farmington, a suburb of Hartford, Connecticut. Most of the girls are boarders, but a few are day students from the neighborhood. The most remarkable thing about the adolescent girls who go there is how utterly at ease they are with adults. They look you in the eye, smile, say hello, and are unafraid of strangers, as if to say, "If you are here, you must belong here, just like I do." Nancy Tuckerman's explanation of what made the school tick in the 1940s was that it was "very much a family school. My mother went there, her sister went there, my sister went there. Jackie's sister, Lee, went there, and their half-sister, Janet Auchincloss, went there too." All that was long ago, before the school started reaching out to nontraditional constituencies in hopes of increasing diversity and reducing its reputation for exclusivity, but even now the place has the feeling of educating polished, confident girls who will one day have a chance both to earn and to inherit everything good that life has to offer. Everybody thinks that Jacqueline Bouvier was the sort of girl who was made for Miss Porter's, but in fact an important part of her never entirely fit in there.

She was shy, something of a loner, and looked for ways to spend time by herself. At the end of the day, when the girls would gather in one another's dorm rooms before lights-out to talk and gossip about the day, Jackie preferred to stay alone in her room reading a book. "Often French literature," Nancy Tuckerman reminisced, distinctly pronouncing it "lit-ra-toor" and conveying the idea of the very proper school Miss Porter's was when she and Jackie were there together. One girl's mother wouldn't have her daughter rooming with Jackie because she thought one of the points of Miss Porter's was to socialize and meet people. Rooming with Jackie would mean rooming with someone who didn't much like to mix with the other girls. It wasn't that Jackie was unpopular or disliked by the other girls, but she was private, reserved, and aloof long before the paparazzi ever pointed a camera in her direction. She had friends, but books and literature were her real intimates.

Girls near graduation who had good academic records were allowed to spend study hall in their rooms. Jackie had this privilege. The room she shared with Tuckerman was at the top of a big Classical Revival house built in 1800, their two single beds wedged in under sloping eaves and their window looking out on old shade trees. Sometimes they would both be up there together, reading their books in bed. Tuckerman loved to laugh and was drawn to Jackie's sense of humor. The friendship Jackie extended to her was so rare a privilege, it would have been hard not to prize it, even when sometimes, late in the day, Tuckerman would think it was all right to raise some conversation, only to be interrupted by Jackie, who would say, "Ssh! I'm reading" and give her a look that made them both lie back laughing against the pillows.

Despite Jackie's love of books, she spent a lifetime trying to prevent people from writing them about her. Yet she did authorize one biography, written and published by Mary Van Rensselaer Thayer. Thayer was a member of one of New

England's founding families. Her ancestors had settled in the Hudson River valley as far back as the days when New York was New Amsterdam. She was a friend of Jackie's mother, and her book, *Jacqueline Bouvier Kennedy*, was published in 1961 as part of the publicity blitz that accompanied the beginning of John F. Kennedy's presidency. The book is far from a tame whitewash of Jackie's early life, however. When Jackie found that in an early draft of the book Thayer was quoting from letters that her mother had lent to Thayer, she asked her mother and her friends to stop cooperating. Jackie did not stop the book, but she made her displeasure with some of what the book revealed known.

Thayer noted that when Jackie was still young, she started putting together a little library of her own of books about ballet: "She knew she could never be a ballet dancer but she did think, for a bit, that she might be part of the show, by designing ballet and theatrical costumes." That sense early on of what she could *not* do was at the nub of Jackie's self-image as a reader. Coupled with the sense of limitation was a determination to work around it, to participate in the creative and artistic activity that gripped her imagination. The little girl who decided before she was in her teens that she could not be a dancer would grow into a woman who published books on half a dozen of the most important dancers of the twentieth century.

Thayer's biography tells of the books Jackie read when she was young. She read *Gone With the Wind* three times. There were ways in which some of the operatic characters from the book resembled people in Jackie's own family. Jackie's mother, Janet, divorced Jackie's father, Jack Bouvier, in 1940, when Jackie was eleven years old. The man who had got his nickname, "Black Jack," from his permanent suntan spent the rest of his life in a succession of New York apartments, sometimes looked after by girlfriends, sometimes not, spending beyond his means and trading on the stock exchange. Janet remarried in 1942. Her new husband, Hugh Auchincloss, was a rich man, the heir to Standard Oil money, which he used to found a stock brokerage in Washington, D.C. He maintained a big house called Merrywood in Virginia and another, Hammersmith Farm, in Newport for the summer. He had a son from a previous marriage, just two years older than Jackie, who was known in the family as Yusha. Yusha Auchincloss remembered that Jackie also loved the movies, and *Gone With the Wind* was one of her favorites. "Rhett Butler reminded her of her father, Scarlett O'Hara of her mother," he said. The grand southern house of the movie, Tara, reminded her of Merrywood and Hammersmith rolled together. Jackie's stepbrother also thought that Jackie "had a lot of Scarlett's qualities, the same ones as her mother had, good and not so good." Jackie grew up patterning herself on one of the most famous temperamental divas of the 1930s and '40s, both the character in the book and Vivien Leigh's depiction of her on the screen. Scarlett O'Hara could be shrewd and selfish as well as self-sacrificing, and it's difficult to tell which of those features drew Jackie to read about her again and again. Jackie might also have seen that her own family dramas sometimes paled before the melodrama on the page, and in that sense the saga of Scarlett and Rhett was a comfort.

Jackie learned to look for men in books, too. Yusha Auchincloss recalled that "as a teenager she devoured Tolstoy's *War and Peace* and Sir Walter Scott's *Ivanhoe*. Courage and chivalry were tops on her list of qualities she admired most in men." Another model for how men should behave was in the children's story *Little Lord Fauntleroy*, by Frances Hodgson Burnett, about an American boy living in Brooklyn who discovers that he is heir to an earldom when his English grandfather, the earl, sends a lawyer to visit his mother. The American boy, undaunted by the prospect of a big house and a title, inadvertently teaches his grandfather about kindness and compassion toward the less well-off. Jackie wrote in her essay for *Vogue* that little Lord Fauntleroy's grandfather was one of her heroes. It is interesting that she identified with the corrupt old aristocrat rather than the hero of the story. Perhaps she dreamed of high caste and riches, as many little girls do, but appreciated adult wickedness, too. All three of these books imagine a life lived in castles and palaces, among reckless and courageous European nobles. The humble March sisters of Louisa May Alcott's *Little Women* were not for Jackie.

Nor is it surprising to find her a little in love with Lord Byron, the bad boy of English Romantic poets, a dandy who had affairs with young men and his own half-sister as well as a string of eligible women. Thayer notes that as Jackie "edged into her teens, Lord Byron became a beloved companion. She read and reread his poems and lived his life through the pages" of Byron's biography. Her father, who was a dandy too, who was rumored to have been bisexual (he had been a friend of Cole Porter's at Yale), and who had the insouciance to be photographed holding the hand of one of his girlfriends as he stood behind his wife's back, was about as Byronic a man as one could find on Long Island in the 1930s. Rhett Butler, Byron, and Black Jack Bouvier merged together in Jackie's reading life to sustain her image of where she came from as well as to give her an idea of where she might like to go.

One of the letters from Jackie's father that Mary Thayer put into her book tells of how much he was going to hate losing her when she found a boyfriend or a husband. Black Jack wrote that he supposed "it won't be long until I lose you to some funny-looking 'gink' "—slang for an odd boy—"who you think is wonderful because he is romantic-looking in the evening and wears his mother's pearl earrings for dress-shirt buttons, because he loves her so." In other words, he was afraid she'd marry a mama's boy who wore ladies' pearls in his shirt-front. As a snazzy dresser himself, perhaps Bouvier was projecting some vision of himself that she might like to marry, but there's no question that she remained attached to him long beyond the grave. As an adult, she kept no pictures of JFK or Onassis in her library, her favorite room in her New York apartment. The biggest framed photo sitting on a side table was of Black Jack.

Romances by the Book

A few years later, one of the ways in which Jackie first connected with JFK was via books. When she went to Europe on an assignment in 1953 for the *Washington Times-Herald*, her companion remembers, Jackie loaded her suitcase on the return trip with books to take back to the young senator she was dating. One of JFK's favorite books, Lord David Cecil's biography of the nineteenth-century British prime minister Lord Melbourne, captured the very era in which Byron flourished. Melbourne's first wife, Lady Caroline Lamb, had been one of Byron's lovers. The biography describes untamed aristocrats who were committed to public service at the same time that they did not give a damn what the public thought about their louche private lives. In that era, before many people could vote, they did not have to care. JFK had first learned to admire the idea of a wealthy aristocrat's obligation to serve the state—noblesse oblige—when he had lived in London with his father, who was the American ambassador to Britain in the late 1930s. This idea of state service combined with playing a role in history and doing whatever you pleased in private life was one of JFK's key points of contact with Jackie.

As a reader of history and lover of books, Jackie was highly conscious of the way in which European monarchs had encouraged the creation of works of art by becoming patrons of artists. In the White House she saw her job as nothing less than raising the profile of the creative arts in America. Book collecting was one of the most important attributes of European kingship. The core of the British Library, one of the best collections in the world, was the product of King George III's passion for book collecting. The gift of his library to the British nation was one of his legacies, more memorable than his blindness about the American colonies. Jackie refused to accept the traditional cultural divide between Britain and America, between European and American attitudes toward the arts. She took European court culture as her pattern. One of Jackie's lesser-known projects in the White House years was beginning the work to found a White House library, later completed under President Johnson. She asked the academic editors of the Adams Papers and the Jefferson Papers to advise on the creation of such a library, one that would be appropriate to a house built in the early decades of the nineteenth century and to the shared philosophy of the nation's founders. What books should it have? She wanted the library to be available for use, not just for show. In 1962, Arthur Schlesinger, on leave from Harvard while he served on JFK's staff, was helping her to select a book to take as a gift to Jawaharlal Nehru when she went on a state visit to India. They agreed on a first edition of Thoreau's *Civil Disobedience* as being intellectually related to the philosophy of India's founding statesman, Mahatma Gandhi. She wrote a letter to Schlesinger agreeing that "a library is dead if not used." She also observed that White House staffers were entirely capable of "pinching" the books and teased

Schlesinger by asking him to sit in the library dressed in historic costume to discourage theft.

Late in her life, in a note to Carl Sferrazza Anthony, who was writing a book on American first ladies, Jackie went out of her way to say how she cared about American history. Anthony had started doing his research early. When he was a boy in the 1960s he began writing to Nancy Tuckerman in the White House, asking her for memorabilia. Perhaps because of this persistence and the fact that both women could remember that he had written to them years before, Jackie was unusually frank with him. It still bothered her that many Americans considered her unpatriotic—in the 1960s some had accused her of being too French or European. Jackie told Anthony that she remembered her step-uncle, Wilmarth "Lefty" Lewis, the editor of the Horace Walpole Papers at Yale, telling her as a girl that of the three greatest men alive in the eighteenth century—Denis Diderot, Benjamin Franklin, and Thomas Jefferson—two were American. She did not want to make the White House European. She wanted to raise the public profile of a long intellectual tradition that stood behind the American presidency, one that was the equal of any European court.

In the aftermath of JFK's assassination, Jackie was deeply depressed. People who spend their time reading in private corners often struggle more than others with depression, as they withdraw from companionship when company is what they most need to feel better. She developed a confidential correspondence with the former British prime minister Harold Macmillan, with whom JFK had had a warm relationship, not only because JFK liked him but because both Macmillan and JFK's sister had married into the family of the Duke of Devonshire. She wrote Macmillan a searing letter early in 1964, telling him how full of despair she was. Macmillan replied, comforting her and encouraging her to write more. She did not write to him very often, but her correspondence with him was more revealing than any of her other letters that have been discovered to date. In September 1965, reporting on a summer in Newport, where sunburns, sweet corn, and clambakes had returned her to a semblance of her previous composure, she said how important her reading was in helping her recover. She had been reading *Report to Greco,* a spiritual autobiography by Nikos Kazantzakis: "The Greek way seems to me to be the only way you can see the world now." Kazantzakis was a Greek writer who enjoyed a vogue in the 1960s, when *Report to Greco* was translated into English and his novel *Zorba the Greek* was made into a film starring Anthony Quinn. In that same era, Aristotle Onassis had invited Jackie to stay on his yacht to recover from the death of her baby Patrick, and her sister, Lee, had begun an affair with him. There was something about the culture of the eastern Mediterranean, about the mythological dimensions of Kazantzakis's work, which recalled Homer's *Odyssey,* that particularly attracted her. In Dallas and at the funeral afterward, her own life had suddenly assumed mythological proportions: she had become at once a human widow and the iconic Widow, an archetype, a goddess, recognizable the world over for the rest of her life, whether she liked it or not. Reading Kazantzakis may have helped her reflect on her own reluctant mythology. Reading Kazantzakis, she told Macmillan, had given her peace.

Kazantzakis also came up in a letter she wrote to Arthur Schlesinger in May of 1965 about his book on the Kennedy administration, *A Thousand Days.* She objected to Schlesinger's characterization of Adlai Stevenson as a politician typical of Greek classical antiquity while Jack Kennedy was typical of classical Rome. She concluded from reading Kazantzakis that the Greeks had warred with the gods, that a desperate defiance of fate was characteristic of Greek tragedy and the Greek character. That epic struggle reminded her of Jack. It was unlike Roman politicians, who had more prosaic and practical ideas about power. "Lyndon Johnson is really the Roman—a classic Emperor—McNamara—maybe even George Washington are Roman—but not Jack." She read her way into identifying with what she understood to be a Greek frame of mind long before she married Aristotle Onassis in 1968. Just as reading about the world of Byron and Melbourne had been a bridge from Black Jack to JFK, Kazantzakis led her to Onassis.

When she married Onassis, the changes she made on his yacht *Christina* were not all to do with the carpets and furniture. Peter Beard, a handsome photographer who has been described as "half Tarzan, half Byron," spent a summer on Skorpios. He was having an affair with Lee, who was five years older, and was vaguely employed to look after the children. As he recalled, Jackie "stacked the library of the *Christina* with the works of new authors—poetry, nonfiction, art books, everything" and disappeared every afternoon while others napped to read by herself. "She was a voracious reader." Beard's assessment was that she did not have the confidence in her own ability and talents to pursue the life of an artist. "It frustrated her." At an exhibition of Beard's work, she took him aside to tell him, "I wish I could do what you're doing—but I can't."

In one of the few times she ever ventured into print as an author, she wrote an afterword to accompany one of Beard's books of photography. Beard had found some old photograph albums of one of the servants of Karen Blixen, who under the pen name Isak Dinesen had written an autobiographical account of her attempt to run a coffee farm in Kenya, *Out of Africa*. Jackie confessed in her afterword to Beard's book that she admired Blixen. Like *Gone With the Wind*, *Out of Africa* tells the story of an abandoned young woman living in a rarefied social circle who has to learn to make do, manage an estate on her own, and deal with unfaithful men—some of the story Jackie had lived herself.

Aristotle Onassis complained that Jackie spent all her time reading. Another of Jackie's intimates sensed the same thing. Dorothy Schiff was older than Jackie and the powerful publisher of the *New York Post*. Schiff hoped to use her intimacy with Jackie for the paper's benefit. In the 1960s Robert Kennedy needed the *Post*'s support if he were to succeed as a senator in New York, and Jackie kept up her friendship with Schiff as a service to RFK. Schiff's note of what she recalled of a personal tour around Jackie's apartment mentions that "next to the living room but not with a door through was a library. She said she spent most of her time there." Schiff looked hard to find a television but could not see one. Instead, she remarked on "a sofa covered in brown velvet, stained from where people had spilled drinks and things. There were bookshelves all around, with sets of books and single volumes." Even in the bedroom, "at the foot of her bed was a long settee with books and magazines flung on it in haphazard fashion." Not satisfied with her own eyes, Schiff had a translation made of the account in an Italian magazine of what it was like to work for Jackie, written by one of Jackie's former maids, Greta, who had been fired. Greta's chief complaint, like Onassis's, was that Jackie spent a lot of time reading, and sometimes read past the dinner hour, so that her food was cold or overdone.

Models and Mentors

In the late 1960s Jackie commissioned Aaron Shikler to paint a portrait that would hang in the White House. Shikler did a number of studies for this portrait. The one Jackie told him she liked best depicts her lounging on a sofa reading a book. The portrait is similar to a famous portrait of one of Jackie's heroines, Madame de Pompadour, a mistress of Louis XV, who helped give Versailles its reputation for being a center of France's artistic life. Pompadour had been a friend of Voltaire. She aided and defended Diderot and d'Alembert, whose *Encyclopédie* was one of the most famous works of the Enlightenment. She helped found the manufacture of Sèvres porcelain. She was a patron of architects who laid out the Place de la Concorde and of painters like François Boucher, who flattered her by showing her the way she saw herself: on a sofa, in a beautiful dress, with a book. It is also significant that a Boucher painting of Pompadour with a book, similar to Shikler's drawing of Jackie, appeared in one of the first books to which she lent a hand as an editor, Princess Grace's *My Book of Flowers*. The patronage of creative artists, passion for eighteenth-century France, loving to hide herself away in a library from all those who wanted to inspect her in public, yet

choosing an image of herself for public portrayal depicting her bookish intelligence: Jackie as a reader is the theme that connects all these different selves. In the Shikler portrait she took a step out of the closet toward declaring herself publicly.

Jackie has often been written about in terms of her two husbands, but the key transformative moment in her life—her decision to go to work as an editor—resulted from listening to and being advised by other women. Dorothy Schiff had been born to riches and privileges, but she planted the seed that ultimately bore fruit when she told Jackie how important work had been in her life. It is true that she was trying to persuade Jackie to write a column for the *New York Post,* which had scored a surprise hit when Eleanor Roosevelt first agreed to write a column. Nevertheless, Schiff was also trying to fill a void in Jackie's life and knew that work could help heal Jackie's wounds in a way that living on a yacht and decorating a house on Skorpios never would. Jackie realized that she wanted to work while she was married to Onassis. She put the idea to her husband, but he would not let her; a working wife would have undermined his Mediterranean manhood. So she could not put her career plan into action until he died in 1975. She took Schiff's suggestion of working for the *Post* seriously, even letting herself be given a tour of the newspaper's offices. Schiff was surprised when one day Jackie turned up very late for a simple lunch in her office at the *Post*. The cabbie had gone the wrong way, and Jackie seemed a little distracted. Schiff examined her outfit and found that she was wearing a blouse that was unbuttoned in the middle, with her net brassiere showing underneath. Schiff looked at her in surprise, and Jackie quietly buttoned it. It must have been hard for her when women examined her more meticulously than men did.

A more appealing suggestion came from her former White House social secretary Letitia Baldrige. Baldrige, like

Schiff, knew the ins and outs of high society, and like Jackie had attended Vassar, but she also had a career, working, among other jobs, as an assistant to the American ambassadors in Paris and Rome. Later she wrote books on etiquette. As a social secretary, Baldrige was eventually too strong for Jackie, and in 1963 Jackie put Nancy Tuckerman in Baldrige's place at the White House. However, the two stayed in touch, and Baldrige was certainly a model of how a working girl from a good family could stay afloat in decades when marriage was most women's only option for economic survival. Baldrige suggested that Jackie try contacting Thomas Guinzburg, publisher of the Viking Press, to see whether a place could be found for her there.

Guinzburg was a Yale friend of Jackie's stepbrother, Yusha Auchincloss. Jackie and Guinzburg were only two years apart in age and had known each other since they were both in school. He was also one of the founders of *The Paris Review* in the 1950s, with another of Jackie's old friends, George Plimpton. In the early 1960s Guinzburg had shared a mistress with President Kennedy, so he had no particular awe of the Kennedy mystique. He was utterly at ease with Jackie. Unlike most people, he was unafraid of her. Guinzburg leapt at the idea of Jackie's joining Viking. She may have known nothing about how to edit a book, but her contacts were superlative. She might bring in any number of big names as authors, and having her on staff would be a public relations coup for the firm.

The most important influence on Jackie once she got to Viking in the fall of 1975 was Diana Vreeland. Vreeland had been a towering figure in the fashion world for decades, most famously as the editor of *Vogue* from 1963 to 1971. She had her hair lacquered into a black helmet that was said to make a metallic noise if you hit it right. In later life she wore strik-

ing tribal jewelry. The fashion press paid attention to her pronunciamentos, that the bikini was the most important thing since the atom bomb, for example, as if she were Wittgenstein. When the publishers of *Vogue,* incensed at her extravagance, fired her, Vreeland remade herself as special consultant to the Costume Institute of the Metropolitan Museum of Art. Her all-red drawing room had design affinities with Boucher's painting of Pompadour, and she became Jackie's mentor. When Vreeland died in 1989, at age eighty-six, after a long illness during which she kept most callers at bay, Jackie was the last person she allowed in to say goodbye.

Jackie's first project at Viking came to her via Vreeland. In that era of détente, Thomas Hoving, the director of the Metropolitan Museum of Art, was fostering increased cooperation with Soviet museums. He forged an agreement with the Hermitage in Leningrad to borrow some Russian art treasures for their first display in the West. Vreeland was working on a show of Russian costumes at the same time. She suggested that Jackie should put together an illustrated book to accompany the exhibition. This was the origin of *In the Russian Style*, a big coffee-table book published in 1976 with detailed historical commentary on illustrations of Russian clothes through the ages, chiefly those worn by the aristocracy and in the court of the tsars. In a publishing career of nearly two decades, Jackie allowed her name to go on the spine only on this book.

A Philosophy of Reading

What Jackie derived from Vreeland, however, was bigger than this single book. Vreeland had a philosophy which she put into *Allure,* a book on the secrets of desire and erotic attraction, which she had learned from a lifetime of looking at striking images. Jackie edited the book. Vreeland had a key insight on why women wanted to make themselves look good: it was not about vanity, it was about aspiration. To make her point, she turned to Cecil Beaton and Truman Capote. Capote had made a bitchy remark about Beaton's becoming legendary for designing upper-class images, remarking that "out of the middle classes of England it's rather curious to get such an exotic flower." Vreeland disapproved of Capote's cattiness. "Still," she wrote, "Truman was getting at something and we should give it a name. It's a form of wanting to be. We all want to be. You are and you want to be. How is it you do it?" You might deride this as social climbing or wearing clothes to get ahead, but in fact the best of us all aspire to be something bigger and better, smarter and wiser, than we were in the place where we were born. Diana Vreeland's wisdom was to say that this was not snobbery but wholesome ambition. This was at the core of what Jackie learned from Vreeland, and reading was the path she chose, compelled by her intellectual aspiration. You are. You want to be. You read a book to find out how. Moreover, reading a book is adorning the mind, just as wearing a pretty dress is adorning the body. Jackie's collaboration with her fashionable friend reached a peak of productivity when she persuaded Vreeland to put that principle into writing in *Allure*.

Two other of Jackie's authors also managed to put into the books she edited words that had long remained inchoate or unspoken in her own personal philosophy. That was the magic of being an editor: to read a manuscript and to find there elements of a life, or fragments of philosophy, that are deeply familiar to you yet at the same time strikingly new because articulated for the first time. This is to find almost biblical reassurance for your own life. A "good book" confirms or expands or suggests exciting potential alterations in your own guiding principles. Of these two authors, the first was Martha Graham, the premier modernist dancer and choreographer of the twentieth century. Jackie's achievement was to persuade Graham to write her autobiography. Imagine, then, Jackie's satisfaction when she read this portion of Graham's text: "I have a holy attitude toward books. If I was stranded on a desert island I'd need only two, the dictionary and the Bible. Words are magical and beautiful. They have opened up new worlds to me." Nor were Graham's choices in books always the hard or highfalutin ones. She liked spy stories. "I'm a very strange reader; I like espionage. Nothing lets me think more clearly through a problem than reading and alternating between two mysteries at the same time. Odd, but it works." Graham said that from her earliest days as a dancer, she would go home in the evening, "gather some of my favorite books around me in bed, and take excerpts from them in green stenography notebooks." Graham had built one of the foundations of her art on the practice of being a reader and argued here for the first time that a problem in movement could be sorted out by dwelling on the solution of a detective story. Jackie thus found two of her great passions, books and ballet, united in a text that brought prestige to her publisher and for which she alone was responsible.

The second of two authors whom she particularly admired was Bill Moyers. Moyers had served as press secretary and a key adviser to President Johnson, though he was originally a Kennedy appointee. He and his wife, Judith, had met the Kennedys in the White House, but they did not become friends with Jackie until later, when they all found themselves in New York and Moyers was establishing credentials as a commentator on PBS. What Jackie admired about Bill Moyers was not only his crusading, progressive politics but also the broad curiosity that spurred him to take up and investigate, on air, topics like mythology and alternative healing strategies in medicine. It was Jackie who first suggested that his series of interviews with Joseph Campbell, a specialist on comparative mythology, could be made into a successful book. Moyers did not believe her. She insisted. *The Power of Myth,* published in 1988, became one of the smash hits of her editorial list. Moyers wrote in his introduction that Campbell wanted to remind people that myth was not something to be experienced only through exotic travel or witnessing tribal ritual; rather, "one sure path into the world runs along the printed page." The wisdom, solace, and insight on life offered by mythology were there to be had in thousands of the world's religious and literary texts.

Jackie was someone who had always been more comfortable alone with books than in a crowd of people. Her good luck was less in marrying rich men than in finding a way to turn being a reader into something that might offer her a workable new life in the years after her children were grown. Being an editor was not the first thing that occurred to her. She had always had her work as a writer praised by adults and even friends who were professional writers. Part of her journey to a desk at a publishing house involved trying to be a writer, and that story, with its small victories and some hard knocks too, is just as important in revealing who she was.

chapter 2

I KEEP THINKING WHAT POWER
A GREAT WRITER HAS.
—*Jackie to Truman Capote*

•

Many people who knew Jackie well when she was a young woman have talked about her talent as a writer. Her mother said that she always thought Jackie "had the temperament and talent of a writer, that perhaps she could write novels, poetry, or fairy tales." One of her instructors at George Washington University, to which she transferred in 1950, after leaving Vassar and spending a junior year abroad in Paris, said that Jackie "could write like a million. She didn't need to take my class." Another English professor told a family friend after JFK's election that he always knew Jackie would make a name for herself, "but I really thought it would be by writing a book." One of the *Vogue* judges for the Prix de Paris said, on the basis of her application, that Jackie was clearly a writer. So why did she become an editor instead?

In fact Jackie tried to be a writer and ultimately rejected writing as something she might take up as a career. Although previous biographers have known of them, Jackie's published and unpublished works have never been given much attention, even though to look at them together is to find out more about who she was and how she presented herself on the page than if one were to discover an old trunk of her love letters. She revealed herself in the process of writing works of both fiction and nonfiction. Here are her devotion to her father, her barbed wit, her self-mockery, and her uncertainty about sexual desire. Here are traces of her melancholy nostalgia for lost days. Any writer who sits down to commit herself regularly to print reveals something of herself, for all writers are to a certain extent lovers of themselves, narcissists, trying on varieties of sentences as an actor tries on different personas, admiring the voice they choose to put in writing just as an actor practices before a mirror. The writing Jackie is a Jackie with her dark glasses off, speaking to us directly about what mattered to her.

Long after Jackie tried to be a writer herself, she formed a deep friendship with a younger woman, Carly Simon, her neighbor on Martha's Vineyard. They published four children's books together, an unmistakable mark of Jackie's confidence and admiration. As for Carly Simon, when invited to look back on those days, she recalled: "Jackie and my mother were the two most important women in my life." She discovered that in writing two of her children's books for Jackie, she had inadvertently revealed a terrible passage of her own childhood. Between the ages of six and fifteen she had a stammer that crippled her speech. Of all her family, only her mother understood how to help her. "She never finished my sentences. If I was having trouble finishing, she'd suggest that I tap my foot and sing it, even if it was only 'Please pass the butter.'" When she reflected on these two books, she found to her surprise that both of them "had to do with me." They were about finding music and ceasing to be mute, about a character rediscovering "her note" and so finding her voice too. "I hadn't thought of that before," Simon said, surprised at what had turned up in the conversation. Her children's books with Jackie were a way of revealing a hurt she had had as a child and overcoming that hurt by turning it into song.

Unpublished Papers

A close examination of Jackie's work turns up similar discoveries. In the fall of 1950, when she submitted her Prix de Paris application to *Vogue*, she was just twenty-one. In the essays for the magazine, at the very moment that she was making her bid for the editors' attention, she cast herself as already reconciled to never being able to become a writer. She said she'd had dreams of locking herself up and turning out children's books and *New Yorker* short stories, but her current ambition was to be a Condé Nast editor because her writing talent was not "pronounced enough." Working on the magazine's editorial staff, she maintained, would allow her to keep up with new ideas in the arts that excited her. *Vogue* in the 1940s and '50s was a more serious magazine than it is today. It published all the heavyweights of the writing, fine art, and photography worlds. So for Jackie even to have made the first cut in the Prix de Paris competition, when there were as many as one thousand applicants from three hundred schools and when the magazine took its cultural criticism seriously, says a great deal about the talent she certainly had, even if she downplayed it. Applying to *Vogue* also speaks of ambition.

Jackie famously remarked in her application to *Vogue* that the three men in history she would most like to have met were Oscar Wilde, Charles Baudelaire, and Serge Diaghilev. All three were artists who stood in defiance of the old Victorian convention that the purpose of art was to teach people morality. They all believed that rather than serving as a means to teach people how to behave well, art existed for its own sake.

Art was valuable as pleasurable and aesthetic experience in its own right. Wilde was a playwright, Baudelaire a poet, and Diaghilev the ballet impresario who first put the dancer Vaslav Nijinsky on stage in a see-through leotard. Two were gay, two were dandies, and the older generation regarded all three as decadent. Compare this to what is known about Jackie's father. A silk handkerchief came spilling out of his breast pocket. He wore two-toned shoes and unbuttoned suit-coat sleeves turned back to reveal his shirt cuffs. He lived beyond his means and preferred showing up on Long Island for the weekend in a convertible roadster to saving money for a rainy day. He lived above the rules that governed most people's style and morality. Jackie's tribute to men like Wilde, Baudelaire, and Diaghilev suggested that she saw in them the same elevation of style for style's sake that she knew and loved in her father.

It was daring for Jackie to play with gender stereotypes in those conservative postwar years under President Truman. A dandy is a feminized man, whose exaggerated attention to dress suggests a woman's attitude to clothes. For her *Vogue* application, Jackie proposed that the magazine do a spread on women cross-dressing as men. She imagined an entire issue of the magazine dedicated to "nostalgia," with women dressed in men's outfits that recalled "the Directoire Dandy." The Directory was an era in France when revolutionary violence was out and austere neoclassical decoration was in. That time's most famous representative on the other side of the Channel was Beau Brummell, the man who pioneered the black dinner jacket. Jackie suggested that as a tribute to one of Brummell's successors, who also made an art out of dressing up, "we all wear a green carnation," just as Oscar Wilde had done. She also favored the sort of suit that her father might well have worn in the decade she was born: "a 1920s gigolo air, boxy tapering jacket with wide revers [lapels] . . . slim skirt, like the man-

nish suits shown by [French designer Jacques] Fath last fall."
Before she married and had children, her inspiration came
from French and English history, from fin-de-siècle dance and
literature, and from imagining a stylish gender-bending that
was no longer immoral or decadent, only a bit mischievous.

She showed a more cautious side of herself in a short story
she submitted for a writing class she was taking in her senior
year at George Washington. It's about two young Americans,
about her age, living in Florence, possibly as students or summer travelers. What might have been about the sexual ini-
tiation of two twenty-somethings swept away by a feeling of
freedom at being so far away from home turns out to be about
a young woman in love with language. They are going out for
dinner. The girl asks the boy to teach her something in Italian,
not "thank you" or "good morning" "but something really Italian." He proposes a flirtatious proverb: *"Come bello fare l'amore
quando piove,"* or "How beautiful it is to make love in the rain."
The girl says it over "slowly . . . And then faster. What a lovely
Italian thought! I didn't think it would be very beautiful to
make love in the rain, but it was so pretty to say so."

After dinner they go for a walk and decide to cross the
Arno at a treacherous point where the river runs deep. In
order to get across, the boy has to hold the girl aloft, their bodies pressed together on a warm evening. She does not enjoy it.
Neither does she like the physical contact, nor his naked feet
underwater looking "like dead martyr's feet in paintings,"
nor the water rat they encounter on the other side. The story
conveys her love of exotic European adventure and her love
of language and the feel of it on her tongue rather than the
prolonged contact with a boy. She enjoys learning the Italian
phrase more than being carried in the boy's arms.

Sarah Bradford had a key insight on what the story says
about Jackie. Bradford is the doyenne of British biographers,

author of more than a dozen books, and Jackie's most reliable biographer to date. The daughter of a brigadier and the wife of a viscount, Bradford knew Jackie's social world from personal experience, and she observed that Jackie was always slightly uncomfortable with the sexual side of herself. Like Marietta Tree and Evangeline Bruce, other prominent women from posh backgrounds, Bradford thought that Jackie was always envious of Pamela Harriman, who had used her sexual appeal to land a succession of husbands from Randolph Churchill to Averell Harriman, and to influence presidents from Roosevelt to Clinton. Jackie thought she could never do what Pam did. In this story she wrote when she was twenty-two, Jackie revealed that sexual shyness, whether she intended to or not.

There was a gap between the 1950s, when Jackie wrote these pieces, and the 1970s, when she tentatively started writing again, this time for publication. In the meantime she had married twice and raised two children, who were now old enough to be away at boarding school. Like many of the bright women who had come to adulthood in the postwar era and who had been raised mainly to be supporters of their husbands, she was faced with the difficulty of how to forge a career in her forties. In the early 1970s, when Betty Friedan and the National Organization for Women were beginning to make feminism mainstream, it no longer seemed enough to be the keeper of a household and a mother to children. To launch any new career is difficult; to get started again when you are entering middle age is tougher still. The women of Jackie's generation had not been trained for it. Many of them had begun college and never finished, when the work of being a wife had greater urgency and cultural approval. Jackie had been among the first presidential wives ever to have finished college, but even her college career—Vassar, a Smith junior-year-abroad program in Paris, George Washington University—was a patchwork of spur-of-the-moment decisions rather than a plan to enter a profession. The majority of the first ladies who followed Lady Bird Johnson had some experience of higher education, and many of them completed degrees, but it is nevertheless interesting how recently in American history presidential wives have been expected to have educations that equal those of their husbands. Jackie was ahead of the curve in having been to college; she would be ahead of the curve in taking paid work beyond her mothering years too.

Written for Publication

In the 1970s, when marriage to Aristotle Onassis was neither occupying all her time nor fulfilling all her expectations, Jackie began to allow a few of her written pieces to appear in print. The first of these was a brief reminiscence of her friendship with Randolph Churchill. Sir Winston Churchill's son was an arrogant and charming alcoholic who, because of his father, had met many of the famous personalities of the twentieth century. Randolph died in his fifties, having failed to fulfill his promise and having lived most of his life in his father's shadow. Like many young people who lived through the Second World War, Jackie revered Winston Churchill and Franklin Roosevelt. Counting both men's sons among her friends was part of her way to have contact with some of the great events of the century. In 1971, a friend of Randolph's, Kay Halle, put together a collection of memories, and among them was Jackie's.

She recalled a visit Randolph had made to Hyannis after JFK's death and the impression he had made on her son, John. She remembered that Randolph didn't alter himself to suit the little boy but was the same larger-than-life character who so entertained the adults. John was fascinated. Randolph later sent John all forty-nine volumes of his father's collected writings in a tin trunk, as a gift. "John is always taking one out," Jackie wrote, "and asking me what it is about." It was important to her to pass on her own love of books to her children, and Randolph Churchill had assisted her in this. She noted that JFK had always been interested in Winston Churchill's writings, too, and had had some of his volumes when he was a student at Harvard. Jackie thought that when John grew older, if "he finds in them what his father found in them—that would be this strange touching legacy of Randolph's."

She identifies herself mainly in this short piece by her connection to men—to a prominent friend, to her former husband, to her son—but at least one passage shows her own talent for evoking a sense of place. When JFK was still alive, Randolph came to the White House to accept honorary citizenship of the United States on his father's behalf. Both men were nervous lest they spoil a tribute to Sir Winston, of whom they both stood in awe. After the ceremony was over, when both men had spoken well and without mistakes and when most of the invited guests had gone, the president returned to the Oval Office. Jackie remembered it was "a spring day after rain, with the afternoon sun streaming into the Green Room." A small group of friends had stayed behind to relax with Randolph. "We sat around a table . . . with glasses of warm champagne." In that after-party glow, he was a genial man whose friends appreciated him not for being the son of his father but for who he was in spite of his faults.

Jackie's sister, Lee, though younger and less talented as a writer, still had influence on Jackie. In 1974 Lee persuaded her that it would be all right to publish a scrapbook they had made for their mother in 1951, when they had gone on a summer vacation to Europe together. Published as *One Special Sum-*

mer, the book features cartoons drawn by the girls and stories narrated in their distinctive separate handwritings about their adventures on the Continent when they were twenty-two and eighteen. Although they had written the book twenty years earlier, the fact that Jackie allowed Lee to publish it toward the end of her marriage to Onassis, who died the following year, suggests another of the ways in which she was trying out being a writer in the 1970s.

That the sisters' relationship could be difficult is evident early on in the book, when Jackie insists they go out to a party in Paris rather than spend the evening in their hotel. Lee moans, "Oh I don't even want to go." Jackie replies, "Don't you ever want to meet fascinating people," or did Lee just want to spend all her time with her "dreary little American friends"? Like most older children, Jackie could be a bit of a bully. At a very young age, she was also sure that more interesting people could be found in Paris than at home in Newport. Boys in Brooks Brothers shorts, content to spend their lives collecting dividends, did not interest her.

Jackie could also be very funny. She wrote two waspish sections in which she makes fun of herself and her sister trying to flirt with boys they find abroad. Both times she satirizes her own certainty that the boys are likely to be better when they are found in France. On the first occasion they go in search of Paul de Ganay, the son of a marquis. They have met him before and they know him to be a cadet on army maneuvers in the countryside. They arrive at the maneuvers in their little car in the midst of munitions exploding like fireworks. Jackie writes: "I rolled up the windows to deflect shrapnel, crouched on the floor of the car and yelled 'Come on Lee—You can make it if you really try!'" They drove into a clump of trees and "screeched to a stop at the feet of the 2 best looking officers this side of Paradise. They wore blue berets and had lovely gold cords twining underneath their arms. We tumbled out, patting our hair into place and inquired if anyone knew where we could find L'Aspirant de Ganay. The Lieutenant smiled. I had to put on my sunglasses to intercept the ardor of his glance." The lieutenant blew his whistle, and in a few minutes de Ganay magically appeared, "trotting through the trees." "'Paul!' we cried, and sprang for him. He recoiled and greeted us very formally. We were crushed. It would have been such fun to kiss him on both cheeks the way they do in newsreels. He stood there, a ramrod of agony and disapproval while we toed the ground nervously, wishing we had sweaters to cover up our strapless sun-dresses." Jackie was making fun not only of the awkwardness of two forward American girls meeting this boy in full view of his commanding officer, but also of her mother, who had been prompting them in her letters to behave and to dress in a ladylike fashion while they were abroad.

Jackie was also aware of the fun in her comeuppance at the hands of another boy they met, an American whom she called Ace. She and her sister were in Cannes. Ace proposed they go together to visit one of the casinos farther along the Riviera. "It took us an hour to drive there and all the way he [Ace] kept exploding: 'Gee—do you realize we're going to Monte Carlo! That glittering den of iniquity! The hangout of the Gay International Set, where Empires are won and lost nightly.' We got there and at

the end of the ballroom were three truck drivers playing poker and sucking wet cigars." Still only in her early twenties, Jackie already suspected that the "Gay International Set" was not all it was cracked up to be, but it would take another twenty years for her to reach that conclusion via prolonged experience with Mediterranean yachts and smart society.

Late in 1974, her sense that she had to do something to get a career off the ground grew. She began discussions with William Shawn, the editor of *The New Yorker*, about whether she might contribute to the magazine. Few people know that her preferred social set in New York included writers like Philip Roth, editors like Shawn and Robert Silvers of the *New York Review of Books*, museum curators like Cornell Capa, and the New York Public Library's president, Vartan Gregorian. One of the hazards of being Jackie O. was that influential people were willing to give her a great deal more rope to hang herself than a beginning writer would ordinarily be given. Shawn agreed that she might write a short piece for *The New Yorker*'s Talk of the Town on the opening of a new museum of photography. She had known the new museum's director, Cornell Capa, a long-haired Hungarian, since he had taken photographs of JFK for the 1960 campaign. Though she was at ease with Capa, for a new writer to publish in that magazine was a bit like making a TV debut in primetime. It was a frighteningly prominent place, with highly educated and critical readers, to try out one's self-conscious sentences. The only protection she had was that in those days all contributions to the Talk of the Town were anonymous.

The new International Center of Photography, she wrote in the magazine's issue for January 13, 1975, was housed in a Fifth Avenue mansion once occupied by the Audubon Society. She described the house in a three-word sentence with surprising syntax: "Lovely it is." She also made fun of the magazine's convention whereby all writers referred to themselves as "we." Cornell Capa and Karl Katz, an influential force in the ICP's founding, were going to show her around. "Mr. Capa put one arm around Mr. Katz and the other around us, and began to steer us through." European monarchs used the royal "we," too, but no one could tell that this anonymous writer in the magazine was "America's queen." As in her unpublished work, however, she could not help but reveal a rather private side of herself in this short piece. She chose to give special emphasis to a slide show at the museum that had a voiceover by the famed French photographer Henri Cartier-Bresson. "I love life," she quoted Cartier-Bresson as saying. "I love human beings. I hate people also . . . I enjoy shooting a picture, being present. It's a way of saying, 'Yes! Yes! Yes!' . . . And there's no maybe." Photography helped Cartier-Bresson overcome his shyness by his engagement with the subject of the picture. The *New Yorker* editors grasped that this was the point of Jackie's piece and gave it the title "Being Present." The question she had before her was whether writing such pieces for *The New Yorker*, fulfilling an ambition she had had ever since she was in her twenties, would help her overcome her shyness and be present in a new way as well.

The year 1975 was among the most significant years of her life. Not only had she successfully written this short piece for America's foremost literary magazine, but Onassis died, freeing her at last to take up a career. In the autumn of that year she joined Viking. She traveled to Russia to do research for *In the Russian Style* and to encourage the Russians to be more forthcoming with Vreeland's requests for loans of historic dress. She commissioned an expert, Audrey Kennett, to write a historical introduction to the book, but Jackie chose the pictures, composed captions, and wrote short introductory sections for each chapter. Once again she displayed her talent as a writer, at the same time revealing herself in the elements of Russian history she chose to emphasize. For example, here is the writerly Jackie introducing the late-seventeenth- and early-eighteenth-century tsar Peter the Great: "A huge man six feet seven inches tall, cruel, crude, and devoted to Russia, Peter was a contradictory figure." She manages alliteration ("cruel" followed by "crude") as well as a surprising reversal of direction in midsentence ("devoted to Russia"), when the reader least expects it. Here, too, is Jackie identifying with that portion of Russian history which she most aspired to emulate: while only seven books a year had been published under Peter's reign, she pointed out, eight thousand were published under Catherine the Great in the eighteenth century.

Moreover, mindful of criticisms from the Kennedy family, from Onassis when he was alive, and from a hostile press—that she was unduly extravagant, likely to plunk down $60,000 for a snuffbox from her favorite antiques and jewelry shop, Manhattan's A La Vieille Russie—she filled the book with historical illustrations drawn from the archives of the store. "This is who I am, and who I want to be," she seemed to be saying. "Take it or leave it."

The problem with publishing a book and putting your name on the cover is that it invites criticism. Detractors can take potshots at you in public journals. As a good deal of ego tends to be invested in a writer's work, that criticism can hurt. Jackie was shocked to find that a prominent intellectual, a Russian composer now living in the United States and a man whom she considered a friend, Nicolas Nabokov, was willing to attack her book in the *New York Review of Books*. Nabokov said that her book was filled with inaccuracies and sloppy history. It was the work of a dilettante, not a professional historian. He ended his review with a line aimed directly at

Jackie: "Beware of well-meaning but muddle-headed amateurs, however illustrious their names may be." If writing her first piece in *The New Yorker* was an unusual privilege, being attacked in the *New York Review of Books*, a journal of record for the American intelligentsia, was a very public flaying. Even though her friend Leonid Tarassuk, a senior research associate in the department of Arms and Armor at the Met, came to her defense and published a number of letters in succeeding issues that took aim at Nabokov's points, she still felt humiliated in a new and uncomfortable way.

Jackie had been taught from before she was ten that when she was thrown from her horse, she had to get back on and keep going. So once again she followed Diana Vreeland, writing a piece for an exhibition catalogue to accompany a new show at the Costume Institute. The exhibition, entitled Vanity Fair, was Vreeland's answer to the seventeenth-century Puritan attack on vanity written by John Bunyan. Jackie's accompanying essay, "A Visit to the High Priestess of Vanity Fair," a tribute to her mentor in the shape of an interview with Vreeland, appeared in 1977. The essay is unparalleled not only because of its writing, but also because it is the only place Jackie ever appeared in print explaining why she cared about clothes.

In the essay, Jackie writes of following Vreeland around on a personal tour of an exhibition mainly of the fine craftsmanship that went into women's historical dress. She begins her essay by choosing two unusual metaphors. Vreeland was "whippet boned" and looked "like a high priestess, which in a way she is, and her temple is on the ground floor of The Metropolitan Museum of Art." Here was Jackie's teacher, resembling both an elegant animal and the celebrant of a sacred rite. Jackie quoted Vreeland's explanation of why women ought not to be ashamed of dressing up. "Do not be too hard on vanity," Vreeland said. "Some may think it vain to look into a mirror, but I consider it an identification of self." She observed further, "The feel of a perfect piece of silk to a woman is a very exciting thing. It's the greatest projection of pleasure. And what's wrong with pleasure?" For Vreeland, fashion was also about the exquisite craftsmanship of women's clothes, itself an art, not inferior to painting or writing or photography. It was important for women of means to sustain this art; otherwise the knowledge of the craftsmen—the sewing, the cutting, and the intricate beadwork—would die out. To wear a beautifully intricate dress was to keep that knowledge alive, and it was also about a kind of hedonism in which women ought to indulge from time to time. As if to cap off her praise of the vanity Bunyan would have regarded as sinful, Vreeland remarked of a daring dress that Pauline de Rothschild wore to a Parisian ball in 1966, "Nothing is illegal in France, as we know." Jackie had indeed known what it was like to be young in Paris, and it was for some of the same reasons that her mother had called her home and forbidden her to accept the *Vogue* internship in Paris when it was awarded to her.

Jackie took Vreeland's lesson and put it into words she chose herself. She discovered an anonymous verse found on an ancient Egyptian papyrus, probably part of the inscription at a burial place of the pharaohs. The tombs and chapels of famous men are all temporary, says the verse. They crumble and fall, just as people do. That is why you should "follow your desire while you live," and "increase your beauty," because "no one goes away and then comes back."

The verse Jackie quoted is similar, both in sentiment and in the eastern Mediterranean geography of its origins, to the Cavafy verse her friend Maurice Tempelsman quoted at her memorial service. That poem wishes that the traveler will have "many summer mornings when

with what pleasure, what joy,
you enter harbors you're seeing for the first time;
may you stop at Phoenician trading stations
to buy fine things,
mother of pearl and coral, amber and ebony,
sensual perfume of every kind—
as many sensual perfumes as you can;
and may you visit many Egyptian cities
to learn and go on learning from their scholars."

Tempelsman was reiterating a point Jackie had made long before in her essay on Diana Vreeland, on which the two of them were in warm agreement.

In writing this piece, Jackie learned something else. To collect and commission beautiful things—whether beautiful dresses or beautiful books—was itself a form of creation, of worthwhile knowledge, because it stimulated the work of other artists. Sartorial connoisseurship is a stimulus to creation in fashion. Editorial connoisseurship stimulates the production with pen and ink of the work of others. She showed with her metaphors and her quotations from obscure but illuminating sources that she had a writer's talent, but it was not necessary to write herself to participate in the creative process. This is evident from another work that appeared in the next year.

Jackie's travel to Russia for *In the Russian Style* had piqued her interest in Russian clothes, Russian history, and the Russian visual arts. In the 1970s she also met Andreas Brown, the proprietor of the Gotham Book Mart, where she set up charge accounts for herself and her children. Brown showed her some rare books illustrated by Boris Zvorykin, a Russian artist and illustrator who had been in the circle of Diaghilev and Stravinsky before he emigrated to Paris after the Russian Revolution of 1917. At Viking, Jackie brought out a new edition of Zvorykin's illustrations, *The Firebird and Other Russian Fairy Tales*. Later in her publishing career she would seldom do what she did with this Zvorykin edition, which was to write the introduction. Zvorykin had had to start all over in Paris. He had presented this collection of folktales with illustrations to his publisher, Louis Fricotelle, as "a gift of gratitude for a new life, celebrating all he valued and missed in the old." The artistic circle around Diaghilev had fascinated Jackie when she was applying for the *Vogue* prize in the 1950s. Twenty years later, it was as if she were fulfilling the dream she had had then of doing something to educate herself and disseminate the genius of those turn-of-the-century Russian artists.

The last of her written works from the 1970s was an introduction to a collection of photographs of the famed French photographer Eugène Atget. One of Jackie's editorial choices was to emphasize photographs of royal parks and palace gardens. This was a passion that had been present in the White House and would resurface later in her editorial career. The tabloid press and one of her biographers called her "America's queen," not always in admiration. Nevertheless, she embraced that title by showing her interest in what European historians call "court studies": the history of the costumes, architecture, and customs of kings after the fall of the Roman Empire. The black-and-white photographs in the Atget book captured Bourbon palace gardens at Versailles, Sceaux, St. Cloud, and the Tuileries.

In writing about the vanished grandeur of the French royal court in her introduction, Jackie noted that the avenues, axes, and vistas laid out in the seventeenth century were often still extant today: "The royal vision lingers wherever the antique lines they imposed long ago on the landscape still survive, despite all the vicissitudes of time." She acknowledges with regret that middle-class people now occupy the spaces once designed for kings. Atget was photographing royal gardens in the early twentieth century, when many of them had become public parks. For example, "In the Luxembourg," Jackie wrote, "the fountain has become a family gathering place. We find these photographs troubling because we can connect to them. The time is bourgeois here, and our grandfathers sit in black serge suits along the paths laid out by kings and queens." Her father's family, the Bouviers, had originally come from France, and it unsettled her to see bankers and cabinet-makers seated with such ease around a royal fountain. Some of Atget's photos reminded her of "a wild Greek island with terme and tree torn by wind."

Still, what impressed her most was the beauty of the photographs. Atget had been successful in preserving memories of these distinctive spaces in the art of his photography. Jackie quoted a member of the French Academy, Georges Duhamel, as saying, "In the present disorder of the world, to conserve is to create." This is what Atget had achieved: his act was a double act of creation, for not only had he taken beautiful photographs, he had created something new by conserving and preserving the genius of these crumbling royal gardens. Jackie also quoted Edith Wharton, who was, like Jackie, an American who lived as an expatriate in France for many years: "Of the art of France, Edith Wharton said that we had only to look around us and 'see that the whole world is full of her spilt glory.'" In this piece Jackie showed that she had ability to be the writer she sometimes dreamed of being, quoting widely from dissimilar experts, making daring passes at telling her own life story, and using the alliteration of her remembered Greek island's "terme" and "tree."

Something else was happening in her writing of the Atget introduction, however. What may well have dawned on her was that what most attracted her was not textual but visual material—a Russian costume, a turn-of-the-century illustration, a photograph of a royal garden. For a shy woman who wished to control as much as she could of what the world learned about her, it was maybe too bold to start a discussion in her own words of the Bouviers and of what she recollected of Greek geography. If "to conserve is to create," if to recognize and give shape to the artistry of another is itself a form of artistry, perhaps her safest and most fulfilling role could be as an editor, to choose what was brilliant in the work of others rather than to be a writer herself. This, too, was a form of creation.

Fading into the Background

In the 1980s, Jackie's published writings came to an abrupt halt. She wrote only three short pieces, all briefer than her works of the 1970s, all to advance specific projects she cared about, and spent more of her time learning to be an editor who faded, unacknowledged, into the background. Acknowledgment was not what she craved anyway; what she wanted was to be a part of the creative process.

The three brief pieces she did allow into print in the 1980s are nevertheless just as expressive of her personality and her passions as the work she had already published. She wrote a foreword to accompany *Grand Central Terminal,* a catalogue published by New York's Municipal Art Society to accompany a traveling exhibition. Jackie had played an important role in standing with preservationists who saved the Grand Central building from destruction. Two bankrupt railroads had proposed to improve their balance sheets by tearing it down and building an office tower. The 1963 destruction of the old Pennsylvania Station and its replacement by the present Penn

Station in a dirty basement underneath Madison Square Garden can give an idea of what might have happened to Grand Central. Jackie was justly proud of her role in saving Grand Central. She began her foreword with a flourish. The writer James Agee had collaborated with the photographer Walker Evans to expose rural poverty in the American South during the Depression in their crusading book, *Let Us Now Praise Famous Men*. Jackie wrote of her crusade, "Let us now praise Grand Central Station."

She rued the loss of the old Penn Station. She argued that "old buildings are a precious part of our heritage, and . . . we cripple ourselves if we destroy them." History had to be our guide when we sought what was valuable in great architecture. If we value only what is modern, we will have lost wisdom about architecture that our ancestors had. "Great civilizations of the past recognized that their citizens had aesthetic needs, that great architecture gave nobility and respite to their daily lives." To preserve Grand Central, to republish Atget's photographs, to restore the White House to the Monroe era of its original construction, was to point out the magnificence that was open to all if they were to step into the structures built in the past.

Preservation of the rural countryside is the theme of another of Jackie's short pieces from the 1980s. Marshall Hawkins was a photographer known for his work documenting the rural hunts she had participated in on horseback since she was a child. Hawkins had taken a famous picture of her falling off her horse in Virginia when she was first lady. In fact, Hawkins had startled her horse and was partially responsible for her fall. Jackie had asked JFK to prevent Hawkins's photo from being published. The president had responded, "When the first lady falls on her ass, that's news," and had allowed the photograph to be printed over her objections. More than twenty years later, when she was asked to write the foreword to a group of Hawkins's photographs, she showed no particular resentment over the earlier incident. What she recognized was a much more urgent problem: "The inexorable press of modern development has steadfastly reduced the perimeters of our natural environment, not just for horsemen, but for nature-lovers all. Everywhere we look, we are reminded of the countryside which once was, and we wish for earlier times." Hawkins's photographs are less impressive as images of a lucky few who own horses and riding coats than they are of a vanished countryside. But once again she sounded the elegiac note. Hawkins's subjects—and she included herself here, because there is the photo of her being thrown as well as a shot of her getting up afterward, uninjured—valued these images as "intensely felt, vanished moments now fixed forever." Many of Jackie's written pieces expose this side of her personality: her nostalgia for vanished grandeur, whether in the built or the natural environment, whether in beautiful clothes or in royal gardens. She was nostalgic not for a simpler world, but for one that was more elaborate, more formal, and more hierarchical.

The last of her published pieces, one that had appeared in 1988, is a brief foreword of no more than a few lines to Michael Jackson's memoir *Moonwalk*. She says much by saying little. It was not a project she particularly enjoyed. It was a book she felt she had to do for the company's bottom line, and as everyone expected, it was a bestseller. Jackie felt she ought not to say very much, as it would have been dishonest to praise Jackson effusively. Jackson and his representatives had pressed her to write a foreword, and she wrote one, asking, "What can one say about Michael Jackson?" as if with an ironic wink.

What she learned in the interim period, mainly in the 1970s, when she published works under her own name, was that she need not be a writer herself in order to assist at the creation of the work of other artists. Jackie's friend Jane Hitchcock modeled a character on Jackie, Clara Wilman, in a novel she wrote after Jackie died called *Social Crimes*. The narrator of the novel looks up to Clara Wilman, just as Hitchcock had intensely admired Jackie. Hitchcock put words into Clara Wilman's mouth that Hitchcock acknowledges having heard from Jackie first: "The secret is not so much knowing how to do it yourself—it's knowing whom to *choose*."

Jackie had remarked to Dorothy Schiff that she thought she was not a bad writer herself, but it took her a long time to write anything. She said it was "agony." It was also pretty painful to be taken to task for the "shabbiness" of her work by Nicolas Nabokov in the pages of the *New York Review of Books*. In later life she would publicly go to bat for her authors' books and stand up to defend them against criticism, but this was a personal and painful experience that she cannot have wanted to repeat. Jackie adored stylish things—beaded jackets, formal parterres, marbled concourses—but in these published works she also showed that she could produce a stylish sentence herself. One part of herself revealed in writing was that she valued flourish and swagger and poise not as marginal extras but as things worth having in their own right. Of Atget's photographs, she concluded, "His conquest of us [his viewers], like that of his own visible world, [is] complete." Having learned that lesson, she moved into the background of her books, allowing her authors to have pride of place, but with no less ambition to achieve complete conquest of us as her readers.

chapter 3

I WANT TO BE THE
KIND OF EDITOR YOU WANT ME TO BE.
—Jackie to one of her writers

•

The Jackie that no one knows is the one her colleagues remember sitting down on her office floor, cigarette clenched between her teeth, laying out illustrations for a book. "This very grand woman getting down on the office floor to arrange photographs, literally abasing herself," was how her assistant Scott Moyers put it. Another colleague remembers hearing, while sitting at a desk outside her office, *"Oy vey,"* loud and low, in a deep voice. He went into her office to see if she was all right. He was surprised to find her down on the floor doing her filing. Jackie as a working editor was not the gossamer creation that she appears to be in many of her photographs. She was a down-to-earth woman who struggled with office politics, messy files, and authors who always wanted more four-color photographs than the higher-ups would pay for. The strange thing is that office life, far from tying her down, set her free. She went from being a shy celebrity recruit to a respected editor with a long list of books that were not only distinctively hers but that even today make publishing executives shake their heads in admiration of what she accomplished. Taste is not some evanescent thing that people are born with: Jackie acquired hers by sitting quietly in the presence of people who knew better than she did, by having the courage to say what she loved, and by making sacrifices in order to bring what she loved to life.

Jackie was given her chance to try out being an editor because she was a publisher's chance for increased publicity, but she ended as an editor who had produced a number of commercial successes. Although she allowed her new employer to trumpet her employment and put her picture in the papers when she arrived at Viking, she ended by publishing most of her books silently, unheralded, and usually without the use of her name. Even today, a Jackie book is indistinguishable from the dozens of others produced at Viking and Doubleday in the same era, because many, perhaps the majority, of them do not have her name anywhere on them—not on the cover, not in the acknowledgments, nowhere. She wanted her books to succeed because something deserved to be said or shown, not because of her "celebrity"; even the word made her shiver with an instinctive dislike. How she did all this, and how the two decades after 1975 transformed her life, can be seen in the story of how she arrived at Viking in the first place and was forced to change jobs two years later. She then spent sixteen years at Doubleday, first very much in the shadow of editors who knew a lot more than she did but slowly emerging from that training period on the basis of book projects she took the initiative in selecting. It is a story that has her not only getting down on the floor but holding the hands of her authors, getting money for them, spotting talent, encouraging writers by showing interest in what they had done, and sometimes telling them no. She once remarked to Mabel Brandon, "Oh, Muffie, aren't we lucky we work?" Jackie's discovery in these years was that reading by herself in a corner, sailing on a yacht, and buying couture clothes in Paris were all a great deal less sustaining than going into the office and drinking coffee out of a Styrofoam cup.

When Jackie and Lee had sought out the art historian Bernard Berenson in Italy during the summer of 1951, he had told them, "The only way to exist happily is to love your work." Going to see Berenson, a distinguished intellectual and art dealer, when she was only twenty-two was among the first indications that Jackie was a good deal more than a shy debutante. She was at odds with her era, because in the 1950s and 1960s, "work" for most women was tending to husbands and households, getting married and raising children. Although Jackie had briefly had a job doing a column as a photographer for a Washington newspaper, she had never collected a salary for long or aimed at a career. Like many women of her generation, however, she began to think about work when her children gave signs of soon needing her less. Aristotle Onassis's death in March 1975 gave her further reason to reorganize her life. She remarked to an acquaintance, "I have always lived through men . . . Now I realize I can't do that anymore."

Though Dorothy Schiff had never persuaded Jackie to write a column for the *Post*, she had kept in touch with her. In 1975, after Onassis died, Schiff impulsively put a new proposal to her: Jackie should run for the Senate as a Democrat to unseat New York's conservative senator James L. Buckley, brother of the right-wing ideologue William F. Buckley, Jr. Jackie played with the idea for a short while. Did Schiff think she could do the job on only three days a week—Tuesday, Wednesday, and Thursday—in Washington? Schiff told Jackie she thought four days a week was the minimum. Jackie's question and the fact that she turned down Schiff's idea after only one night to sleep on it show that the job she had just started at Viking was holding her interest. She had worked only three days a week when she was in the White House, spending long weekends either in Virginia or at Hyannis. She would keep to that same three-day-a-week schedule when she worked at Doubleday. It was not because she did not intend to work; the evidence is that she worked with authors in her apartment and at her summer houses. One of John's friends wandered out onto the terrace of the Hyannis house one summer afternoon and was surprised to find his friend's mother working on a manuscript instead of a tan. She was working on, in his words, "some language conundrum." It didn't really interest him, but he did note that she had an unusual grasp of language and that because of her, John had developed a surprisingly large vocabulary. Jackie knew that a person with her shyness around people could not stand more than three days a week of constant face time. New York was the center of the world she loved, and she was not about to give it up for a return to Washington, where she had been simply a political wife.

Moreover, she had no intention of working nine to five. She later established a routine at Doubleday that was more like eight-thirty in the morning to twelve-thirty in the afternoon on Tuesdays, Wednesdays, and Thursdays. Then she was gone. She was also absent for about three months in the summer, when she was on Martha's Vineyard. This was an enormous privilege, and it caused resentment, even though she could honestly say that she was on call in the afternoon and in the evening, at home and at the beach. She often met authors for editing sessions at 1040 Fifth Avenue, occasionally attended sales meetings on Long Island, traveled to California and Washington on book business, and lunched with a wide variety of people whose manuscripts she hoped to bring into the office. Nevertheless, she did not like being reminded that the three-day-a-week privilege extended to her was not extended to all, even to the most accomplished of her colleagues. One fellow editor of Jackie's generation, who had been at school with some of her Kennedy in-laws, once spoke with Jackie about the number of books they worked on. The two had a little laugh together about how to fill out what seemed a pointless new Doubleday form. Jackie's colleague remem-

bered saying, "Oh, but of course you only work part-time." It was a gaffe, and the mood changed abruptly. Jackie stiffened when she realized that her work was regarded as part-time. Her colleague backpedaled furiously. To speak of her privilege or her celebrity in her presence was one sure way of making Jackie angry, yet privilege and celebrity were also two of the reasons why she had been hired in the first place and, perhaps more revealingly, two of the subjects that she had most success exploring in her list. Understanding that contradiction and finding out how it animated her as well as sometimes causing friction with coworkers is the story of her life in the office at Viking and Doubleday.

Shall We Tell Jackie?

Thomas Guinzburg's father had founded the Viking Press, and the business was still family owned when Jackie signed on in the fall of 1975. To one of her later authors, she recalled enjoying the fact that when in 1953 her sister, Lee, married Michael Canfield—the adoptive son of Cass Canfield, the head of the publishing house that has since become Harper-Collins—she had new contact with writers. Going to Viking, she imagined hopefully, would be more of the same. When she accepted Guinzburg's offer that she should be a consulting editor and join Viking in September 1975, her salary was $10,000 a year. This was not a huge investment: in the late 1970s, a full-time editor at a major publishing house would probably have been earning double that, though a beginner starting with as little experience as she had might have expected to be paid even less. Jackie posed next to Guinzburg for a photograph on her first day and looked happy with what she'd been offered.

She spent two years at Viking, and though she was associated with only five or six books, she was immediately assigned to work on a book celebrating women's roles in the history of early America, *Remember the Ladies*. She was also working on biographies of Thomas Jefferson's mistress Sally Hemings and Chicago mayor Richard Daley, as well as *In the Russian Style* and Boris Zvorykin's illustrated *The Firebird and Other Russian Fairy Tales*. She recalled being involved with a book on the nineteenth-century photographer Mathew Brady's photos of Abraham Lincoln. All this was interrupted in 1977 when Guinzburg decided to publish a novel by Jeffrey Archer, *Shall We Tell the President?* Archer was a British thriller writer, who served as a member of Parliament, deputy chairman of the Conservative Party, and was admitted to the House of Lords before he was convicted of perjury and sent to jail. In the novel, a figure clearly modeled on Jackie's brother-in-law Edward Kennedy is the target of an assassination attempt. It is unclear how much Jackie knew about the book when it was acquired. Doubleday editor Lisa Drew had told Jackie and Nancy Tuckerman at a lunch that she had turned down Archer's proposal for Doubleday as she thought it was particularly unsavory trash, but that it had sold to Viking. This may well have been the first Jackie heard of it, and she approached Guinzburg for reassurance. According to Guinzburg, when Jackie was told it might be profitable for Viking, she decided she didn't want to stand in the book's way.

However, when the novel was published, the influential critic John Leonard wrote as the last line of his review in the *New York Times*, "Anybody associated with its publication should be ashamed of herself." In comments to the *Times*, Guinzburg waffled about how much and when Jackie had been involved with the project. She always claimed that Guinzburg had acquired the book without consulting her. After Leonard's review, and under pressure from the Kennedy family, she resigned from her job at Viking and released this statement: "Last spring when I was told about the book . . . I tried to separate my lives as a Viking employee and a Kennedy relative. But this fall, when it was suggested I had something to do with acquiring the book and that I was not distressed by its publication, I felt I had to resign." Sixteen years later, when she agreed to a rare interview with *Publishers Weekly*, the magazine's editor, John F. Baker, remarked, "It is clear that memories of the incident are still upsetting to her." The truth of the matter is that Guinzburg probably got a little greedy. For a long time afterward, Jackie told her friends that she had not forgiven Guinzburg for what happened. Guinzburg had probably given her some advance warning of the book, but she had not anticipated that Leonard's review would blame her, or the wrath of her former husband's family. She got caught between her own publicity value to Viking, on the one hand, and the Kennedy family, on the other.

Once in a Lincoln Town Car going down to the Morgan Library after lunch with one of her favorite authors, Olivier Bernier, Jackie confided, "You know, in the 1960s dealing with the Kennedys wasn't easy." Bernier remembered that she said this as they passed Grand Central. It surprised him, because it was not the sort of thing she usually discussed and he would not have dared to raise it with her himself. "I'm sure it wasn't," he replied neutrally. "I'll tell you about it sometime," she said. She never raised it again. Dealing with the Kennedys in the 1970s was not always easy either, and the Viking episode was one way in which the sleeping volcano of her old life could still occasionally erupt to destroy her new one. Guinzburg did not have a happy ending either. He sold his family firm to Penguin, and the new company summarily fired him the next year.

A Rare Bird in a Common Nest

In the autumn of 1977 Jackie found herself again without a job, but she had had a taste of a world she liked very much. Dorothy Schiff recalled of Jackie that year that "she had never been so happy, and I must say she looked it." The famed photographer Alfred Eisenstaedt, who often worked for *Life* magazine, took her picture for Viking on her first day in the office. He said she resembled "a kid straight out of college," younger-looking than he had ever seen her before, "all excited about her first job." One more fringe benefit, Jackie confessed to Schiff, was that her fourteen-year-old son found her more interesting after she went to Viking. She was not about to give that up.

Much of her work at Viking had been with Bryan Holme and the Studio Books division, which specialized in large-format illustrated books. Jackie was friends with the ballet critic Francis Mason when he was also the assistant director of the Morgan Library. She asked Mason to introduce her at some small publishing firms that specialized in illustrated and art books. They went downtown several times for a number of informational interviews. That is why Mason was "shocked" when a few months later, early in 1978, Jackie took a job as an associate editor with Doubleday. In the era after the Second World War, Doubleday was the biggest publisher in the world, known for producing poor-quality books for a middlebrow readership via the Doubleday book clubs. Doubleday did not specialize in the sort of illustrated book Jackie loved. The company had also acquired a bad reputation in the industry for having tried to suppress Theodore Dreiser's classic novel *Sister Carrie* because the owner's wife objected to the heroine's adultery. Edna Ferber, a Pulitzer Prize winner, once remarked that the main achievement of the founder's son Nelson Doubleday, was "devising schemes for putting books in the hands of the un-bookish." In Jackie's era, the grandson of the firm's founder, Nelson Doubleday, Jr., preferred baseball to books. His father once remarked, "I sell books, I don't read them." In the publishing world, Doubleday books were known for being physically ugly, at their worst looking like "rubber stamped on newspaper." It is hard to imagine Jackie going to a publisher more at odds with her own personal style.

Nevertheless, what counted more with her was that Nancy Tuckerman was doing some work there for Nelson Doubleday, Jr. She was a built-in safety net, someone to whom any problems at the company could always be submitted first. Another mark in favor of the firm was Jackie's friend John Sargent, the president, who was married to Nelson Doubleday's sister. Sargent asked Tuckerman whether she would object to having Jackie join the firm. When Sargent asked Jackie why she had selected Doubleday when she could have gone anywhere, she replied, teasing her old friend a little, "Why, Nancy's having such fun there."

Early in 1978 Jackie joined Doubleday and was assigned a windowless cubicle, the sort of office that most assistants had. Immediately Nelson Doubleday came to call on her and in a friendly way proposed that the company should find some art-work for her cubicle walls. "I don't need any artwork," Jackie answered. "I like my office as it is." Jackie's main work was not with the grandson of the company founder but with a series of skilled younger editors who made it their job to show her what they were doing, to teach her what they knew, and to provide major assistance with the practicalities of book publishing. Among them was a cadre of younger women, such as Lindy Hess, Lisa Drew, and Shaye Areheart, who provided a loyal and protective phalanx around Jackie. Of course, following the Viking debacle, Doubleday was anxious to assure Jackie the utmost privacy. It was an unspoken rule that no one should speak about her, and the company undertook not to publish anything remotely connected to Jackie's life or to the Kennedy family. Jackie also had an expert way of her own to line up protection. She had a way of seeming to confide in some of her coworkers that made them anxious and willing to protect her. Scott Moyers remembered, "She immediately brought you into a sense of complicity with her. She managed, without being overt about it, to make you feel protective of her privacy, make you shield the outside world." The young Texan novelist Elizabeth Crook also thought that Jackie had silently reposed a large trust in her. Jackie trusted her, for example, not to ask her anything remotely connected to her fame or private life: "I felt that in a small, implicit way I had been enlisted as another guardian of Camelot."

Jackie had a slow start at Doubleday. Although her combined list at Viking and Doubleday would later grow to include nearly a hundred books, those books are concentrated in the period after the mid-1980s. In the ten years up to and including 1985, she was connected with the publication of about twenty-five or twenty-six books. She was not solely responsible for all of them. On some projects she helped to acquire the book, while colleagues did the technical work of bringing it to press. Or she merely assisted other editors with projects they had acquired. In the ten years after 1986 she was connected with almost seventy books, and with the majority of these she took some significant share in the work herself.

Sandy Richardson, a Doubleday editor in chief during Jackie's time there, saw her as not accomplishing very much early on but confirmed that she began to do a lot better later in her career. He characterized her job objective as bringing in books by other celebrities, and he noted that she continued to take on visual projects that seemed like a continuation of her time at Viking. Herman Gollob, another editor in chief, thought Jackie lacked business smarts. Her books had small print runs and seldom had a major impact on the culture. He conceded that she was of public relations value to the firm and that she was a magnet of some note for authors who wrote books of which the company was proud. Not understanding the business side of publishing, though, was "a major flaw in an editor," said Gollob.

Nevertheless, by the mid-1980s Jackie had significant books in the pipeline which gave her the confidence to gather forward momentum in her career. Books often take a long time to make it into print. They frequently come in to the publisher as promising but half-baked ideas which the editor has to tease out, or as proposals, or as half-completed manuscripts, so it is hard to pinpoint exactly when Jackie could look back on what she had done and feel that she had accomplished something significant. There are groups of her books whose publication dates cluster from the mid-1980s to the early 1990s where it is clear that she was doing a good deal more than merely bringing in celebrities. Perhaps she left the business side to others, but there are certainly five significant kinds of books that emerge as landmarks of her publishing list.

Making a List, Checking It Twice

In reflecting on Jackie's list, Nancy Tuckerman observed that she liked "things of a scholarly nature." Jackie brought out a new edition of the Marquis de Custine's famous nineteenth-century journal of his travels in Russia, and his notes on the Russian national character. Custine's notes on Russian despotism showed the tragic, illiberal continuities between the tsarist and Soviet systems. Jackie also republished the rare diary of a French soldier on Napoleon's march to and retreat from Moscow, unusual in providing the point of view not of the officer class but of the ordinary fighting man wearing poor boots, hungry, and cold. Jackie commissioned the memoirs of a distinguished art historian, John Pope-Hennessy,

for many years the director of several of London's top museums. She may not have been a PhD herself, but she had a certain genius in identifying scholarly subjects that might have
crossover appeal to a broader audience.

Another group consists of works of considerable prestige that brought the company some welcome publicity, and
in some cases money, too. These included memoirs by Martha
Graham and André Previn, as well as a trilogy of novels by the
Egyptian Nobel Prize winner Naguib Mahfouz. In each case
Jackie was the sole figure who had enough weight to bring the
author to Doubleday. She made the personal connection that
encouraged each author to sign the contract. Alberto Vitale,
one-time CEO of the group of companies that included Doubleday, remembered that his initial collaboration with her on
contacting Mahfouz led in time to the company's acquisition
of the rights to more than a dozen Mahfouz titles of considerable commercial value. Because Vitale has sometimes had a
reputation in the publishing world for valuing cash over culture, this is a significant tribute to Jackie.

The third group consists of works of particular artistry,
beautifully produced books that were works of art in themselves. These include two books by Naveen Patnaik on India,
one by the interior decorator Mark Hampton with his own
watercolor sketches, and another by the photographer Toni
Frissell, for which Jackie personally selected and arranged the
photographs. These remarkably designed books justify Jackie's claim to having achieved something tangible while working as part of a creative team, and working against the grain
of Doubleday's reputation for book design that "used to be
quite bad," as she herself put it. Particularly at the beginning
of her career, she liked working on large-format illustrated
books, such as Diana Vreeland's *Allure* and Deborah Turbeville's *Unseen Versailles*. "These are the books I most love to do,"

she wrote in 1980. They can be dismissed as mere coffee-table books only by missing the fact that the images in them were as striking and unusual as she was. Although her list became more varied as her career lengthened, these illustrated books were certainly one of her trademarks.

The fourth group consists of works of political passion. Among them is a book by Carl Elliott, the first recipient of the John F. Kennedy Library's Profile in Courage Award. Elliott was a southern congressman who stood up for the rights of his impoverished constituents. His career ended in a political contest with the South's most notorious racist, George Wallace. Jackie also championed a biography of Judge Frank Johnson, a civil rights hero of the 1960s, who was responsible for important decisions striking down segregation laws and forcing Wallace to permit Martin Luther King's march from Selma to Montgomery. Writers have often described Jackie as not interfering in White House politics, but her publishing record shows that she was deeply committed to some of the causes both JFK and Bobby Kennedy also cared about.

The last group consists of bestsellers. By the late 1980s, Jackie already had three: a tell-all memoir by the ballerina Gelsey Kirkland, a first-ever book by Michael Jackson, and a book fashioned from television interviews conducted by Bill Moyers. Any editor lives and dies by the sales figures of books on her list. Jackie could show with these three authors that she had added significantly to the company's bottom line, independently of her unquantifiable publicity value to Doubleday.

Today when publishing professionals look over her list they point to its variety and eclecticism, its combination of arcane, highbrow interests, which were uniquely hers, and crowd-pleasers, which spoke to her instinct for sales. The British editor and author Ion Trewin said he was "amazed" at the range of high and low in it: her list went from an earnest tract by the town planner Raquel Ramati, *How to Save Your Own Street*, to a book on how to set the table in *The New Tiffany Table Settings,* from Mahfouz to Michael Jackson. People who rode on horseback with Jackie in the hunt country of Virginia were surprised at how competitive she could be. She did not necessarily have to win, but she wanted to compete with distinction. Similarly, Steve Rubin, the head of Doubleday during many of her most productive years there, recalled that "she hated to lose money." He found that telling her a project she was enthusiastic about might lose money was a way of causing her to pause and think. Her list was put together out of this combination of considerations: subjects and authors that caught her fancy and a determination that she would not just be a spoiled socialite who always published books independent of commercial calculations.

Her longtime assistant Bruce Tracy sometimes filtered the proposals that came across her desk. He reeled off a list of the subjects that would usually interest her: ballet and modern dance, India, French and Russian history, anything by Bill Moyers and others whom she had known from her days in Washington, design and interior decoration, and photography. Another editorial colleague, David Gernert, now a literary agent, described her list as "high culture and famous friends." Steve Wasserman, one-time editor of the book review section of the *Los Angeles Times,* who briefly overlapped with Jackie when he was at Doubleday, characterized her list in a different way. He identified the concentration of works by dancers, on courtly life, on Hollywood, and on myth in her list. He thought that many of her books were about being the exotic bird in a gilded cage. The bird in the cage wishes to escape but makes its peace with being always on view. Her books are about the discipline, the rigor, the ritual it takes to perform in the gilded cage, as well as about the secrets that are not on view. He regarded the most significant theme in her list as the hard work that went into an effortless, stylized appearance. The theme in her list, Wasserman said, was also a theme of her life.

Working Girl

There are also themes in her daily office life that show us a side of Jackie that is unfamiliar. The single most repeated recollection of her as an editor has her down on the floor laying out photographs and illustrations to see how they look in sequence. It was something she had learned from Diana Vreeland, who liked to lay out a prospective issue of *Vogue* by placing the feature pages and advertisements on the floor along the office corridors and in conference rooms. In her interview with *Publishers Weekly* in 1993, Jackie said, "I want my books to look as beautiful as possible." She took a larger role than many other editors not only in selecting the illustrations for the interior but in choosing the image for the cover. She showed *Publishers Weekly* the image that she had found for Edvard Radzinsky's biography of Nicholas II, *The Last Tsar*, a gloomy picture of the former tsar sitting on a tree stump, seemingly aware of the horrible murder that the Soviet revolutionaries had in store for him. She compared it with the less moving image of the entire Romanov family Ion Trewin chose for the English edition of the book, noting that that edition had not sold as well as Doubleday's.

Jackie did not regularly interfere with the work of Doubleday's designers; rather, she encouraged them by enjoying and appreciating what they produced, and occasionally by buttering them up. Olivier Bernier went down to one designer's office once with her in order to ask for wider margins and better paper on his next book. He watched the designer "melt" when she told the man, "I'm sure you're just going to surpass yourself" on the design of Bernier's book. Peter Kruzan, a designer whom she singled out for particular praise in her interview with *Publishers Weekly,* could remember only one time, though he worked with her on dozens of books, when she suggested a change to him. On Radzinsky's *Last Tsar* he had proposed a baroque filigree around the border of the book's cover. "Do you think it might be a little too fanciful for so sad a book?" she asked him. Kruzan recalled her delicacy in pointing this out to him: "She made it a question" rather than a change she wanted made. Her celebrity may have been a factor in persuading these designers to take the work in a direction she wanted, but above all she loved the books they worked on together and enjoyed being a part of the shared enterprise of putting them together.

When Whitney Cookman came on as a senior creative director at Doubleday, he was surprised that Jackie never summoned him up to her office. Instead she phoned him up herself and asked if he had a minute so she could "lope on down" to see him. Cookman thought of her less as an editor and "more as a curator." She "assembled a book as if it were an exhibition." While working together on *The Diary of a Napoleonic Foot Soldier*, they went to the New York Public Library to examine nineteenth-century illustrations. Cookman also thought Jackie was like a patron of the arts. Though she could not do all the layouts and design work herself, "she did love to be around those who could."

Marysarah Quinn was another designer whom Jackie admired. She was part of a new regime introduced by Nancy Evans, who when she became head of Doubleday decreed that the books should look better. Quinn was just a young woman in her twenties, but Jackie made a point of going to her office, welcoming her, and saying that she looked forward to the design department's having its shackles removed. Jackie also felt that it was her job to introduce this new recruit to a senior designer who worked independently for Doubleday on occasion. She and Quinn got in a cab to go uptown to meet him. The women discovered that neither of them had enough cash to pay the taxi driver. As Quinn put it, "I was only twenty-five and had no money." Neither did Jackie, because . . . "Well, because she was Jackie O." They pooled the small change from the bottoms of their purses, paid the man what they had, and then got out early to walk the rest of the way. Quinn felt instinctively that it was her responsibility to guard Jackie as they walked up Broadway and was relieved when passersby only smiled at her.

Quinn also recalled Jackie's friendly rivalry with Nan Talese. Talese had acquired and edited *The Hat Book,* by the photographer Rodney Smith. Quinn had designed a large red grosgrain ribbon that tied across the cover of the book, an unusually expensive flourish. "How did she get to do that?" Jackie said as she held the book up enviously in her hands. The woman in the pillbox hat remained visually alert and tuned in to questions of book design throughout her publishing career. The nineteenth-century critic Walter Pater, who inspired Wilde and the other fin-de-siècle artists Jackie admired, observed that there was a point to enjoying art, poetry, and beauty in the world: it was to live always at a high pitch of intense artistic experience, "to burn always with this hard gem-like flame." Whether she was stroking a grosgrain ribbon or selecting a picture of a deposed Romanov, Jackie also believed in that elevating, transfiguring effect of a book's design.

Of course, she did many of the humble things that all editors have to do. She held the hands of nervous authors while they produced their manuscripts. Elizabeth Crook was, like

Quinn, a young woman for whom Jackie had a protective maternal instinct. Crook wrote two novels for Jackie. As she was writing the second one, *Promised Lands,* a historical novel set during the Texas war for independence from Mexico in the 1830s, she asked Jackie whether she would like to see each chapter as she wrote it or groups of chapters. Jackie replied that it was probably better to show her groups of chapters. "But if you need some hand holding through the forest," she wrote, "you must do whatever makes you feel best." When Ann Waldron, whom Jackie had commissioned to write a biography of Eudora Welty, asked whether she should send in research reports, Jackie replied, "I want to be the kind of editor that you want me to be." She was a book geisha. She cultivated the art of charming and pleasing the people who wrote for her, trying to sense what they wanted from her so she could provide it and they would produce their best work.

She got those who outranked her at Doubleday to approve money to offer authors as advance payments on royalties. She did this somewhat less often than other editors, but still she was involved. When Doubleday wanted to make an offer to Jackie's friend and Martha's Vineyard neighbor Carly Simon, Herman Gollob gave Jackie instructions on how to proceed. Gollob recalled, "We told her to offer $150,000, and go as high as $250,000 if necessary, but if it goes beyond that come back to us and we'll discuss it." Jackie talked to Simon's lawyer. Then she went back to Gollob and said, "He took the one-fifty—what do we do now?" "We make a contract. Nice work, Jackie." "But," she said, "you told me we could go as high as two-fifty." Gollob replied, "But only if he continued to bargain. He took the first offer." She said, "Then we're screwing Carly." Gollob concluded in mock exasperation, "It was hard for her to understand the negotiating process." She had to learn the job, like everyone else, and she did not like preventing her friend from earning the full amount the company had considered paying her.

Stories like this are relatively few and far between. It seems that in later years, Shaye Areheart or the deputy publisher, Bill Barry, did a lot of negotiating for her. Barry, for example, was the person who discussed the amount of the advance with Radzinsky's agent, Lynn Franklin, when it came to buying both *The Last Tsar* and a biography of Stalin that appeared after Jackie died.

Sometimes, even when Jackie felt passionate about a project—about the autobiography of Judge Frank Johnson, for example—she was not able to get enough money to give the author the time off he needed to write the book. In fact, the book on Judge Johnson came into being only many years later when a journalist, Jack Bass, proposed writing about him. Judge Johnson, having had earlier contact with Jackie and suspecting that she was still interested, told Bass cryptically, "Jackie Onassis would like to edit this book"—an amazing revelation to Bass, who thought he might be writing what another editor had called merely "a regional book" on an obscure southern judge.

Above all, Jackie's job was to spot talent and acquire books. She was expected to be the hunter: to bring in big game in the way of high-profile names and celebrities. She did do some of this, as Michael Jackson, André Previn, Martha Graham, and Carly Simon all demonstrate. But it is perhaps more revealing to see the names that got away. She wanted to do something with Ken Burns, the producer of such famous PBS documentaries as his film on the Civil War, but never quite succeeded. She learned that the director and producer Oliver Stone had written some novels before his Hollywood success with the film *Platoon* in 1986. She asked if he would let her see them. He said, politely, no. Stone asked Jackie in turn whether she would come to the premiere of his new film, *Wall Street*. She also said no. Jackie asked General Norman Schwarzkopf to consider Doubleday for his memoirs at the height of his fame following the first Gulf War. He thanked her, but he took his project to a higher bidder. Diana Ross, Frank Sinatra, and George Cukor all eluded her.

Rather, her usual sources for books were elsewhere. A number of books came to her via her contact with the Metropolitan Museum, the city's main public art gallery, just across Fifth Avenue from her apartment. There was her work with Diana Vreeland, but also with the museum's director, Thomas Hoving; with Leonid Tarassuk from the department of Arms and Armor; with the museum's special curator of Islamic and Indian art, Stuart Cary Welch; and with Karl Katz, who headed up a division intended to take the museum's collection to a broader audience via film and television. Another source of projects was the New York Public Library. She attended the library's annual literary lions dinner, which honored prominent writers. She relied on the library's special expert in Slavic studies, Edward Kasinec, who helped her with several of her books. Jackie also got ideas from the press. Some of her books originated in articles written for *Rolling Stone,* whose editor, Jann Wenner, was a friend. Others came from *Vanity Fair, People,* and the *New York Times*. She relied on contacts from the White House years, too, and in addition to her books with Bill Moyers, she published books with LBJ's press aide Jack Valenti, who was on the plane back to Washington from Dallas in November 1963, when she was photographed next to the new president at his swearing-in, and with JFK's secretary of the interior, Stewart Udall. Above all there was a small group of writers with whom she repeatedly published books, because she trusted them, admired them, and had fun working with them. In that group is the *Rolling Stone* writer Jonathan Cott, a Chicago writer who left the priesthood to teach psychology, Eugene Kennedy (no relation to her first husband's family), and Tiffany's design director, John Loring.

Sometimes editors are unable to move ahead the projects that interest them. This also fell to Jackie's lot. She encouraged a piano duo who had become biographers to start working on a book on *Vogue*'s one-time photographer Baron de Meyer. Ultimately she could not get the Doubleday brass to approve it. She had to write to Arthur Gold and Robert Fizdale and apologize because she couldn't take it any further. Fascinating projects on the photographer Berenice Abbott; on the man who walked a tightwire between the World Trade Center towers, Philippe Petit; and on the architecture of American houses, from those of presidents to those of pioneers, by her good friend John Russell, were ones that she tried but failed to move forward. Jackie even had to tell Cathy Rindner Tempelsman, Maurice Tempelsman's daughter-in-law, that her book had not met with the approval of the reader to whom Jackie had submitted it. Though Jackie was a powerful force at the company and could swing some deals with a clout other editors simply did not have, she could not advance a project that would have meant much to Tempelsman. Her rejection of it shows that she sometimes had to put the company's interests before her own.

Working Side by Side

Bill Barry worked for many years as Doubleday's deputy publisher, a powerful figure who kept track of the money and served as Steve Rubin's right-hand man. Barry originally thought of becoming a priest. After deciding against the priesthood and leaving the seminary, he joined Doubleday's religion department, hoping to become an editor. He soon began working on an MBA at night and then rose through the ranks, learning to manage the different divisions of the company. Now a publishing consultant in his fifties, he's still a good-looking man, who, behind half-closed eyes, gives the impression of a Roman senator who has witnessed every variety of human power and excess. When Jackie knew him, he was significantly younger than she was and would have been one of the most handsome men in the company.

Barry remembered that Jackie employed a variety of ways to get what she needed at Doubleday. She thought of men as "either puppy dogs or alpha males." With some she could be "absolutely seductive"; with others she could be a "fierce advocate" on behalf of the authors and projects she wanted to publish. At times her manner was "almost schoolgirlish," in deference to what she, at least, thought of as much greater and more creative talents than her own. But she often got her way. In the days after Jackie died, the PBS talk show host Charlie Rose chaired a panel discussion on his program remembering her. In addition to Bill Barry and George Plimpton, the panel included Jackie's friend Brooke Astor, the one-time White House photographer Jacques Lowe, and the legal counsel of the Metropolitan Museum of Art, Ashton Hawkins. At one point Plimpton recalled that Jackie had once asked him to go to a children's party dressed as a pirate. Did he do it? "I did. I did everything she told me to do." Ashton Hawkins added wryly, "We all did." All the men in the group laughed heartily.

At Doubleday, Barry remembered, Jackie sometimes agreed to do things she didn't particularly want to do. He told her that she could win special favor for her books and motivate the sales force if she came for lunch before presenting her titles later that afternoon at a sales meeting on Long Island. Jackie agreed. "So she comes out early," Barry explained. "I get a select group of the sales reps around the table. I escort her into the dining room of the Garden City Hotel, and she sits down at the table. As the lunch started off, one rep thought it was important to tell the whole table about his recent dental surgery. Having noshed on the bread plate, he takes out a newly installed dental bridge" to show the table.

This quickly defused any collective nervousness. Barry remembered her reaction. "She was unabashed." She went on to ask everyone what his territory was, what books he'd recently read. "She couldn't have been more engaged, more cordial. It wasn't a veneer. It was genuine. One asked if it wouldn't be too much of an imposition for him to take a picture of her with the group, something which normally she would have been repelled by, but she agreed to it with a smile."

Barry concluded, "So she was very good at doing what she had to do and came across as a very strong advocate for her books. I don't think these things were easy for her. I don't think they came naturally. I know she realized she didn't have to do them, but that was her commitment." Her performance, he thought, was both "honorable and pragmatic." If the guy taking out his bridge was doing something odd because of his social anxiety, she wanted to put him at ease and charm him so he'd sell her books to all the right bookstores. She didn't particularly like to use her fame to promote her authors' books, but if someone like Barry told her it would help sales, she was willing to go along.

Barry remembered too, though, that she was especially pleased when he invited her into his office in the 1990s to talk about her salary. Her performance and her longevity at the company had been rewarded with successive increases as she moved from associate to senior editor. Now her salary went over $100,000 for the first time. "She was as proud of herself as she could be. This was something she had clearly attained on her own. It had no relation to her husbands, how much money she had, or the covers of magazines she would be on every week. This was Jackie Bouvier who had distinguished herself with an editor's skill, by her own lights, with some mentoring, but also with close attention to how the business got done."

Barry wasn't always in the driver's seat in his relationship with her. Jackie went out of her way to introduce the younger man to some of her most powerful contacts, once delegating him to represent Doubleday at a Washington publishing party, hosted by Senator Edward Kennedy, in honor of Carl Elliott. Barry was aware that Jackie rarely visited Washington, and understood that as much as she wanted to be there to fete Elliott in person, "she also wanted all the attention to be on the former congressman and didn't want to risk diminishing the celebration of him that might have happened had she attended herself."

If she knew instinctively how to win over the salesmen on Long Island, she also occasionally knew how to sell Barry on a project that he was skeptical about. She and her longtime collaborator, Shaye Areheart, wanted to do a children's book by the leggy A-list supermodel of the 1980s Paulina Porizkova. Jackie had had success with Carly Simon's children's books, and Scott Moyers thought she was proud of initiating the whole genre of children's literature by well-known personalities. Barry wasn't convinced that the book was a good idea. "I was very resistant to giving her whatever amount of money she wanted. I understood the commercial viability of Carly Simon's books and some of the others, but this wasn't an obvious match." So one day, unannounced, Jackie walked Porizkova into Barry's office, saying, " 'Paulina was just visiting and I thought it would be good if you two met.' I have no doubt that Jackie had coached Paulina in terms of what she should do. She sat down and stretched one willowy leg out and bent it over the other. I was being worked. I knew I was being worked. I let Jackie know that I knew that I was being worked. In the end I just decided to relent, because it wasn't so much money."

Jackie and Barry also worked together on trying to convince Richard Gere to do a Doubleday book. They weren't sure whether he would be willing to do an autobiography or a book on Eastern spirituality, but they both knew that deploying Jackie might do the trick. Gere and one of Jackie's authors, Jonathan Cott, started talking about producing a series of television programs on alternative healing therapies. Their hope was that a book might result from the TV series. Jackie was worried that Cott's tastes, like her own, ran to arcane and not particularly marketable ideas (English eccentrics, Egyptian myths, and Emily Dickinson poetry were all the subjects of books Cott did with Jackie). She reasoned that if Cott could coauthor a book with Richard Gere, it might give him some financial independence. So she was particularly close to the Gere negotiations, not only because a Gere book would help Doubleday, but because it would help Cott, about whom she felt especially protective. As with any Hollywood personality, the negotiations were long and carried on through lawyers and other third parties. In the midst of this, one of the tabloids published a photo of Gere pinching the bottom of supermodel Cindy Crawford, whom he eventually married. Jackie did a little sketch of a devil with horns on the picture and sent it along with a note to Barry: "What do you think of our author now?" Jackie was not above taking an interest in the scandal sheets. Her playful flirtation with Barry was a way of both amusing herself in the office and enlisting his continued financial support of her book projects. The Gere project never got off the ground, but her friendly collaboration with Barry flourished.

As they grew comfortable with each other, Barry could sometimes cautiously engage her on the subject of her own fame. "I was in her office with the door closed," Barry remembered. "She had bummed a cigarette. She was an occasional social smoker. The window cleaners were coming down the outside. They were right there. They look in and they recognize Jackie. The way her desk was situated, she was peripherally aware of them, but I was looking at them head-on. I said, 'He's mouthing *Jackie O.*' So she turns around, she gives that beaming smile, and she notices 'Javier,' the name stitched on the pocket of his uniform. 'And he's Javier,' she replied, completely neutral. In other words, I am who I am. He is who he is. It wasn't said with any condescension." Most of the time Jackie didn't like anyone to refer to the commotion her celebrity caused, but she would allow Barry to see that it had become something which she found completely unremarkable. By this time in her life, she neither loved the attention she attracted nor hated it. It was just there.

Barry continued, "I somehow used that as the jumping-off point, and I said, 'Have you thought of doing your own autobiography?' She made a gesture indicating someone who was a real pain," and here Barry imitated her famous whispery voice, "'Oh Bill, I can remember when I was working with Michael Jackson.' She would be up on Martha's Vineyard and Jackson would be on the phone complaining to her about the burdens of celebrity." On the phone she was sympathetic to Jackson, but she really didn't want to rehearse in print her own reaction to the events that had made the world take notice of her. She told Barry, "'I can remember just repetitively tracing the floral pattern' of the upholstery where she was sitting, listening to Jackson, 'looking out to the sea and thinking I would never squander my time writing my memoirs when there are beaches to be walked.'"

Barry would not take no for an answer. "I challenged her a bit on that—we had the kind of relationship where I could go at her. I said to her in a friendly gibe, 'And what about your obligation to history?' She said something along the lines of— and with a seriousness she was absolutely entitled to—'I think I've honored my obligation to history.' Now, that could have referred to a whole bunch of things. It may have referred to the fact that she'd done these tapes about the assassination that had a seal on them," which weren't to be released in her lifetime, "or that she had discharged so many obligations with such generosity and aplomb that she simply wouldn't be saddled with the self-revelation that an autobiography required." Jackie had in fact already tried being a writer and rejected it as a path forward, so memoir-writing was out of the question. She wanted to be responsible for the written work of authors who she considered had more interesting things to say than she did. There is fragmentary evidence that she kept a visual diary of some of her travels, and perhaps she considered leaving this behind as one record of her life. She once showed Raquel Ramati a little sketchbook she kept of the places she had been and some of the scenes she had witnessed. She kept this occasional visual memoir, but she showed it to very few people, and it has never been published.

Jackie and Barry once flew down to Washington together. She was interested in working out a publishing relationship between Doubleday and the National Gallery. They were late to the airport and the last to arrive on the plane. Their seats were in the back, so they had to walk all the way down the aisle of the plane, with a hundred fellow passengers craning their necks to look at them. "Look, Bill," she whispered with her head down when they finally reached their seats and sat down, "everyone knows you."

Noticing her fame and joking about it were okay as long as she was doing the joking and she was with someone she trusted. It was generally not okay to refer to it at any other time. While Barry was flying down to Washington with Jackie, the flight attendant leaned over him to tell Jackie, "I've always admired your fashion sense." Jackie gave her "a polite smile and recognition, but it was not anything she wanted to be noted for. Ever. Whereas her books she was passionate about. If someone was knowledgeable about one of her books, she would be spontaneously engaged. In the absence of the autobiography she had no inclination whatsoever to write, her books were as good an insight into her as exists outside of a very small group of her intimates." Her list, then, was both Jackie's achievement and her most revealing testimony about who she was. It is the tangible legacy of a woman who spent nineteen years transforming manuscripts into published works.

If the story of her office life has her moving from a shy celebrity recruit to a senior editor with an established list, there are equally compelling stories told by the list itself. Her books tend to cluster around the roles she herself had played. She never spoke in public about what it was like to be married, or how she grew into a new woman after her marriages were over, but the books she decided to publish tell the story for her.

chapter 4

DADDY, IT'S THE DEAD PRESIDENT'S WIFE.

—*A child announcing Jackie on the phone*

Jackie regularly consulted one of her writers, Mike D'Orso, who lived in the South, by telephone. One of the times she called, D'Orso's seven-year-old daughter, Jamie, picked up the phone. He could tell she was talking to an adult by what she was saying. "Fine." Pause. "Second grade." Pause. "Playing with my dolls." Pause. Then she called out to her father across the room, "Daddy, it's the dead president's wife." That was the paradox of Jackie's fame: she lived for three decades after her first husband, married another man, edited dozens of books, and collaborated with scores of writers, but she remained famous for having been the wife of JFK. Children remembered her for something adults usually knew better than to mention to her.

Her devotion to silence about her two husbands is part of what feeds the curiosity about what those marriages must have been like. What was it like to be married to Jack Kennedy and to put up with his infidelity? How did she feel about having the nation's sex symbol, Marilyn Monroe, as one of his admirers? What was it like to be married to Ari Onassis, legendary for his vulgarity as well as for carrying on a public affair with Maria Callas while still married to Jackie?

Jackie's biographers have speculated on these questions, going over and over what little information can be found in

public documents or gleaned from the guarded remarks of
Jackie's friends about her marriages. All along, however, the
most revealing information has been hiding in plain sight. In
Jackie's books she commented in the most public way possible about what she thought of the institution of marriage,
about presidential mistresses, about what it was like to have
a career in order to circumvent unhappiness in a marriage,
about Marilyn Monroe's sex appeal and Maria Callas's eyes,
and about how a woman might guard her privacy in the midst
of a marriage the world regards as public business. Six of her
books, spread out over sixteen years, show her choosing to
back authors who wanted to deal precisely with these questions. Jackie was intimately involved in encouraging Barbara
Chase-Riboud to publish her historical novel about Thomas
Jefferson's relationship with his slave, *Sally Hemings* (1979).
She also had a role in helping Princess Grace to step away from
her marriage-turned-stale to Prince Rainier by sponsoring
the American publication of *My Book of Flowers* (1980), a first
attempt by Grace to have a career of her own that was not in
acting. Diana Vreeland's *Allure* (1980) paid tribute to the pri-
mal eroticism of both Monroe and Callas. Jackie stood behind
young novelist Elizabeth Crook in *The Raven's Bride* (1991), a
story of what it was like for an extremely private woman who
loved horses to be married to a prominent elected official more
devoted to his career than to his marriage. Finally, Dorothy
West's novel *The Wedding* (1995) makes both philosophical
and poetic remarks about marriage that Jackie endorsed by
putting them on paper between hard covers. Jackie never came
out and said more clearly what her marriages were like than
in the way she chose to become involved in these book projects. All of them have a unity on the question of marriage, and
a wisdom, achieved sometimes painfully, sometimes pleasur-

ably, that ran parallel to, echoed, and emerged from her own experience.

A President and His Mistress

Barbara Chase-Riboud is an American sculptor and poet who lives in Paris and Rome. She grew up in Philadelphia, finished degrees at Temple and Yale before moving to Paris in the 1960s, where she married the French photojournalist Marc Riboud, and had her artwork shown in museums and galleries. When she first met Jackie, Chase-Riboud had also had a volume of poetry published at Random House, with Toni Morrison as her editor. The Ribouds had some friends—also friends of Jackie's—who vacationed on a Greek island near Skorpios. Jackie regularly invited them all over to Skorpios, and Chase-Riboud remembered everyone's reluctance to go. Jackie sometimes had to beg her friends to come visit her in Greece. She once telephoned when Nancy Tuckerman was already in Greece, stopping to see other friends before a planned visit some weeks later to Jackie, and saying, "Nancy, can you come *now?*" She was sometimes lonely and needed friends, and she could afford to send a helicopter to pick them up.

Soon after they met, Chase-Riboud found herself on the beach with Jackie, tête-à-tête. In the distance speedboats circled the island with cameramen whose telephoto lenses were pointed in their direction. It was one of the things that discouraged Jackie's friends from visiting her. Jackie had to work hard to put everyone at ease, calling Skorpios "the island of Dr. No," a reference to the hero's evil rival in the first James Bond film. But Chase-Riboud was charmed by the former first lady and attracted to her dry sense of humor. She told her she couldn't bring herself to call her Jackie, and used the French *Jacqueline*. Jackie laughed, saying that "only you and my mother call me that."

Chase-Riboud had recently read a new biography of Thomas Jefferson by the historian Fawn Brodie, who presented evidence that Jefferson had had a long relationship with one of his female slaves, Sally Hemings, and fathered several children by her. Chase-Riboud was so moved by the story that she went to Toni Morrison with the idea of writing an epic poem on Hemings. Random House said no. The house was interested in offering an advance if she wrote a historical novel, but the editors didn't think they had a market for epic poetry. Chase-Riboud told all this to Jackie in 1974, when Onassis was still alive and Jackie was still some time away from becoming an editor. Nevertheless, she was excited by Chase-Riboud's idea, telling her, "You have *got* to write this story."

The story appealed to both of them on many levels. Part of Sally Hemings's time with Jefferson took place in Paris, where Jackie and Chase-Riboud had both lived during important years of their young adulthood. Jefferson's Monticello was in rural Virginia, which Jackie knew well. She and JFK had built a house not too far from there when they were in the White House. Jackie hunted on horseback in Virginia all her life. Most of all, Jackie knew about presidential mistresses, a fact that did not escape Chase-Riboud, who thought as she described the story to Jackie on the beach, "Here I am telling the former first lady about a former first mistress." Although Random House's rejection initially discouraged Chase-Riboud, Jackie's enthusiasm impelled her to reopen her notes and start working.

In the following year, when Jackie went as a consulting editor to Viking, she arranged for Chase-Riboud to be given a contract for a historical novel on Sally Hemings. Jackie had moved from Viking to Doubleday by the time *Sally Hemings* was published in 1979, but she was certainly the prime mover in making the book happen. The book, although fictional, is based on thorough research. It suggests that when Jefferson's wife died, he was attracted to Sally Hemings because she was of mixed race: she had been sired by his wife's father and was thus his wife's half-sister. It was not uncommon then for slave owners to sleep with and father children by their female slaves. After Martha Jefferson died, Jefferson went to Paris as American ambassador to the court of Louis XVI. Hemings joined him there when he sent for his youngest daughter, whom Hemings accompanied to Paris. She spent almost two years there, where according to French law she was free. Hemings returned with Jefferson to the United States, thus choosing effectively to reenslave herself, although she might have stayed in France.

This was one of the tough facts that Chase-Riboud found hard to imagine, and she recalled Jackie offering her insight on why Hemings might have chosen to stay in bondage to such a man "despite everything." Jefferson was a brilliant man whom Jackie and JFK had both admired. One of JFK's most famous quips when he was in the White House was at the dinner Jackie had arranged for all the nation's living Nobel laureates. JFK said it was the greatest gathering of minds in the White House "since Thomas Jefferson dined alone." Jackie had been taught to love Jefferson and his era by her step-uncle, Wilmarth Lewis, a great expert on the late-eighteenth-century Enlightenment, in which Jefferson was a prominent figure. She had two of Jefferson's chairs in her collection of furniture on Fifth Avenue. She also made reference to Jefferson jokingly when she told Dorothy Schiff, whom she wanted to invite to lunch, that she couldn't find her telephone number, so instead she was writing her a note, "Thomas Jefferson's way." Jackie's admiration for Jefferson was in no way diminished by the fact that he had slept with Sally Hemings.

This was not the case for many readers of *Sally Hemings*. The novel became an immediate bestseller but was greeted by howls of protest from some historians who claimed that Chase-Riboud was sullying the reputation of one of America's greatest presidents on the basis of fiction and hearsay. The historian and lawyer Annette Gordon-Reed has written a recent Pulitzer Prize–winning account of the Sally Hemings controversy in which she points out that Chase-Riboud's book sold more than a million and a half copies and that it has had a bigger impact on the popular view of Jefferson than Fawn Brodie's biography, which inspired it. She thinks Chase-Riboud's fiction somehow struck a chord with the reading public, who wanted to believe in the story. CBS, hoping to capitalize on the book's success, proposed to do a television miniseries. Learning of the television plans, two southern white men decided to use their power to stop the spread of what they regarded as a scandal. Dumas Malone, the author of a multivolume biography of Jefferson, and Virginius Dabney, the editor of one of Richmond's newspapers and himself a descendant of Jefferson's, went to Bill Paley, the head of the network, and got the proposal quashed. They would not have Chase-Riboud's story about Hemings and Jefferson distributed any further.

Jackie played no public role in the controversy, and there is no mark of her involvement in the book's gestation or in the book itself, but she remained a staunch supporter of Chase-Riboud through the post-publication aftermath of the book and long beyond. When Chase-Riboud published a novel, *Echo of Lions*, on a slave revolt aboard a ship bound for America, Jackie sent it to Steven Spielberg, suggesting that it had film possibilities. Jackie's letter was important evidence when, years after Jackie died, Chase-Riboud brought a suit against Spielberg's production company claiming that his film *Amistad* had stolen scenes from the manuscript that Jackie had originally submitted to him. Spielberg settled out of court with Chase-Riboud for an undisclosed sum. Afterward, Chase-Riboud owned houses in Paris and on Capri.

When Chase-Riboud decided to divorce her first husband, Jackie helped her again by providing sympathy and advice. "She got me through my divorce," Chase-Riboud remembered. Jackie counseled her not to return to New York as a divorced woman, speaking of the vulnerability of divorced women of a certain class in the States. She was better off in France, Jackie thought, where divorced women were "not lonely occupants of Park Avenue bars." They saw each other only occasionally, going to lunch sometimes at the Stanhope, the hotel just down Fifth Avenue from Jackie's apartment. They sometimes found themselves on the same Air France flight from Paris to New York.

More developments in the Sally Hemings story took place after Jackie died in 1994: Jackie's friend James Ivory and one of her authors, Ruth Prawer Jhabvala, helped put the Sally Hemings story on the screen as *Jefferson in Paris* in 1995, with Nick Nolte as Jefferson and Thandie Newton as Hemings. Further, DNA testing from the later 1990s tended to prove what Fawn Brodie and Chase-Riboud had argued all along: that there were living descendants of the children Jefferson had by Hemings. Reflecting back on all this, Chase-Riboud said, "I never thought about what a daring choice Jacqueline made in publishing *Sally Hemings,* although no one expected the controversy and reaction it provoked . . . In a way, it became a strike against the way public history was written in America . . . including her own."

By encouraging Chase-Riboud to write *Sally Hemings,* Jackie had given a woman who had never spoken before a historical voice. She had also placed a president and his mistress on the page without feeling any of the scandal or awe or intimidation or prurience that such a subject usually inspires. *This is how men and women are,* she seemed to be saying. Undoubtedly she was also alive to the power difference, which put many more of the cards in Thomas Jefferson's hands than in Sally Hemings's. She certainly felt that even in the 1980s divorced women, alone and uncoupled from their husbands, even in cosmopolitan New York City, were at a comparative disadvantage.

Another motivation for encouraging Chase-Riboud was to reflect on her own White House marriage to JFK. She has often been written about as the wronged wife of a man who was a kind of sex addict, who had so many mistresses that the CIA might have lost count of the different young women ushered into his bedroom when Jackie was away on weekends. It seems more likely, given Jackie's role in the Chase-Riboud story, that she was more sympathetic to the dependent position of the mistresses than to the supposed injury done to her marriage. She had been told by JFK's friend Lem Billings how many girlfriends there had been before she married him and that JFK was unlikely to stop fooling around after the wedding. She had allowed Mary Van Rensselaer Thayer to publish her own flash of insight, on first meeting Jack Kennedy, that here was a man who didn't want to be married, who was happy to have his freedom. Jack Kennedy told more than one person that he was only marrying Jackie because he was thirty-seven and people would think he was "queer" if he didn't marry soon. Given the way JFK's sexuality resembled similar roguish traits in her father, she might not have been surprised when what Lem Billings and others had warned her about came to pass.

In fact, there is evidence from that old Kennedy loyalist Arthur Schlesinger that she exploited her husband's roving eye.

Once when they were attending a rare after-theater party that Jackie was enjoying, she feared that Jack might grow bored and make them go back to the White House early. She told Schlesinger to find some pretty girl and take her up to JFK so he would want to stay. Jackie was too well versed in the sexual mores of the aristocratic classes in Europe in the eighteenth and nineteenth centuries, when discreet marital infidelity was fine as long as the marriage was upheld in public, to be too shocked or scandalized by JFK's sexual appetite. It may have liberated her to go off and do exactly what she wanted to do. As one of her more careful biographers has remarked, "Her silent acceptance of what others considered intolerable offenses freed her to explore precisely where she could flourish, and to discover to which life she could bring the best of herself." Jackie's role in the publication of *Sally Hemings* indicates her fellow feeling for women who struggled against their economic reliance on men, but she was hardly shocked by what men did with their liberty. Championing Barbara Chase-Riboud in her fight with the Virginia historical establishment showed that Jackie was unafraid of controversy over the reputations of great men in the White House, but no less in awe of the work of one of the nation's founders. In pushing Chase-Riboud forward, Jackie showed with actions rather than words that whether black or white, descended from the enslaved or the free, American or expatriate, women had better stick together. Hers was that "second wave" feminism born of the post-Woodstock generation's realization in the 1970s and '80s that women deserved and could demand better.

Grace Notes

Princess Grace grew apart from her husband, Prince Rainier, in middle age. Married in Monaco only three years after Jackie's marriage to JFK in 1953, Grace and Rainier often lived in separate houses, one in Paris and the other in Monaco, two decades later. Grace's excuse was that she had to be in Paris during her children's schooling. She actually preferred to be in a different house from her husband. She had begun a hobby of hiking in the mountains above Monte Carlo with the children when they were young. She would collect flowers, press them in telephone directories, and then put them together in collages. She had a sale of these collages in a Paris gallery and was pleased when all the artworks sold. The proceeds were to go to a charity in her name. When her husband and friends arrived at a restaurant after the show to celebrate, Rainier crumbled up the petals of a flower from one of the tables and put them on an empty plate. He held up the plate and cried out, "Sold!" Grace laughed to show that she could take a joke, and she understood that the value of her collages had something more to do with her fame than with her talent, but she was hurt, too.

Grace, like Jackie, longed to find a role other than pretty face or princess-on-demand. Finding a new career became especially pressing as her children grew older and prepared to leave home. Rainier blocked Grace's attempts to go back to the stage or to films as inappropriate for their position in Monaco. She thought she'd found something in this flower project, only to be made fun of by her husband. Jackie recognized the predicament. The two women had known each other for a long time. They were the same age, both having been born in 1929. Both of them had made marriages that sent the media wild. When they were both newlyweds, Jackie had persuaded Grace to cooperate in a stunt that was essentially another way to poke fun at Jack's inability to stop fooling around with other women. With Jackie's help, Grace dressed up as a nurse and appeared without warning in JFK's hospital room while he was recuperating from a back operation in the 1950s. Grace and Rainier had both visited the Kennedy White House. Later on, Rainier and Onassis were sometimes rivals, sometimes enemies, sometimes wary business colleagues. Jackie and Grace both knew what it was like to live as American expatriates, at the whim of temperamental European husbands under the Mediterranean sun.

Grace and Jackie had also worked together on a tribute to Josephine Baker, the African American woman who grew up poor in St. Louis but shot to European stardom when she sang and danced nearly nude with the Folies Bergère in Paris. She never had the same success in America, though Shirley Bassey acknowledged Baker as her model and mentor, calling her *"la grande diva magnifique."* Baker refused to perform before segregated audiences in America. In the 1950s she accused the owner of the Stork Club in New York of racism when the restaurant refused to serve her. Grace Kelly rushed over, took Baker's arm, and publicly stalked out of the restaurant, vowing never to return, and she never did. Grace and Baker were friends forever afterward, even to the extent that Grace offered Baker a villa and an income when she fell on hard times toward the end of her life. Baker died in 1975. In 1976 Grace arranged a gala tribute to Baker in New York, with Jackie as her co-chair, the proceeds going to benefit underprivileged children. Since Jackie very rarely made public appearances for charities, this says something about her devotion not only to Josephine Baker but also to Princess Grace.

Josephine Baker, like Barbara Chase-Riboud, and even to an extent Sally Hemings, was an African American woman who found greater freedom, appreciation of her talent, and acceptance in France than she had at home. All three were outsiders who had to leave their native country to feel at home. Though Jackie looked to the world like an ultimate insider, she often said she felt like an outsider. Whether it was because of her Catholicism, her parents' divorce in the 1940s, when that still carried a considerable stigma, or her own shyness is not clear.

Part of Jackie's role at both Viking and Doubleday was to bring in as authors big names whom she knew from her social rounds. Bringing Grace's book to Doubleday, where it was published in 1980 as *My Book of Flowers,* was a way of both helping Grace and doing precisely what she had been hired to do. This was very early in Jackie's career as an editor, when so much of the detailed work of negotiating the contract and shaping the text was taken care of by others. The book nevertheless shows unmistakable signs of Jackie's hand and collaboration. The book is heavily illustrated, with many pictures of Grace in Monegasque gardens, as well as pictures of the flowers at her wedding to Rainier and her daughter Caroline's wedding to Philippe Junot. It includes Grace's flower collages, but it is also a book about flowers in art, architecture, dress, and furniture-making. Here is Grace describing her wedding, which might as well be drawn from the wedding of JFK to Jackie: "I was told how magnificent the flowers were at my wedding, but all I remember is that the flower arrangements in the cathedral were filled with Rolleiflexes, Hasselblads, and Nikons with telephoto lenses and flashbulbs."

Grace also paid tribute to one of Jackie's favorite French authors, quoting prominently from Charles Baudelaire at the head of her chapter on potpourri and perfume: *"Je suis un vieux boudoir plein de roses fanées"* (I am an old boudoir full of faded roses). After her run-in with the critics over *In the Russian Style* in 1976, Jackie often preferred to keep her name out of her books. Nowhere in Grace's book is Jackie's name mentioned, but there is a tribute to Rose Kennedy, toward whom Jackie had begun to feel more affectionate in the 1970s, as having "the regal bearing of a proud rose."

Grace and Jackie concluded by putting a shared but secret joke on the back of the book's jacket. It tells of Clark Gable in the 1950s on location in England and filming a scene that took a long time to set up. The director Delmer Daves wanted to distract his star, so he took him to look at some flowers in a nearby field, asking Gable, "Have you ever looked into the heart of a flower?" As they were standing there, looking closely at flowers, strangers drove up and asked for directions. After having driven off, they came back. "Are you Clark Gable? You *are* Clark Gable, aren't you?" the driver said. Grace tells the rest of the story: "Gable leaned all those six feet over and answered, 'My good man, have you never looked into the heart of a flower?'"

Jackie certainly experienced at the hands of Onassis a humiliation that was similar to the effect of Rainier's crumbling the table flowers onto an empty plate in front of Grace's friends. Kiki Moutsatsos, Onassis's longtime personal assistant, was close enough to her boss and his sisters to be invited to family suppers from time to time. She published a book several years after Jackie's death that includes several accounts of chilling scenes between Jackie and Onassis. The one that would have mortified Jackie the most, cut her to the quick, was when she was brought up short by her husband in the midst of the kind of intellectual speculation that she loved. Onassis's sister Artemis was married to a Professor Garofalidis. Jackie, Ari, Artemis, the professor, Kiki, and others were gathered one night in Artemis's house in Glyfada, which was near the runway for the Athens airport. Even though it was a big villa and opulently furnished, landing jets could kill the conversation with their roar. Ari liked the noise. It was the roar of money. He owned Olympic, Greece's national airline, and it was his planes that made the noise. Jackie had that day been reading a biography of Socrates and asked Professor Garofalidis whether he thought Socrates had been one man or Plato's invention to cover many men, a whole school of philosophers. The professor replied that he didn't know and perhaps it was the same as Jesus Christ. Who knows whether he was one man or many? Onassis went into an ugly tirade: of course Socrates was one man. He asked roughly whether they hadn't seen Socrates' statue in the center of Athens. Jackie was so upset at being spoken to in this way that she tried to walk out the door into the rain, but she was pulled back inside by one of the men. Onassis sent her jewelry in the morning but did not apologize.

Why had she married Onassis in the first place? She told the journalist Pete Hamill, whom she dated in New York a decade after the death of Bobby Kennedy and who later wrote about her in *Newsday*, "I wanted to go away . . . they were killing Kennedys and I didn't want them to harm my children. I wanted to go off. I wanted to be somewhere safe." Nancy Tuckerman always regarded Jackie's marriage to Onassis as "a mistake." She rejected the idea that Jackie wanted to get out of the country in 1968 for the safety of her children after the assassination of Bobby Kennedy. Jackie had continued to live mainly in New York, because the children were still in school there and had spent comparatively little time in Greece. Five years after JFK's death, she was still depressed and had not entirely recovered. She was tired of being the president's widow. She had been boxed into a role she didn't want to play for the rest of her life. Marrying Onassis was not only getting outside the box but destroying the box.

Very early on, Jackie and Onassis decided to remain married but to go their separate ways. She knew precisely what Grace was going through with Rainier, and publishing Grace's book was giving Grace a way out that Onassis had never allowed Jackie when he was alive. After Onassis died in 1975, she never spoke critically of him to her authors or colleagues. She would occasionally pepper her conversation with his name. One of John's friends remembered her saying, when she wasn't sure whether she'd found the right restaurant, "I think this is where Ari took me."

A Geisha and a Diva

There was another enormous wink, an in-joke about Jackie's marriages, that readers would discover only if they paid close attention to the small print of the acknowledgments of Jackie's next book, with Diana Vreeland. The idea was to produce a big-scale picture book of ideas from fashion. Vreeland had spent a lifetime selecting such images for *Harper's Bazaar* and *Vogue*. Now she would reprise that role for Jackie, selecting not just pictures of women in wonderful dresses but also news photos, pictures of face-lift surgery, and newsreel images of royal ceremonies. The broad, hold-all concept was "allure," which Vreeland defined by saying, "Allure *holds* you, doesn't it? Whether it's a gaze or a glance in the street or a face in the crowd or someone sitting opposite you at lunch . . . you are *held*." Vreeland decided that as she would be approaching some of the most powerful photographers in the world, and their most famous sitters, for permission to reprint their work, she would need a letter of introduction. So she asked Jackie to write her one. There was something funny about this. Vreeland was herself a figure of world renown at this late stage in her career. She counted the likes of Andy Warhol, Jack Nicholson, and the Duchess of Windsor among her friends. It was rather like Mao Zedong asking for a letter of introduction from Zhou Enlai.

Jackie's letter, on Doubleday letterhead, begins with a kind of absurd contradiction, typical of Vreeland, who probably wrote the letter for Jackie to sign: Vreeland's book on fashion photography "would not be limited to either fashion or photography." It would include "even the work of the paparazzi [sic]." What must the recipients of such a letter have thought? Here was Jackie, legendary for her lawsuit against Ron Galella and other paparazzi in order to keep them at a distance from her, writing to introduce Vreeland, who, at least in the world of fashion photography and celebrity, needed no introduction, and defending Vreeland's choice of work by the paparazzi. Maybe Jackie's misspelling of "paparazzi" was her single slip to show that Vreeland was taking her for a bumpy ride and she was holding on tight. It seems more likely that they were both fairly good-humored about Vreeland's outline for her project. Jackie sincerely admired the magnificence, the drama, and the magnetism of Vreeland's photograph selections. Further, Jackie endorsed Vreeland's selections of pictures of her husbands' best-known mistresses. Marilyn Monroe had had a brief affair with JFK, and by 1980, when Vreeland's *Allure* was published at Jackie's behest by Doubleday, this was well known. Indeed, Monroe had made it almost embarrassingly public by singing him a sexy "Happy Birthday" when he was in her audience at Madison Square Garden. Monroe had committed suicide during the very week that Vreeland was taking over the editorial position at *Vogue*. She began work just as the outgoing editor was putting together the finishing touches on an issue which, by chance, included an article with a tribute to Monroe and several photographs. Vreeland's colleague wanted one of the photos taken out. It was too *"triste"* in light of what Monroe had just done. Vreeland replied, "You can't leave that out! You *cannot!* It's got all the poignancy and the poetry and the pathos of the woman in it!" That was in 1962. In the late 1970s, Vreeland explained what she loved about this photo to Christopher Hemphill, a protégé of Andy

Warhol's and Fred Hughes's who was helping her assemble *Allure*. "Marilyn Monroe! She was a geisha. She was born to give pleasure, spent her whole life giving it—and knew no other way." Some people said the same of Jackie. The art historian and Picasso biographer John Richardson told Sarah Bradford that Jackie had a geisha quality: "She did have this tremendous charm, that wonderful soft voice—I think pleasing was what she was about." What did Jackie say to Vreeland about the Monroe photograph? Probably nothing, but the fact that she silently allowed Vreeland to include it shows Jackie content to acknowledge Monroe's *ur*-sexiness, a quality that Jackie did not think she shared with the screen icon.

It seems as if Jackie was able to separate her editorial self from the woman whose husband had had a public fling with Monroe. She was thrilled, about the same time she was working with Vreeland on *Allure,* when a proposal came into Doubleday that promised pictures from Bert Stern's last photographic session with the actress. "Marilyn Monroe!!!" Jackie wrote in a memo to her colleague Ray Roberts. "Are you excited?" She proceeded to the businesslike details of how much they might bid (somewhere between $50,000 and $100,000) and what writer they might find to write the text to accompany the pictures. Vreeland's treatment of Monroe was probably like this for Jackie too: a publishing opportunity rather than a moment to reflect on a personal injury. In any case, if injury there had been, she was able to rise above it.

Not content with having touched on Jackie's personal history only once, Vreeland included in *Allure* a whole series of photos of Maria Callas. She was an opera diva who was also celebrated as the mistress of Onassis. Callas had gone out with Onassis before his marriage to Jackie, but they started to be photographed together again shortly after Jackie married Onassis in 1968. Nor did Callas withhold bitchy remarks about

Jackie, speculating publicly to reporters that Jackie was not making Onassis happy, hence his willingness to be photographed once again with her. The sense of Callas as a much more powerful, dangerous, and temperamental rival than Marilyn Monroe is captured in the pictures Vreeland selected. One of them shows Callas as Medea, very angry indeed. Vreeland said of one of the Callas photos, "If eyes were bullets, everyone *in sight* would be dead." Another showed a process server, having delivered a legal document to Callas in her dressing room, informing her of an action against her by one of the companies with whom she was under contract and being given in return a piece of the diva's mind.

Vreeland also captured another, different side of Callas, which ran parallel to Jackie's own experience. It was the fact that Callas could be a magical, nearly mythic character onstage, with a voice of inhuman proportions, and the next moment be an ordinary woman with money problems, a woman who had to eat and drink, who gained weight, who lost her voice as she grew older and sounded more like a gravel truck than a goddess. Vreeland recounted the story in *Allure* of how she had once invited Callas to her apartment in New York for Thanksgiving. Vreeland was a collector of celebrated artists. She awaited the diva's arrival. Callas made her entrance. Before sitting down to the table, she enchanted the guests. She was a marvel of emotion, drama, and theatrical-ity. But seated before a plate of turkey, "She was as common as mud." This vibration between Callas's two selves, queen and ordinary woman, an icon who was only flesh and blood, Cinderella turned back into a serving girl—this was a vibration that everyone around Jackie felt, too. It was an effect over which Jackie had only limited control. More than one of her authors and colleagues remembered that she sometimes liked to play with it. Her routine was to stand by the elevator door at Doubleday, where she knew she'd be seen, wishing her guest a whispery goodbye while everyone inside the elevator after the doors had closed craned their necks to see whom the American goddess could possibly have been addressing. Publishing Vreeland's photos of Maria Callas and Marilyn Monroe was far from Jackie's revenge on two husbands who had cheated on her. By the time she published Vreeland's book in 1980, she was paying tribute to their allure.

Texas Romance

Jackie admired Bill Moyers, and his opinion mattered to her more than that of many others. Moyers brought a manuscript to her that he was sure would interest her. It was a novel about a young woman who had been married to an ambitious man already in high elective office. The young heroine of the story was shy, loved horses, and fiercely protected her privacy. The marriage went wrong, possibly because of her husband's adultery, but almost certainly because he put his love of power before love of his wife. The two split up after only eleven weeks, and the man left the governorship of Tennessee in the scandal. He went to live among the Cherokee. His wife returned to live with her father. Afterward, hounded by intense public curiosity over what went wrong with her marriage, the woman ordered that all images of her be destroyed, that all her papers be burned, and that she be buried in an unmarked grave.

Moyers brought the novel to Jackie precisely because of its similarity to her own story. It was a novel about the marriage of Sam Houston, one-time congressman and governor of Tennessee, who later fought Mexico in the successful war to claim Texas and became the Republic of Texas's first president, before it joined the United States. His marriage to Eliza Allen, a woman from a good family, came apart after only a few weeks, with neither one making any comments about why they split. Eliza wished to be buried in an unmarked grave to forestall public curiosity about the details of her private life. There are many parallels to Jackie's life. For example, she was significantly younger than JFK, who was already a senator when they married. She quickly found that he spent more time on the road campaigning for higher office than he did at home in Georgetown with her. Of course, Jackie's first marriage ended under different circumstances, but her determination to protect her privacy matched Eliza Allen's. Like Allen, Jackie even instructed her children in her will to do all they could to prevent the publication of any of her letters, and she burned a few herself.

Bill Moyers's wife, Judith, recalled, "I absolutely do see the parallel between Jackie's life and Eliza Allen's. We saw that parallel. We thought that was why Jackie might be interested in the book." Another feature of the novel that interested Jackie was that Sam Houston had figured in a chapter of JFK's book, *Profiles in Courage*. That book, which Jackie had suggested he write when he was laid up, recovering from one of his back operations, examined politicians who had sacrificed their careers for important matters of principle. Houston, long after his marriage to Eliza Allen broke up, sacrificed his political career in Texas by refusing to swear loyalty to the Confederacy when Texas seceded from the Union.

The novel's author was a young woman, Elizabeth Crook, the daughter of a Johnson administration official who had served as the American ambassador to Australia, among other positions. She had known Moyers since she was a child and had worked for him briefly. This was her first novel, and she had suffered its rejection by many editors before Moyers recommended it to Jackie, who decided quickly to buy it. When Jackie telephoned Crook, she could barely believe her ears. Like the writer she was, she dwelled on Jackie's words over the phone, saying incredulously to herself over and over, "Mrs. Onassis wants to acquire it." It was two miracles at once: first, to have Jackie as her fairy godmother, and second, that her much-rejected novel would now actually be published.

Jackie's sponsorship of Crook was a lot like her support of Chase-Riboud in telling the Sally Hemings story. Both were young writers who were out to rescue wronged women whose names had been nearly erased from the historical record. Both chose fiction rather than biography or history while working much of their historical research into the characters' stories. The *Houston Chronicle,* in its review of *The Raven's Bride: A Novel of Eliza Allen and Sam Houston,* Crook's novel, which took its title from Sam Houston's nickname, "The Raven," among the Cherokee, quoted Crook as saying that she wanted "to write about a woman overlooked or misrepresented by history." Although the manuscript had already been edited before it arrived on Jackie's desk, she did try to tinker with its subtitle. Jackie suggested the subtitle "A Novel of Sam Houston's First Wife," preferring it to "Sam and Eliza Houston," which Crook had proposed, "because," as Jackie pointed out to Crook, "that sounds like an old married couple nodding into the sunset." That didn't adequately describe Allen's marriage to Houston, and it's interesting that Jackie should have taken an interest, because it didn't describe either of her marriages either. The novel was fascinating precisely because it described a tempestuous and ill-suited match that was the opposite of "an old married couple nodding into the sunset." In the end, they compromised, and Jackie allowed Crook's subtitle to go forward, the only revision being that Eliza Allen came first: "A Novel of Eliza Allen and Sam Houston."

Jackie had a special affinity for younger women writers and did much to advance their work. She was especially excited about Crook's novel and did more to promote it personally than she ever agreed to do for Michael Jackson. Steve Rubin remembered that Jackie "was insane for Elizabeth Crook." Jackie went out of her way to attend the launch party that Bill and Judith Moyers threw for Crook in their New York apartment. She allowed photographers to circulate, even though at some other book parties she had the guests informed in advance that cameras were forbidden. She also persuaded her daughter Caroline and her husband Ed Schlossberg to come, as well as her Martha's Vineyard neighbor Walter Cronkite. White wine was served in the library, where Bill Moyers's Emmy was on display, and sushi was passed among the guests, who also included the actor Tony Randall and the gossip columnist Liz Smith. A picture of Jackie looking as radiantly proud of Crook as if she were her daughter and standing with both Moyers and Rubin was taken at the occasion. The fact that Jackie is also pulling at her cuticles, a frequent habit, showed that the camera's presence was costing her some effort.

Jackie wrote Judith Moyers a thank-you note that same night and had it hand-delivered to the Moyerses' apartment the next morning at the same moment they picked up their morning paper. It includes a little of her trademark flippancy and her genius for a funny non sequitur. Jackie wrote that the party had made everyone happy and left them feeling better about their colleagues and themselves. "People go to Califor-

nia and roll around on the grass for days to get that feeling (I hear!)—but it's ersatz." Going to California as a false path to joy is an indelible Jackie image. If she had to go to a party at all, a book party in Manhattan was more her idea of fun than a cast party in Beverly Hills.

If Jackie was drawn to Crook's first novel because of parallels to her own life, it's interesting that in that same era she was also sitting down with young women of Crook's age and advising them—playfully, but advising them nevertheless—not to marry, and not to mix their money with their husbands' money if they did. Karen Karbo, an essayist, novelist, and author of *Motherhood Made a Man Out of Me* (2000), sat on a panel of judges to award a literary prize that was to be given in a ceremony at the Kennedy Library. Jackie was in attendance and sat next to Karbo onstage. Karbo had two memories of that evening. They had to sit there "listening to an HOUR-long keynote speech by George Plimpton about his love of fireworks." It was far too long. Jackie "crossed her legs when we first sat and didn't move a muscle from that moment on. I could see why—every so often a photographer would swoop in front of us and snap her picture. She was as still as a lizard on a rock. She wore sensible beige spectator pumps and a beige pants suit."

Most of all Karbo remembers the part of the evening before the speeches. They were walking from the preliminary cocktail party with one of the library staffers, another young woman, who had been assigned to show her and Jackie where to sit on the stage. Karbo had just had a baby; the other young woman had just been married. They were chatting about this when Jackie interrupted them to say how much she admired modern young women, how many choices they had, all the things they were free to do in their lives. Then she made her show-stopping remark: "But you know what I always say! Never marry, never mix your money!" Karbo thought she was teasing, saying the sort of thing you might say to charm a stranger at a party, but she also remembered that Jackie brought this up on her own. The other two women were too in awe of her to initiate anything. Karbo, who later made the subject of being married to a husband who didn't contribute his share to their marriage into an essay in the *New York Times,* ended up thinking about what Jackie had said a great deal, and ultimately agreeing with her. Both *The Raven's Bride* and her laughing conversation with Karen Karbo show Jackie to be content with Americans giving greater freedom and independence to women than she had ever known with Kennedy or Onassis.

The Wedding

Toward the end of her life, Jackie was working with another woman, this time one who was more than twenty years her senior. An amusing irony of these later years was that Jackie, at a time in her life when she was truly and happily finished with being married, and Dorothy West, an African American writer in her eighties who had never married, should have been collaborating on West's novel called *The Wedding*.

Scott Moyers is now a respected literary agent. He has a square jaw, an open manner, and what looks like a dueling scar on his forehead. In the 1990s, not far beyond his college years, he sat outside Jackie's office in the corridor at Doubleday as her assistant. He remembers the day a package arrived with a Martha's Vineyard postmark; it contained several chapters and an outline for Dorothy West's novel. The package also included an edition of her 1948 novel, *The Living Is Easy*. West was one of the last writers of the Harlem Renaissance, and had been friends with American literary greats such as Langston Hughes and Zora Neale Hurston. "Hot spit!" Moyers remembered Jackie saying and rubbing her hands together as she did whenever she was excited about a project. Here was just the sort of book she lived for, something with real literary merit, historical interest, and the author a Martha's Vineyard neighbor to boot. She lost no time in contacting West and telling her she wanted to publish her new novel.

What Jackie and Scott Moyers did not know was that the material they had just read had been written in the 1950s, when the novel had been under contract with Houghton Mifflin. Even with a new Doubleday contract in her hands, West had lost momentum and found it hard to finish the book. But Jackie made West her mission. Whenever she was on the Vineyard, she would drive her blue Jeep to West's house on Oak Bluffs, a prosperous African American community with a historical presence on the island. The two established a friendship: Jackie in her sixties, West in her eighties, the two of them from very different worlds but warm and affectionate collaborators nonetheless. Dorothy West remembered, "I think I was as unique to her as she was unique to me. I was without self-consciousness and so was she. Neither of us felt we had to apologize to the other for being who we were. I was born and bred in a very special circle of colored Bostonians for whom the now descriptive word 'black' had not yet been invented as a rallying cry. So neither of us felt embarrassed at being different from the other and indeed were enchanted by the difference."

The trouble came when Jackie grew ill in 1994. West's novel was still not done. As she worked on the book, the quality of her writing diminished, and she grew reluctant to see it in print. Doubleday had it scheduled for 1995, and the company wanted the book published. After Jackie died, West appeared to lose interest, and there was pressure by the publisher to get the novel finished whether West herself wrote the end or not. One of West's colleagues read the final draft of the novel and remarked, "This sounds like a white person wrote it." Scott Moyers worked with Dorothy West at the very end, after Jackie died. He remembered that West had a very detailed outline of where she wanted to go, but added that she definitely needed more help. Beyond that, he would only say that the relationship of a writer and an editor is privileged, like that of lawyer and client.

The first portion of the novel is written in a poetic prose that includes biblical language and is reminiscent of a Negro spiritual; the very last portion is not. This did not detract from the book's success, however. The publication of *The Wedding* led to a resurgence of interest in Dorothy West's earlier work and to a celebration of the author on Martha's Vineyard that Hillary Clinton attended. Oprah Winfrey put the weight of her publicity machine behind the book and produced the novel as a television miniseries starring Halle Berry, though the events of the story were significantly altered and the sad ending turned into a happy one.

Had Jackie lived, it's doubtful whether she would have allowed a second author to finish the book. Probably she could have coaxed Dorothy West to complete it in the same voice that Jackie so admired in the book's beginning. As it is, the novel is a wonderful look at the black upper middle class in the 1950s, living a life of prosperous ease on the East Coast's most exclusive island, worrying about interracial marriage and the different shades of skin color that resulted from those marriages. It includes a marvelous line about one character on her way to a wedding in the late 1800s. Josephine is a poor white woman from a plantation-owning family in the South, but in the post–Civil War era, broke and fearful of being forever an old maid. She takes the train north to marry Hannibal, the black son of one of her grandfather's slaves. Feeling so poorly that she might collapse, "Josephine boarded the train, and did keel over twice before she reached New York from the heat of the bridges burning behind her." What fun Jackie must have had reading that. She and Josephine had something in common.

As the novel reaches its climax, one of its heroes, himself the veteran of an unhappy marriage, sits down to tell his daughter the truth about the love everyone thinks is supposed to underpin a married partnership. This daughter is about to be married in the wedding referred to in the book's title. Clark tells his daughter, Shelby, "Sometimes I think romantic love is just another scourge put on this earth by the Lord, another measuring rod that no one thinks they quite measure up to, a simple idea that never seems to fit the two messy lives it's assigned to cover." Jackie would have been ready to testify to the truth of that, too.

In the space of a two-decade editorial career, Jackie had many manuscripts before her about marriages that rise to a more transcendent understanding of human love. She went from editing books by Barbara Chase-Riboud and Princess Grace to having a philosophical detachment about men's infidelity and the imperfections of marriage with the books of Diana Vreeland, Elizabeth Crook, and Dorothy West. Her comment to a friend who complained at lunch about men sleeping around outside their marriages was a simple "Well, all men are unfaithful anyway." Jackie was not a victim. She had the last word on marriage with both of her husbands, by chance, because of their early deaths, and by choice, because of the books she selected to edit. The question "What was it like to be married to them?" she answered best in her relationship with Maurice Tempelsman: better never to marry, and keep your money separate.

There was also wisdom about marriage in Jackie's book with Bill Moyers and Joseph Campbell. In *The Power of Myth,* Campbell tells Moyers, "Marriage is not a simple love affair, it's an ordeal, and the ordeal is the sacrifice of ego to a relationship in which two have become one." Toward the end of her life, Jackie could not regard JFK and Onassis as brutes or herself as the victim of marital unhappiness. She couldn't take her history that seriously. She sprinkled her conversation with their names, and none of her authors could remember her being critical of either one. She found that casually dropping a memory of Jack into a conversation with any male was one way of charming him. The normally skeptical *New Yorker* writer Adam Gopnik was moved by her mentioning Jack to him in a dinner-table conversation, but she did that with lots of men. Yes, her husbands had caused her some pain, but they had also given her children, money, and scope to get started again once they were gone. She lived to tell the story and could certainly joke about them. Bill Barry remembered sitting one day in her office when she was telephoning Maurice Tempelsman to make an appointment. Tempelsman's assistant answered the phone, and Jackie said, "May I speak with Mr. Onassis, please?" The assistant, knowing whom she really meant to speak to, briefly put Jackie on hold. While Barry looked on, Jackie took off her shoe and pretended to chew on it.

However, it was no Freudian slip that Jackie also mentioned Tempelsman's name in the opening paragraphs of her will, before she even got to the money and property she was leaving her children. In the first paragraphs, she named two Indian miniatures she wanted to leave to her friend Bunny Mellon. Next came Tempelsman, to whom she gave "my Greek alabaster head of a woman." She would not deny her past with JFK, next to whom she chose to be buried, nor her marriage to Onassis, with whom she collected Greek antiquities. Tempelsman was a man who could comprehend all that, give her the ample space to be the woman she'd always wanted to be, and love her, too.

chapter 5

AN EDITOR BECOMES KIND OF YOUR MOTHER.
— *Louis Auchincloss, remembering Jackie*

Jackie often told friends and even casual acquaintances that her proudest achievement was having raised her children. Pete Hamill knew her well enough in the 1970s to become a warm semi-paternal friend to her son, John. Books, Hamill thought, would never cease to be written about Jackie. One of the most important things those books had to make clear—one of the most difficult things to dramatize without cliché—was that "she loved her children." Many people scoffed when she first went to Viking, saying that she had no experience for the job. Her genius was to take what she had learned from being a mother and make it the foundation of her success as an editor. How she did it, how that late-in-life mothering led her to important new relationships and some beautiful books, is one of the best episodes in her life as an editor, and one that shows in a surprising way how much she had learned from bringing up Caroline and John.

In the mid-1960s, when she was still trying to recover from what had happened in '63, she confessed to Harold Macmillan one of the strangest of her feelings about being a mother. She had been invited to go to England with John and Caroline in 1965 to inaugurate a memorial to JFK at Runnymede. Britain was paying him a significant tribute, because Runnymede was also where King John had signed the Magna Carta in 1215, a charter that limited his power, acknowledged the freedoms of his subjects, and established a precedent for the rule of constitutional law in the English-speaking world today. She told Macmillan she was pleased with the way the children had behaved at Runnymede, but she was also grateful to them, because they were, in her post-assassination slump, the only reason she had to keep living. She had tried not to think of JFK in order to concentrate on the children and raise them to be the sort of people he might have admired. "Probably I will be too intense and they will grow up to be awful," she wrote. She worried about passing on her own depression to her children. She apologized to Macmillan for burdening him with her worries, but remarked that he was a useful substitute for writing a diary or undergoing psychotherapy.

In another letter to Macmillan a few months later she said she had begun to feel a bit stronger and better. But there was still something oddly ragged about her feelings toward child rearing. Again she wrote of her delight at the children they were becoming, but she also said that "if they grow up to be all right—that will be my vengeance on the world." She didn't blame Lee Harvey Oswald or the Texan radical right, which had been fomenting hatred of JFK in advance of his visit there in 1963, but "the world" for Jack's death and what she had been put through. She wanted revenge on the world and the world's nonstop scrutiny of her life. Some of the energy that went into raising her children was not only understandable recuperation from a tragedy but also a more complex rage.

Even before the assassination, Jackie sometimes teased her children in a way that sounds as if it were in the English tradition of being a bit cruel rather than the American way of giving unilateral approval. Arthur Schlesinger remembered coming upon Jackie with her two children in a corridor of the White House. She had recently taught Caroline to curtsey and John to bow. When they encountered Schlesinger, Caroline dutifully curtsied, and instead of bowing, John curtsied, too. Jackie said she thought this was "ominous," and Schlesinger laughed. John, having overheard and understood the joke at his expense, complained that he *had* bowed rather than curtsied. Perhaps Jackie's insistence on these correct, courtly forms related back to her mother, whose climb up the social ladder had been fairly steep, and whose insistence on correctness may have accompanied a feeling of social insecurity. Jackie's wanting her own children to observe the forms is reflected in a photograph from Runnymede, which shows John Kennedy doing a proper bow by putting his head down as he reaches out to shake hands with Queen Elizabeth II. For Jackie, teaching her son to behave correctly around royalty was as important as saluting his father's casket. The 1960s were more formal days than today, but Jackie's child rearing still had a European, Old World discipline about it.

Jackie also passed on traits for which her children remained grateful. She was a reader, and she hoped to make

them readers. Her daughter, Caroline, published a book in 2001 of the poetry her mother had taught her to appreciate. The cover illustration she chose was of Jackie reading to her as a young girl. A few years later, when there was another sale at Sotheby's to auction off her mother's belongings, Caroline put a memory of her mother in the sale catalogue. She explained the number of books in the auction by saying, "My strongest image is of my mother reading, whether on a winter afternoon in the city or a summer evening by the sea." In 1968 Jackie commissioned a portrait from Aaron Shikler of her two children with books. Loving her children and loving books at the same time were the part of motherhood that came most naturally to her.

The White House majordomo J. B. West said in his memoir of working with Jackie that he had the feeling that she was often "performing" her role as first lady, but that she was at her least self-conscious around her children. Nearly thirty years later, Bill Barry observed the same thing. When he was in public with her, she would hold herself in a way that suggested she knew she was being watched. Once, at a book party held in the New York Public Library, Barry watched Jackie as her son, John, arrived. For a moment, all the attention shifted away from her and John was in the spotlight. She was without envy and had a look of intense pride. "A lot of times in public she had a 'face,' but that was as natural a face as I've ever seen on her anywhere," said Barry.

There are relatively few surviving video images of Jackie interacting with her children, but two that do survive show the same thing. One is a campaign film aired in September 1960, in which Jackie is sitting with Caroline on her lap while JFK is making the pitch that he should be elected president. In the concluding frames Caroline points to her mother's microphone and says, "What's that?" The stilted smile Jackie has been giving the camera vanishes, and ignoring the millions of viewers for whom the film was being made, she turns to explain it to the single viewer she is holding in her arms. Another is a film of Jackie at John's graduation from Brown in 1983. John is in a procession walking by the spot where Jackie is standing. "Hi, Mummy," he says to her, and again her guard drops: she claps her hands together under her chin as if every wish she has ever had has been granted. Whatever the kinks in her own personality, some of which she had even before the death of her first husband, it's clear that motherhood provided Jackie with some of her most sublime moments.

You Probably Think This Song Is About You

Doubleday under Steve Rubin was not a specialist in children's books. When he came to head the company in 1990, he knew the children's book business was an entirely different specialty within publishing from bringing out trade books, or wide-release nonfiction and novels. Books for kids were not a core part of Doubleday's business, he decided. Children's books were expensive to produce, because their illustrations were in color on glossy paper, and they could represent large losses if they did not sell well. That Jackie was allowed to publish children's books was one of the privileges Doubleday extended to her; almost no other editor was permitted to combine books for adults and children on a list. Laughing at the semantic nicety with which he justified Jackie's exceptional privilege, Rubin remembered, "She was allowed to do children's books because we called them 'books for children of all ages.' "

Jackie's interest in children's books predated Rubin's arrival at Doubleday. She had thought when she wrote her *Vogue* essay in 1950 that she would like to write books for children. Bringing up her own children had deepened her interest in the subject. However, she didn't often claim privileges the other editors didn't have, and the story of how she came to do her first children's book is more the story of her adopting a celebrity from the music world and championing her work than it is of asserting her authority.

Herman Gollob is now retired from the publishing business. He went to Texas A&M, served in the air force in Korea, and after a career acquiring as well as editing other people's books, he took an Oxford summer course for which he wrote a paper on *The Merchant of Venice,* then wrote his own book, called *Me and Shakespeare: Adventures with the Bard.* In the 1980s Gollob was an editor at Simon & Schuster. He was riding the train back to New York from Boston when a beautiful woman got on board and sat down in his car. He recognized her as Carly Simon, not only a nationally known recording artist but also the daughter of Richard Simon, cofounder of the company for which he worked. "I can't sit on a train for four and a half hours and not say something to Carly Simon," Gollob thought to himself. He overheard her talking to her traveling companion about a book she wanted to write. This was his opening. He went over and said, "I heard you talking about a book. I happen to be in publishing." "What publisher?" Carly Simon asked. "Your daddy's old company!" They laughed, and talked on the train for a long time. He suggested that she write a memoir of her father. They also discussed other people she might like to write about. "We had lunch two or three times," Gollob said, and he recalled her saying, "I still love James [Taylor], but he'll always be an addict and I can't get back into that." They were close to signature on a deal in which she would write her recollections of the important people in her life when Doubleday offered Gollob the position of editor in chief.

Simon & Schuster was anxious not to lose a memoir by Carly Simon when Gollob moved to one of its rival publishing houses, so he agreed that he wouldn't take the project with him. However, he found a way around this once he was installed at Doubleday. His new colleague Jacqueline Onassis knew Carly Simon from Martha's Vineyard. If Jackie were to telephone Carly and to begin a new conversation with her about writing a memoir, it wouldn't be Gollob's project anymore.

Carly Simon's recollections are a little different, and her first memory of her books at Doubleday begins with a telephone call from Jackie. She thought they had met only once before, at a restaurant called the Ocean Club, then "the" place on the island, when the maître d' had taken her over to a table where Jackie and John were sitting to be introduced. Or possibly they'd met at the Styrons' house. Martha's Vineyard had a small literary community that included people such as the writer William Styron, the playwright Lillian Hellman, and the columnist Art Buchwald. Jackie loved being a part of this circle as much as she loved being at the beach, and it would not have been unusual for her to come across Carly Simon, who lived on the island most of the year, during one of her summers there. However, Carly Simon remembered not knowing Jackie well and thus being surprised when Jackie telephoned around 1988 to ask "in her unselfconsciously but also extravagantly seductive way if I would do my autobiography." Carly Simon was not the only one of Jackie's authors to recall that she had a seductive, even flirtatious manner on the phone, but she was the only woman to say so.

Carly Simon laughed at the memory. "What could I say?" What do you say when Jacqueline Onassis calls you up and asks you to write about yourself? "I told her I'd love to consider it. We discussed how I might do it." Jackie suggested that she devote individual chapters to significant characters in her life. For example, there might be chapters on Mike Nichols, her sisters, her first husband, and her children. "She thought it could be individual chapters about me and that person. A lot of my history would then come out of my description of that relationship. So I began writing."

She started writing about building a house on Martha's Vineyard with her first husband, James Taylor. She wrote something like seventy or eighty pages before she came to an impasse. She realized that much of her story revolved around her father and mother. Her mother was still alive, and she didn't want to hurt her. Nor did she want to write around the topic: "I wanted it to be with teeth. If I was writing autobiography, I didn't want to make it novelistic. In a song you can be untrue." Her twelfth album, *Hello Big Man,* released in 1983, made several references to her parents. When her father first met her mother, he said, "Hello, little woman," and she said, "Hello, big man." The album included a song about her parents. "In the last verse, what happens is the reverse of what really happened. It was a fairy tale about how a child wishes to see her parents love each other forever. But in the autobiography I was trying to write, if I had the memory, I didn't want to beat around the bush. I realized I couldn't do the story without deeply hurting my mother."

Carly Simon's husband at the time, Jim Hart, was aware of her dilemma. He suggested submitting to Jackie instead one of the children's stories Carly had written. This was the origin of Jackie and Carly Simon's first children's book together, *Amy the Dancing Bear,* a bedtime story Carly had dreamed up to tell Sally and Ben, her children with James Taylor. She loved staying at home in New York to put them to bed. "It got me out of the social scene, or attending some event connected with the music business. We'd be all three sitting together on a king-sized bed, one on either side of me holding an arm, hoping the other one would let go of the other arm so they could have me all to themselves. There's never been a time since when there was so much competition over me! I loved it. I would turn out the lights and imagine a story to tell them." When Carly Simon showed Jackie the story, she was delighted. Margot Datz, an artist friend of Carly Simon who had painted murals in people's houses all over the Vineyard, did the pictures for the book. The book tells the story of a young bear who resists her mother's call for her to go to bed and dances all night as her mother falls asleep.

When the book was released, it was a considerable success. The executives of Doubleday's parent company, Bertelsmann, flew over from Germany to congratulate both author and editor at a party. It was the first time anyone had seen a children's book by someone famous in a field outside of writing, a melding of two categories that in 1989 seemed strange. "Wow, what's this, *mann?*" Carly Simon remembered, mocking a hippie German accent, but in fact Jackie had stumbled onto a new genre that is still profitable in publishing today. Most noncelebrity children's book writers aren't thrilled about the development, but Paul Simon, Steve Martin, and Katie Couric have all followed Carly Simon into print with their own books for children.

The success of *Amy the Dancing Bear* in 1989 led to three more children's books: *The Boy of the Bells* (1990), *The Fisherman's Song* (1991), and *The Nighttime Chauffeur* (1993). Although Carly Simon never wrote the memoir that had originally been imagined, elements of her autobiography are intertwined with the stories of the books: not only her childhood stammer, which appears in characters who are "mute" and rediscover their voices, but also her love of her children and her love of her mother. She dedicated *Amy the Dancing Bear* to her mother, Andrea, and her daughter, Sally.

In Jackie, Carly Simon had discovered an older woman whom she wanted to please as deeply as she had longed in childhood to win her mother's approval. They lunched and had tea together in Carly Simon's circle garden on the Vineyard. They once went together to see a matinee in Vineyard Haven with a lunch packed by Jackie's housekeeper, Marta Sgubin. A little boy, prompted by his mother, who recognized them in the street, ran up to Carly Simon and asked for her autograph. Then his mother noticed Jackie standing there as well and told the boy it was the president's wife. The boy ran back and said to Jackie, "Oh, Mrs. Washington, may I have your autograph too?"

As in any close relationship between mother and daughter, there were teases that pinched and small senses of betrayal, too. Jackie and Carly Simon went to hear the Spanish tenor Plácido Domingo, and backstage afterward, the star flirted with Carly. The next morning a messenger arrived with a signed Plácido

Domingo photo that read, "My darling Carly, I will adore you forever." She called Jackie, saying, "Can you imagine? He sent this to me! I think he's in love with me." Jackie burst out laughing and said, "*I* signed and sent that picture to you."

Carly Simon was aware of the differences between the two women's interior decorating styles. She had consciously tried to create a rough, kid-friendly house, almost the opposite of Jackie's more austere style, with its Audubon prints and Proustian chintzes. Once Jackie gave her a boxed set of magnificent reproductions of artworks at Russian palaces, such as Petershof and Tsarskoe Selo. She sent it with an impish note: "If you're ever planning on doing some interior decorating in the next little while, this could give you some ideas." Carly Simon recalled in self-defense, "She loved my little slum here . . . But," she added later, perhaps slightly doubting herself, "I don't know how sincere she was, because I read somewhere that she'd made fun of my house."

Most significantly of all, Carly Simon recalled Jackie giving her a small dinner at 1040 Fifth Avenue before the launch party for their last book together, *The Nighttime Chauffeur*. The party was to come after dinner across the park in Tavern on the Green. She was to arrive in a white horse-drawn carriage, to imitate the events of the book. At the last minute, Jackie told her she wasn't coming to the party after dinner. "You go alone. You'll be fine. It's about you, it's not about me." Carly Simon recalled feeling like a child abandoned in the grocery store. "Jackie!" she protested. Jackie was devoted to Carly, and *Rolling Stone*'s one-time publisher Joe Armstrong, who was Carly's intimate friend, surmised that in Carly Simon Jackie saw the person she "couldn't be anymore." But Carly couldn't believe that Jackie would not come to support her at the party. More than a decade later, it still bothered her: "How hurt I was . . . it was that kindergarten sense of betrayal."

Jackie often avoided parties where she thought she would be the center of attention and take the spotlight off her author. She was not above canceling at the last minute, as she did with at least one of her other authors whom she also counted as a friend. Moreover, the launch of Carly Simon's last book came late in 1993, when Jackie was suffering from unidentifiable symptoms that heralded the beginning of her final illness—something that Carly Simon couldn't have known, as Jackie didn't yet realize it herself. The next year, when Jackie's cancer was diagnosed, she went to a luncheon at Carly Simon's apartment in the city. At the end Carly Simon impulsively stuffed into Jackie's pocketbook the lyrics to a song she'd written, "Touched by the Sun," and intended to dedicate to her. The song talks of wanting to learn from great people who avoid safety and choose a life of danger, like Icarus in Greek mythology, who flew too near the sun. She based the song on a poem by Stephen Spender that she'd loved since childhood and that she'd heard both JFK and Jackie had admired, too. The guitar part of the song was complicated, and she didn't want to play it for Jackie in front of everyone at the lunch, but she made sure that Jackie saw the lyrics. That evening, Jackie telephoned, touched by what Carly had done. She didn't need to be told that the song was about her.

Wearing Her Pearls into the Ocean

Jackie's experience with Carly Simon led directly to her publication of children's books by two other young women, one a musician and the other an artist. They came to her via Jann Wenner, and as with anything having to do with Wenner, there was an element of youthful romance, combined with the unexpected, that helped Jackie renew and prolong her own youth. Wenner was the editor of *Rolling Stone,* and his friendship with Jackie worked precisely because he was between her and her children in age. She wanted someone who could give them some contact with an older person's world but who was not so old that they'd immediately reject him as uncool. For his part, Wenner liked celebrities, and was surprised to find that Jackie didn't mind flirting with him as well.

Claudia Porges Holland, now Claudia Beyer, first met Jackie in the late 1970s. She had been working at *Rolling Stone* for a couple of years on and off. "I used to work for Joe Armstrong before the magazine moved to New York. I was nineteen or something. I then worked for Annie Leibovitz when the magazine was moving from San Francisco to the East Coast. I was helping get her situated and finding her an apartment. Shortly after that I was an assistant to Jann Wenner's assistant, Iris Brown. Those were wild days!" The magazine was known in the 1970s for promoting the "gonzo," or participatory, first-person journalism of Hunter S. Thompson, who joined the Hells Angels motorcycle gang in order to write about them. Its combination of political commentary with rock-and-roll music reporting was in tune with the freewheeling zeitgeist of the 1970s, when the magazine's encouragement of marijuana use and mockery of the establishment made it a must-read for many young people.

Beyer remembers that generation's feeling of being free to do what you wanted. "I went every year at Christmas with my family to St. Martin. One year I decided just to stay on the island. I abandoned my job to go down and live there. I was living in a little shed. I had a little hammock. I used to hitchhike around because I didn't drive. I used to collect my mail at a boutique. One day there was a handwritten letter from Jann Wenner. 'Hi, how are you? I've got a little favor to ask of you. I told Jackie Onassis you were down there and said you might show her around when she comes down in a few weeks.'"

Could she go to La Samanna, the island's premier resort, and meet Jackie? "I was barefoot and dirty," she said, exaggerating how unused she was to receiving celebrities on the island. "I went to the front desk in my little sarong. 'Could you ring Mrs. Onassis?' They weren't going to do it. I showed them Jann's letter, too. 'Okay, okay,' the woman behind the front desk said. I could watch her face fall as she talked to Jackie on the phone. The woman hung up and said, 'She'll meet you at the bar in ten minutes.' My friend Tommy and I met her at the bar. I showed her around. I chartered some boats. She wanted to see my little hut. It was so primitive: a little concrete bunker. She thought it was really funny. I had some pearls that I'd inherited. I used to wear them into the ocean. I showed her a little tiny book of miniature drawings I'd done. 'You should do a book of your life here someday,' Jackie said. 'You remind me of *Wide Sargasso Sea.*'"

Jean Rhys's 1966 novel, *Wide Sargasso Sea*, is about the life of an heiress living in the Caribbean, conceived as a "prequel" to a more famous Victorian novel. It's the story of Mr. Rochester and his first wife, before the beginning of Charlotte Brontë's 1847 novel, *Jane Eyre,* in which Jane meets and falls in love with Rochester. It is sometimes regarded as an important feminist and postcolonial work by critics today, because Rhys gave a sympathetic account of the heroine's descent into madness after her unhappy marriage to Mr. Rochester in England, and also gave West Indians a voice they had seldom had in English literature before. Jackie was entranced, because suddenly, there in St. Martin, Claudia unintentionally brought to life the imaginary world of one of her favorite books. It was almost as if Claudia were playing out an alternative version of Jackie's own youth. Jackie had been the correct young woman in pearls when she married JFK. Here was an uninhibited young woman who romped into the surf wearing her pearls, kept a journal for her artwork, and thought of showing her art to a wider world: all things Jackie would have liked to have done herself.

Claudia ended up leaving St. Martin. She was not often in touch with Jackie, but she did send her a birth announcement for her first son. It was probably ten years later. Meanwhile, via *Rolling Stone,* Claudia had met Jody Linscott, a rock-and-roll musician who toured as a percussionist with the Who and, in addition to working with Pete Townshend and Roger Daltrey, played with many of the best-known rock performers of the later twentieth century. "Jody and I stayed friendly over the years," Claudia said. "We were in New York together in the late 1980s. We started to do this little book just to entertain our kids on the train to Boston. It began with a little alliteration. Jody turned the alliteration into a continuous story. We thought it was a good story, and our kids liked it. I did a few collages just to see what would happen. We didn't have a plan. Then I read somewhere, maybe in *People* magazine, that Carly Simon was doing children's books with Jackie at Doubleday. I didn't want to just call her out of the blue. I thought I'd just write a little note. 'Hi, it's been so long. I've got a little book project and I'd love to show it to you just to see what you think about it.' Three days later there was a message on my machine. One of her assistants called and asked if I could come in to meet Mrs. Onassis. There I go with my little collages and the whole of Jody's text." "This is charming," Jackie said, looking at the material Claudia had brought in to show her. "She turned to Shaye Areheart and said 'Let's do it.'"

The success of her book with Carly Simon gave Jackie the confidence to make such quick decisions. No one was more shocked than Claudia. "I thought it was just going to be a preliminary thing. I hadn't seen her in years when I showed her the book idea." After Jackie agreed to do it, Claudia went straight downstairs, out onto Fifth Avenue, and spent thirteen dollars in quarters at a pay phone to call Jody Linscott in London. She wanted to share the incredible news right away.

Jackie now became the impresario of Claudia and Jody's traveling road show. The idea behind their books was the formation of a traveling band, the Worthy Wonders, who went from place to place, learning about the different cultures they visited on their tour. It was multiculturalism for children *avant la lettre.* The two young women often consulted with Doubleday's designer Peter Kruzan, and would go into Jackie's office wearing elaborate costumes. Claudia recalled, "My illustrations are kind of crooked and a little goofy. Peter Kruzan was shocked that I worked with fingernail scissors and not with some sort of X-Acto knife. Jackie would say, 'You're like a little lace-maker.' She was wonderful to work with. Everything was easy. Sometimes we'd show up with all three of our kids. I remember changing diapers in the bathroom at Doubleday. We used to dress in this very bright hippy-dippy way. It rubbed off from Jody's rock-and-roll sensibility. Jackie loved the way we dressed and took our picture in the office." Jackie's "little lace-maker" comparison, which she had picked up from Diana Vreeland, and the photos of the young women's outfits were both signs that she was enjoying herself with Claudia and Jody.

The launch for the first book was at the Sindin Galleries, then at Seventy-ninth and Madison. "It was our party," Claudia said, "not Doubleday's, but they did end up buying us a case of champagne. We had all the originals framed and sold many of them through the gallery. Jackie bought one. She came to the opening." The young women were disappointed that Doubleday didn't do more to promote the book. "Why no book signings?" they asked. The promotions department replied, "Who would come?" Doubleday, having allowed

Jackie wide latitude to produce an expensive children's book that could not be expected to bring in the sales of something like Carly Simon's books, was unwilling to spend anything further on the project.

Nevertheless, Jackie was enthusiastic about doing another book. *Once Upon A to Z: An Alphabet Odyssey* came out in 1991. The second book, *The Worthy Wonders Lost at Sea: A Whimsical Word Search Adventure,* was slated for 1993. For this book, Jody Linscott had written, produced, and performed some music. It was the first time she ever sang on a recording, and she did it by borrowing a friend's studio. Jody and Claudia had the idea of producing a CD to be packaged and sold with the book. If Jackie could not move Doubleday to spend more money on promotion, she could at least make some calls and use her name to investigate the feasibility of the CD idea. As Peter Kruzan remarked, "Who's going to refuse a phone call from Jacqueline Onassis?" Claudia knew that Jackie was doing a lot for them and was a little embarrassed to complain about Doubleday's failure to promote the book. Jackie's telephone calls to record producers were worth a good deal more than whatever Doubleday might have spent on book signings.

The CD idea never materialized in the production of the first two books, although there were plans for a third book in which the Worthy Wonders visit India, one of Jackie's own favorite destinations. Both young women were hopeful that their music idea might go a bit further with that one. However, Jackie became ill before their next book was finished. Shaye Areheart moved to another publisher. Claudia and Jody couldn't interest Doubleday or other publishers in their third idea. It was sad, both personally and professionally, because they'd had a wonderful ride with Jackie. Looking back on it, Jody Linscott reflected on Jackie's talent as an editor and on what she learned from her. If some of the text needed a little work, she recalled, Jackie "would make a suggestion very delicately that you would have to think about." She knew how to lead people without telling them what to do, a considerable art. "In the music business," said Jody Linscott, "you'd get an 'artists and repertory' or A&R person. They don't have them anymore. When you were a singer or a songwriter or a band or whatever, they'd stand by you, stick with you, help develop your idea. They'd help bring the art out of you. It has all changed now. That's in the past. But Jackie was very old-fashioned like that. My grandfather Robert Linscott was a senior editor at Random House. He discovered Truman Capote. He edited William Faulkner. He and Jackie had this similarity" in their attitude to bringing along authors. "I had a kind of understanding of the publishing business through him, even though I was a musician. I really appreciated how she worked, because I'd heard stories of how my grandfather worked. If you're going to take somebody on because artistically you believe in them, you just want to bring out what they can do. That's the call of an editor, and that's the call of an A&R person with an artist. There's a *rapport* between you, and it becomes personal." In losing Jackie, Jody and Claudia lost something more than an ally. She was almost a parent who helped them give birth to their art.

Claudia learned something from Jackie about staking your all on a project that animates you, however arcane or unpopular it might be. Whenever she and Jody went into the office, Jackie would press free copies of her other books into their hands. "We never left her office without an armful of books. She did things she was passionate about. It seemed so obscure to do a book called *The Frenchwoman's Bedroom,* but it was beautiful. She was also crazy about Peter Sís," the author of a children's book called *The Three Golden Keys,* published, like Claudia and Jody's last book, just before Jackie died. What remained of Jackie long after she was gone was not only the physical books she had edited, but also, and more important, the idea deep in the belly of creative artists that someone powerful had once believed in them, and might do so again.

Prague Spring

For most of the three decades between the building of the Berlin Wall in 1961 and its destruction in 1989, much of Eastern Europe lay shut off from the West. Civilians who tried to escape from East Berlin, controlled by Moscow, to the western part of the city, allied with NATO, were killed by Communist snipers. When President Kennedy went to Berlin in 1963 and said, *"Ich bin ein Berliner,"* he was showing Western support for the Germans whom Moscow was bent on annexing for the East. For most of the cold war, however, the Western European democracies and the United States decided that East Germany, Poland, Czechoslovakia, and Hungary were—at least geographically—within a sphere of legitimate Soviet influence. Even when the Czechs rebelled against the Soviets during the "Prague Spring" of 1968, no armies from the West went to their assistance. Russian tanks crushed the rebellion. It was not until the late 1980s, when Mikhail Gorbachev decided that the Soviets could no longer afford the military expenditure that made control of Eastern Europe possible, that one by one the former eastern bloc countries began to declare their independence from Moscow.

Jacqueline Onassis made a small but determined contribution to the renaissance of Western interest in Eastern Europe beginning in the late 1980s by commissioning the Czech artist Peter Sís to write a children's book about his homeland. Sís had come to America in 1982 and fought off feelings of alienation in a strange country. Sent to assist in the making of a movie about the 1984 Olympics in Los Angeles, Sís was ordered home when the eastern bloc canceled its participation in the Olympics as part of its cold war conflict with the United States. Sís refused to go back and was granted asylum in this country. He longed to visit Prague, but both American immigration restrictions and the hostility of the Communist regime to Czechs who had left for the West prevented his return even for a brief visit. He made a successful living as an illustrator of children's books and attracted the attention of a scholar of children's books, Michael Patrick Hearn, who introduced Sís to Jackie.

Jackie knew right away that she wanted to publish a book that Sís would illustrate, and she was sure he had something to say, so she wanted him to write it too. His artwork was different and darker from that in standard children's books, even the ones she'd already published herself. They owed something to the monstrous images of Maurice Sendak, whose *Where the Wild Things Are,* published in 1963, had been criticized for resembling children's nightmares. An interview with Sendak helped Sís to find his first work in America. Part of Jackie's commitment to Sís was long discussions during which they talked about what he should write. They started by considering adaptations of stories that were as much for adults as for children, such as the French novelist Alain-Fournier's *Le Grand Meaulnes*, in which two teenage boys search for a lost love. They also thought of Italo Calvino's *Baron in the Trees,* set in the eighteenth century, in which a boy escapes from a cruel baron, his father, to live his life in the trees. These were both well-known authors with major reputations in European literature. Jackie may have been working on a book for children, but in collaborating with Peter Sís she was also following her passion for serious writing by authors of acknowledged literary standing.

Sís remembered that "finally Jackie was the one who came up with the idea of doing a book about Prague." He had tentatively raised this idea with other publishers, but they weren't interested in Prague. They wanted more reliable subjects of interest in the West, such as Paris or Venice. Jackie's instinct was that because Prague was meaningful to Peter, because he was even tortured by the memory of it, he could write an unusual book about it. "She talked about things without commercial considerations," he said. They didn't discuss money. Shaye Areheart did the book deal and discussed the amount of the advance with him. "It was never quite clear whether we were talking about children's books or adult books," he recalled. Jackie encouraged him to "be as free as you want to be" and not to worry about making matters too dark for children. "This was a chance for me to really let go. I was still trying at that point to make everything children-friendly." He was still agonizing over his childhood memories of wonderful freedom in Prague combined with the lack of political freedom that had compelled him to leave everything that he loved behind. "Suddenly I could deal with all these feelings and subjects." She gave him the license to do whatever he wished.

Telling Sís to do whatever he wanted might well have horrified the money managers at Doubleday. Jackie said to him, "Why thirty-two pages?" which was the standard length for a children's book. "She didn't feel limited by the market," he said. She selected Italian marbled paper and the book was printed in Italy, an expensive proposition. Shaye had to apply the reality principle whenever she could. Although the book came in at more than sixty pages, the commercial artist in Peter felt compelled to point out that "I was only paid for the book as if it were thirty-two pages." Even so, Shaye might well have felt a tinge of what JFK and Onassis felt when they had to pay Jackie's bills.

Even Jackie may have regretted some of the license she had given her author. Sís said, "I had no idea how long it would take me to do the book, and I ended up needing double the time allotted. 'Take all the time in the world you want,' she said, and the project occupied almost a year. At one point she got nervous. We had just had a little baby. I was in hot and humid New York trying to re-create Prague." The centuries-old city of his youth couldn't have been more different: one of his strongest recollections was of the cool air blowing out of cellars onto the street. He was finding progress difficult. Jackie went downtown by herself one day to call at Sís's house and rang the bell. Finding him not at home, she walked over to a building housing artists' studios at Lafayette and Spring Streets in Soho. She decided to try finding him there, without knowing precisely which studio was his. She created a stir in the building, wandering around different studios in her dark glasses and surprising artists at their tables by knocking unannounced on their doors: "Do you know where I can find Peter Sís?" "She finally found me," he recalled, and she was happy with the incomplete work that he showed her, even though it was beyond the deadline. "Take your time," she told him, but he knew very well that what she meant was to hurry up.

When he finally finished, he had to take all his artwork in to Doubleday. "We had a meeting in a conference room that was all glass," with a view over the towering buildings of midtown Manhattan. "We spread all the art on the floor. For an immigrant, this was the most amazing moment. I had all my art above New York and Mrs. Onassis was down on the floor looking at it." She looked, she admired, she approved. Better than citizenship, a green card, or a passport, this was Peter Sís's moment of arrival.

He sensed that Jackie personally would be responsible for the book's success—or perhaps he wished, like many of her other authors, to ensure its success by putting her name on it. But she would not allow him to dedicate the book to her. Instead she said the book must be dedicated to his baby daughter, Madeleine. He followed her advice, and indeed the narrator of *The Three Golden Keys* tells the story to Madeleine, born in New York with no knowledge or experience of her father's native country. It's a dreamlike recollection of being led around Prague by a black cat, who gives him three golden keys, ancient Czech legends that will reopen the door to his childhood. "She didn't particularly like cats," remembered Sís, but she permitted him to leave the cat in. He also put in "Thank you for a dream J.O." on the reverse side of the title page.

The book is not a standard children's book. Its predominant colors are shades of black. It includes quotes from André Gide, who called Prague a *"ville glorieuse, douloureuse et tragique,"* and from Albert Camus, who felt lost and desolate in Prague's "opulent Baroque churches." It has a happy ending—the narrator unlocks the door to the remembered warmth of his childhood home—but again Jackie had pushed the limits of what was considered permissible in children's literature. With Peter Sís's work, she aimed at an unusual crossover audience of adults suddenly curious about one of the jewel-like Eastern European cities that had been off-limits to Westerners for the past thirty years.

The benefits that accrued to Peter Sís were stunning, even though Jackie's early death prevented him from ever doing another book with her. His next publisher, Farrar, Straus & Giroux, allowed him to publish a book of sixty-eight pages, greater than the still-standard thirty-two, simply because his previous book had been with her. He remembered shyly, almost a little ashamed to recollect it, that she used to write him letters in which she called him a genius: "From the depths of my mind, thinking back, maybe she planted the seed for the awarding of the MacArthur grant." In 2003 he was awarded a so-called genius grant when the MacArthur Foundation made him a fellow and gave him a stipend that freed him for several years from working for publishers.

Jackie benefited too. She told *Publishers Weekly* in 1993 that she loved editing any book that took her on a journey into something she didn't know before. Her collaboration with Peter Sís led her to go incognito with Maurice Tempelsman to Prague in 1991 to meet the Czech president, Václav Havel. Sís had first started talking to her about Havel before the Communist system fell apart. It fascinated her that a playwright like Havel might actually replace the Communist leadership. It seemed as if a true "republic of letters" was in the process of being born. Sís told her a story that delighted her of all the new Czech leaders coming to New York. Some of them were, like Havel himself, poets, playwrights, and dissident intellectuals. Before they began their round of official visits, someone told them, to their surprise, "Now, you must have a jacket and tie." They were all wearing leather jackets. Jackie so loved the trip to Prague and the meeting with Havel that she started work on a book (one that never came to be published) that was to be a recounting of the Czech "Velvet Revolution," whereby the Communist system was overthrown nonviolently and writers occupied the seat of power. Her wish to throw her weight behind Havel and his cohort was thoroughly consistent with the speech JFK had once made in Berlin. It was almost as if she wanted to say publicly and in print, "I'm Czech, too."

"She's just a rich lady pretending to be an editor," Peter Sís said he thought at first, when he recalled their work together. "That's the stereotype people have of her. But in fact she was one of the most inspiring editors I ever worked with. She was always flying up there in the air and curious about all subjects." She was as free intellectually as she encouraged him to be in his work. She modeled that freedom, as a mother does for her children. But he knew, too, that it was also his good luck to have been taken up by a woman who had as much power and who was given as much liberty as Jackie had at Doubleday. "Every artist gets to meet his Medici," Sís said, referring to the powerful Florentine family whose patronage supported artists like Michelangelo during the Italian Renaissance. In Jackie, Peter Sís met his Medici.

All My Children

Publishing children's books was not the only way in which Jackie applied what she'd learned as a mother to her career. She pressed, prodded, and protected a score of younger writers and junior editors. These young people were shocked to find that the world's most famous woman acted less like a celebrity and more like their moms. The Texan novelist Elizabeth Crook was born in 1959, in between Jackie's own two children, who were born in 1957 and 1960. In the 1990s, when Jackie was editing her two novels, Crook was in her thirties and still wore her blond hair in a long braid down her back. One of her very first memories was the death of JFK; she was four years old. Any American child who was alive in 1963 felt the world shudder and change at that moment, just as a younger generation did on September 11, 2001. It was a particularly meaningful instant in Crook's family, because her mother was getting dressed to go and meet President Kennedy when he was killed. Her father had been an unsuccessful Democratic candidate for a congressional seat in east Texas. She was in the room with her mother and was surprised to see her weeping. "I had never seen her cry before. She and my dad had been scheduled to meet with the president later that day in

Austin—Bill Moyers had arranged it. My dad was the president of the San Marcos Baptist Academy and outspoken in favor of President Kennedy among Baptists. The president was going to talk with him, because it was unusual for a prominent Baptist to speak up in those days in favor of a Roman Catholic. My mother was getting dressed for the meeting when the news that the president had been shot came on the television. I was in the room with her. She was trying to fit into a dress—she had just given birth to my sister a few days before and was trying to find something she could wear to the meeting. The television was on, and the news broke in, and I was very suddenly aware that the world had turned upside down."

Crook also had to cope with the surprise of Jacqueline Onassis entering her life when she agreed to publish her novels. "Oddly enough, it was her shyness that put me at ease," Crook remembered later—that and the fact that Jackie was "motherly." It was not always a matter of being wrapped in a warm blanket, however. Crook found that she was still a little afraid of Jackie and used to hope, when an issue came up and she had to telephone Doubleday, that Scott Moyers or Bruce Tracy would answer the phone. Jackie was softspoken in person and on the phone, but her written comments, especially on early drafts of Crook's second novel, *Promised Lands,* were not only direct but also brutal. "CUT" and "DELETE," she wrote in all caps. "Overkill." "Cloying." "This is pretty trite. Can you recast?" "Overwritten, overwrought." "Melodrama; I'd eliminate." All these appeared in Jackie's handwriting in the margins of Crook's manuscript. At one point Crook had dwelled too much for Jackie's taste on the stump of a dog's tail, and Jackie said it should come out. Where Crook had put in a section on bringing up a baby, Jackie wrote that it was enough to put the reader off babies. Still, Crook recalled that "I would get off the phone after talking to her and feel just thrilled. Then I would realize that she had just told me the book had big problems, that a lot of work would have to be done. I can remember thinking 'Why do I feel excited? She just told me to start over.' She had a gift for criticizing a book without demoralizing the author. Her comments were blunt—especially her written comments. But I always felt she believed in my books and more generally in me as a writer. I always felt we were on the same side."

David Stenn was another of Jackie's younger authors who responded to her combination of editorial direction and personal warmth. He was a young man who, just out of Yale, had had success writing and producing television shows such as *Hill Street Blues, 21 Jump Street,* and *Beverly Hills 90210.* He didn't lack confidence, but like many writers, in the midst of one of his Hollywood biographies for her, he reached an impasse. He decided to take her up on her offer to contact her at home if need be. He felt comfortable going over to her apartment on Fifth Avenue to talk because he felt her maternal interest in him. His own mother was dying of cancer. He was confused about where his manuscript was going. He turned up at Jackie's door wearing moccasins and shorts. She made him speak about his mother's illness and sorted out his confusion about the manuscript over crustless sandwiches and tea.

Jackie also extended her protection to young people whom she worked with in the office. Lindy Hess, a former Double-day editor who had moved on to direct a pre-publishing training program at Columbia University, helped Jackie hire Scott Moyers to be one of her assistants. He remembered that on the first day he met her he was nervous about what she would be like, but she just connected "things I'd told her about in my life with aspects of her own children's lives, just to normalize it. 'I'm a mom. I have kids. I work.' She just put it on that plane. It was very reassuring. I remember finding her impossibly glamorous. She had on very subtle but beautiful jewelry. You know she had this fantastic carriage, presence, life force, *ch'i.* If anybody had *ch'i,* Jackie Onassis had *ch'i.* She was just fully turned on." Working with Jackie, however, wasn't always a matter of observing this beautiful life force floating down the hall. Scott also said, "If she had some criticism to make . . . Boy, she didn't have to criticize very sharply for it to be ringing in your ears. I think because my feet lifted off the ground at first and everybody called her Jackie in the office, I remember somebody telephoned from the outside my first week there, and I said something like 'Jackie can't do this.' It was somebody who actually didn't know her. Afterward, I remember her very gently saying, 'Scott, could you please use *Mrs. Onassis?*'" Shaking his head and laughing, he said, "I never did that again."

Moyers had the sense, though, that he was genuinely being looked after in the office. "My mom had died of leukemia. She knew that," he said, and when he ran a marathon to support the Leukemia Society of America, "Jackie wrote a big check to sponsor me." She also offered him money when he hurt his knee after being hit by a drunk driver. She cautioned him about coming to work with his hair wet in the morning and bought him a blue wool hat to cover his head in the cold. When he came down with the flu, she made him take Theraflu and sent him to her own doctor for an appointment.

Bill Barry recalled one other example of Jackie looking out for her assistants. When the raise Doubleday proposed to give one of her assistants was what Jackie regarded as too small, she proposed to supplement the assistant's salary from her own pocket and effectively embarrassed Doubleday into further increasing the assistant's pay.

Another young man she took under her wing was Paul Golob, now the editorial director of Times Books, a partnership of Henry Holt and the *New York Times.* When he worked briefly at Doubleday as a young man in 1990 he got caught in the middle of office politics. The man who had hired him had to leave Doubleday in a hurry after his own patron, Nancy Evans, was fired and Steve Rubin came in to replace her. Paul was sitting at his desk at four in the afternoon. Jackie came looking for the man who had hired him, who was out of the office. "She stuck out her hand and pronounced her name in the French way: 'I'm Jacqueline Onassis.' 'I just started here,'" Paul said, struggling to his feet and explaining that the man she was looking for was away. Should he leave a message that she had called? "'Yes, if you could.' She left; I sat down and tried to stop my heart from racing."

After the man who had hired Paul left the company, "She noticed that I was kind of alone and unmoored. She would come to see how I was doing. She asked if I knew anything about Herbert Block, the cartoonist. 'I'm thinking of doing a book with him. Would you have time to look at that?'" She asked Golob to write a report on the manuscript. "That was the thing where she felt she could continue talking to me." It was clear that Jackie was giving Paul some work to forestall the company from firing him.

"They moved me to a desk in the middle of nowhere. I came back from lunch one day and there was a note from her. 'I saw your office was empty and thought the worst. Please come see me.' I think she had a mother hen thing. I'm a few years younger than her son was." Eventually Golob left Doubleday for another publisher, but he kept in touch with Jackie, who invited him for lunch after the summer was over. "My feet didn't touch the ground for a while. The fall came. I screwed up my courage to call her at Doubleday. I spoke to the assistant and said I'd like to have lunch whenever's good for her. It had to be postponed several times. Finally the message came: can you come to her apartment for tea? It was the first week of December 1990. I was instructed to come at five P.M.

"I show up at the appointed time. I go up the elevator and it opens. There she was, standing in the entrance hall." He had expected a housekeeper or a butler. "She was right there. Someone materialized to take my coat. She took me into this sitting room; a fire was going. It was a smallish room. Tea came in, and finger sandwiches. She started asking me questions. 'Tell me what you're working on.' She was interviewing me. It was all about me. I started telling her about a book I was editing, *The United States of Ambition,* by Alan Ehrenhalt, about who chooses to run for office in America. Its argument was that the sorts of politicians we now get are based on the people who offer themselves for election, not especially the best people as picked out by experienced politicians. Those people determine the character of the government. In the old days party bosses chose people. Now people choose themselves. Ehrenhalt talked about the decline of deference. Young people used not to put themselves forward so much. That's what prompted Jackie to say, 'I remember when I was first married. I remember that Jack took me to the Senate to the visitors' gallery and we sat up there and I remember him pointing to the different senators, the reverence in his voice—"That's Senator Russell, that's Senator Mansfield."' He as a young senator was still part of the old deferential system. It was an intimate moment. I didn't expect her to be sharing it with me. It was as if I was talking to my own mother. That was so natural. It was her life. 'If I can be of any help, if you need endorsements, let me know,' she said. We talked some more. It was about six. Next thing I knew I was walking toward the door, down the elevator, and out. My carriage had turned into a pumpkin and I was walking home."

The Cinderella or fairy godmother effect that Jackie

often worked on her writers and younger colleagues is something that many of them still remember now, almost two decades after she died. She knew she had this effect on them but didn't particularly value it, because it didn't cost her much energy or effort. Of greater value to her was the sense that she had raised her children well, and that also, in working as an editor, with tangible books to her credit, she had worked off some of the need for revenge against the world that she had written about to Harold Macmillan in the 1960s. Although her sense of grievance lessened over time as she contributed productively to the work at Doubleday, she remained alive to the presence of injustice in the world. One of the injustices she felt most keenly was that the value of women's work had been persistently underrated or denied, that the roles and careers open to them were much more restricted than those open to men. If the hard work of being a mother was both undercompensated and undervalued, she was also interested in the way that women's other economic, cultural, and political contributions had been underrated. A significant number of her books addressed women's contributions to history. She was ahead of her time in commissioning writers to work on this topic, which is now a standard part of university history curricula. However, it wasn't exactly grim political campaigning, because she had some fun with it as well.

chapter 6

SHE'S A CLOSET FEMINIST.
—*Betty Friedan on Jackie*

In 1975, John Warner, head of the Bicentennial Administration, and later a Republican senator from Virginia, teased Mabel Brandon that her hometown of Plymouth, Massachusetts, where the *Mayflower* landed, was not participating in the Bicentennial. Brandon was then the wife of the Washington correspondent of London's *Sunday Times,* Henry Brandon. She had recently been involved in a historic preservation fight in Plymouth to buy the eighteenth-century house where the colonial playwright, poet, and historian Mercy Otis Warren had lived. Both Warner and Brandon came from Jackie's world: Warner's first wife was a Mellon; Brandon was known to her friends as Muffie, had attended Miss Porter's School, and would later serve as social secretary in the Reagan White House. Brandon reflected that millions of dollars were being spent on Bicentennial programs "deifying men and wars." She took issue with this. "Who was talking about what life was really like—the toll the wars took? That's where the women were." About a meeting of the Bicentennial Administration, she said, "They had no right to have a closed meeting to discuss spending public funds . . . A man with a big cigar blew smoke in my face and said through clenched teeth, 'Make it quick, baby.'" Forced to seek other channels of funding, Brandon and her friend Joan Kennedy decided to approach the big corporations who spent money advertising to women and ask them to support a proj-

ect. Their idea was a traveling exhibition of documents, arti-
facts, clothing, and paintings that would celebrate the lives of
preindustrial American women. The show would begin in
Plymouth and then travel throughout 1976 to other American
cities, half a dozen in all. Brandon approached her friend Tom
Guinzburg at Viking and asked him to produce a hardback
book to accompany the exhibition, eventually entitled *Remember the Ladies: Women in America, 1750–1815*. The title of both
the show and the book came from a letter by Abigail Adams,
who had written to her husband, John Adams, in 1776, "In the
new code of laws I suppose it will be necessary for you to make,
I desire you would remember the ladies and be more generous
and favorable to them than your ancestors."

Today the idea of an exhibition examining colonial
women sounds uncontroversial, but the Bicentennial occurred
just four years after Congress had passed the Equal Rights
Amendment, or ERA, a proposed constitutional amendment
guaranteeing that there should be no discrimination on the
basis of sex in federal, state, or local law. Although President
Nixon endorsed the ERA and it quickly gained more than a
dozen state ratifications, its opponents guaranteed that it failed
to gain the thirty-eight ratifications necessary for it to become a
permanent amendment to the Constitution. The ERA ran into
its most serious opposition in the Bicentennial year from conservative Republicans such as Phyllis Schlafly, who denounced
it as "antifamily."

The first lady, Betty Ford, along with Nancy Kissinger
and Joan Kennedy, went to the opening of the exhibition Brandon had conceived in Plymouth in June 1976. When Betty Ford
said before cutting the ribbon that the exhibition would help
"focus attention on the unfinished business of our revolution for
full freedom and justice for women," she was booed by a group
of anti-ERA protesters. They heckled her and carried signs say-

ing "Stop ERA" and "Equal Rights Amendment Stamps Out the Family." They chanted "Go away, ERA" and were met by proponents of the amendment chanting "ERA, all the way."

Remember the Ladies was the first book Jackie worked on at Viking to come to publication. Although she was not in Plymouth for the opening, Mabel Brandon thanks her in the preface as one of the book's editors. An article in *Ms.* magazine called Jacqueline Onassis, somewhat more accurately, one of the show's "patrons." Most of the work on the book was done by others, and Jackie's first association with it came from Guinzburg's pushing it in her direction, but the subject of the book—strong women in history who asserted themselves despite the conventions of a male-dominated society—is a theme of her subsequent books as an editor. She may not have gone to Plymouth wearing Givenchy and waving a pro-ERA placard, but her books allowed her to make a distinct contribution in favor of expanding the recognition of women's role in history while she herself appeared to remain silent.

Much of the text of *Remember the Ladies* might have been describing her own experience, though the events it concerned took place two centuries earlier. One of her later authors, who was an expert on eighteenth-century history, found that Jackie was remarkably well informed about Abigail Adams, the most independent-minded and articulate among American first ladies. The book has Martha Washington, lonely and rather shy, telling a friend that while she was in Washington during her husband's presidency, she never saw anyone. Her comment "Indeed I think I am more like a state prisoner than anything else" would certainly have echoed Jackie's own feelings at times in the 1960s White House. The book also describes Dolley Madison as being such an inveterate and extravagant shopper that the duty alone on a shipment of her clothing from France was $2,000.

In addition to the experience of presidential wives, the book examines that of humbler women, pointing out that in the second half of the eighteenth century the death of young children was commonplace: "There were few mothers who did not bury at least one child." Jackie had had her own problems with miscarriages and had buried two babies who did not live many hours beyond their birth. The book also gives her newly chosen career some weight by pointing to a historical precedent. One of the areas of colonial work in which women had specialized was printing and newspaper publishing, so to have joined Viking was less a new departure than a return to an earlier tradition. That must have appealed to a woman as history-minded as Jackie.

Conover Hunt was formerly the deputy director of a museum at Fort Monroe in Norfolk, Virginia, and has a distinguished résumé listing her other museum curatorships. She has a cultivated voice that suggests the Virginia of colonial plantations as well as a mint julep wit. In the 1970s, when Muffie Brandon hired her to be the curator of the Bicentennial exhibition, she was just out of her twenties. She was amazed at the broad-based coalition of supporters Brandon had put together. There were both blue-blooded ladies and left-wing activists who thought of marriage as counterrevolutionary. "Among the sponsors were the Mount Vernon Ladies' Association and the National Organization for Women," she said. She paused a moment and added, "Fortunately they never saw each other in the same room." Hunt recalled going to an editorial meeting at Viking in New York, where Jackie was present with other editors who were working on the design and layout of the book. "I thought she would be as big as Mount Everest. Instead, this tiny little woman in black slacks and a white silk blouse comes in. Very quiet. Said nothing. Great presence in her quiet way. Very, very reserved. She had obviously become that way by experience. She was not going to open up. The one time she opened up was when we talked about her children." Hunt also remembered Jackie's wearing "nine million gold chains—remember, this was the 1970s," and listening attentively when a designer suggested that the captions to the photographs should be "flush left, ragged right." Jackie said, "Now, explain that to me." The designer replied, "That means, Mrs. Onassis, that everything is going to line up on the left-hand side and there's not going to be margin justification on the right." And she said, "Well, it's just like it *sounds* like it is." Hunt could see that working on the book was mainly a learning experience for Jackie and that her Viking colleagues were still learning themselves how to get along with her.

As Hunt was frantically trying to put together an exhibition in less than nine months, a call from *People* magazine came in offering free publicity if Hunt could arrange an interview with Jackie. This was ordinarily something that would have been handled by Muffie Brandon, but Hunt's instinct was that, however tempting, the opportunity had to be turned down. " 'Out of the question!' I said and hung up." She laughed, remembering this. She and her team were working in the refurbished attic of Brandon's Washington house, now owned by Hillary Clinton. "Muffie came in and said 'What happened?' and I said, 'Well, you know, c'mon! It's Jackie!' Muffie replied, 'Darling, I'm so glad you know how to handle the phones.' I was just trying to get this exhibit up on time. I thought, what is this nonsense?" Guinzburg may have wanted Jackie on board at Viking for her connections and her publicity value, but the women around her knew instinctively that she wasn't going to talk.

The women of Jackie's social background were a good deal less sentimental about her than some of the middle-class authors whose lives she came into as a kind of apparition. To Muffie Brandon, now Muffie Cabot, since she married into one of Massachusetts' founding families following the death of Henry Brandon, Jackie was mere flesh and blood. As she saw it, Jackie's joining Viking in 1975 was less a publicity coup for Guinzburg than it was a great favor he had done her, one that perhaps she didn't altogether deserve. "Tom Guinzburg did her a very great service in giving her that job," she said. When she fell out with Guinzburg over the Jeffrey Archer book, Muffie Cabot noted a parallel. "She also fell out with Ben Bradlee over his small book. She was very sensitive. She was protecting the flame, her version of Camelot. It happens." Bradlee had produced an affectionate memoir of his friendship with JFK while he worked at the *Washington Post* during the Kennedy presidency. Jackie believed that Bradlee had exploited his friendship with JFK for profit. She never spoke to him again, cut him on the street in New York, and even refused to acknowledge him when they were vacationing in neighboring cabanas on St. Martin.

Muffie Cabot's unsentimental attitude toward Jackie also derived from a later project they worked on together. This book, about Muffie's mother, which Jackie encouraged but which was ultimately produced by a different publisher, showed not only that Jackie had a continuing interest in strong women who did daring things that were unusual for their time, but also why Muffie was not particularly in awe of her as an editor. Muffie's mother, Janet Elliott Wulsin, set out with her husband in the 1920s on an exploratory expedition through the Far East that included China, Mongolia, and Tibet. They rode horses and camels, took with them Chinese collectors who amassed biological and zoological specimens, and also documented Buddhist rituals. Initially, Muffie thought she would write her mother's story as a novel. She produced an outline as well as a sample chapter and showed them both to Jackie. "I love it," Jackie said. "But I want to have someone help you."

Jackie proposed Emily Hahn, a well-known writer for *The New Yorker,* who had also traveled in China. Hahn was a bizarre character who, according to her granddaughter, smoked cigars, held "wild role-playing parties in her apartment," taught her grandchildren Swahili obscenities, and whooped "passionately at the top of her lungs" when she passed the gibbon cage at the zoo. This was Jackie's mistake: to pair a Hahn with a Cabot. Muffie remembered Emily Hahn as "a very tough, very takeover" sort of woman. "We didn't get on." Ultimately, Muffie told Jackie she didn't want to do the book. They parted as friends. Muffie concluded that Jackie "didn't have enough confidence in me as a writer." She then added, with charming self-deprecation, "She was right. I was very green." Her book about her mother did eventually appear, in 2003. The fact that Muffie persisted with her project and managed to find another publisher for it suggests that at this stage in her career, Jackie was green, too.

Ms. Jacqueline Onassis Publishes a Novel on Working Women

In the late 1970s Jackie came to know a power couple in publishing, William and Roslyn Targ. Bill Targ was a distinguished editor who had recently retired from Putnam, where his most famous coup was signing Mario Puzo's *The Godfather,* in 1968. Putnam paid Puzo a $5,000 advance and sold the paperback rights alone for more than $400,000. Roslyn Targ was a literary agent. In retirement Bill Targ set up his own company to produce handmade books on heavy paper in limited editions. The books were unique works by highly regarded authors such as Tennessee Williams, Norman Mailer, and Saul Bellow—precisely the sort of publishing that most attracted

Jackie. When Targ produced a memoir of his career, *Indecent Pleasures,* in 1975, Jackie wrote to him out of the blue to say she loved it, and this was the start of their friendship.

Jackie did not often take lunches with literary agents, one of the main avenues by which editors find new books for their lists. Scott Moyers remembered that she would see a few agents whom she knew, but if she started going out with others, every agent in New York would want to take her out. Jackie preferred to take on new projects from people she already knew and trusted. She made an exception for Roslyn Targ, who told Jackie of a manuscript by a Massachusetts novelist whose first work Bill Targ had published at Putnam in 1977. The author was Nancy Zaroulis, and her new novel was about a woman who worked in a textile mill in Lowell, Massachusetts, in the 1830s. The novel explores the fierce independence of this woman and her oppression at the hands of men and mill owners, but it also ranges over all American history of the period up until the Civil War. Jackie liked the story and she trusted the Targs' judgment, so she acquired it as her first novel for Doubleday.

Nancy Zaroulis's *Call the Darkness Light* appeared in the summer of 1979. It had a significant commercial success. Doubleday profited by selling the paperback rights to New American Library. *Family Circle* ran serial excerpts from the novel. A publisher in England bought the foreign rights for more than six figures. It's hard to know exactly why it was such a commercial success, as Zaroulis's subsequent novels never sold that well, but some of the reason may have been the publicity blitz in advance of publication that connected the book to Jackie. As with *In the Russian Style,* the late 1970s were years in which she was finding her way in publishing, and she never allowed her name to be used in connection with one of her books in quite so forward a fashion again.

Throughout the early months of 1979, her involvement with the book appeared repeatedly in the press. Gloria Steinem, one of the founders of *Ms.* in the early 1970s, did a cover story on Jackie in March 1979 featuring Jackie's picture and a headline, "Why Does This Woman Work?" Unusually for her, Jackie cooperated with Steinem—the only other magazine interview she agreed to in her post–White House years was with *Publishers Weekly*—and told her about the projects she was acquiring, including Zaroulis's novel on nineteenth-century working women. Steinem admired Jackie and hoped she would be a model for other middle-aged women who might also strike out and find fulfillment through work that had previously been denied them. Steinem asked this rhetorical question: "Given the real options of using Kennedy power or of living an Onassis-style life, how many of us would have the strength to return to our own careers—to choose personal work over derived influence?" Here Jackie also set out the parallels between Zaroulis's heroine and her own experience. "What has been sad for many women of my generation," said Jackie, "is that they weren't supposed to work if they had families. There they were with the highest education, and what were they to do when the children were grown—watch the raindrops coming down the windowpane? Leave their fine minds underexercised? Of course women should work if they want to. You have to be doing something you enjoy. That is a definition of happiness . . . It applies to women as well as to men. We can't all reach it, but we can try to reach it to some degree."

The article also quoted Jackie's exchange with a cabbie who drove her to work one morning. "Lady, you work and you don't have to?" he asked. She said yes. "I think that's great," he replied. Maybe he also appreciated that she had left her Lincoln Town Car behind and was paying him for a ride in his democratic taxi instead.

The evidence that Jackie was pleased by Gloria Steinem's piece lies in the fact that she kept a framed copy of the *Ms.* issue with her picture on the cover, signed by fifty of the magazine's staffers. Of the hundreds of magazines that had appeared with her picture on the cover, it was the only one that she kept and that survived among her effects until the sale held at Sotheby's in 1996. One *New York Times* columnist, Frank Rich, remembered that even Betty Friedan had claimed Jackie as "a closet feminist," because she set an early example of how to be a working mother. Not everyone was entirely happy with this, however. Linda Grant De Pauw, the historian Muffie Brandon hired to write the text for *Remember the Ladies*, spoke out publicly after Gloria Steinem's article appeared. De Pauw said that far too much influence had been ascribed to Jackie for the book. In De Pauw's experience, Jackie had had nothing to do with it, and De Pauw had certainly never had any contact with her famous editor at Viking. Steinem's homage had touched a nerve of resentment of Jackie's money, privilege, and exaggerated accounts of her achievements.

De Pauw's denunciation of Jackie and Gloria Steinem added to the frenzy and furor that preceded the publication of Zaroulis's novel. Jackie's association with the book was trumpeted in the *New York Times,* the *Chicago Tribune,* and the *Washington Post,* among others. Jackie even talked to a reporter about the new novel when she turned up at a fundraiser thrown by Lally Weymouth, the daughter of the *Post*'s owner and publisher, Katharine Graham, to benefit a library on the history of women that Arthur Schlesinger and his wife were founding at Radcliffe College. Doubleday used to have a suite off Fifth Avenue where the publisher held book parties to celebrate new publications. Steve Rubin, an old hand in publishing who had seen everything, was nevertheless amazed at the turnout for the Zaroulis book. It was the first time he saw Jackie's drawing power in action. The correspondent from the *Washington Post* was appalled at the behavior of the crowds and estimated that several hundred people had gathered on the sidewalk outside the suite hoping for a glimpse of Jackie. When her colleagues tried to smuggle her out of the party through a side door, the crowd broke and ran toward her. There was mayhem, and it was a terrifying experience.

Zaroulis remembered that Jackie had very little to do with the actual publication of her book. "I didn't know Mrs. Onassis well . . . I didn't really work with her because the book was published as I wrote it." Jackie had acquired it for Doubleday, but other editors had taken care of the publicity and production questions. The first time Zaroulis met Jackie was at the publication party. All this might seem to support De Pauw's indignation that Jackie should be given any credit for her own book, but that would be unfair, because Jackie's labor was often symbolic as well as of the sort that required pencils and erasers. The reporters who covered Zaroulis's book noted that in 1979 Jackie had just turned fifty and had found occupation with Doubleday that was a kind of middle-aged renewal. Several of the newspaper articles noted the connection between Zaroulis's examination of exploited female workers in the nineteenth century and Jackie's finding new satisfaction in her life as a working woman. Jackie's lending her weight to the Schlesinger Library's new emphasis on women in history and Zaroulis's novel about working women in nineteenth-century Lowell were both steps on the long road toward female emancipation in America, according to another article. Although Jackie may not have had to get her white cuffs dirty with an inky manuscript, she was certainly setting an example in the same way she had in 1963.

Conover Hunt, who went on from *Remember the Ladies* to curate an exhibition space in Dallas devoted to remembering the assassination, grew suddenly serious when the conversation turned from the Bicentennial project to her later work. "I was born in 1946," she said. "I had no model. We looked at Jackie O. When she died we all had lunch at the Palm, including many of Dallas's women leaders, to salute a woman who in finding herself had helped us find a way." When it was suggested to her that Jackie's contribution had been "significant," Hunt said, "No," her voice vibrating with emphasis. "It was *remarkable*. It was *phenomenal*. She could have caved. She could have lost it that day in Dallas, but she didn't. There are millions of women who watched and remember that. She not only survived but she led the way, led the whole country through that awful weekend. And then went off and found, after doing her child rearing, after assuring the security of the children, her life, her intellectual interests, which she had certainly not brought to the forefront when she was with President Kennedy, but which were always there." In the 1970s, Jackie, like many women, felt it was time for women to have more prominent jobs and careers. "There was a great sense among the leadership," Hunt continued, "with people like Lady Bird Johnson, and Mrs. Onassis in her own way," that the time had come for women to make a stand, have a voice, play a part. *Remember the Ladies* and Nancy Zaroulis's *Call the Darkness Light* were both books typical of an era when the American women's movement was ceasing to be the preserve of radicals and becoming more popular. Hunt concluded by saying of Jackie in the '70s, "She was a woman of her time, even though she has become a woman of all times."

You Are an Eighteenth-Century Woman

With a few exceptions, Jackie was never again as prominent promoting one of her books in the press as she was with

Nancy Zaroulis. Nor was she as far forward as other first ladies—for example, Betty Ford and Lady Bird Johnson—in promoting the ERA. Her instinct was to do things quietly and behind the scenes. Her only antidote to mob scenes on the street was to keep as low a profile as she could. In the 1980s she was involved—more actively as an editor than she had been with either *Remember the Ladies* or *Call the Darkness Light*—with a group of books on the lives of privileged women in history. These books came from the pens of two New Yorkers whom she knew socially, Olivier Bernier and Louis Auchincloss.

Bernier was educated in Paris and at Harvard. Auchincloss told the story of how Bernier's stepmother, Rosamond Bernier, was in such a hurry to leave the Paris apartment of her husband and end her marriage to Bernier's father, Georges Bernier, that she was on the verge of walking out the door without taking any of her things. Then she saw Olivier, and decided on a whim that he looked so lonely she'd take him. Rosamond Bernier later married John Russell, an English art critic working primarily in his later career for the *New York Times*. So Olivier Bernier was raised in the world of art dealing, art criticism, and connoisseurship on two continents. His father and Rosamond Bernier had edited and contributed to France's foremost art magazine, *L'Oeil*. He was an art dealer himself in New York for a decade and then devoted himself to writing popular books on European history and lecturing at the Metropolitan Museum of Art. Nowadays he guides tours sponsored by the Met to the princely houses, châteaux, and castles of Europe, often those that are still in private hands and closed to the general public. Auchincloss said of Bernier, both archly and a little enviously, "Olivier Bernier would have been very much Jackie's dish."

Jackie was part of a circle of well-heeled enthusiasts of eighteenth-century art, history, ideas, style, and culture. Her friends Charles and Jayne Wrightsman were in the same circle and gave several galleries of ancien régime furniture to the Metropolitan Museum. Though Jackie was not herself an avid collector, the most valuable pieces of her own furniture, auctioned by Sotheby's after her death, were from the same period. Women who knew Jackie often thought of her as modeled on one of the aristocratic courtesans, originally court ladies but ultimately "favorites" or girlfriends of the monarch, from this era. Dorothy Schiff told Jackie in 1964, "You are an eighteenth-century woman. You should be the mistress of a king or a prime minister." So when Diana Vreeland did a show at the Costume Institute in 1981 on eighteenth-century women, Jackie was a natural to commission a book to accompany the exhibition and be sold in the shop.

Olivier Bernier wrote the text and assembled the art for the book, *The Eighteenth-Century Woman,* which is arranged in brief chapters on individual women, such as Abigail Adams, Madame de Pompadour, and Georgiana, Duchess of Devonshire. Jackie also helped to arrange a public seminar at the Met to which Bernier, Louis Auchincloss, and Erica Jong were all invited. The invitation of Jong is an important indicator of Jackie's unblinking attachment to at least one variety of the new feminist politics. Jong had written the runaway bestseller *Fear of Flying,* published in 1973. In the novel the heroine unashamedly explores sexual desire beyond the confines of marriage. This was an important step forward for feminism because the novel openly celebrated female eroticism, which had often been veiled, denied, or silenced in previous writing about women. Jong's novel was the *Sex and the City* of her day, but a lot racier, because it was more taboo then than now.

Jong believed that she was invited to the Met seminar because she had just published *Fanny,* a novel about an eighteenth-century woman in England. Bernier remembered being invited to Jackie's apartment for dinner after the seminar. Auchincloss and Jong were also there. He recalled the men turning pale at the dinner table as Jong launched into graphic details about the birth of her daughter, born in 1978. Bernier noted that Jackie sat there unflinchingly, merely nodding and affirming what Jong was saying. Jong was interested in the subject because the research for *Fanny* had turned up evidence that the eighteenth-century profession of *accoucheur,* practiced almost exclusively by men, was more lethal for pregnant women than the old-fashioned midwives, who were always women. Jackie was clearly on Jong's side when it came to discussions of childbirth, whether ancient or modern.

Jong recollected that Jackie was "passionate about books. She was a reader. She was a lover of poetry. She was fascinated by the eighteenth-century woman. In a way she *was* an eighteenth-century woman, especially in her pragmatism about marriage. She married two men who were useful to her both financially and socially." She implied that Jackie was ready to deal with the consequences of such matches and that such pragmatism was characteristic of upper-class eighteenth-century women, too. Jong pointed out that Jackie's mother, Janet, "was the same way. She married a man, Hugh Auchincloss, who was said by Gore Vidal to be impotent." Auchincloss nonetheless had great wealth and social position. While Erica Jong and Jackie were not best friends, they were on friendly terms. "She frequently called me for blurbs," quotes that she could put on the back of her books' jackets to sell them, Jong said. "She was serious about her work, not a dilettante."

One mark of the fact that Jackie was not a dilettante was that she published enough books on eighteenth- and nineteenth-century women to become a specialist. From Bernier she commissioned a subsequent book on the Duchesse d'Abrantès, a woman who not only witnessed but also participated in the rise to power of Napoleon Bonaparte. This book was entirely Jackie's idea. She also encouraged Bernier to do an English translation of letters among European crowned heads about the French queen Marie Antoinette. Bernier remembered having a dilemma, as many of the letters talked about the queen's troubles persuading the king to have sex with her. Jackie agreed that it was strong stuff but said that he had to go ahead and she would publish it. That book became Bernier's *Secrets of Marie Antoinette*.

Bernier loved working with Jackie. Their editing sessions together often began with a cocktail in her apartment on Fifth Avenue. She smoked cigarettes with a long white cigarette holder, like Cruella De Vil. Bernier saw the same pragmatic toughness in her that Jong had seen. She could be very sweet, and she gave him a little plate with an image of Louis XV on it in memory of one of their books together, despite the fact that he left Doubleday to go to another publisher which offered him a bigger advance. "She was considerate and thoughtful, but she was no innocent waif," said Bernier. "She made very sure she could live in the style she wished." In other words, she forgave him for holding out for a bigger advance from another publisher because she had done the equivalent herself. Bernier saw her more than once at a party coming in and standing all by herself. Not only were people afraid to go up to her, but her shyness sometimes put people off. Once she went to a book party at the Seventh Regiment Armory that was filled with literary and urban notables. She went in and stood by herself in the middle of the floor for several beats. No one approached her until a couple from the Midwest, total strangers to her, rushed up and began gushing.

Another of New York's Park Avenue personalities with whom Jackie worked in the 1980s was Louis Auchincloss. Auchincloss's father was a cousin of Hugh Auchincloss,

Jackie's stepfather. He was a kind of distant relation of hers by marriage. Like Bernier, who made the history of the French court his specialty, Auchincloss knew the history of American blue bloods the way adolescent boys once knew baseball cards. Auchincloss was the author of more than a dozen novels that described the moral dilemmas of rich people from old New England families. His models were Henry James and Edith Wharton. If he never received the critical standing of those two Gilded Age novelists, he nevertheless carved out a niche for himself. His books sold well enough to make the publisher of his novels, Houghton Mifflin, happy. So Jackie was pleased to have him join her at Doubleday to do a little nonfiction.

In 1981 Jackie asked Auchincloss to write a historical introduction to a work of photography on Versailles by the fashion photographer Deborah Turbeville. They worked together more intensively on a family diary that had come down to Auchincloss via his wife's grandmother, Florence Adele Sloane. Sloane had been born a Vanderbilt and lived her entire life with the benefit of an immense fortune. The diary covers a crucial period in the young woman's life, including her debut in high society at the turn of the twentieth century, contemporary with James and Wharton. The idea was to publish long excerpts from the diary, with Auchincloss providing the necessary historical commentary to explain the context. Auchincloss put in such turn-of-the-century curiosities as the diarist's train ride in a private car, noting that her uncle was going up to the front to drive the train, as he actually owned the railroad. Jackie, on the other hand, was interested in the way in which this very rich young woman was in fact imprisoned by her privileges. She wrote Auchincloss a note on a draft he'd produced, saying, "Being an Edith Wharton fan from way back there was no way I wouldn't enjoy a diary from this period, but even beyond my own interest . . . I found myself being involved in Florence Adele as a young woman . . . She was bright, articulate, and frustrated as hell at times with her own life. There are virtually no published diaries of that period available. The upper class woman was the most strictly guarded of all. Could you put in something about the rites of society—how young women were presented—how many years did they have to find a husband before they were considered old maids? Love and a happy marriage was the only adventure for these spirited, protected women." Jackie's sympathy here was for a debutante whose life must have been even more constricted than her own. We look at Jackie, who had been dubbed by one New York columnist as "debutante of the year" in 1947, and see only glamour and promise. Jackie looked at a debutante of the 1890s and wondered, "How many years did this woman have to find a husband before she would be shunned as an unmarriageable spinster?" We look at Jackie's wedding to JFK and see nothing but the sheen of a Newport summer. Jackie looked at Florence Adele Sloane and saw her marriage as her only chance to break free.

Doubleday published Sloane's diary as *Maverick in Mauve,* because the 1890s are sometimes called "the Mauve Decade." The publicity echoed Jackie's letter to Auchincloss. An ad that ran in the *New York Times* in November 1983 to accompany the book's publication reads: "Years before it was quite respectable, Florence Sloane had a mind of her own." The body of the ad explains that "this enchanting, romantic young Vanderbilt heiress kept a diary. To read it now is to hear the authentic voice of a real-life Edith Wharton heroine: a passionate young woman prisoner to a gilded age."

A young reporter from *Vogue* went to the book party at the Museum of the City of New York, which Doubleday and Auchincloss threw to celebrate the book's publication. Marie Brenner was surprised to find not only that Jackie was there, but that she didn't shy away from talking to a reporter. "There was no trace of the baby-doll voice as we talked," Brenner wrote of her encounter with Jackie. "What had interested her in the diary was not the detailed descriptions of the Mauve Decade, she told me, but the character of Adele Sloane herself. She used the words 'survival' and 'survivor' several times, and it was impossible not to believe that her fascination for this diary had something to do with feelings of identification. 'What was so moving to me was the spirit of this woman, and the dignity with which she lived her life, and her basic character,' she said. 'That her life would seem to be ideal, and then tragedy would strike her—losing her child, for example. And that her life was not going to be so perfect after all, that she would have enormous difficulties, but somehow her spirit and her character would carry her through. You realize, especially when she writes so movingly about the death of her child, how difficult her life could be.'" Brenner concluded that Jackie had chosen the book because the book was about her life, too.

Perhaps for that reason Jackie next encouraged Louis Auchincloss to do a book on women who had made something of the extraordinary privileges to which they had been born. In 1984 she edited *False Dawn,* in which he looked at more than a dozen women from the late seventeenth and early eighteenth centuries, the era of Louis XIV. Individual chapters tell the stories of women such as La Grande Mademoiselle, the German wife of the heir to the French throne, who had to put up with an openly homosexual husband but also turned out to be one of the most detached and best-informed writers about daily life at Versailles, and Madame de Sévigné, a marquise whose husband died in a duel before she was out of her twenties but who made an art from her polished letters to her daughter in writing that is still fresh and memorable today. Auchincloss makes a telling point in analyzing a Molière play that makes fun of bookish women. "What one can see today in these plays is the opportunity that books offered to women, hitherto bound either to domestic servitude or the cloister, to operate on equal terms with the other sex." Books leveled the playing field for these literate, privileged women. Through the written word, these women left a mark on the world when most of their sisters were silent and thus largely absent from history.

Doubleday's advertising once again stressed that this was about seventeenth-century women who made "strides toward emancipation . . . remarkable in a male-dominated age." However, the book's reviewer at the *New York Times* did not buy this claim: Auchincloss had argued that "despite the age's chauvinism, it produced an unusual number of women of accomplishment. But the age was a 'false dawn' because these gains were lost during the next century. This theory is interesting, but, for the most part, the women Mr. Auchincloss considers are not typical." Auchincloss tended to agree with this criticism. *False Dawn,* he said, "laid an egg" because it seemed to promise more than it delivered in the way of women's liberation. "The idea of the book, the importance of women of that kind: they were important if they were *born* to the job. You had to be born to it." That was disappointing for American women in the 1980s, when birth counted for almost nothing and getting out and doing was all.

But was it? What Jackie had done by promoting the books of Olivier Bernier and Louis Auchincloss was to show the trials of women who, though born to wealth and power, still had to exert effort, intelligence, and ingenuity if they were to overcome the obstacles put in their way by men. This was less a celebration of aristocratic privilege than it was an evocation of the same kind of passion and determination found in those pioneering women who, a century later, sacrificed to found American schools and colleges for women. Miss Porter's School and Vassar College had been lampooned at their founding in the 1800s as useless institutions. "Why educate a woman and teach her to read books if she is only going to raise a family?" argued men of the Civil War era and beyond. Similar arguments that slaves needed no education had also been made in that era. The founders of the first women's schools fought hard to establish the principle that women needed to be educated if they were going to take an equal place with men in their society, and that principle had its origins in the rage for equality that dated from the French Revolution in the late eighteenth century. Jackie's books with Bernier and Auchincloss were her small way of keeping that education-for-women and education-about-women spirit alive. If she could fantasize at the same time about living her life in a Boucher canvas or in a boudoir furnished for a marquise, that was all the better.

From Privileged Women to Everywoman

"Just think, Nancy, he's a professor of psychology who used to be a priest, and now he's *married*." Nancy Tuckerman remembered Jackie's enchantment—part human interest, part plain gossip—with the life stories of her authors. Among them, Eugene Kennedy had a more interesting story than most. He left the priesthood to marry and remained a tenured professor in the psychology department of Chicago's Loyola University. He was not related to the Hyannis and Palm Beach Kennedys; rather, he was a prolific writer and journalist who reached out to a wide, nonacademic audience. In the 1970s alone he had published books on counseling, on love and friendship, on religious belief, and *The New Sexuality: Myths, Fables and Hang-ups* (1972). Jackie had read a newspaper piece he wrote on Chicago mayor Richard Daley and encouraged Kennedy to write Daley's biography. They enjoyed working together, and when Kennedy wrote a piece for the *New York Times* on a rebel politician, Jane Byrne, who had upset the all-male apple-cart of Cook County's Democratic machine, Jackie and one of her Doubleday colleagues, Lisa Drew, called Kennedy into the office for a talk.

Jane Byrne was an official in the administration of Chicago mayor Michael Bilandic. Bilandic fired her in the late 1970s, and she plotted her revenge. She challenged Bilandic at the next mayoral election and beat him in 1979. She served until 1983. She was the first woman mayor of that city and still carries the record of having served as the only woman mayor of a U.S. city of Chicago's size. She was an unpredictable and often a colorful figure. At one point, to bring public attention to the high crime rate in one of Chicago's most notorious public housing projects, she went to live in Cabrini Green, an area of high-rise apartment buildings where cabbies refused to drive, let alone stop. She was also the first Chicago mayor to recognize the city's gay constituency and to urge passage of a ban on handguns.

Jackie and Lisa Drew told Kennedy that he should write a book about Byrne, and he agreed. He didn't dare to do nonfiction, but he did produce a novel about a woman's surprising rise to political power in Chicago, called *Queen Bee,* in 1982. The book was not entirely admiring of this character's performance. A *Washington Post* review said the heroine had "all the innocence of a cobra." Jackie asked Kennedy whether he'd have to leave town as a result of his book's critical portrait of the city's sitting mayor. Although there was no one-to-one correspondence between Jane Byrne and the heroine of Kennedy's novel, the book's tone echoed some of the newspaper criticism of Byrne's tough-minded but also operatic leadership style. Jackie was no universal supporter of women in positions of power, nor was she uncritical of the women who reached political prominence. She was ready for one of her authors to have a little fun at Jane Byrne's expense. Nor was she afraid to correct Kennedy when he produced the draft of another novel with a female character who did not adequately resist men's bad behavior. "No woman would react that way to a man," she told him. "A real woman would kick him all over town."

In the later 1980s, Jackie's book projects that deal with women have this gritty pragmatism: a continuing attraction to the stories of strong women, but women who were more often American than European, not highborn, not perfect, but inventive, persistent, and determined to survive the odds against them. Her book projects in the second half of her publishing career were more often about Everywoman than about elite women.

In 1976 Doubleday had had a stunning success with the publication of *Roots* by Alex Haley. This novel, loosely based on Haley's historical research in Africa and America on his own ancestors, tells the story of an African named Kunta Kinte who is forced into American slavery and his heirs' evolution over centuries of living on American soil. The book was made into a popular television miniseries starring LeVar Burton, Ben Vereen, and Cicely Tyson. For the first time genealogy was not only the preserve of those who could trace their descent from the *Mayflower*. Haley's book represented a new cultural flowering of the civil rights movement whereby people who had once called themselves "black," because of the revolutionary Black Power movement of the 1960s, now became "African American," a more settled and established American ethnicity with a historical dignity that came from distant origins long before slavery. Haley later had to settle out of court when plagiarism claims were made against him, but this did not diminish the landmark status of his book.

Inspired by Haley's novel, a woman named Dorothy Spruill Redford began doing research on her own family background. She wanted the dignity for her daughter and granddaughter that Haley had achieved for his. She envied Africans and West Indians who knew their family history. Through painstaking research in local archives, she discovered that the first slave of Somerset Place, a plantation in eastern North Carolina, was an African ancestor of her family. She organized two homecomings at Somerset, in 1986 and 1988, to which she invited both the black and the white descendants of slaves and slaveowners at the plantation (Haley himself attended one of the parties). She began to organize to save the house at Somerset from destruction as well. Her historic preservation effort added another dimension to her story. This was picked up by *People* magazine and by national television in an era when anything *Roots*-inspired was still big news.

Either Jackie saw the article in *People* or someone pointed it out to her. She sent a colleague, Marshall De Bruhl, himself a southerner proud of his white-columned plantation background, down from Doubleday to try to put a writer together with Dorothy Redford so she could tell a book-length version of her story. The first writer they tried, a female academic, didn't work. Then they hired the journalist Michael D'Orso, who worked for the *Virginian-Pilot*, the main newspaper in Norfolk, Virginia. D'Orso remembers spending long hot summer afternoons with Redford. He would lie on the floor of a housing project apartment with his tape recorder as Redford looked after her baby granddaughter while her daughter was at work. Redford was a powerful and determined woman, and her story moved him. Doubleday published their book together as *Somerset Homecoming* in 1988. The *New York Times* noted in a favorable review that the book's story "is as much about a remarkable woman as about an American people."

D'Orso remembered sitting at his desk at the newspaper the first time Jackie called him from New York. As he cared about his writing, he worried about writing a book with someone else. She reassured him of his authorial control and was pleased when he said he could do the job in six months. She called him occasionally to find out how he was doing, but when he sent in the text, the line editing was done by her assistant. He thought her strength instead was recognizing an idea that was worth exploring at book length and putting the people together to make it work. In D'Orso's opinion, this was what made Jackie great. "She made books happen. She spotted the subjects and put together the projects. That was her forte." In publishing *Somerset Homecoming,* Jackie acquired another favorite collaborator in Michael D'Orso, but she also did what successful marketers always do, publishing a *Roots* for women which built on Doubleday's previous coup. She also grew from the young woman who read everything she could about the Palace of Versailles to an acquisitions editor who could look clear-sightedly and with fellow feeling at women who spent some of their lives in public housing projects.

Jackie was also adept at recognizing the passion and sympathizing with the ambition of her authors. David Stenn, for example, wanted to take the screen stars of Hollywood's past and give them their due as artists. When he started working on a book about Clara Bow, the only thing most people knew about her was the legend that one night at a party in L.A. she had had group sex with the USC football team. Here was a beautiful woman with an unfairly tawdry reputation who deserved more credit for the work she had done. Jackie agreed. After she had published Stenn's biography of Clara Bow, *Run-*

nin' Wild, to good reviews in 1988, she would occasionally call him in Hollywood, where he'd gone back to producing and screenwriting. "When are you going to come back? When are we going to do another book?" Jackie asked him. She wanted him to do another biography. She suggested Norma Shearer, and though Stenn did not take up her suggestion, Jackie's very mention of Shearer is revealing. One historian of Hollywood has described Shearer as one of cinema's feminist pioneers: "the first American film actress to make it chic and acceptable to be single and not a virgin on screen."

Asked how he got started on Jean Harlow, the subject he ultimately chose, Stenn responded by saying of the 1930s, "A woman in that era of Hollywood, navigating in a man's world, is just inherently interesting." Both author and editor wrestled with the evidence Stenn turned up that the glamorous Harlow had lived for a long time with her mother, that she was a passive figure and had allowed herself to be abused by men. "I remember saying to Jackie, 'I feel like I have a choice here. I can invest her with a lot of strength, which she didn't have, but it will make the book more lively. Or I can depict her as she was, but it's frustrating.' It was a rhetorical comment, because obviously I wasn't going to do anything inaccurate. That's why *Bombshell* was more challenging" to write than his book on Clara Bow. Asked whether there wasn't a quiet and committed feminism in Jackie's sponsorship of two books that wanted to recover artistic dignity for the work of two actresses that had been considered merely "commercial," Stenn replied, "Absolutely! You know what her Farmington quote was. In the Farmington yearbook she said her ambition was *not* to be a housewife. That was heretical in the 1940s." Although publishing biographies of Clara Bow and Jean Harlow would not have been heretical when Jackie did them, there remained a subversive motif that connected her schoolgirl days with her publishing days, and that was her insistence on telling a woman's true story beyond the retouched photographic image.

Jackie often invested as much in an author as she invested in a subject. In the fall of 1993, she and David Stenn had lunch to discuss his next project. He'd run across a scandal and cover-up at Hollywood's biggest studio, Metro-Goldwyn-Mayer. In 1937 the studio had invited more than a hundred chorus girls to attend what they thought was a casting call, but was really a stag party meant to entertain visiting salesmen. When one of the dancers, Patricia Douglas, realized that she'd been tricked and tried to flee, she was raped. She sued the studio, which brought out its most expensive legal guns against her, driving her out of Hollywood and into hiding. Stenn told Jackie that he didn't know where the story would take him. "There's this story and I can't make heads or tails of it. It's just in the newspapers. I don't know what became of this woman." Jackie replied, "Well, if anyone can find out what happened, it's you."

Thinking back on that conversation, his last with Jackie, Stenn said, "When someone like Jacqueline Onassis, who has kept company with some of the great artistic figures of the era, has that kind of faith and confidence in you, you don't even consciously realize what a motivator it is. It becomes almost unconscious. She meant it. That gesture of complete faith was almost like a sly command." It led him to find Patricia Douglas, six decades after the original scandal, and persuade her to appear on camera in his film about the crime and the cover-up, *Girl 27.* In the film, she is a wonderful old woman, nearly in her nineties, with a face as creased and lined as that in an old picture of W. H. Auden or Lillian Hellman. It's impossible to keep your eyes off her whenever she's on camera. Stenn's film is a tribute not only to Douglas's courage in suing MGM, but also to her survival and willingness to talk about the scandal so many decades later. She lived to tell the tale, and though Jackie did not live long enough to see Stenn's film, her spirit presides over it.

Steve Wasserman was another young man whose work Jackie encouraged in the 1990s. He had been her colleague briefly at Doubleday. After he left to become an editor at Times Books, he was thrilled that she agreed to have lunch with him at Michael's, a restaurant on Fifty-fifth Street in New York known for its big windows, white tablecloths, and media power brokers who converged there on weekdays at lunchtime. He remembered the table at the back where they sat, away from the prying eyes of the front room but where, because of his lunch companion, he at last earned the recognition of the restaurant's famously discriminating owner. Jackie ordered an appetizer-sized portion of scallops for her lunch. When it came, there were four scallops on the plate. She ate three and left one. Wasserman also remembered telling Jackie about a biography he was editing, the story of a turn-of-the-century American woman, a contemporary of Adele Sloane, who traveled around the world and who at one time pretended to be insane in order to write a newspaper exposé of how asylum staffers were abusing their mentally ill patients. The book became *Nellie Bly: Daredevil, Reporter, Feminist,* written by Brooke Kroeger and published in 1994. Wasserman later wrote of Bly that "her feats of personal courage and social conscience were peerless. She was an extraordinary inventor of her own life." Jackie listened quietly and then sighed, saying, "How remarkable, don't you think, to have lived such a life. It is how I would have liked to live my own." This may have been the practiced modesty of a woman brought up never to speak about herself, but it's hard not to conclude that this was precisely how Jackie did live her life.

chapter 7

WEREN'T YOU ONCE A PHOTOGRAPHER YOURSELF?
— *Reporter's question to Jackie*

●

Jackie fit many people's definition of what it was to be beautiful. Under Diana Vreeland in the 1960s, *Vogue* coined the term "beautiful people" to describe the Kennedy family, which had brought not only good looks but also youth, glamour, and high culture to the White House. Jackie was irritated by the fact that, over time, the high culture seemed to be forgotten and people only remembered her for high fashion and how good she looked in photographs. She couldn't stop people from wanting to photograph her, but Doubleday had given her the opportunity to be active rather than passive. Through the books she commissioned she could explore what beauty meant, why some women come to be thought of as beautiful when others are not, why we are attracted to certain images, why they have such compelling power over us. The art critic for the *New York Times,* Grace Glueck, noticed this activist agenda after Jackie died. She compared Jackie to an evangelist who "wanted to convey her beliefs to the world around her, to pass on her ideas of what was beautiful, what was appropriate, what was right. And in so doing, she had a whim of iron." Jackie had once been an aspiring photographer, and her books on photography not only reprise the first paying job she had taken, right out of college, but continue the journey she started there.

As a wife with young children, Jackie was a dream for JFK's publicity team. One 1960s film, shot to advance JFK's political prospects, shows her sitting nervously on the wooden porch of a house in Hyannis. She has a tense, self-conscious smile. Off camera comes the disembodied voice of a reporter, who asks whether she wasn't once a photographer and reporter herself. Her mouth is very wide as she answers, "That's right." Then, after a stiff pause, she adds, "I preferred to be on the other side of the camera."

That person on the other side of the camera was who she became. She went from being a figure caught in the glare of flashbulbs every time she walked on the street to being a woman who helped put enduring statements of why art matters into print. She was a woman who had been brought up on fashion magazines and had made a college-girl pilgrimage to visit Bernard Berenson at his villa, I Tatti, without knowing that he was a bit of a scoundrel. She was also a woman who chose photographs she found beautiful and took the risk of annoying critics by putting them between hard covers in order to make them available to a wide audience. Jackie shaped, shared, and illuminated the power of beautiful images.

Nineteen Blackamoors

Diana Vreeland runs like a persistent motif not only through Jackie's publishing career but through much of her entire life. Just as Vreeland's *Allure* offers insights into Jackie's approach to fashion, sensuality, and the attractiveness of women such as Maria Callas and Marilyn Monroe, it also sets out a statement of what beauty is and why it matters. Jackie was about the same age as Vreeland's two sons, whom she knew before she met and corresponded with their mother. It is only from the beginning of JFK's presidency that the first letters from Jackie show up in the papers Diana Vreeland left to the New York Public Library after she died. In these rather formal letters Jackie asked Vreeland for advice on her clothes in the White House. She had hired Oleg Cassini to design her dresses in an agreement with Joseph Kennedy, Sr., who quietly paid the bills. She could thus avoid any scandal that would arise from dealing with couturiers who might disclose what she'd paid them. She was ambivalent about her appearance. She wanted to look good, but having her clothes and her body inspected so closely made her feel uncomfortable. There is a revealing metaphor in one of Jackie's letters to Vreeland about Cassini: she said she would appreciate it if Vreeland occasionally helped him, as he valued Vreeland's opinion and "would make me a dress of barbed wire if you said it would be pretty."

Vreeland was also insecure about the way she looked. She told a journalist from the *Washington Post* who interviewed her about *Allure* that she had been an ugly child. One of the things no one mentions about Vreeland is that in her pictures she looks as if she might have been of mixed race, although she always claimed to have been born plain Diana Dalziel to a prosperous British father and an American socialite mother in Paris. When Vreeland was born, in 1903, being of mixed race would have been nearly unspeakable. The *Washington Post* reviewer was surprised to find in Vreeland's apartment when he arrived there a collection of nineteen blackamoor figurines, a convention of eighteenth- and nineteenth-century European domestic decoration. They were probably Vreeland's idea of a small joke, but then Jackie was joking about the dress made of barbed wire, too.

Both women were also insecure about money. Diana Vreeland married a banker whose income was not adequate to their shared aspirations. She opened a lingerie business to supplement their income when they lived in England and worked for fashion magazines when they returned to America, neither of which paid her particularly well. Of her more than two decades of working for the Hearst Corporation at *Harper's Bazaar,* she remembered later, "San Simeon must have been where the Hearst money went—I certainly never saw any of it." Her husband, Reed Vreeland, died in the 1960s, and when *Vogue* fired her in 1971, she had to find another paying job, even though she had a severance package from the magazine. This was why she went to the Metropolitan Museum to curate shows at the Costume Institute. Even there she was not well paid by the standards of the New Yorkers she saw socially. Jackie recalled that a group of her friends each contributed to make up a "paltry sum" (Jackie's words), an annual income of $30,000 a year, as the museum refused to pay her from its own budget. When fashion luminary André Leon Talley, who got his start by serving as Vreeland's unpaid assistant at the museum, raised his own money difficulties in hopes of getting some help from her, she looked at him blankly. It was something that could not be discussed. So for Vreeland to begin *Allure* with the rather aggressive statement "There's no pictures of poverty in this book!" suggests that she constructed a life for herself that denied parts of her own past.

Jackie, too, was aware that her tastes often outran her budget. Born to a father who had more class than cash and raised in a household where all the money was to be inherited by Auchincloss children rather than by those who were there by marriage, Jackie made marrying for money one of her priorities. In those days, when women from her background didn't work, many women considered a prospective husband's finances before they married. JFK certainly had money, but when he died, Jackie discovered that much of his cash was tied up in trusts for her children. After Onassis died, she certainly found herself in funds, but a lifetime of worrying about money had already engraved itself on her consciousness. William

Ewing, who curated exhibitions at the International Center of Photography and became friendly with Jackie, didn't quite understand when the ICP's director, Cornell Capa, told him never to ask Jackie for money. When Jackie once asked Ewing how he would put together funding for an upcoming show, Ewing was at ease enough with her to say he hoped she might help him with some money. Jackie's reaction told him it was the wrong thing to say. "She shrank to half her usual size and had a pained expression. 'Bill,' she said to me, 'don't you know any *rich* people?'"

When Vreeland wrote in *Allure* that "fashion must be the most intoxicating *release* from the banality of the world," she might well have been talking about finding a fantasy relief from the banality of her own appearance and bank account. In the 1957 film *Funny Face,* the actress Kay Thompson played a character based on Vreeland, a madcap fashion editor who in one musical number commands her staff to "Think pink!" as she dances around the office scattering papers. Vreeland's biographer Eleanor Dwight argues that the movie had a serious point to make, because it "illustrated Vreeland's own conviction that fashion is an authentic art form, and is important because it makes life more beautiful." Vreeland had a philosophy that might well have been taken out of Oscar Wilde. She didn't want to dwell on mundanity or everyday worries. Rather, "you had to exaggerate and embellish the world, make it more vibrant and beautiful." Or, as Wilde put it when he was criticizing the characters of Émile Zola, a French novelist who described low-life drunks and other down-and-outers: "They have their dreary vices, and their drearier virtues. The record of their lives is absolutely without interest. Who cares what happens to them?" What Wilde wanted in literature was "distinction, charm, beauty and imaginative power. We don't want to be harrowed and disgusted with an account of the

doings of the lower orders." Jackie and Vreeland wanted the same in their book of photography. This is heady stuff when you think that it was endorsed by the woman who once served as first lady in a democratic republic that prides itself on its egalitarianism.

Jackie did what she could to enhance Vreeland's artistic credentials. She arranged an exhibition of Vreeland's selection of photographs from the book to be staged at the International Center of Photography, where she served on the board, in the autumn of 1980. A photographer captured the two together at the party, clasping one another. Their eyes and lips seem less like those of two lovers of fashion than of two powerful women determined to advance commercial projects. Jackie also spoke openly to the press about the book and her role in it in a way she would later give up doing. She told *Newsweek* that Diana Vreeland was "an original," and the reporter from the *Washington Post* sent out to interview Vreeland was surprised to find just how original she was. Vreeland had a strange, fashion-model walk, bent over backward, "as if she might put her hands on her hips and break into cheerleader's kicks at any second." She smoked with her Lucky Strike cigarette hanging "from the corner of her mouth, gangster style." He also noticed that she rouged the back of her jaw line, the sides of her forehead, and even her ears. "It sort of widens the face," she told him. "Don't you think? Mm-hmmm? *C'est merveilleuse.*" This was the strange creature Jackie was backing to the hilt.

Jackie told the press that she had helped select the pictures for the book at Vreeland's apartment. Some of her comments say as much about her passions as about Vreeland's. Jackie said that Vreeland's "visual sense" was a combination of the Ballets Russes and the *Arabian Nights:* "She sees like Diaghilev and tells stories like Scheherazade." *Newsweek,* the *New York Times,* and the *Washington Post* all responded with rave reviews. The highbrow *Christian Science Monitor* went one further and pointed precisely to what the two women were trying to do. *Allure,* wrote the *Monitor*'s critic, suggests "a contemporary theory of beauty." Referring to one of Vreeland's most famous phrases, "Elegance is refusal," the critic explained that elegance is "the refusal of convention, of taste, and even of fashion in favor of the most flagrant expression of one's own uniqueness. Without excuses. Without apologies. But with lots of artifice and style . . . Now *that's* character. And *that's* allure." The *New York Times* agreed. What was startling about the most beautiful photographs—for example, a paparazzo snapshot of Greta Garbo—was "the revelation of character." This was how fashion's oddest dictator and the world's most photographed woman decided to define beauty in 1980. Jackie wanted to publish work about Vreeland's legacy even after Vreeland died. She wanted someone to write Vreeland's biography and found a connection via Cecil Beaton to a writer she thought would be ideal, Hugo Vickers. Vreeland had often commissioned Beaton to work for *Vogue.* Before he died, Bea-

ton had chosen Hugo Vickers as his official biographer. Vickers met Vreeland in 1980 via Beaton's secretary. Whenever Vickers was in New York, he had dinner with her. When Vreeland died, in 1989, he came to the United States for her memorial service held in the Metropolitan Museum. Vickers discovered Jackie among the mourners, and when she left the service, he snapped two photos of her as she got into her car. The snapshots show her doing what she did every day: facing a phalanx of photographers. What they reveal of her character is a wary dislike of a familiar situation, an elegant forbearance. Does she show a little surprise, too, that someone she recognized from indoors at the service should have left the museum before her to join the paparazzi outdoors? Perhaps the best revelation of her character ever captured by the paparazzi was the photograph of her walking down Fifth Avenue, oblivious of her surroundings, reading a book (see page iv).

Vickers thought she might have been a little annoyed at his photographing her, but the following year, when they

began discussions about writing Vreeland's biography, Jackie
seemed to have forgotten. In 1990 Vickers began talking with
Vreeland's sons and the literary agent Andrew Wylie about
writing Vreeland's biography. Jackie wanted to be the editor, so she called Vickers into a meeting in her office. Vickers
wrote up the meeting in his diary and left a wonderful image
not only of Jackie at work but also of why she thought a Vreeland biography needed to be written.

When Vickers came into the lobby of the floor at Doubleday where Jackie worked and waited for her assistant to come
fetch him, he was surprised to see Jackie coming herself, "walking slowly, not slinking, but gentle, casual, friendly. She wore
dark slacks and a cashmere pullover with gold jewelry . . . She
has pale, soft skin, a tiny diamond mark on her right cheek,
and tiny lines round her eyes." Her hair, he thought, "looked
like an enormous lampshade," and she played with it, scooping
it in her hands and putting it up, as she spoke to him in her
office. He told Jackie that he thought Vreeland had exaggerated in her storytelling. Jackie disagreed. She thought most of
Vreeland's stories were true. She thought Vreeland had been
ill-used by the Metropolitan Museum. The museum directors,
Jackie said, were "stuffy and pompous. Hoving was better than
Philippe de Montebello," but even Tom Hoving had demanded
to know what Vreeland's academic qualifications for coming
to advise the Costume Institute were. Vreeland had replied,
"What do you mean, academic qualifications? You know I
have no academic qualifications. That's not why I am here.
I'm here to get people into the museum." One of Vreeland's
predecessors, Margaret Case, had committed suicide by jump-
ing out the window of her apartment after *Vogue* fired her, so
Jackie thought that Vreeland was brave to make a new career
at the Met on a small salary. "There was never any self-pity,
and it can't have been easy for her," Jackie told Vickers. She

also pointed to Vreeland's achievement: she transformed what was "previously a sleepy, neglected backwater," the Costume Institute, into a new destination at the museum. The annual December gala, where Jackie herself was usually the star guest, "each year brings in so much money." Thus, in commissioning Vickers to do a Vreeland biography, she was commemorating not only Vreeland's elevation of costume to high art, but also her own role in making it happen. The Vreeland biography was eventually written by the wife of Vreeland's lawyer, but Jackie made it clear that Vreeland stood at the cornerstone of what interested her most about art and photography. What drew Jackie to Diana Vreeland was the way she could wrap together fashion and photography, describing both in such an offhand, offbeat way as to render them closer to art than to design. Vreeland gave Jackie the confidence to select for publication the bizarre as much as the beautiful.

These Worn-out Girls at $1,000 a Day — They Kill Me

Deborah Turbeville was a remarkable photographer whom Vreeland had commissioned for *Vogue*. One critic has characterized Turbeville's work as "ghost stories," combining the "*hauteur* of post-Punk" with the plain odd. Turbeville came to Jackie's Vreeland party at the International Center of Photography on the arm of Vreeland's *Allure* collaborator, Christopher Hemphill. The world of fashion photography could be very small, but Jackie wanted Turbeville to go beyond fashion in a book project she outlined for the photographer. Jackie's star turn during JFK's presidency had been her appearance at Versailles for the French state dinner. Jackie had always been interested in French history, and President de

Gaulle had praised her knowledge of the subject. In later years, Jackie had been back to visit Versailles and had been shown the *petits appartements,* or private living quarters of the royal family, as well as the back stairs used by servants and private visitors of the people who lived in the palace. Jackie wanted a book of photographs to examine the rooms that were off the beaten path, unseen by tourists, who saw only the grandest of the public rooms. This was the contradictory and probably unconscious impulse of a woman who spent all her life trying to quash the publication of tales of her own private life in the unseen rooms of the White House.

Jackie asked Louis Auchincloss to write a literal-minded introduction to the subject that would give a detailed history of what had gone on inside the palace in the seventeenth and eighteenth centuries, at the peak of royal power. From Turbeville she wanted something much less literal and more atmospheric. Jackie wrote in her Editor's Note, hiding anonymously behind a royal "we," that "we wanted to match Louis Auchincloss' formal portrait of Versailles with Deborah Turbeville's dream; to unite a master of the precise and mistress of the poetic."

Turbeville had come to fame as a fashion photographer with an unusual vision. As the critic Vicki Goldberg wrote in the *New York Times,* Turbeville was known for her "soft-focus style that combined poignancy and dislocation, lyricism and stark loneliness." Her women might have appeared in a film by Ingmar Bergman or in Woody Allen's *Interiors.* As Diana Vreeland put it, "I adore Turbeville's girls. These worn-out girls at $1,000 a day—they kill me. We don't know who they are, or why they are, or why they are so beautiful." Goldberg said that though many people had photographed Versailles, only the turn-of-the-century great Eugène Atget had left as personal a stamp on images of the palace as Turbeville had.

It was no coincidence that Jackie had brought out those Atget images as a book too.

Turbeville remembered Jackie asking whether she had read Nancy Mitford's *Madame de Pompadour* or her biography of Louis XIV, *The Sun King*. "I think in a way Jacqueline felt that she was a kind of Madame de Pompadour. Because she was such a patron of the arts. She was a very romantic figure. 'Oh dear,'" Jackie told Turbeville, "'but you have to read this Nancy Mitford book.'" Jackie loved grand architecture and specifically chose Turbeville for this project because she remembered that her photographs conveyed a great feeling for buildings. Jackie also loved royal ritual and aristocratic manners, but she had the same playfulness on the topic that Nancy Mitford had, which somehow kept displays of social hierarchy in perspective. Both of them could appreciate elaborate courtesies as a form of art, but neither of them could take it all that seriously.

Jackie stood behind Turbeville and backed her up with the authorities at Versailles when the photographer wanted to bring in monkeys, piles of dead leaves, and models in costume. Jackie talked to the curators and advised Turbeville not to mention the monkeys in advance. When one of the curators complained to Jackie that Turbeville was creating soft porn à la David Hamilton, Jackie's support didn't waver. She also spoke to Vicki Goldberg at the *New York Times*. "On the back stairs," Jackie told Goldberg, "everybody was throwing chamber pots out, sellers were trying to sell laces, Voltaire was stomping up, love letters were passing hands, and assignations were going on. All those lives, you can just feel them, like ghosts." In short, what Jackie imagined on the back stairs was the same irreverent history Mitford had described—grandeur and great philosophers mixed with turds, corsets, and adultery. Those "ghosts" reappeared in Jackie's Editor's Note, where she said that Turbeville had captured at Versailles a "labyrinth peopled by ghosts of her imagination," a vision inspired partly by Watteau but also by Salvador Dalí and Edgar Allan Poe. Many of Jackie's visual projects, and the photography projects most of all, have that sense of recapturing something in the past, something unnameable, something beautiful, often strange, but also vanished.

Guns and Bourbon

In stark contrast to *Unseen Versailles* was a book of photography that Jackie picked up from her editorial colleague Jim Fitzgerald as he was preparing to leave Doubleday. Fitzgerald had decided to move to a better position with a rival publisher and needed to parcel out his Doubleday projects to other editors before he left. He asked Jackie whether she would be willing to take on a book of photography by William Eggleston, to be entitled *The Democratic Forest*. Eggleston was not well known outside the world of art photography. A Museum of Modern Art curator, John Szarkowski, had helped launch Eggleston in the 1970s as the first major American photographer who worked in color. Fitzgerald was surprised to learn that Jackie not only knew Szarkowski, but was well-informed about Eggleston. She was happy to take on the project. Fitzgerald had been born in Texas; Eggleston was from Tennessee. When Fitzgerald telephoned Eggleston in Memphis to say that Jackie was to be his new editor, Eggleston replied, "Well, my man, I'd best be gettin' up there to meet mah new editor, then." Both men enjoyed teasing New Yorkers with elaborate good-old-boy accents. In Eggleston's case, the accent concealed that he'd come from a privileged plantation background. It also concealed the photographer's alarming eccentricity. Jackie may well have had the chance to wonder what she'd got herself into.

When Eggleston arrived in New York, Fitzgerald took him to Jackie's office to introduce him. He was then called away for a few minutes for a phone call. Fitzgerald recalled, "I came back about twenty minutes later and he was on the top of her desk with these boots on, illustrating a Prussian soldier's march. She was just sitting there, delighted. They were both kind of wacky in a really weird way. But it just jived really well. So then we were going to lunch. Now, lunch with Jackie was always a calculated thing. You couldn't just go to a deli or something. There was this new hotel just up the street that had just opened up—the Peninsula, I think. So we go there and

they knew her and they gave her a table in the back. We sat down. The waitress came up and Bill ordered a drink. 'Well, I'm sorry. We just opened. We don't have our liquor license,' the waitress said. This was tantamount to the Civil War still being on. So Bill said, 'I'll be right back.' We sat and chatted. I don't know where he went or how he did it, but I think he was back in about ten minutes with a bottle of Old Crow and three glasses and some ice. He thought we were going to all sit there and get plowed under . . . Well, two of us did." Jackie didn't care for bourbon.

She did respect artists, though, and even before she met Eggleston, she was fascinated to hear of Fitzgerald's first visit to the photographer's home in Memphis. "I drove over," Fitzgerald remembered. "He was in the swimming pool with a tuxedo jacket on and his underwear and he was painting the pool blue. 'What's wrong with this picture?' " he asked himself. "Nothing. You're in Eggleston's house. A lot of guns. A lot of bourbon." The critic for *Newsweek* who reviewed *The Democratic Forest* when it came out in 1989 had a similar though more unsettling feeling when he first met Eggleston. "Looking every lanky inch the elegant Southern gent in a tailor-made, three-piece suit, the photographer William Eggleston meets a visitor to his Memphis home with one hand outstretched in greeting, the other gripping a revolver." Once inside, the critic found that Eggleston had enough "antique guns to stock a modest arsenal."

The idea for the book had originated with an editor at an English publisher, Secker & Warburg, and Fitzgerald did much of the work for the Doubleday edition before he left. Nevertheless, Jackie's consent to be associated with it highlights the way in which the book intersected, in some ways jarringly, with her typical visual concerns—for example, her passionate hatred for the skyscrapers taking over the city—as well as with her own history. Eggleston and the English publisher had recruited the novelist Eudora Welty to write an introduction to the book. The book's only works of conventional beauty are of the countryside near the plantation where Eggleston had grown up. Most of the photographs are of litter, urban sprawl, fluorescent lighting, and chance views through windows where he has asserted that the composition and color of the photo itself possess a beauty that surpasses the subject matter. Welty points out that Eggleston has focused on Atlanta skyscrapers, proliferating like weeds and rearing up "like bullies." Rarely are human beings in the pictures, and Welty says of the skyscrapers that "no last drop of humanity" could come from these cityscapes we've allowed to spring up "like fortifications." As if to underscore this ominous tone, she then moves to Eggleston's photograph of the Texas School Book Depository on Dealey Plaza in Dallas, which she describes as "indelible in the world's memory as the source of the gunshots that killed President John F. Kennedy." But Welty refuses the notion that Eggleston has dwelled on the negative. Rather, she says that his work shows all that the "mundane world so openly and multitudinously affirms" and thus his "fine and scrupulous photographs achieve beauty." Yes, the building in which Lee Harvey Oswald stood to kill the president has awful historical memories for us, but these memories contrast with the spare elegance of Eggleston's photograph. Eggleston's aesthetic was almost the reverse of Vreeland's: where she wanted to ornament, to embellish, and to reject the mundane world, he wanted to look closely at it to see what beauty, in the careful framing of his photograph, he could establish was already there.

With Eggleston, Jackie moved beyond the teaching of her original mentor. She could embrace two very different notions of photographic beauty. She was able to look in a clear, dry-eyed way at the ghosts of her own past. Maybe she never fully overcame the horror of the assassination, but it says something about her bravery, her practicality, and her sense of the priority of art that she was willing to take on the Eggleston project. That the Dealey Plaza photograph appeared in *The Democratic Forest* was a coincidence. Fitzgerald hadn't thought about it before asking her to take over the project, but she didn't shudder and ask that it be sent back to him when she found it. She went straight ahead with it.

In fact, Jackie had some of the same easy familiarity with Fitzgerald, a younger man with whom she sometimes shared a cigarette and who wasn't afraid to tease her, that she had with Bill Barry. Twice a year Doubleday would have a big sales meeting in which the new season's books would be presented to the sales force. In the old days there had been a party atmosphere and free spending from company expense accounts, so Fitzgerald looked forward to going. One year the sales meeting was to be in Texas. Fitzgerald remembered, "She had a sense of humor." He could get her to acknowledge even the most sensitive subjects. "I asked her if she was going to the sales conference in Dallas." Said Jackie dryly, "I think I'll pass on that one."

Jackie's Orientalism

One of the first important writers to inspire Jackie was André Malraux, Charles de Gaulle's minister of culture, whom she met in Paris in 1961. Malraux had been an archaeologist, a novelist, and a fighter in the French Resistance during the Second World War. When Jackie met him, the two fell a little under one another's spells. Letitia Baldrige overheard one of Jackie's friends asking her what was so great about Malraux. He wasn't even attractive. "The First Lady shot two thunderbolts straight into the questioner's eyes. 'He happens to be a war hero, a brilliant, sensitive writer, and he happens to have a *great* mind.'" Malraux was equally taken with Jackie, and promised her the loan of Leonardo da Vinci's *Mona Lisa* from the Louvre; the painting came to Washington's National Gallery in 1962. Malraux was also the one who raised the alarm about Egyptian antiquities being flooded by the building of the Aswan Dam, starting in 1960. This resulted in Jackie's work to save the Temple of Dendur, originally built around 15 BCE, and bring it to America. As a young man Malraux had been on a dig in Cambodia and written a novel about the experience. This led directly to Jackie's visit to the ancient Cambodian temple at Angkor Wat in 1967. Malraux was the first to interest her in the non-Christian civilizations of Asia and the Near East. So when Jackie was married to Onassis and sat down to dinner in Paris with French photojournalist Marc Riboud, she was excited to hear that he'd been in Cambodia as well and that he'd made Asian subjects, even in Communist China and North Vietnam, one of his specialties.

In about 1974 Onassis and Jackie invited Riboud to dinner with them at Maxim's, then Paris's most exclusive restaurant, where you had to be Jackie to get a table and you had to be Onassis to pay for it. Riboud was a little shocked at Onassis's coarseness. He made rude jokes, which Riboud called "below the belt." Jackie tried to keep the conversation on a higher plane. She wanted to talk about their mutual friend Cornell Capa. She encouraged Riboud to go and photograph Angkor again. They struck up a friendship that outlasted her marriage to Onassis. One of her assistants who dealt with Riboud at Doubleday when Jackie signed him up to do a book of photographs on a Chinese mountain, *Capital of Heaven,* remembered Riboud as a strangely sexy older man. Riboud wasn't afraid to flirt with Jackie, either.

Riboud had traveled extensively in China and had been struck by a particular mountain range, the Huangshan, from the top of which there were spectacular views. "It was not only a beautiful view," he recalled, "but a sensation. A mystical experience." It was customary for young married couples to hike up to the top of one peak in the range. Couples who for some reason could not get married also went there to commit suicide. Riboud's voice was vigorous and friendly over the phone from Paris. "I told her about these mountains. I told her, 'You should come. Let's go there.'" Jackie never went with Riboud to the mountain sometimes called Capital of Heaven, but she did go to China for the opening of I. M. Pei's new hotel there, the first time the renowned architect had ever built a structure in the country where he had been born. Jackie knew Pei from the building of the Kennedy Library in Boston, and when she found Riboud would be there at the same time, she agreed to meet him in Beijing to help him with some photography he had planned to do for *Time* magazine at a new Chinese university. While there, they found a photography studio where newlyweds went to have their pictures taken. It was unusual for Jackie to travel and not be recognized, but the Chinese seemed not to know her, so she was relaxed enough to go into this studio and have a photo made with Riboud. The next time he was in New York and he was invited to Jackie's apartment with Maurice Tempelsman, Riboud was able to announce over his predinner drink, "Jackie, I have the picture of your wedding with me." He explained, "I showed her the picture. *Voilà*."

The photographs that appeared in Riboud's Doubleday book are of cloud-enshrouded peaks. In the book he thanks Jackie for championing his work, saying that she "was the first to believe that those misty snapshots could make a book." She and Riboud asked François Cheng, the first member of

the Académie Française of Asian origin, to write an introduction. Cheng recalls going to the top of one peak with fellow travelers and admiring a sudden view through clouds: "We remained long silent, profoundly moved by a splendor which we felt should endure forever, but which we knew deep in our hearts to be fleeting." The note of nostalgia returns. In Jackie's books of photography, beauty is often of the past, evanescent, never to come again. There's an element of sadness because it's so hard to recapture, even in a photograph.

When the book came out, Riboud wrote in the copy that he presented to her, "For Jackie, who has always been on the top of CAPITAL OF HEAVEN. I am expecting more summit meetings." It was their only book together, although they continued to have a warm friendship. Still, Riboud wouldn't do everything she asked him to do. "She wanted me to do a book on the vegetable *jardin* of Versailles. She heard about this *jardin* from someone. When I went there it was a total jungle." He took one look and then phoned her in New York to say "*Non.*"

Riboud's project on China and Jackie's discussions with him about Malraux and Angkor fit together with a book of photography she did on Egypt: in both she imagined herself embracing the East. Before becoming an editor, she went to India as first lady and traveled to Egypt with Onassis, in addition to making forays into Cambodia and Pakistan. She loved what she found. When the Egyptian writer Naguib Mahfouz won the Nobel Prize for Literature in 1988, she knew of his work from having read it in French and wondered whether there wasn't some way for Doubleday to get the rights to publish Mahfouz in English. Alberto Vitale, then the chief executive officer of the holding company that had recently purchased Doubleday for the German media company Bertelsmann, had the same idea independently. He had spent part of his childhood in Cairo and wanted Mahfouz as well. He knew the competition among American publishers would be fierce, so he went to Jackie, someone he knew would have the clout to reach Mahfouz, and found her willing to help.

Jackie knew David Morse, a prominent New Yorker who had served as a labor advocate in the Truman administration and as director general of the International Labor Organization, which had itself been awarded a Nobel in 1969. Morse in turn knew the Egyptian foreign minister, Ahmed Esmat Abdel-Meguid. Morse told Jackie he would call Egypt. Jackie remembered, "I said to him, 'David, what time is it in Egypt?' He replied, 'It's three A.M., but he won't mind. He's a friend— we used to be law partners.'" Abdel-Meguid sent his son to find Mahfouz, and Mahfouz accepted Doubleday's offer when Vitale flew out to arrange the details.

Doubleday took over a large number of titles from Mahfouz, and by 1992 the cumulative sales for twelve different books was about half a million copies, an impressive figure in publishing. They sold well because the Nobel, and Doubleday's publication of new translations of many of Mahfouz's novels, coincided with the beginning of the first Gulf War in 1990. There was a great curiosity in the English-speaking world about the domestic life and worldview of Muslims. Jackie was excited to be involved in this, not only because Mahfouz was an author of real literary merit, but also because she knew some of the culture and conventions of the eastern Mediterranean from her own experience. She told her Doubleday colleague Martha Levin that the father figure in the Cairo Trilogy, three Mahfouz novels that followed the same Cairo family through several generations, was someone she had encountered herself. Levin remembered one conversation when Jackie told her, "You know, I've spent a lot of time in Greece." There was silence while Levin thought to herself, "Who doesn't know that, Jackie?" but murmured assent instead. "And the main character, the father," Jackie continued, "he really reminds me of the men in Greece."

Palace Walk, the first novel in Mahfouz's Cairo Trilogy, is an attack on the unreasonable power of the father, who wields absolute and ill-tempered power over his wife and children.

He's a hypocrite and an egotist who rages to his wife about his opposition to a proposed marriage, "No daughter of mine will marry a man until I am satisfied that his primary motive for marrying her is a sincere desire to be related to me . . . me . . . me." The same story was played out in Onassis's opposition to his daughter Christina's romantic relationships, which Jackie witnessed firsthand.

Still, it didn't make her think less well of Egypt, for which she had an enduring fascination. She chose historic black-and-white photographs for the covers of the books in the Cairo Trilogy, and was proud enough of these particular books to take them along as part of her show-and-tell for the *Publishers Weekly* interview. So when the young photographer Robert Lyons wrote to her out of the blue, saying that he'd taken some pictures of Mahfouz and asking whether she would be interested in one for the jacket art of any future Mahfouz books, she picked up the phone and called him in California.

When Lyons had first heard of Mahfouz, he had flown to Egypt to meet him. He showed the writer some of his photographs of Egypt, and Mahfouz promised him the use of one of his short stories for Lyons to include in a book of these photographs. Jackie looked at the same photos and said she wanted to publish the book. She told Lyons that she saw him as being in the tradition of two nineteenth-century travelers: the photographer Roger Fenton, who'd done studies of his sitters in oriental costume, and the scholar Richard Burton, famous for his translation of the *Arabian Nights*. Lyons's book with Jackie, *Egyptian Time,* came out in 1992.

Jackie also set up an exhibition of Lyons's work at the International Center of Photography and attended his launch party there. All Lyons could remember of that night was the hubbub of the crowds in the galleries but a great hush when she descended the staircase to the downstairs gallery where his pictures were being exhibited. She allowed Lyons to fly to Hong Kong, at his own expense, and supervise the reproduction of his images as they came off the press so they were exactly as he wanted them, the kind of direct participation in production that a publisher almost never allows an artist or a writer. For her part, in this new third-party collaboration with Mahfouz, she found that her ideas about beauty were taken to a new level in the way the novelist described the childhood origins of our aesthetic sense: "Life's first love," Mahfouz wrote in the story that appeared in *Egyptian Time*, "is of food, especially sweets . . . They are the first exercise in the love of beauty. A child runs, grasping his tiny coins, never satisfied or jaded, to taste with keen craving everything good and delicious, crowning his campaign with knafeh, baklava, cake and chocolate."

Learning to Look

Jackie's last book of photography was one that pulled together all the things she loved about the medium. Toni Frissell was a photographer working in the 1940s and '50s, known not only for her work in fashion magazines, but for her photojournalism in Europe during World War II. One of the curators at the Library of Congress's photographic collection called Toni Frissell's daughter Sidney Frissell Stafford in the 1990s to say that the library had received some telephone calls from people interested in writing about her mother's career in fashion photography. Sidney Stafford thought to herself that really there was more to her mother's work than fashion photography. "Why don't I do a book?" She put together a proposal and sent it to several publishers. When she got a call from a voice identifying herself as Jacqueline Onassis, Stafford recalled, she was surprised. Once she had talked to Jackie and gotten over the shock, she knew she'd found the right editor. Frissell's life in many ways ran parallel to Jackie's. Not only had Frissell known Jackie's mother and photographed Jackie's wedding in Newport, but both of them loved the aura of old money now mainly spent and the tattered opulence that remained. George Plimpton, whom Jackie hired to write the introduction to the Frissell book, quoted Toni Frissell as saying, "When we give a dinner party, the people who serve wear green jackets and white gloves, but my drawing room curtains are in shreds." Or, in the case of Frissell's photograph of the Vanderbilts at tea in Florida in 1950, the money had not been spent and nothing was in tatters.

Both Jackie and Frissell had an irreverent view of fashion. Frissell dropped one of her models into the dolphin tank at Marineland in Florida to achieve an effect that was lovely, otherworldly, and at the same time don't-try-this-at-home-ladies. Jackie chose this shot for the cover of the book.

Like Jackie, Frissell was impatient with being known for her work on fashion, so when the Second World War came, she took the opportunity to photograph soldiers, bomb destruction in London, and children displaced by the Blitz. Toni Frissell was also the first to photograph the Tuskegee Airmen, a group of black pilots trained in the South who fought and flew missions together during the war. Her photographs helped pave the way for the recognition of African Americans' contribution to the war and for the integration of the armed services after the war.

Jackie and Frissell loved hunting on horseback. Frissell made a portrait of Miss Charlotte Noland, who had founded Foxcroft, a girls' school in the country around Middleburg, Virginia, where Jackie rode. Frissell captured the tailored elegance Jackie also adored about hunting costume, as well as her admiration for the unmarried, old-fashioned women who

ran girls' schools before the war. "Ride like hell, little darlings! Ride like hell!" Frissell remembered hearing Noland call out when she visited the school with her mother and saw the head-mistress riding out—sidesaddle—with some of her students.

Jackie led a group from Doubleday down to the Library of Congress in Washington to look through the negatives Fris-sell had left there and make one of the initial rounds of selec-tion for the book, even though many of the photographs had not been catalogued. The only people who had the historical memory and the knowledge of the social milieu to identify the people in the photographs were Frissell's daughter, Sidney, and Jackie. So while Sidney and Jackie leafed through photos,

saying "Oh, that's old so-and-so," librarians were standing in the background, ready to scribble down the pair's identifications. The two women spent a long day going through album after album of photographs. They had brought with them a group of disposable cameras in order to take rough shots of the Frissell images they wanted to use. Someone snapped Library of Congress photograph curator Beverly Brannon with Jackie and Sidney Frissell Stafford at work. Set to one side were the photographs Toni Frissell had taken of Jackie's wedding to JFK in 1953. Peter Kruzan, Doubleday's art director, remembered, "We had gone through pages of photographs, and of course there was that pile [of wedding photographs] still sitting on the table. That was the white elephant that no one wanted to talk about. We finally had to just sit down and say, 'Okay, Jackie, the last thing we have to do is your wedding.' And she went through it." Sidney Stafford remembered the same awkward moment: "It was kind of uncomfortable for all of us. Jackie just said, 'Of course we have to use one of the wedding pictures from my mother's house. Let's use that one.' It

wasn't one of the more glamorous pictures of her. Her choice surprised me."

Sidney Stafford told the critic from the *New York Times* assigned to review the book that it was "not your typical coffee-table photography book." She called it a "photobiography." It was not just her mother's photographs but "the story of a woman." Two women, actually. Whether consciously or not, Jackie summed up her own affinity with Frissell in the jacket copy for the book, over which she would have had direct control. Frissell, says the book's jacket, "stretched the boundaries of the privileged world into which she was born and became one of the most innovative and renowned photographers of her time." The books Jackie edited spoke to her stretching of the boundaries of her world as well. During the declining months of her life, Jackie had come to identify herself so completely with her job that she preferred going into Doubleday to staying at home in bed. The Frissell book was one of the last she ever worked on.

She had persuaded the editor in chief at *Town & Country*, Pamela Fiori, to run excerpts from the Frissell book timed to coincide with its publication. The magazine's photo editor Bill Swan remembered that when the *Town & Country* staff visited her in 1994, Jackie was physically strong, though she was already ill and had a big bandage on her cheek. What struck Swan most when he came into the conference room and was introduced to Jackie was the contrast between the famous photos of her and the way she behaved in person. In her photographs, Swan remembered, "she has just a blank, middle-distance stare." In person, he was surprised to find, she was more animated than he expected, more "engaging, almost little-girl-like" in her enthusiasm for the work she was showing them. It was hard to believe that the Jackie who warned off paparazzi with a cold glance could be the same as this neat woman wearing pencil-leg trousers and Chelsea boots, who came over and asked him to write his name in her book. Jackie O. wanted his autograph.

Pamela Fiori was also aware of Jackie's lymphoma diagnosis. "I was sitting in a chair and she plopped—yes, plopped—on the floor next to me and began showing and telling [photographs], with the enthusiasm of a seven-year-old. As she did, she would point to something and look me in the eyes. I prayed she wouldn't look too closely, because she would have seen that my own eyes had welled up. Here was the world's most famous woman sitting on the floor beside me, hoping I would be interested in what she was showing me." Enthusiasm for one of her book projects was what Jackie *did*. It was natural. It wasn't work for her. She was also surrounded by a Doubleday team that was devoted to her. Swan noticed of Jackie's colleagues, "It wasn't what you'd expect. The relationship wasn't stiff or formal at all. It was very casual. You could tell they loved her." When the *Town & Country* people prepared to go, Jackie took them to the elevator and treated her visitors affectionately. When the elevator doors opened, she said, "Now, scamper in, scamper in!"

Sidney Stafford remembered that by the time the first finished book was in her hands, in the summer of 1994, Jackie had already died. She told the *New York Times* about Jackie's role in the publication of the book, saying, "I don't think my mother ever had an inkling that I would do this book . . . But I think that she's up there, somehow saying it's O.K. and especially pleased with whom I did it."

Perhaps an epitaph of which Jackie would have been prouder still appeared in a different book, one she had edited a few years earlier. John Pope-Hennessy was a British art historian who was an expert on Renaissance sculpture. He had headed up two distinguished London institutions, the Victoria and Albert Museum and the British Museum, before coming to New York to chair the department of European art and sculpture at the Metropolitan Museum. Jackie knew many of the curators at the Met, and her friend John Russell, the art critic for the *New York Times*, had been instrumental in boosting Pope-Hennessy's career at the Met by writing approvingly of his rearrangement of the Met's European collections. Pope-Hennessy had written an article in the *Times* in which he had sketched out a few reminiscences of his career. Jackie asked him to flesh this out as a full-scale memoir, which she

published at Doubleday as *Learning to Look* in 1991. Early in
the book, Pope-Hennessy explains why art matters. It has no
utilitarian ability to feed the poor, "but works of art have always
seemed to me to have a supernatural power, and I believe that
visual images constitute a universal language through which
the experience of the past is transmitted to the present, and by
whose means all lives can be immeasurably enriched." This is
a fine example of an author putting into words an idea that,
inchoately, Jackie herself had put into a collection of her books
on photography. Pope-Hennessy's emphasis on "the experience of the past" enriching the present was an idea Jackie often
returned to in the images she selected for publication. Moreover, all her books aimed to capture varieties of beauty in the
visual world that included an element of what Riboud called
the *"surnaturel"* and the poetic.

For Jackie, of course, you could find beauty in places
besides photographs. One of those places was dance, movement, and ballet. Jackie told *Publishers Weekly* that all little
girls were interested in ballet, and that preserving the little-girl
fascination for dance in herself was another way of fueling her
journey of self-discovery. If her books of photography were
about exploring beauty, her books on ballet were about exploring the body.

Jacqueline Kennedy, 1957, by Yousuf Karsh. She told her Doubleday colleague Ray Roberts that she remembered the picture being taken at "ten a.m. in full evening dress, and he scared me to death!"

(ABOVE) Jacqueline Onassis with Jann Wenner at the Oyster Bar, Grand Central Terminal, 1977. When Wenner moved *Rolling Stone* from San Francisco to New York, Jackie took him under her wing. They later collaborated on a book about John Lennon and on an anthology of the best writing in the magazine.

"Vassilissa the Fair," one of four stories illustrated by Boris Zvorykin in *The Firebird and Other Russian Fairy Tales*, which Viking republished in 1978 with an introduction by Jackie. She was interested in the Romanovs, Russian costume, and strikingly illustrated books.

(LEFT) Jackie at Viking in 1977 with copies of her book *In the Russian Style*. Diana Vreeland sold the book at a party in the Metropolitan Museum, calling out to the crowd, "Buy a beautiful book!" but Nicolas Nabokov attacked it in the *New York Review of Books*.

(ABOVE) Jackie with American ambassador to India John Kenneth Galbraith in 1962 during her visit to India. She later edited several illustrated books featuring Indian artists. Galbraith said of Jackie's trip to India that while the visit might have had some diplomatic value, mainly it was about having fun.

Jackie and William Howard Adams at a benefit for the ICP, where she served on the board. Adams wrote the text for *Atget's Gardens* (1979), a collection of turn-of-the-century photographs of French royal gardens. Jackie wrote that Atget's photographs reminded her both of her Bouvier ancestors and of Greek islands in a windstorm.

(LEFT) Jackie and former JFK aide William Walton at the International Center of Photography (ICP) for an exhibition of dance photography in 1978. She wanted to edit *Fleeting Gestures*, the book accompanying the show, but couldn't persuade Doubleday to do it. She had better luck producing a book of nineteenth-century letters with Walton called *A Civil War Courtship*.

Jackie sitting with photographer Berenice Abbott and architectural historian John Harris in London at a party for the Atget book. Abbott was one of Atget's greatest champions. Jackie also wanted to do a book on Abbott's photography and planned to fly in a private plane with ICP curator William Ewing to Abbott's house in Maine to discuss the project. "Bill, do you want to reserve the plane, or should I?" Ewing told Jackie that she'd better do it.

(RIGHT) Gloria Steinem with Jackie. Jackie gave a rare interview to Steinem at *Ms.*, and the magazine ran her picture on the cover with the headline "Why Does This Woman Work?" in March 1979.

(ABOVE) Jackie and Nancy Zaroulis in 1979 at the Doubleday suite, where book parties were held. Zaroulis's novel *Call the Darkness Light*, which followed the story of a female factory worker in the nineteenth century, was one of Jackie's first commercially successful projects.

Jackie permitted Diana Vreeland to reprint this image
of Marilyn Monroe in *Allure*, the book they did together in 1980.
She also wanted Doubleday to acquire a book on Monroe's
last photo session with Bert Stern.

HOW TO SAVE YOUR OWN STREET

RAQUEL RAMATI

Saul Steinberg's cover for Raquel Ramati's *How to Save Your Own Street*, published in 1981. Jackie's interest in architectural preservation and urban planning had begun in her White House years.

(BELOW) Title page of *To the Inland Empire*, 1987. Former Kennedy cabinet member Stewart Udall and photographer Jerry Jacka produced the book after a hiking trip in the Southwest with Jackie. She cared about the design of her books and wanted them to be as beautiful as possible.

TO THE
INLAND EMPIRE
*Coronado and
Our Spanish Legacy*

STEWART L. UDALL

PHOTOGRAPHS BY
JERRY JACKA

Doubleday
LONDON TORONTO SYDNEY

Jackie and Philip Johnson, 1983. Jackie commissioned a book on Philip Johnson from her friend Rosamond Bernier. Both women were disappointed when they discovered Johnson had authorized another, similar book at the same time, and their project had to be dropped.

(RIGHT) Jackie and Peter Beard, 1983. Jackie told Beard at one of his photography shows, "I wish I could do what you're doing—but I can't." Jackie wrote the afterword for one of Beard's books that had been inspired by Isak Dinesen's *Out of Africa*, a memoir they both loved.

(ABOVE) Jackie with Eugene Kennedy at the launch of his novel *Father's Day* in 1981. He was the only author who moved with her from Viking to Doubleday in 1978. Kennedy recalled working on a manuscript at Jackie's apartment, where she smoked from an ivory cigarette holder and served cucumber sandwiches.

Carly Simon and Jackie on Martha's Vineyard in 1989 for the launch of *Amy the Dancing Bear*, one of Simon's books for children. They did four books together between 1989 and 1993.

Egyptian novelist Naguib Mahfouz won the Nobel Prize for Literature in 1988. One of Jackie's greatest coups was to bring Mahfouz's books to Doubleday.

(ABOVE) Bill Moyers, Maurice Tempelsman, and Jackie in 1992. Jackie edited *The Power of Myth*, Moyers's interviews with Joseph Campbell, which discussed how an ordinary person could be transformed into a myth.

BILL MOYERS

HEALING
· AND ·
THE MIND

(RIGHT) In the year before her last illness Jackie was working on this book about untraditional medicine. She was instrumental in winning the right to reproduce a Georgia O'Keeffe painting for the book's cover and told colleagues that to her the nautilus shell represented "infinity" or "eternity."

chapter 8

David Stenn recalled his first attempt at writing a Clara Bow biography. He wanted to make his work different from the poorly researched Hollywood biographies that had been published previously, so he'd thrown every fact, detail, and statistic he had discovered about Bow into his partly completed draft, which he then submitted to Jackie. She returned his manuscript to him covered with suggestions for cuts, changes, and revisions. "It was eviscerated," he remembered, laughing. She understood how hard he had worked on the research for his subject, but her advice to him was "Be like Fred Astaire. Don't let the hard work show."

Jackie had been fascinated with dance ever since she was little. A significant subset of the books she acquired addressed great American dancers in different traditions: classical ballet, modern dance, and Hollywood. She did three books with Gelsey Kirkland. She commissioned a book on Fred Astaire soon after he died. She asked Rudolf Nureyev to write an introduction to stories by Alexander Pushkin, one of which had inspired one of the greatest ballets in the classical repertory, *Eugene Onegin*. She worked with Martha Graham on her autobiography and agreed with Graham's friend the ballet critic Francis Mason that Doubleday should publish a book of recollections about the choreographer George Balanchine after he died. She also asked for an autobiography from Judith

Jamison, a dancer who headed the Alvin Ailey American Dance Theater soon after the death of its founder.

Many of the books on ballet that Jackie commissioned are books about how the dancer's body needs to be forced into unusual poses in order to execute the required movements of classical ballet. They deal frankly with eroticism, seductiveness, and sensuality. Sometimes they tell about the mutilation of the dancer's body in order to achieve a greater physical perfection. These books are not just about Jackie's love of ballet, they may well be about her consciousness of her own body. There are links between the dancers' stories and her own.

Dancing on Her Grave

Gelsey Kirkland, a principal dancer with two of America's most important ballet companies, the New York City Ballet and the American Ballet Theatre, was one of the most famous prima ballerinas of the twentieth century. The artistic director of the New York City Ballet, George Balanchine, put her in starring roles while she was still a girl and created a new staging of Stravinsky's *Firebird* for her before she was eighteen. Growing restless under Balanchine's direction, she left the New York City Ballet to join the ABT, saying that she wanted to perform in more traditional ballets. There she created memorable roles with Mikhail Baryshnikov, who was also her lover. A high-profile life on the stage and universal acclaim in the 1970s brought with them an addiction to cocaine, which she was able to sustain as one of the most bankable ballet dancers of that decade. Reviewers in the early 1980s, however, began to notice that her dancing had become more erratic. She missed rehearsals and even performances. The management of the ABT began sending her threatening letters about breach of contract. Early in 1984 she scraped bottom: she missed a flight from New York to Boston, where she was due to begin a tour with the ABT, in order to buy cocaine from one of her dealers, a former boxer who lived with his family in, as she described it, "one of the rankest places on earth, a basement apartment in the Forties near Eighth Avenue." Outside she met a young man, Greg Lawrence, who was also trying to find some coke. Lawrence was a part-time freelance reader of books for a film studio. He also managed a TV production company across the street and was, in his own words, a "glorified bookie." He was also a writer and poet, though until he met Kirkland he had published none of his work. They couldn't wake their dealer, so they returned to Lawrence's two-room apartment, which had "no furniture whatsoever, only a mattress on the floor, books and papers scattered everywhere." Lawrence's girlfriend was away. They found that together they had a small supply of cocaine, so they decided to spend the night together.

This was the beginning of a romance during which they did drugs but talked of quitting. Kirkland was well aware of the difference between her star earning power and her new lover's garret existence. She feared that Lawrence might be taking advantage of her. She didn't know whether it was "intuition or wishful thinking," but she hoped he was different from the men who had let her down. "We seemed to be deeply in love, but the trust between us was wavering," she recalled. Once he disappeared for an entire night without telling her where he was going. She accused Lawrence of manipulating her.

Lawrence, who had dismissed his former girlfriend, persuaded Kirkland that their life might be better if they were off drugs. She broke her contract with the ABT and they went to live on a farm in Vermont where she could end her addiction. With Lawrence's help, she began writing a memoir of her childhood and growth as a dancer. It was a form of therapy and a way to exorcise her demons. She wanted to reflect on her own life as well as warn others away from the traps into which she had fallen. It was Lawrence's idea to organize the writing of her memoir around the men in Kirkland's life: first her father, then Balanchine, followed by Baryshnikov, and finally Lawrence himself. In August 1984 they signed a contract for the book that was to become *Dancing on My Grave,* and Jackie, whom Kirkland knew in part because Jackie served on the board of the ABT, was to be their editor. Jackie was in awe of Kirkland's dancing and no doubt thought she might help a struggling artist regain her place in the limelight. She could hardly have known in advance that the finished manuscript would prove to be as controversial a bestseller as it became.

Kirkland traced her problems to an alcoholic father. She believed that she had learned in childhood to rebel against her father and that this was the origin of her passive resistance to Balanchine. At first she was a fanatical devotee of the master: "I had to please him. I loved him more than my own father." Later she decided to believe in rumors she heard of his sexual impotence and admitted, "I developed the habit of mentally undressing him, without any attraction, simply fascinated to know if he possessed all the attributes of the male anatomy." Thus she had a strange Electra complex whereby she eroticized her relationship with her father. She saw her relationship with Balanchine through the same lens.

Indeed, much of her relationship with the world is experienced via sex in the book. She recalled that her first introduction to competition and performance was through horseback riding. At a summer camp she lost her confidence and was thrown from a horse after the other girls convinced her to do a belly dance in front of the counselor who was her riding instructor. She gave up competitive riding for good and never told anyone why.

One of the most scandalous parts of the book was Gelsey Kirkland's attack on Balanchine. She was not only a dancer attacking her teacher but also a prima ballerina attacking a master of the dance world. She accused him of encouraging the self-destruction of children. For example, he required young girls to deform their bodies by twisting the femur bone in its socket in order to achieve the proper "turnout," with feet splayed at a 180-degree angle. She also said he encouraged jealous rivalry among his female pupils and created an atmosphere that "was a mixture of convent and harem." The young Kirkland wanted to show that she could stand up to him and walked out of one of his classes where he dared to criticize her heroes, Rudolf Nureyev and Margot Fonteyn. Afterward, they snubbed one another and didn't speak for more than a year. Indeed, Kirkland sometimes provided more damaging revelations about herself than she did about Balanchine. She had had breast implants and snipped off her earlobes. She had also had silicone injected into her ankles and lips. She suffered from anorexia. On tour in Russia, she had decided that the radio in her hotel room was being used to spy on her, so she smashed it with a hammer.

In the book, she also went into detail about her love life with Mikhail Baryshnikov. Seeing Baryshnikov perform made her decide to leave the New York City Ballet to become his partner. In 1974 he defected from the Soviet Union and they both joined the ABT. They first slept together before he had even learned English and while she knew no Russian, returning after a supper with friends to her mother's Upper West Side apartment, where she decided that they couldn't have sex in the room where she had grown up so chose her brother's room instead. "After groping with buttons, belt, and zipper, Misha appeared for a brief moment to be a statue . . . a pedestal of rumpled clothes at his feet. He seemed embarrassed, like a bashful god. I shared his discomfort and dimmed the lights to conceal my own naked form. Our embrace did nothing to relieve the pressure. This would be our first performance. We were both suffering from stage fright." The star of the Russian ballet, so daringly quick onstage, proved also to be rapid in bed. "Sensing what was expected of me, I waited for him to be done. I felt no need to fake what had not taken place, what could not have taken place in the time that had elapsed. After he came to rest in my arms, we both turned back into stone. It was over." Her father, then Balanchine, then Baryshnikov: she had hero-worshipped all three and all three had disappointed her.

Reviews of the book were almost uniformly hostile. One reviewer in the *New York Times* said of Kirkland that "so intense and panicky is her focus on herself that her insights into other people and events are blurry." Another called it "one of the saddest stories ever written." The *Washington Post* spoke of the "crudely sensationalist tactics of the book," and in the *Ballet Review* another critic called Gelsey Kirkland "the Judy Garland of ballet," saying that the grave she was dancing on was one she'd dug for herself. Perhaps because of the intemperate reviews, and because of word of the book's revelations about Baryshnikov, who was a sex symbol in the 1970s and '80s, the book sold extremely well. It was published in 1986 and was one of Jackie's first bestsellers.

This did not mean that bringing out the book was easy for her. The book ruffled feathers at the ABT, and some believed that it had caused trouble for her there. The memories of the book at Doubleday were not all happy ones, either.

Although it was a commercial success, almost everyone who worked on the book remembered Kirkland, and particularly Lawrence, as being exasperating characters. Steve Rubin recalled of Kirkland, "She's a little nuts," and added of Lawrence, "He's the problem. He's always been the problem." Another colleague echoed this assessment, calling Lawrence "a very difficult man." Bruce Tracy said that they were both "high-maintenance." Scott Moyers remembered that Jackie was proud of the book's success, but said that there had been little person-to-person contact between her and the authors: "There wasn't much of a direct relationship there." Herman Gollob, then editor in chief, laughed when he was reminded of the book. Kirkland had gone on a book-signing tour as part of her contract with Doubleday. She wanted to break the contract and come home when she got bored midway through. Jackie persuaded her to go on.

The success of *Dancing on My Grave* led to two more books, one on how the newly drug-free Kirkland returned to the stage and created new roles in London, *The Shape of Love* (1990), and a children's book about a little girl whose twin loves are ballet and horses, *The Little Ballerina and Her Dancing Horse* (1993). Neither book sold as well as the first one. Like Gelsey Kirkland, Jackie was the daughter of an alcoholic father. She, too, had loved ballet and horseback riding from an early age. She, too, grew to be legendary for performances exhibiting her carriage and grace on a worldwide stage, though the role she created was her own rather than one from the classical dance repertory. She would have been sympathetic to Kirkland's self-consciousness about her body, for women who are objects of constant attention are encouraged to edit the way they look, not only through their clothes but through dieting and cosmetic surgery. Jackie was herself on a constant diet, and when her son returned home from school, he asked their cook, Marta Sgubin, to serve something other than "diet food." Even Jackie's closest friends, among them the Irish writer Edna O'Brien, worried at how thin Jackie kept herself. O'Brien remonstrated with her once when Jackie leapt up on a ledge in her apartment to arrange a curtain and O'Brien remarked on how little of her there was. Jackie shot back, "Edna! I've always been thin." Other people also worried over the way Jackie treated her body. Karl Katz, one of Jackie's friends at the Met, noticed the way she would tear at her hands, her fingernails, and cuticles, particularly if she had to sit through a boring speech.

Jackie continued to respect Balanchine and brought out a book that was a monument to his memory after she edited Kirkland's book. She continued to serve on the board of the ABT long after Kirkland left. While she produced some commercial books that critics might deride as "crudely sensationalist"—Kirkland's is only one of them—her personal presentation remained modest, low-key, and the reverse of self-revealing. This very contrast, however, points up interesting disjunctures that highlight who she was and how her mind worked. She rarely talked about Black Jack, but her unreliable father loomed large in her relationship with two romantically unreliable husbands. She told a friend from Miss Porter's how self-conscious she was and how much she'd hated being forced to undress in semipublic with other Senate wives as they got into Red Cross uniforms for a charity event. This made the friend laugh, as she suspected Jackie of wearing particularly flossy underclothes in anticipation that the other women would inspect her. She exercised, sacrificed her appetite, and exerted self-control to withstand all that scrutiny: this was the work required to achieve her outward appearance of grace and serenity. In revealing her secrets, Kirkland revealed the secrets of many women, perhaps even Jackie.

She Had Quite a Naughty Spark to Her

Sarah Giles worked for *Vanity Fair,* which became one of the hottest magazines of the 1980s. In 1987 Fred Astaire died, and the magazine's editor, Tina Brown, assigned Giles to write an article based on interviews with Astaire's friends, including their comments on his life and work. One day after the article had appeared, Giles was working under another deadline at her desk when the telephone rang. Giles remembers, "I picked it up and said hello. Then came a sultry whisper, which said, 'Hello, this is Jacqueline Kennedy Onassis.' " Giles replied, "Yeah, and I'm the Queen of Sheba. Who the hell is it? I'm busy." Slowly, as the voice on the other end of the line calmly reiterated her identity, it dawned on Giles that it actually *was* Jackie, whom she had never met, and, swallowing hard, she made her apologies. Jackie told her not to worry. It happened all the time. She was telephoning because she'd seen Giles's article on Fred Astaire and she wanted her to turn it into a book.

Giles was usually not impressed by big names. Her father had been the editor of one of Britain's most distinguished newspapers, *The Sunday Times,* and her mother, Lady Kitty, was a Sackville, one of Britain's oldest aristocratic families. Nevertheless, she was immediately seduced by Jackie's manner and by the flattering way in which she talked about England, saying she had once met Fred Astaire there. "She was so flipping charming," remembered Giles, perhaps because "she had quite a naughty spark to her." Jackie wanted Giles to expand the list of people she'd talked to about Astaire. Instead of going to the usual celebrities, Jackie wanted Giles to interview noncelebrities—for example, Astaire's housekeeper, the man who made his shoes, and his chiropodist. Jackie wanted to know all about these people behind the scenes who were helping put on Astaire's show. She also wasn't confident that Alex Gotfryd, Doubleday's art director, was up to producing a jacket for the book that was as beautiful as she wanted it to be. Jackie told Giles, "We love him. We just *love* him. But are we really sure he's the right man for this?" Jackie's question, Giles thought, was her rather wicked way of inviting Giles to find someone from outside who could produce a glossier, more glamorous book.

Jackie also pressed Giles to try to find some romantic gossip about Astaire. Astaire's first wife, Phyllis Potter, had died relatively young, and there was a long period when he was on his own before, late in life, he married a much younger woman, Robyn Smith. "Are you *sure* he didn't have a mistress?" Jackie asked. "What about Cyd Charisse?" who was Astaire's dancing partner. Giles found nothing, but she was amused by Jackie's persistence. Jackie's repeated questioning seemed blind to the endless newspaper speculation about her own romantic life.

Giles and Jackie had active cooperation from Astaire's daughter, Ava, and many of his friends, but Astaire's widow, Robyn, threatened to sue both of them if they published their book. "Jackie dealt with it through Doubleday's lawyers. She told me to have no qualms about it, other than to lay off Robyn. She said, 'I don't think we're going to get this dame. She's obviously got something in the closet. She's determined not to have it come out.'" Jackie liked to talk tough, using that 1940s language in which women were "broads" and "dames," to show she was going to support her author and resist Robyn Astaire.

She also supported Giles by telephoning her at home on a Sunday when at last the book appeared and a hostile review came out in the *New York Times*. "Sarah, I just want you to know," said Jackie, "whatever you're feeling at the moment, that it is fantastic. Listen! It's going to sell books." Giles remembers feeling that Jackie could have waited until Monday morning when she got into the office, but "she was perfect. She was spot on when I was feeling all torn up."

However, when it came to the publication parties, Jackie refused. Tina Brown wanted to use the book's publication as the excuse for major parties where Jackie would be the star attraction and help promote *Vanity Fair*. One party was held at the Royalton Hotel, the first of a new generation of boutique hotels, developed by the former owners of the nightclub Studio 54. Another was to be in Los Angeles. "Jackie wouldn't come near either one," Giles remembered. "She was not going to be used for a photo op. She was savvy."

Jackie also wanted to have it both ways. She wanted to resist Robyn Astaire's suit against Doubleday for intruding on her privacy and tinkering with Astaire's reputation, yet within a few years she herself would threaten to sue *Vanity Fair* to protect her own when one of the magazine's reporters did a long feature on her. She might resent *Vanity Fair* for going after her, but she was not above urging Sarah Giles to discover new material about Fred Astaire's love life. The difference, if there was one—and perhaps it's slight, but it's important nevertheless—is that what Jackie wanted primarily was an anatomy of Astaire's style. He was the personification of male elegance. He had influenced not only popular dancers like Michael Jackson, but also Balanchine, Nureyev, and Baryshnikov. That part of Astaire's life was public, open to inspection and analysis. Jackie regarded what she'd done in the White House as the only thing of hers that belonged to the public. Everything else was off-limits, and she wanted those limits respected. Whether this was genuine shyness and modesty on her part or simply the unilateral assertion of a powerful woman who had the resources to keep the world at bay is hard to say. She wanted to be a good editor who commissioned hard-hitting biographies, but she also wanted to protect her own privacy.

The most fascinating parts of Giles's book, *Fred Astaire: His Friends Talk*, are those in which Astaire's friends speculate on the elements of the dancer's style that were clearly Jackie's style, too. For example, Nancy Reagan thought Astaire's shyness and his elegance were somehow mixed up together. One contributed to the other. Another friend of Astaire's, Whitney Tower, said of Astaire's longtime love of thoroughbred racing that he believed "Fred liked racing for the graceful movement of the horses." The woman who rode horses for much of her life, and who preferred reading a book by herself to mixing in big parties, would have understood those two ingredients of Astaire's self-presentation well.

Nureyev Asked to Write as Well as Dance

Rudolf Nureyev was a soloist for Russia's Kirov Ballet before he defected to the West in 1961. He helped create a legendary partnership with Margot Fonteyn, from Britain's Royal Ballet, and danced all over the world in the 1970s and even into the 1980s, when he reached his fifties. On one of the rare occasions that Jackie agreed to speak to the press, she had a conversation with John Lombardi for an article he was writing on Nureyev for the *New York Times*. Jackie told Lombardi, "I first saw him with Margot Fonteyn in early 1963 when he came with the Royal Ballet. The tension when they danced was extraordinary. You lost yourself in it. I remember there

were forty curtain calls. People's hands were black-and-blue pulp." It's a little odd that she should follow a tribute to a great ballet performance with that terrible image of bruised hands.

She had flown both Nureyev and Fonteyn to the White House in a private plane and started a friendship with Nureyev that lasted for three decades. She was reputed to be one of the only women he stood up for when she visited his dressing room backstage. For her, Nureyev provided a living link back to Diaghilev and the Ballets Russes. "Seeing Rudolf and Margot Fonteyn dance together has made up for having missed Nijinsky and Chaliapin," Jackie said. "It has been one of the strongest artistic experiences of my life." So it's not surprising that when she became an editor, she involved Nureyev in one of her book projects. Via her friend at the Gotham Book Mart, Andreas Brown, who had first led her to discover the fin-de-siècle illustrator Boris Zvorykin, she decided to bring out a new edition of Alexander Pushkin's fairy tales, illustrated by Zvorykin. She asked Nureyev to write an introduction, in which he pointed out that Zvorykin and Diaghilev had come out of the same artistic movement, the Slavic Revival, in the 1890s.

The dance critic Francis Mason suspected that someone else wrote the introduction for the dancer's signature. Whether Nureyev wrote it or not, he was certainly involved in planning the book with Jackie. Edward Kasinec at the New York Public Library remembered Jackie and Nureyev coming to look at a rare edition of Pushkin illustrated by Zvorykin in the library's collection. It had been signed by the Russian empress to one of the readers of the New York Public Library, Isabel Hapgood. Jackie and Nureyev also socialized with one another in the 1970s and '80s. Jackie visited Nureyev's house on St. Bart's in the Caribbean and warned her friends away from it, saying that it was filled with awful plastic furniture. Nureyev and his boyfriend also had a ranch house in Virginia near where Jackie hunted.

More important, when Mikhail Gorbachev finally gave permission in the late 1980s for Nureyev to return to Russia to visit his ailing mother, Nureyev alerted Jackie. She asked Ted Kennedy to raise this as an issue with the Russian ambassador in order to guarantee that the Russians made good on their promise to let him return to the West. Nureyev's relationship to mother figures had earlier attracted Jackie's attention. "Every time I see *Swan Lake* performed by anyone else, I realize what an actor he is," Jackie told Lombardi. "When he kisses his mother's hand, you see, you begin to understand feudalism and, at the same time, the homage, the duty, the respect he has for the idea of a mother. It takes a great, great artist to distill that feeling." One twentieth-century term, "mama's boy," was a derisive way of referring to male homosexuals or male effeminacy. Sensing that Nureyev's homosexuality was an issue that needed to be addressed, she told Lombardi that Nureyev had helped challenge sexual stereotypes. After his athletic dancing brought people from all fifty states to see him, she noted that "people come from Utah now to see dance in New York—men who used to think it wasn't manly." Nureyev had cracked the stereotype of the effeminate homosexual.

Jackie had many gay friends, and there was a higher proportion of them among the authors on her list at Doubleday than in the population at large. She also seems to have gone out of her way to teach herself about homosexuality. One of the few books left behind in her library in which she had turned down many pages for easy reference, and which she'd annotated in her own hand, was a history of homosexuality. Her commitment to Nureyev was not in spite of the dancer's sexuality, nor because of it, but certainly it interested her. It was one more way ballet taught her to think about the body.

Martha Graham Wrote for Jackie, Too

Francis Mason served for decades on the board of Martha Graham's dance company, and twice as its chairman. He had also served as cultural attaché at American embassies abroad and in the 1960s had promoted Balanchine's and Graham's companies in London. This enhanced the reputation and success of both companies in America. He was the longtime dance critic on New York's WQXR-FM radio station as well. He died in September 2009, but some months before that he recalled how Jackie had helped Martha Graham's company with her presence, not her cash: "She gave some money. Everybody knew her heart was in the right place. She didn't have a big pocketbook, or didn't display it conspicuously." Still, that was enough, because Jackie's renown helped the company. "She was influential: we could get in anywhere with Jackie." More important, "Martha liked her."

Ron Protas was Martha Graham's assistant before she died, a young man who helped her overcome alcoholism and depression late in her career. He also helped her regain enthusiasm for her company's work. Graham made Protas her heir before she died. He interpreted her will to mean that he owned the copyright to all her dances, and even to her dance technique. After Graham's death, in 1991, he sued her dance company to try to prevent it from performing her choreography. A lengthy and expensive legal battle ensued. Much of the battle took place when Mason headed the board of the company after Graham's death. Mason said of Protas to the *New York Times*, "Martha gave him the world on a platter, made him anew, and he wrecked it." For several years the legal difficulties even closed the company down and prevented it from performing. Eventually most of the choreographic rights were restored to Graham's dance company and performances resumed. Protas faded from the scene.

When Jackie was involved with Martha Graham's company, however, Protas was front and center. Protas played a role in persuading Graham to record some of her memories for transcription with the idea of making them into an autobiography, and by his own recollection, he was important in telling Jackie about the recordings. "In 1986 after a gala performance I brought Jackie backstage," he said. "I told her about the taping sessions and said to her, 'If only I could persuade Martha really to do a book with them.' Later that night Martha said to me, apropos of Jackie, 'We could work together.' And then she used the Quaker image 'We walk the same way.'" Aaron Copland had composed the score to accompany one of Graham's most famous ballets, *Appalachian Spring,* which had at its core a Shaker melody. The Shakers were a sect thought to have evolved from Quaker Protestantism. Graham's reference to the Quakers was thus a significant tribute to Jackie. When the book was ultimately agreed to and a contract was signed, Protas recalled, Jackie went to visit Graham in the afternoons, sitting "at her feet like a kid, taking notes, helping her out. It was fascinating, because Martha really didn't enjoy most women, but she liked Jackie. Martha was fearful about the book, afraid she would fail. It didn't come easily. But toward the end, after she became ill, she pushed herself, saying, 'Jackie believes in this. We mustn't let her down.'" By 1991, when Graham's book came out, Jackie had given up her earlier practice of speaking to the press about her books, but in lieu of words she did agree to show the reporter from *Publishers Weekly*, "with a kind of talismanic wonder, an ancient Han dynasty Chinese jade disk that Graham had given her."

The freelance writer Howard Kaplan, who had once worked for Doubleday and also written for Francis Mason's *Ballet Review,* transcribed Graham's tapes and pieced them together into a narrative while consulting with Graham and Jackie. Graham called the book *Blood Memory* to convey the generations of blood and family inheritance that direct a dancer's instinctive steps, which sometimes come without preparation or instruction.

The book's most interesting revelation was the way its author, the self-assured dance legend, confessed that she still suffered from fear. She explained her decision to work on an autobiography this way: "Always I have resisted looking backward until now, when I began to sense that there was always for my life a line through it—necessity . . . Necessity to create? No. But in some way to transcend, to conquer fear, to find a way to go on."

Over and over Jackie testified to her interest in the creative process artists undergo to make their art. The passage in which Graham chose an Icelandic phrase, "doom eager," to discuss that creative process would certainly have had Jackie's attention: "You are doom eager for destiny no matter what it costs you. The ordeal of isolation, the ordeal of loneliness, the ordeal of doubt, the ordeal of vulnerability which it takes to compose in any medium, is hard to face. You know when this thing is coming on you. You know when you walk the streets by the hour. When the restlessness comes, when you are sick with an idea, with something that will not come out." Graham added that "the artist is doom eager, but never chooses his fate. His is chosen, and anointed, and caught."

Not all of Graham's memories were about the artist vying with dark destiny. There are one or two elements of camp humor. Graham recalled having to resist congressmen who wanted to censor her work because of its eroticism, but she conceded that her frankness sometimes got her into trouble. In Japan one of her dancers went off with several sailors and missed a performance. She told a friend while in a taxi afterward, "'She never would have been a great dancer. She doesn't move from her vagina.' The taxi driver nearly swerved off the road. 'You understand English?' I asked. He turned and smiled. 'Yes, ma'am. I was raised in Brooklyn.'"

Graham said she had been "a devotee of sex, in the right sense of the word. Fulfillment as opposed to procreation, or I would have had children." That statement would certainly have gotten her into trouble with the religious right. "In the early days when I still had an active life I wouldn't be caught dead in bed without a light makeup. But I was never promiscuous . . . My philosophy of lovers and boyfriends? When I loved them I loved them. When I didn't, I left. That simple." Graham even described a moment during a dance with Erick

Hawkins, whom she married briefly in the late 1940s, when she adored his male bottom. "Just before I tapped Erick with the flower in *Every Soul Is a Circus*, I thought, 'Where did you come from? I could eat you up.'" Jackie put Graham's comment under this picture in the book.

Jackie's book with Martha Graham embraced sexuality as openly as Gelsey Kirkland's, only Graham's book was funnier. Jackie was willing to have a little fun with the pictures and the captions of Graham's memoir. Of course, any publisher would have been happy to have Martha Graham's recollections. That the great dancer felt she could write with Jackie what she could not and would not write with others is testimony to the way in which Jackie not only admired the creative process from a distance but dared to enter into it sympathetically, and collaboratively, with one of the century's great talents. Jackie's books were often braver, more unconventional, and more off-color than the way she presented herself to the public. When she was working with dancers, she was often at her best.

Cut It

Two dance books that appeared toward the end of her time in publishing, however, do not consistently match the high quality she reached with Graham or the high sales she achieved with Kirkland. After George Balanchine died, in 1983, Francis Mason had the idea of bringing out a new edition of the book he had done with Balanchine, first published by Doubleday back in the 1950s, a scene-by-scene retelling of the stories of the great ballets. This book had been a tremendous success and gone through many editions. Mason remembered, "I went to Jackie and said, 'Look, can I do a book?' She said, 'Yes, but you've got to do it in a year. Catch everyone while the memory is green.'" That careless but evocative metaphor, that Mason should go speak with dozens of aging ballerinas while their memories were still fresh and "green," is vintage Jackie. What she might not have anticipated, though, was that Mason would take much longer than a year. Balanchine died in 1983, and Mason's book wasn't ready until the beginning of the next decade. Further, his manuscript was much too long. His contract called for 60,000 words and he produced 650,000. "Cut it," she told him frankly. If he offended some of those he had interviewed, Jackie said, "Blame it on me. I'm the editor." She offered him her office to do the work while she was away and gave him two months to do the job. Even after Mason's cuts, the book came in as a door-stopping monument to a dance hero rather than a slim, readable book. When it came out in hardback, it was more than 600 pages long.

Jackie might also have been tougher on another of her dance authors. Shortly after publishing the Balanchine book, Jackie approached another great of the dance world to ask for her autobiography. Judith Jamison had long been one of the principal dancers of the Alvin Ailey dance company, and after Ailey died, in 1989, she took over the leadership of the company. Ailey had won fame in the 1960s and '70s not only for bringing black dancers to the stage but for choreography that described the experiences and was often based on the music of African Americans. Jamison's book, *Dancing Spirit,* was to be published to coincide with the thirty-fifth anniversary of the founding of the Ailey company, so in publishing the book, Jackie was also promoting the company. It fit together several of Jackie's passions: not only her love of dance, modern as well as classical, but also her commitment to honoring the work of African Americans in history.

Jackie enlisted the same writer who had helped assemble Martha Graham's book to work with Jamison on putting together her story. Kaplan recalled an adventure with Jackie in which they went to watch a rehearsal of the Ailey company. At the studio there was no stage separating the audience from the dancers: the dancers were right in front of them, performing breathtaking movements, nearly nude. The book also has some touching moments, as in the description of a time when Jamison traveled to the Vienna State Opera for an engagement. She was surprised to be greeted backstage by a group of little girl ballerinas all wearing pink tights and pink shoes, who curtsied to her and said, *"Grüss Gott."* She then realized that this was the etiquette of the institution. "I was the star dancer from America and I was treated as such."

Judith Jamison understood that she was working with the same powerful woman who had told Mason in no uncertain terms what he had to do with his book. Jamison's mother was the same way: "I just come from a legacy of very strong women so Jacqueline Onassis can join the ranks there." Jamison danced with Alvin Ailey, and Ailey had studied with Martha Graham. He had what Jamison called "blood memories" of spirituals, gospel music, ragtime, and folk songs from growing up in Texas, all of which inspired his dancing and choreography. Jamison was also aware of the scandal created by Gelsey Kirkland's book, and she decided to take the opposite approach. She held her cards close to her chest, and although the book is called an autobiography, it leaves out the details of romances and personal life. Jamison's book reveals little and says of her meeting Gelsey Kirkland with Mikhail Baryshnikov in Europe only that "she was having trouble in those days." Jamison says that a dancer is at her most moving when she makes herself vulnerable onstage, but she refused to make herself vulnerable in her book in the same way that Graham and Kirkland had.

The critics responded unfavorably. Some of them even pointed, without naming names, to Jackie's role in the book, calling it "carelessly edited and produced." It sounded as if Jamison had chatted at random to a tape recorder. The book had no index, no list of its striking photographs, and an entire page had been devoted to a bibliography of only four books. Another critic pointed out that the book did not mention that Ailey and other dancers, such as Nureyev, had died of AIDS. Thus, although Jamison's book exposed the prejudice African

Americans experienced in the dance world, it reinforced the stigma felt by gay men who were dying in a health crisis that disproportionately affected the dance world.

The Visitors in the Room Froze, but Mrs. Kennedy Rose

Jackie's love of dance went back a long way in her life. Even her girlhood horse, which she took with her to Farmington, was named Danseuse, though she shortened that to Donny, just as Jacqueline in her family had been shortened to the more prosaic Jackie. With Jackie, though, even if there was an informal and prosaic name on the surface, there was always a formal and controlled embrace of a poetic ideal underneath. When Robert Kennedy began, as senator from New York, to strengthen his ties with Harlem in the 1960s, Jackie, too, became a patron of a tuition-free school in Harlem called the Children's Storefront. An episode one observer remembered of her behavior there speaks to the kind of ballet-like performance she could summon up: "Her physical manners were . . . polished. She always jumped to her feet when she was introduced to someone. Once she was visiting the Children's Storefront school in Harlem. As she sat in the office of Ned O'Gorman, the founder, a drunken homeless man wandered in. The visitors in the room froze, but Mrs. Kennedy rose. 'How lovely to meet you,' she said as one friend held her back."

On a small scale, Jackie's gesture was similar to her movement and carriage at the funeral in November 1963. Hers was the application of principles from the dance world to the manners and courtesies of everyday life. Whether arriving at the door for a society event to benefit the ABT or shaking the hand of a homeless man in Harlem, she aimed with her movement to bring a dancer's sense of occasion to the most mundane and ordinary of everyday ceremonies.

Gelsey Kirkland remembered that as a young girl, what had impressed her about George Balanchine's ballet classes was the way he kept alive an Old World sense of courtliness and ritual. "The rules of classroom decorum implied an aristocratic tradition that went back to the court dances of the Renaissance," Kirkland wrote. "At the end of class, we always observed the quaint ritual known as the reverence. Each dancer bowed or curtsied for the teacher." It was to return to that world of ritual and courtly romance where she felt most at home that Jackie sponsored books on the best-known of Europe's royal dynasties, the Bourbons and the Romanovs, as well as the lesser-known but no less elaborate rituals of Mughal India and pharaonic Egypt. In the world of ballet and in these historic courtly societies, grace and carriage was all.

chapter 9

CIRCUS QUEEN.

—Jackie's girlhood prediction of her own future position

Among the many roles Jackie inhabited in her lifetime—reader, writer, and editor; wife, mother, and myth—probably the one most often publicly associated with her is queen. She was the most unforgettably regal of twentieth-century first ladies. Her only real rival, Eleanor Roosevelt, chose an identity nearer to the mother superior of an order of powerful nuns than to the royal persona Jackie slipped into so easily. Roosevelt told Marietta Tree privately that she distrusted JFK's "meretricious charm" and disliked the "court" the Kennedys created at the White House, but the rest of America loved it. Nor could anyone question that Jackie's planning of the 1963 funeral and her own performance at it were the closest things Americans had ever witnessed to a royal ritual. The universal feeling was that she had single-handedly saved both the nation and the world from prolonged despondency as a result.

What's more surprising is that Jackie should have been preparing for this role long before she married Jack Kennedy. After he died, she commissioned more than a dozen books on kings, queens, and royal courts; on royal patronage of the arts and on the prostitutes or courtesans who attended royal men; on vilified royal ladies blamed for spending too much money and their husbands, who were put to death when they were still young. A review of the royalism of her early life is an important introduction to the books she was publishing at the end of her life. Together they show us a dimension of her personality that seems to have been present from her earliest years and persisted well into her middle age.

"Little Edie" Beale, Jackie's cousin of *Grey Gardens* fame, thought Jackie in childhood was an odd combination of "tomboy and dream princess." She remembered that when Jackie was a girl, she played with a cardboard crown and wanted to run away from home in order to become "queen of the circus." A more reliable source, Mrs. Thayer, noted in her authorized biography that Jackie had written a send-up of various family members when she was young and imagined a comic future as circus queen for herself. Jackie's stepbrother, Yusha Auchincloss, recalled from traveling in Europe with her that she was particularly interested in the kings and queens of England. He also witnessed firsthand how Jackie could sometimes behave in a queenly way. He remembered her criticisms, which "could strike with severity and then serenely turn sympathetic. She would stamp her foot, clap her hands, point her finger, and then hug." Even the loyal Nancy Tuckerman recalled these brief flare-ups as "you know, hands-on-hips" sorts of thing. Not everyone was willing to put up with what they thought of as a regal act that was out of place in a domestic or a democratic setting. When as a young bride-to-be Jackie told the Kennedy family that the proper pronunciation of "Jacqueline" was the French one, Ethel Kennedy raised a laugh by saying in a stage whisper, "Hmmm, rhymes with 'queen.'"

Jackie wasn't going to be deterred from being who she was by Ethel. Even before Jack was elected president, Jackie wrote to Diana Vreeland to consult her on what she might wear for the inaugural balls. Had her husband, then still only a candidate, seen this letter, it would have gotten her into trouble, and she knew it. Jackie was well aware that she was going to be attacked as a "let-them-eat-cake fiend" for lik-

ing Parisian clothes. Marie Antoinette, the last French queen before the French Revolution, was reputed to have suggested that the hungry crowd rioting for bread in Paris should eat cake instead. The queen's reported comment on the riots was a myth meant to stir up displeasure with the monarchy. Marie Antoinette was one of the royal ladies with whom Jackie identified, because she knew well how people were willing to connect being beautifully dressed with self-indulgence and supposed blindness to the needs of others. Nevertheless, she pressed on. Jackie told Vreeland that she wanted the inaugural gown to be very simple, possibly in white, "as it is the most ceremonial color," and added that "I suppose it's undemocratic to wear a tiara—but something on the head." She closed with her usual stroke of self-deprecating humor: if Jack was not elected, she would wear the dress to watch the balls on TV. Come hell or high water, however, she wanted to wear diamonds in her hair.

The fashion choice was indeed regal, so it is no wonder that Jackie as first lady sometimes gave the impression of being in competition with the queen of England. When she and JFK made a state visit to Britain early in his presidency, they posed next to Queen Elizabeth II and Prince Philip for a formal photograph. Jackie made the queen look as if she'd chosen her frock out of the Missouri closet of Bess Truman. Her own dress looked space age, as if she were ready to meet George Jetson and his boy, Elroy. Perhaps the queen recognized what Jackie was up to and wanted to put her in her place. The palace had politely inquired whom the Kennedys might like to meet when they came to the state dinner. The queen resented the American request that Jackie's sister, Lee Radziwill, then living in London, be invited to the party, because there was a ban on receiving divorcées at the palace. Jackie had also suggested inviting several of the queen's racier relations, including her sister, Margaret, and Princess Marina, who had moved among Hollywood actors before the war. After the state dinner was held, Jackie confessed that she'd been beaten: "The Queen had her revenge. No Margaret, no Marina, no one except every Commonwealth minister of agriculture they could find."

Jackie did have some queenly habits, however, which other practiced observers noticed and admired. Philip Mansel and Lady Antonia Fraser are two English historians of court life who between them have written more than two dozen volumes on European kings and queens. Connoisseurs of courtesy, both were surprised when they met Jackie to discover what notable manners she had. When the British government invited Jackie and her children to inaugurate the memorial to her husband at Runnymede in 1965, the Frasers, who had known Jackie since she was first married, invited her to their house on Campden Hill Square, just down the road from Notting Hill. Fraser remembered, "We had an old Scottish cook. She wasn't our cook, but she happened to be having a holiday here from Scotland. She was really old, and as she was here, she said she'd cook dinner for Mrs. Kennedy. It was rather a thrill for us. She also looked after the children's tea. After dinner, Jackie said, 'Can I see the lady who cooked the dinner?' She went into the kitchen, found Mrs. Hepburn, and said 'Did you cook that dinner? Did you make those sandwiches the children had?' I couldn't get over this. She went into great detail. That is what we *think* royalty do, but on the whole, they don't. But she did. She made one old Scottish lady intensely happy."

This has to be balanced with another repeated observation of Jackie: she could have an imperious manner. She gave tongue-lashings even to those she considered friends and allies. Her correspondence with Roger Stevens, who was chairing the committee that built the Kennedy Center for the Performing Arts in Washington, shows her giving commands as if he were a mere pawn. She told Stevens that after the center was built, its director "must be acceptable to me." If the center was not what she thought JFK would have liked, "I will ask Congress to change its name—which they will do"—a reminder of her nearly sacred status in the post-assassination and pre-Onassis era. She also told him she had to have a representative on the board of the center: "I must have one—or I wish to pull out of the whole thing right now."

Jackie was equally curt with William Manchester, who had written a fawning pro-JFK biography and whom she and Robert Kennedy had selected to write the one authorized account of the assassination. After Manchester had finished, she got wind of a prepublication deal whereby the author would be paid several hundred thousand dollars by *Look* magazine to run excerpts from the book. She changed her mind and tried to forbid him from publishing, even though he'd resigned from his full-time job and given several years of his life to the project. She refused to face the fact that she and Bobby had commissioned him to write the book in the first place. News leaked out that she was trying to suppress his account and destroy the author: it was the first time in the post-assassination period that her reputation was tarnished. After some revisions and excisions, and the author's commitment to donate the bulk of the money promised him to the John F. Kennedy Library in Boston, the book was published as *The Death of a President,* in 1967.

Even ex-Kennedy loyalists, longtime supporters of the Kennedy Library, and staunch defenders of JFK against revisionist historical attacks on him could come in for Jackie's wrath. Theodore Sorensen served Kennedy both in the Senate and in the White House as a speechwriter and a close adviser. Sorensen wrote in his book *Counselor,* published in 2008, that Jackie was deeply involved in protecting her husband's reputation, mainly through the supervision of the library built in his name and academic programs named for him at Harvard. He thought she was "misguided" in her fury at one head of the John F. Kennedy School of Government's Institute of Politics at Harvard for directing programs that were not in the original spirit of the family gift to the university. Sorensen noted that Jackie could write well herself, but he ultimately "found that the writer of such moving, sensitive, and beautiful letters could also be volatile on rare occasions, turning those eloquent words and powerful feelings against even close friends if they seemed to err." He gave as an example his plan to bring out a collection of JFK's speeches. Jackie thought he wanted to take credit for the speeches himself, as well as to profit from the sale of the book, something that always made her angry, even though she was rich herself. He was "crushed" to receive her letter condemning the proposed book. He was able to get another member of the Kennedy family to intercede for him with Jackie and explain it to her better, "but I have never forgotten the impact of that one brief but ferocious rebuke."

These stories continue into the Doubleday period. One fellow editor, Tom Cahill, was surprised to find how protective she was of her relationship with Bill Moyers. When he had followed up a suggestion of hers that he contact Moyers about reviewing a manuscript he was considering, she telephoned him and to his surprise asked him, "How dare you use my name?" A stream of vituperation followed, and although she didn't quite say, "You little nobody," he recalled that that was the drift of what she said to him on the phone. When he asked her to wait and reminded her that it had been her suggestion that he contact Moyers in the first place, she said quietly, "In that case, I apologize," and hung up the phone. But they didn't speak for a long time afterward.

Her relationship with Bill Moyers was also the center of a dispute Herman Gollob recollected at Doubleday. Jackie's assistant Judy Sandman had expressed an interest in meeting Moyers, so when Gollob was taking Moyers out for lunch, he invited Sandman to join them. But Jackie regarded Moyers as her author, and soon afterward she met with Gollob in his office to tell him she didn't appreciate having her assistant invited out with her authors behind her back. Gollob defended the lunch, but he was a little taken aback at Jackie's possessiveness of Moyers and her resentment of Sandman, who served her loyally.

Which was the real Jackie, good queen or bad queen? Or perhaps the better question is, what was going through Jackie's mind as she gave these different performances? The fact that she did eight books on the Bourbon court at Versailles and the Napoleonic court that succeeded it, as well as books on courtly life in India, in ancient Egypt, and in Russia under the Romanovs, gives ample room to explore what interested her in the worlds of European and oriental monarchies. Her own life intersected with these books in four different contexts— France, India, Egypt, and Russia—which together tell a story about her that she was never willing to tell in her own lifetime.

What a Cruel Fate! She Must Have Been an Extraordinary Woman

In her correspondence with Oleg Cassini about the clothes he was designing for her to wear in the White House, Jackie said that she had in mind three royal women whose fates she wanted either to avoid or to emulate: Marie Antoinette, Josephine Bonaparte, and the Princesse de Réthy. Early on in JFK's presidency, she already thought the press reports about her clothes were getting "vulgarly out of hand," and she had no wish to be "the Marie Antoinette or the Josephine of the 1960s." She understood that this would have a negative impact on JFK's administration. Her problem was partly Cassini himself. He and his brother, a gossip columnist, were from a White Russian family, descended from nobles prominent in pre-Soviet diplomacy, so they were socially okay, but both of them were also self-promoters. Before the Kennedy presidency was long under way, Cassini was using the fact that he was designing for Jackie to sell his collection, and thus there was more publicity than she liked. She tried to get him to desist by reminding him that he was "a gentleman"—a hint that he was not—and by saying that she wanted prior approval before he released anything to the press. She used this tactic again in her editorial years when she told Howard Kaplan, one of her writers, that "a gentleman never tells whom he's sleeping with." She wasn't sleeping with Kaplan, but she didn't want him talking to the press, or to his friends even, about what it was like to work with her as an editor.

Jackie's remark to Cassini underscored that she knew Queen Marie Antoinette had not been the wicked queen her detractors made her out to be. They said that she spent extravagantly on clothes; that she had lovers, both male and female; that she meddled in the king's political business. None of this was true. It was part of the sexism of the era, when a woman could be made the scapegoat for the French monarchy's problems. When the French monarchy fell in the 1790s, Marie Antoinette and her husband, King Louis XVI, were both guillotined by the revolutionary regime. They were convicted of plotting against the revolution, and they symbolized an old order— hierarchical, historical, and Catholic—that the revolutionaries wanted to bury for good.

Jackie wanted the French royal family back, or at least that was the impression she gave through her books. She and her friend Jane Hitchcock loved talking about the Bourbon court of the eighteenth century in the period that led up to the revolution. Looking back over those long-ago discussions with Jackie, Hitchcock remembered laughingly, "We were obsessed!" Hitchcock's novel *Social Crimes*, written after Jackie died but with references Hitchcock has frankly acknowledged as her tribute to Jackie, is filled with detailed historical knowledge of Versailles, the French court, and the manufacture of Sèvres porcelain. Jackie owned a number of rare bibelots from this court. After she died, her children sold some of them at Sotheby's in 1996, including a small ornamented box that had once belonged to Marie Antoinette.

Jackie's book with Olivier Bernier, *Secrets of Marie Antoinette* (1985), described the queen's difficulties as a young Austrian woman trying to become accustomed to the French court and to persuade her husband, who was uninterested in sex, to help her produce the children and heirs that it was her duty to provide. Jackie also asked Bernier to write biographies of the king who had plucked Madame de Pompadour from obscurity and given her the latitude to cultivate the French court's reputation for cultural excellence, *Louis the Beloved: The Life of Louis XV* (1984) as well as of that king's great-grandfather, the so-called Sun King, who built Versailles, *Louis XIV: A Royal Life* (1987). The center of Bernier's world was the Metropolitan Museum in New York, where he gave lectures on the French court and where Jackie's friends the Wrightsmans exhibited their Bourbon furniture. Jane Hitchcock's *Social Crimes* points out that for anybody to be anybody in New York in the first decade of the twenty-first century, they had to be on the board or in some other way connected to the Metropolitan Museum of Art. An astute observer of the New York social world, Hitchcock also wrote that bustling New York was more like the French court than most people realized, with ambitious people trying to climb up and others being sent to the provinces in exile. It was almost as if the museum, across the street from Jackie's apartment, had become a kind of American Versailles, the repository of everything associated with taste, social power, and prestige. Jackie's publication of books on Versailles, her long-term association with the Met, and even her geographical proximity to it were her ways of asserting continued interest in being part of the social hierarchy long after JFK and Aristotle Onassis had died. She appeared to sit effortlessly and unconcernedly atop the New York social heap, but she actually possessed a position she did not intend to relinquish, and the books helped her defend it. Only a few, but the few who counted, knew that she had edited them, as her name is usually omitted even from their acknowledgments pages, so she could assert her status without seeming to say a word.

After the French Revolution sent Marie Antoinette and Louis XVI to early deaths in 1793, a series of unworkable experiments in government led to a young army officer's staging a coup d'état and taking power for himself. Napoleon Bonaparte eventually resurrected the French court, with himself at the center. In the 1790s Napoleon had met and married Josephine de Beauharnais, a widow whose husband had been executed in the bloodiest phase of the revolution. She was a stylish society figure with more than one lover. He crowned her empress in 1804, but divorced her in 1810 in hopes that another woman could produce a male heir. Still friendly with Napoleon, she lived in retirement at the Château de Malmaison outside Paris until her death in 1814.

Jackie sometimes playfully imagined herself in the guise of Josephine. On the state visit to Paris in 1961, Jackie, accompanied by André Malraux, had gone out of her way to attract attention not only with her clothes but with saucy references to French art and Napoleonic history. After a visit to the Jeu de Paume, a small museum in the Tuileries that in the 1960s held the Impressionists and other nineteenth-century French paintings, reporters asked her what she had liked best. She picked one of the sexiest canvases on display, Édouard Manet's *Olympia,* considered shocking on its first exhibition for its nude depiction of what appeared to be a rich courtesan. Critics identified the black cat at the end of the naked lady's bed as a cultural symbol of the sitter's profession. Jackie didn't mind being connected with *Olympia.* She later commissioned work from Jacqueline Duhême, an illustrator for a French magazine, who had depicted her and Malraux in cartoon fashion standing in front of the painting. Jackie even had in her own collection some erotica by the French painter Marcel Vertès, known as the illustrator of Colette, someone Jackie identified as one of her favorite writers. Vertès's image is also of a black cat next to a naked lady. Caroline Kennedy disposed of

Le Chat Noir at a Sotheby's sale in 2005, but perhaps her mother enjoyed faintly subversive images of women's sexuality.

After visiting the Jeu de Paume with Malraux, Jackie specifically asked to be taken to see Malmaison. Standing in front of Josephine's portrait and recalling her story, Jackie commented, "What a cruel fate! She must have been an extraordinary woman." Malraux caught Jackie's flirtatious tone and replied in the same vein, "A real bitch!" Later, when Malraux came to visit in Washington, Jackie and Cassini decided that her dress for the reception at the French embassy should be something Josephine might have worn, in the Empire style. More than twenty years later, Jackie still liked to imagine herself in Napoleon's world. She asked Olivier Bernier to edit and abridge a collection of letters from a courtier in Napoleon's circle who knew Josephine well, which Doubleday published as *At the Court of Napoleon: Memoirs of the Duchesse d'Abrantès* (1989). Although Diana Vreeland died in the summer of 1989, Bernier's book coincided with an exhibition at the Costume Institute that December on the age of Napoleon. Jackie was not one to dwell on historical fantasy without figuring out ways to sell her books.

The third royal woman whom Jackie singled out as one of her models—certainly in jest, but the joke is revealing—was actually Belgian. Jackie told Cassini at the beginning of their collaboration that she would like him to design some daytime clothes for her as "if Jack were President of FRANCE—*très Princesse de Réthy mais jeune,*" something a younger Princesse de Réthy might wear. The Princesse de Réthy was a controversial Belgian lady born in 1916 (she died in 2002). The Belgian king had married her after his first wife, Queen Astrid, died in an automobile accident and he was a state prisoner of the Nazis in 1940. Together they decided that she should not hold the title of queen of the Belgians, but this did not prevent her from being unpopular. Astrid had been beloved by many Bel-

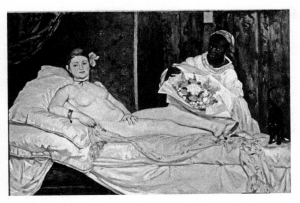

gians, and the king had married his second wife at a time when he was suspected of having collaborated with the Nazis. What the Princesse de Réthy had in common with Marie Antoinette and Josephine was a certain stylish sophistication, which forever inspired distrust of her among the Belgian people, even though this distrust was probably undeserved.

Before the 1980s, the view of academics was that the eighteenth-century French court had been a top-heavy extravagance waiting to be swept away. Most university historians viewed themselves as *amis du peuple,* antiroyalist advocates for the poor. Most of them thought that the revolution of 1789 had been long overdue. A majority of French intellectuals of the post–World War II generation, Malraux among them, were either Marxists or believers in the necessity of a more thoroughly egalitarian reconstruction of the social order. Malraux in his own day had fought shoulder to shoulder with Republicans and Communists in the Spanish Civil War. Jackie's books universally went the other way. They pointed out some of the failings of the French court, but they were pro-monarchy and enthusiastic about the life of art and music, decoration and dance, architecture and literature that thrived at Versailles. In short, her books might have seemed like bits of fluff she did with an amateur historian from the Met, but they were in fact royalist tracts that celebrated the achievements and romanticized the lives of French kings and queens. It takes a woman with some courage, and a sense of humor, to wear a Josephine-inspired dress to dine with André Malraux.

Passage to India

Another of Jackie's star turns as first lady was her 1962 visit to India, where she was greeted by Indian newspapers as

"Amriki Rani," American queen. She went accompanied by Lee, while JFK stayed at home. Although the trip has been described as a way of persuading the Indians of the desirability of alignment with the West during that cold war era, when Americans were anxious to combat the Soviets, it also had a different purpose. It was about fun. The American ambassador to India at the time, John Kenneth Galbraith, a Harvard economist and an intimate of both Jackie's and JFK's, said long afterward that it was "a fraud" to think that such state visits accomplished anything serious. They were meant for the pleasure of the visitors. Visiting the maharajah of Jaipur, nicknamed Bubbles because of all the champagne poured at his birth, and an attractive figure in the jet-setting scene of the 1960s, was just as important for Jackie and Lee as fighting the cold war.

India had not been among Jackie's earliest interests, nor was Hindi among her languages, but in the years that followed she not only began to collect Indian art, advised by Galbraith, but also visited India several times. She even sent her son, John, there to travel and attend the University of Delhi for six months in the early 1980s.

Naturally, as Jackie and Lee were good-looking young women in their thirties, a good deal of romantic teasing was involved. The code name Washington officials assigned to Jackie caused Galbraith some embarrassment in the run-up to the trip, as cables kept being received in India announcing the arrival of Girlfriend. He also had a difference of opinion with the president when it was proposed that Jackie should visit a famous temple with erotic statuary at Konarak, which he anticipated the press would misinterpret. He advised against her going there. JFK cabled back, "Why? Don't you think she's old enough?" When Jackie and Lee arrived in India, the two women were scheduled to stay in the guest quarters

of the American embassy, but the Indian head of state, Jawaharlal Nehru, insisted that these were not good enough and
they should stay with him. Galbraith remembered being surprised by this move and described it later as "not a simple act
of grace. Meeting her at the plane and seeing her later, he was
enormously attracted and wanted to see more of her, which as
the visit passed he did." Lee Radziwill remembered Nehru as
among the most sensuous men she had ever met. A picture of
Jackie together with Nehru on the trip suggests that the sexiest
thing about him was that he made her laugh.

This spirit of sensuality, openly expressed, lives on in a
book Jackie edited called *A Second Paradise: Indian Courtly*

Life, 1590–1947, published in 1985. The publication coincided with a special exhibition on Indian art at the Met and with a show, The Costumes of Royal India, at the Costume Institute. Jackie thanked Diana Vreeland for her "original inspiration" in an editor's note to the book. The book described the many courts that flourished throughout India between the sixteenth century, when the Mughals conquered India, and the twentieth century, when British control of India's government ended. The book has color illustrations on virtually every page and must have been not only expensive but also unusual to produce in those days, when book design was not Doubleday's priority. Galbraith had introduced Jackie to his Harvard colleague Stuart Cary Welch, who curated the Met's show on Indian art, and she wanted him to write the text for her book, too, but he did not have the time. Instead, Jackie's friend the novelist Gita Mehta introduced her to her brother Naveen Patnaik, who agreed to write it. Brother and sister were from a prominent Indian family, and Naveen Patnaik was a social butterfly on the New York party scene. Vreeland sent Jackie to stay with Patnaik in New Delhi when she was doing research for the book in the 1980s. Patnaik told *Vanity Fair*'s regular contributor Dominick Dunne that when Jackie arrived to visit him in Delhi, he was shocked that "she literally had two pairs of slacks, dark glasses, and one gold jacket for evenings, which she wore to even the grandest palaces." Her wardrobe may have been inadequate, but Gita Mehta remembered her brother receiving "pages of research material annotated" in Jackie's own hand. "I know as a writer that to have that kind of attention by a commissioning editor is quite rare," she said.

The book is more eyebrow-raising still, not only for the way its description of Indian courts directly recalls Jackie's specific contributions to the Kennedy White House but also for its frank embrace of female sexuality. Here are two excerpts from the book's jacket copy, which Jackie may well have written herself. In Indian court life, "with the ruler as patron, there flourished great schools of music, poetry, cuisine, philosophy, and painting, taking court life to a peak of subtlety and splendor." The book promises to go "behind the harem wall to reveal the lives of royal women, the training of a courtesan, the preparation of a princess for the bridal chamber, the use of intoxicants to enhance the madness of passion. It describes the ancient ceremonies that raised a king to divinity and reveals the pageantry of court life through its spectacular celebrations." It is almost as if regality entailed both high culture and carnality. Patnaik's book suggested that you couldn't have a court without classical music and courtesans.

Jackie told *Publishers Weekly* that she was particularly proud of *A Second Paradise,* and she "caressed [it] lovingly" while she talked to the magazine's interviewer. Patnaik's text discusses how concubines would plot to enslave a maharajah by using aphrodisiacs and by studying "erotic spells" from the Kama Sutra, the biblical text of Hindu lovemaking. Patnaik also distinguishes between a lowly concubine and an upscale courtesan: "The beautiful courtesan was a woman a man could not possess as he did his wives and concubines, and the courtesans of Lucknow added that element of adventure to a man's life lacking in his crowded harem." Many of the illustrations for the book come from the collection of Stuart Cary Welch. Welch's wife, Edith, wrote the glossary for the book and helpfully explained of a picture of scantily clad Nautch girls, "They're like the Folies Bergères," where Parisian women danced nearly naked in the 1890s. Of another image of an all-female orgy, Edith Welch commented, without disapproval, "Look at all these ladies carrying on."

The Welches and Jackie went to India together several times, Jackie profiting from the learned commentary of a couple who were both exceptionally knowledgeable about Indian art and culture. "We weren't social," said Edith Welch. "We all three sat around and read our books." One of Stuart Cary Welch's younger colleagues, Navina Haykel, now a curator at the Met, remembered that "he talked to me frequently about her. He found her to be a person of some substance. She was not his creature. He couldn't easily move her. He quite admired that about her." Welch opened a generation's eyes to Indian art and was used to being surrounded by adoring students, but Jackie refused to be his acolyte. Like a courtesan of Lucknow, she would not allow herself to be possessed.

Jackie had to do a lot of legwork for the book to acquire the rights to reprint images belonging to different people. She approached Mark Zebrowski, one of Welch's students, then living in London, for permission to use several images that belonged to him. One image alone required four letters to Zebrowski in Jackie's own hand. He ultimately sent Jackie his own book on Deccani painting, for which she wrote him a long thank-you note. She recalled a visit with John to visit the nizam of Hyderabad, one of the hereditary rulers of India, who had been dispossessed after the newly independent Indian state was proclaimed in 1947. She struck a wistful note in this letter and pointed to a last important feature of what inspired and interested her in the former courts of India. Their rulers had become so refined, so devoted to rituals of lovemaking and art patronage, that they did not have the wherewithal to survive. They became decadent. That was what she loved the most.

Jackie remembered having spent a memorable evening with the surviving nizam and his friends, when there were aged musicians playing on a moonlit night. Her noble hosts talked of how their culture was disappearing and how young people appreciated neither the traditional music nor the traditional manners. "This over civilised, rarified world—you could feel it—but you knew it was too rarified to survive. You felt so fortunate to be able to sense for those hours what it had been," she wrote. When she had read his book, she told Zebrowski, "I understood it, what it had been at its zenith. That evening was profoundly sad. My son John told me the next day that the sons of the house had taken him to their rooms, because they couldn't stand the classical music—and had offered him a tall glass filled with whisky and had put a pornographic cassette in the Betamax and the Rolling Stones on the tape deck. They wore tight Italian pants and open shirts, and all the while, their fathers, on the terrace in beautiful shantung, were speaking of how sad the sons made them." She identified with the Indian noblemen who rued the passing of something wonderful, something cultivated, something great; but there is also a sense of mischief behind her description of the boys taking John upstairs in their tight pants and putting a skin flick on the video player. To appreciate and poke fun at the same time— that is Jackie speaking in her characteristic register. She concluded by saying, "Often in art I think I love the periods when you know it cannot last, when it has become over civilised." What couldn't last was her adolescent son's youth, for he, too, was soon to leave home for good. What she could do to make some of that world endure was to put it between two hard covers.

Jackie's spirit and the spirit of rarefied courtly India live on in *A Second Paradise,* a kind of reincarnation of all that she'd marveled at when she'd first gone to India in 1962. But she didn't live entirely in the past. She had no wish to return to her White House days. What she had in the 1980s was vastly better: freedom to travel with obscure academics, to make visits without fanfare, to be attended by her only son, and to leave behind something entirely of her own creation, a finely illustrated book. Naveen Patnaik acknowledges Jackie's contribution, but the reader won't find it without hunting in the back of the book. That so perfectly fit her modest and ironic sense of humor about herself that it, too, has to be called "overcivilized."

Walk Like an Egyptian

Jackie didn't look on all historical courts with regret for fallen grandeur. She was interested in the courts of the pharaohs in ancient Egypt, too, but the book she commissioned that was published in 1987 showed that she also had an affinity for the kooky and the absurd. Jonathan Cott was a regular contributor to *Rolling Stone* in the 1970s and 1980s. He had written articles for the magazine based on interviews with Bob Dylan and John Lennon. Jann Wenner remembered Cott as "very much in Jackie's style. Very intellectual, arcane, dreamy. He was just the kind of person Jackie would like. She loved writers." She had been introduced to Cott by Jim Fitzgerald, her Doubleday colleague, who specialized in popular culture and shared an interest with Cott in Bob Dylan. She then worked with Cott on a book tribute to John Lennon after his death. What Cott submitted to her next, however, was completely different. He had seen a small paragraph in the *New York Times* about Dorothy Eady, an unusual Englishwoman who believed she had been the lover of an Egyptian pharaoh in an earlier life. Eady had forsaken a comfortable life in twentieth-century England to go and live in a mud hut in Egypt, where she participated in archaeological research on what she was convinced was her former life. Strangely enough, when she would say to the archaeologists, "I remember the ancient garden was here," they would dig and discover an ancient garden. Cott was surprised when he went to meet Jackie in her office to discuss writing Eady's story: she had seen the same paragraph in the newspaper and pulled it out to show it to him.

Jackie's interest in Egypt and the archaeology of other Middle Eastern cultures went back a long way. When she redecorated the White House, she said she was particularly proud of the Blue Room, where she had restored the original French furnishings from President Monroe's era with a motif from Napoleon's Egyptian campaign of the same period. André Malraux was also someone with whom she discussed Egypt, and the Temple of Dendur eventually came to New York partially as a result of those conversations. Malraux had sent her a limited-edition book to which he'd written the preface, *Sumer* (1960), which pictured Sumerian sculpture discovered in a region roughly corresponding to modern Iraq. He wrote an inscription in French saying that the book contained images of little goddesses and her special goddess was one of fecundity—was he teasing her?—and he hoped this goddess would bring her the good wishes of Queen Subad, or Shubad, who had lived in Sumer two thousand years before the Christian era. So to Cott's surprise, when he showed Jackie an ancient crown of Queen Subad, that a curator of the British Museum had shown to Dorothy Eady, Jackie already knew all about it. She told Cott, "It's one of the most precious things ever unearthed—so beautiful." Cott still thinks of that exchange with Jackie rather wonderingly, saying, "Jackie had a remarkable but unselfconscious way of bringing the entire world back home." He noticed that she had in her private collection at 1040 Fifth Avenue rare volumes of Egyptian history and ethnography commissioned by Napoleon in the early nineteenth century, the *Description de l'Égypte*. Jackie, like Eady, had all of ancient Egyptian history at her fingertips. She told

Cott that Malraux had introduced her to a curator from the Louvre, Christiane Desroches Noblecourt, who had arranged a King Tut exhibition that traveled to the National Gallery in 1961. Noblecourt had also acted as their guide when Jackie and Onassis and Caroline had gone on an expedition up the Nile to visit Egyptian antiquities in 1974.

When Cott finished his account of Dorothy Eady's strange life in England and Egypt, Jackie arranged for a cover to be designed that captured a bit of the heroine's slightly ridiculous personality. It's a pair of red lips painted on an ancient Egyptian statue. But neither Jackie nor the book's reviewer in the *New York Times* regarded Eady's idea that she had once served a pharaoh and been more recently reincarnated as an ordinary nonroyal Englishwoman as entirely absurd. The *Times* reviewer noted that reincarnation stories often contained the element that Eady's did of a love gone wrong, often with a royal lover. "Perhaps these passionate affairs represent a universal human metaphor for the spiritual quest gone awry; the longing for God invested in another mortal, and therefore doomed?"

Jackie's love of royal ritual may well have had something to do with being a Catholic, since the grandeur, costume, and elaboration of the mass recall something more historical and more divine than everyday human lives. Francis

Mason noted in his review of Jackie's Martha Graham book that Graham admitted to having been influenced by the Catholic Church, "the glamour, the glory, the pageantry, and the regality." Diana Vreeland's emphasis on fashion that achieved a transfigured moment, the ordinary rendered extraordinary, carries some of the same feeling. Vreeland's model was less the Catholic Church than it was either the British coronation ceremony or the Ziegfeld Follies. Having been rendered instantly royal herself in the aftermath of JFK's assassination, a process that must have seemed to her not all that different from Eady's supernatural vision, Jackie became not less but more interested in reading about royalty in history. Perhaps she hoped to find there clues about how to live her own life in the present.

Nicholas and Alexandra

After the French Revolution in 1789, the other most notoriously violent end to a European monarchy came in 1917. Under orders from Lenin, the Bolsheviks murdered the Russian tsar, Nicholas, and his wife, Alexandra, along with their five children and some of their attendants in July 1918. This followed the tsar's abdication in 1917, after he had become discredited during the disasters of Russia's involvement in the First World War. Jane Hitchcock recalled that besides being interested in the deaths of Louis XVI and Marie Antoinette, she and Jackie had also been fascinated by the fate of the Romanov family. She explained they were both "intrigued by the Russian Revolution, the French Revolution, because they somehow seem extremely accessible and also because I think everybody puts themselves in the position of those people. Would they have been able to escape? Would they have done it differently? What were the forces swirling around them?"

Also, these people lived in palaces and wore clothes that were themselves works of art. As Hitchcock put it, "The sheer beauty of the Romanovs was not to be believed." Loving to know more about them was partly about the drama of sudden death, but also about the fate of people who lived ornamented lives because, whether they liked it or not, they served as embodiments of ideas larger than themselves.

Jackie's interest in Romanov history also had a Vreeland origin. Vreeland had asked Tom Hoving to take Jackie with him to Russia in the late 1970s when he was meeting with cura-

tors from the Hermitage to facilitate exchanges with the Met. Vreeland was using Jackie as her secret weapon to persuade the Russians to allow more of their most valuable clothes to travel to New York for one of her shows at the Costume Institute. During this visit with Hoving, Jackie was shown a cape and hat made of swansdown and worn only once by the last Russian tsarina, on a visit to the opera. Hoving snapped her picture after Jackie asked the Russians whether she might try it on.

The Russian playwright Edvard Radzinsky was convinced the first time he met Jackie that she was royal, and remarked later, in heavily accented English, that "she was a tsarina." Radzinsky was equally fascinated with the Romanovs and wrote a long Russian biography of the last tsar, dwelling on the final days leading up to his assassination. The completion of Radzinsky's work happened to coincide with the dissolution of the old Soviet system in 1991, a revival of the Russian Orthodox Church, and a brief movement in the early 1990s to restore the Romanov monarchy in Russia. Radzinsky hated the Soviet system and painted a highly sympathetic picture of the Romanovs. Also in 1991, as the Communist government crumbled, human remains thought to be those of the Russian royal family were discovered at the bottom of a rough grave in Yekaterinburg, in central Russia, to the east of the Ural Mountains. DNA testing and the matching of DNA samples drawn from Britain's Prince Philip, whose grandmother was the sister of the tsarina's grandmother, confirmed that the bones were the remains of the murdered Romanovs. This came to the attention of the New York literary agent Lynn Franklin, who met Radzinsky on a visit to Russia. He agreed to work with her, and she was able to sell a brief English synopsis of a work that still needed to be translated to Jackie at Doubleday. One of the book's strongest selling points was that this was a work of Russian history by a Russian author rather than by one of the Western experts on Russia who had been such a staple in providing information during the cold war. All these circumstances surrounding the acquisition of Radzinsky's book gave it the feeling in advance of a potential bestseller, if it was handled right.

Jackie first met Radzinsky around a conference table in New York, where a group of Doubleday personnel, Franklin, and, via a Russian interpreter, Radzinsky conferred about what to do with the large and unwieldy manuscript in Russian. The Doubleday staff pointed out that Radzinsky had been successful as a playwright but never as an author in English prose. They were universally of the opinion that the book needed to be cut. Radzinsky's English was rudimentary, but he recalled, "I am a writer. I understood the word 'cut.'" The interpreter ignored him. She was hypnotized by Jackie. Radzinsky saw that he had to convince Jackie himself in order to save his manuscript. He had found among the papers of the Romanovs in the Russian archives a poem about forgiveness. He told the people at the conference table that his story was about forgiveness, about the tsar's family forgiving their assassins. Radzinsky remembered looking over at Jackie: "I saw her eyes. She realized what I was saying and she understood. It was a magnificent moment. 'No cuts. Let it all be translated. I want to read the whole book,' she said."

Jackie hired the translator Marian Schwartz, whom she knew via Schwartz's translations of Nina Berberova. She sent Radzinsky out to Austin, Texas, where he stayed for more than a week with Schwartz while they went over the manuscript together. Relations between author and translator were not all smooth. He was a showman; she was an intellectual. Radzinsky suspected that Schwartz did not entirely understand his Russian. Schwartz saw that some of the long digressions on Russian history and some of the melodrama in Radzinsky's text would irritate an English-speaking audience. It was left to Jackie to referee their disputes by telephone.

The tonal differences between author and translator also went to the heart of whether Jackie identified with the assassination of the tsar's family and relived it as a part of her personal nightmare, or not. Radzinsky wrote a sensational account of the royal family's death. Nicholas and Alexandra, along with their four grown daughters and their hemophiliac son, Alexei, had been led into a bare wooden room. A line of their former security guards along the wall suddenly brought out guns and began to fire at them. The tsar's daughters had sewn some of the royal family's jewels into their corsets. They had hoped to exchange these jewels for help in fleeing the country, and for a while the jewels deflected their assassins' bullets. Radzinsky has a theatrical scene in which the killers of the tsar's family reminisced about what had happened afterward at the Hotel Metropole: "They sipped unsweetened tea through a sugar lump, crunched the cube, and told stories about how *the bullets bounced off the girls and flew about the room.*" Radzinsky called the Central State Archive of the October Revolution, where he had found some of these accounts, "the Archive of Blood." He was convinced that Jackie was the perfect editor for this book because she "was the woman who had had the same tragedy." Wasn't he embarrassed to submit text to her calling his source an archive of blood? Radzinsky said she was absolutely conscious of the connection between her history and the story of the book. "She had to be very strong to read this book. It was about forgiveness, but it was also about a cruel assassination, and about the mystery of the assassination. She immediately understood what I was trying to do. For her, it was a mission too. For her, it was about suffering. She wanted to read it."

Marian Schwartz doubts that this was Jackie's motivation for acquiring the book. "I think she was bigger than that," she said. "The parallels probably occurred to her, but I would not assume this hit a nerve. She may have understood the draw this thing had. She lived with people's insatiability for contact with her and wanting to know more about JFK's assassination." Schwartz was more impressed by the way Jackie approached the text as a professional editor. "She knew exactly what she had and what had to be done with it." Schwartz paused and added drily, "You don't sell that many copies of a book with an academic coverage of the subject." She remembered that Jackie line-edited the manuscript and toned down some of Radzinsky's sensationalism. As a professional translator Schwartz was aware that Russian and Anglo-Saxon attitudes to language are different. Russian is a highly colored and expressive language. To render it for English-speaking tastes, some of the emotionalism has to be removed and replaced with understatement. However, a lot of the drama remained even after Schwartz and Jackie had worked on the text. Schwartz recalled three categories in which she could place most of the letters she received after the book was published: "dead Romanovs, fabulous diamonds, and the church." Whether Jackie was thinking of 1963 or not, many readers of Radzinsky's book found it had some of the same compelling ingredients as the death of JFK.

Lynn Franklin is also skeptical about how directly Jackie connected the book to her own experience. Franklin thought the parallel was there for the reader to see, but she didn't think that was Jackie's main concern. "There was something pure about Edvard beneath all the showmanship that she responded to."

The British editor and author Ion Trewin, who helped bring out the British version of Radzinsky's book for Hodder & Stoughton, collaborated with Jackie in collecting photographs for the book. Some of the rarest photos of the Russian royal family came via a connection Trewin's father had had to Tsar-evich Alexei's British tutor. Trewin brought these photos to New York for Jackie to see. He remembered meeting her for the first time. When he got to Jackie's small office, she was sitting there reading something on her desk, with her big glasses pushed up on her head. When she looked up, he half expected to see the face he remembered from dozens of photographs in the 1960s, but in fact the age had begun to show and he could see small lines around her eyes. She asked him detailed and pointed questions about the photographs he'd brought. Had they been cleared for the right to publish them in America? How much did they cost? Why had he brought this one, or that, where the figures were hard to identify? They had a thoroughly professional discussion about what still needed to be done to the book. He wanted her to go through the manuscript and take out some of the Americanisms that might jar on an English readership. He said he would take care of some of the historical inaccuracies—for example, Radzinsky had placed the tsar's visit to Queen Victoria at Windsor Castle right next door to the Tower of London because of his unfamiliarity with British geography. Trewin did not believe that Jackie had been thinking of 1963 while working on the book, though the parallel had occurred to him. He was too shy to raise it with her. Later he stumbled out onto Fifth Avenue, his head reeling after his long meeting with her. The buses were covered with bold advertisements for Oliver Stone's 1991 movie *JFK,* which dredged up conspiracy theories about his assassination. Jackie might have schooled herself not to think about 1963, but the reminders were everywhere.

What was more likely to have attracted Jackie to the book, in addition to its commercial promise, was the way in which Radzinsky evoked the grandeur of a lost civilization. He talked repeatedly with one old lady who could remember

Russia before the revolution. He described these meetings as "our nightly conversations in a Moscow kitchen, our journey to a drowned Atlantis." This is the characteristic note of Jackie's own faintly nostalgic view of history, in which we live today exiled from a land of former glories that can be recaptured only in books or memories or art. Much of the early part of Radzinsky's book is about ceremony, such as those of the old tsar's funeral and the wedding of Nicholas to Alexandra, the sort of ritual Jackie also loved in the court of the Bourbons.

The evidence, too, is that she had buried what memories she had of 1963 as deeply, though perhaps imperfectly, as she could. Nureyev once invited her to the private screening of a film in which he played a role and his character was killed by a gunshot. Jackie shouted out loud and covered her face when the gun was fired. She didn't remove her hands until the lights came up, whispering her apology to Nureyev: "I just couldn't look at that." Cecil Beaton remembered accompanying her to an opera in which several shots were fired onstage. She jumped several feet out of her seat before regaining her composure. Jackie's friend Karl Katz took her to *A Bridge Too Far,* a film set during the Second World War in which there was much gunfire and carnage. "It was a terrible mistake," he later reflected. She was visibly upset during the screening and afterward. One of Jackie's editorial colleagues was once sent a manuscript by a well-known author that had a dream sequence in which Jackie descended a staircase to look into JFK's open casket; next to her husband lay Marilyn Monroe. In the manuscript, she seemed to see this and accept it. Jackie's colleague wanted to acquire the book but consulted Nancy Tuckerman first. Tuckerman thought it would be better not to ask Jackie about the book and just let it go to another publisher. However, the editor was moved by the quality of the manuscript and telephoned Jackie on the Vineyard to ask whether they

might waive the Doubleday rule that nothing was to be published about the Kennedy family. When Jackie came on the phone and the passage in question was described and the word "assassination" spoken, her colleague heard Jackie's sudden intake of breath on the other end of the line. The book project was dropped. The colleague decided that for Jackie, although the assassination was a period in her life that had been consciously set aside, mentioning it could still hit a nerve.

It's possible that Jackie saw herself as a more lighthearted and even comic figure than the grieving icon that Radzinsky and many others believed her to be. When she went to Russia, she tried on Alexandra's opera costume and made no pilgrimage to Yekaterinburg. Her costume at the launch party for Radzinsky's book at New York's Russian Tea Room is interesting. Did she wear a simple black dress, as if she were in mourning for the murdered tsar, or something demure and unlikely to draw attention? No. She wore a dress that recalled a harlequin's outfit from the Italian Renaissance. The harlequin was a stock comic figure in the productions of the commedia dell'arte, something between a jester and a buffoon, whose origins dated from sixteenth-century Italy. Jackie had shown an earlier interest in the harlequin figure when she had purchased a harlequin design drawn by Cecil Beaton and exhibited at a gallery in New York. Now she dressed in a harlequin motif for the party to celebrate the publication of Radzinsky's book. She sat on a banquette with the author and looked vaguely distressed as he told her another of his tall tales. In the courts of kings, queens, and maharajahs, not only princesses, artists, and courtesans were in attendance but also professional clowns, who amused the assembled courtiers after supper. Her harlequin outfit was closer to clown than to queen, and perhaps the circus queen that people remembered her posing as when she was young was nearer her own vision of herself than the perpetual widow of popular imagination.

chapter 10

JUST A SHELTERED SOCIALITE.

—*Jackie on how she was stereotyped in the press*

Jackie resented being considered a socialite. She thought that winning *Vogue*'s Prix de Paris was proof at an early age that she had substance as well as style, that she could compete with other talented young women to be chosen for a job that would require real work. *Vogue* in the 1950s was much more highbrow and socially exclusive than it is today. It published poets such as W. H. Auden, whose work took some training to enjoy, and featured couture clothes that were well out of the range of the ordinary pocketbook. Its models were often East Coast debutantes or young women from titled families in Europe. Jackie was perfect for the *Vogue* magazine of 1951, and that was a reputation she had to spend the rest of her life trying to live down.

Arthur Schlesinger won his early fame by producing volumes of history on American liberalism and the presidency of Franklin Roosevelt. He also had a fondness for the social whirl and liked Jackie from the first time he met her at Hyannis in the 1950s. She liked him, too, and by the time JFK won the White House, they were on comfortable, teasing terms. At one of her most famous White House parties, the Catalan cellist Pablo Casals, who had refused to visit the United States after America's recognition of the Fascist regime in Spain, played for the Kennedys' guests after supper. At another party, in honor of her sister, Lee, many of her sister's 1960s jet-setting friends flew to Washington for the occasion. Afterward Jackie told Schlesinger that she had come up with a test to measure "the artistic sensibilities" of members of the Kennedy administration. Whom would they rather have return to the White House, Pablo Casals or Lee Radziwill? She was making fun of Lee as a party girl, but she was also making fun of Schlesinger, who she suspected would choose Lee before Casals. As for herself, she had enjoyed herself at both events. Schlesinger noticed this about Jackie on another White House evening, when he and his wife were invited to a small dinner party that included Oleg Cassini and his girlfriend as well as a couple from *Paris Match*. Cassini and the rest of international café society didn't bring out the best in Jackie, thought Schlesinger. If she hadn't married JFK, he thought, Jackie would have turned out more like Lee. "But I love her," he wrote in his diary.

If she created books on high culture by publishing artists of the ballet world and novels of a Nobel Prize winner, she also did books on the taste, decorating habits, and manners of social elites in both America and Europe. She was willing to break the American taboo on speaking about social distinction, a topic more dangerous in American conversation than sex, politics, or religion. The Kennedys were the classic case of Americans' desire to look at rich, handsome people having a good time without thinking too much about whether money in their case didn't sometimes trump merit or how they had achieved social prominence. Joseph Kennedy loved Jack's marriage to Jacqueline Bouvier. She put the stamp of good breeding and respectability on a fortune that came from cheap Hollywood films, Wall Street manipulations, and bootleg liquor. However, Jackie could sometimes be too much of a good thing. Jack Kennedy worried that she would tip the scale. It was fine for the Kennedys to be seen playing touch football, a sport all Americans could understand, but in the White House, Jackie's evident liking for French clothes, fox hunting, and fine wines was a political liability. He once remarked that she had "a little too much status and not enough quo." In the summers, when she vacationed with Lee and the newspapers photographed her boating with the Fiat magnate Gianni Agnelli off Capri or with Aristotle Onassis among the Greek islands, JFK wrote to her to protest. She was going too far. He wanted more pictures of the kids and fewer of her with kingpins. However, this was the price JFK paid for his freedom with other women while she was away, and she was happy, within certain limits, to make him pay the full fare.

After JFK died, John Kenneth Galbraith advised Ted Kennedy that if he wanted to be serious about acquiring national political stature, he had to give up all the Camelot nonsense Jackie had devised for his brother's memory. Being "beautiful people" for the short time they were in office was fine for Jack and Jackie, but in the 1970s Ted should not try that himself. Galbraith thought the residents of the White House ought to be drab and compassionate. There should be no black tie evenings with ladies in rhinestones. In short, having Jackie as his sister-in-law could be a liability as well as an asset as Ted planned his career.

It is one of the strangest quirks of Jackie's view of her own social position that she should repeatedly tell people she felt like an outsider in American society while most Americans regarded her as the ultimate insider. Even though she was married in Newport, lived on Fifth Avenue, and rented a house in the hunt country near Middleburg, Virginia, something in her was like a little girl with her nose pressed to the glass, looking in on the lives of those more privileged than she was. This quirk emerges in the books she published on America's most famous shop for luxury goods, Tiffany & Co., on the life of a Vanderbilt heiress living in the 1890s, and on the decoration of bedrooms by baronesses who wouldn't think of sleeping in anything less than a four-poster with velvet curtains. If she hadn't been interested in the aesthetic that joined luxury goods with good manners, she wouldn't have spent so much time commissioning books about it. Her books show her repeatedly supporting four-color anatomies of etiquette and social origins. They offer an opportunity to explore a significant theme in her character.

Three authors whom she repeatedly backed to discuss top-shelf taste, history, and design were John Loring, Louis Auchincloss, and Mary-Sargent Ladd. One was Tiffany's design director for thirty years, another was the novelist of Manhattan's *haute bourgeoisie,* and the third was an American debutante turned fashion model, expatriate, and French baroness. These were all occupations and pastimes that Jackie was particularly drawn to. The story of her relationship with these authors hints at how Jackie may have thought about what Cole Porter and Louis Armstrong called being "in high so-ci-ety."

Breakfast at Tiffany's

John Loring used to lunch regularly with Jackie at New York's most exclusive tables, but he has the sort of charm that suggests he would have much rather been with you. He retired as Tiffany's design director in 2009 and now divides his time between a newly gentrified patch of West Palm Beach and Manhattan, still busy with freelance designing, decorating, and writing.

Loring worked on six books with Jackie, more than she did with any other author, and Nancy Tuckerman remembered that "she liked him, she really did." Pictures of them together show her happy and utterly at ease with him. Loring had a funny story about the origins of their first book together.

Walter Hoving was the founder and president of a holding company that owned Tiffany and other expensive stores, such as Bonwit Teller. Hoving was of Jackie's parents' generation and a friend of Jackie's mother, as well as the father of Tom Hoving at the Metropolitan Museum of Art. Hoving told Loring soon after he was hired at Tiffany that not only was he going to supervise design, but because he had established a reputation as a writer on design in magazines like *Architectural Digest,* Hoving wanted him to write for Tiffany too. Hoving had in mind an illustrated book on Tiffany table settings. "My friend Janet [Auchincloss]'s daughter is an editor over at Doubleday," Hoving told Loring. This was the true *grand seigneur* style—to refer to Jackie without mentioning her name. Hoving called both Loring and Jackie in to an appointment in his office. "He sat us down like two bad children," Loring recalled, "and told us what we had to do." There had been a book called *Tiffany Table Settings* in 1960. Now Loring and Jackie were being assigned to produce a book that would be called *The*

New Tiffany Table Settings when it was published in 1981. For thirty years Tiffany had sponsored exhibitions of tables designed by famous hostesses and decorators in the shop's Fifth Avenue showrooms. Now these table settings would be photographed for a book, as a way of promoting sales of flatware and plates in the shop as well as Tiffany jewels and other Tiffany objects that could be used to decorate the tables.

After the meeting finished, Loring went back to his office thinking, "This is not going to happen. Why would she be interested?" Nevertheless, Hoving's idea had come to Jackie at the very beginning of her Doubleday years, and it must have struck the management at the publisher as a good way to introduce her to some of the ins and outs of producing an expensive illustrated book, since a good deal of the work would fall on Loring's shoulders and she could learn from him. Tiffany paid for the photographs and retained the copyright so the company could use them later for promotional purposes if necessary. Doubleday was a big operation with a good deal of capacity at its printing presses. This Tiffany proposition was probably not an enormous risk for the publisher. In the end, sales of the book made it among the top sellers on Jackie's list. This and the subsequent five Tiffany books had sales that were mainly in the healthy five figures, exceeding those of many of Jackie's books by well-known authors such as Judith Jamison,

George Plimpton, and Stewart Udall, whom Jackie had hand-picked, but which did not live up to expectations. The Tiffany books would not have become such a regular feature of Jackie's working years in publishing if they were not profitable. The fact that Loring went on to produce fifteen more Tiffany books after Jackie died, suggests that she and Loring had designed a winning formula.

Jackie laid down a ground rule with Loring before they got started: "You have to understand that I cannot put my name on a commercial enterprise." She said she looked on their book as a "social document," not advertising. It was going to be snapshots of social customs, social settings, and life in a particular section of American society at a particular time. Several times Loring returned to this point. The book on Tiffany table settings and the other Tiffany books that came afterward were not "advertorials," that is, sales plugs disguised as unbiased editorials. They were not glorified merchandise catalogues, even though the photographs are gorgeous, printed on beautiful paper, and the designers came up with theatrical settings for plates and silverware, most of which could readily be found for sale in the shop. Of course, Tiffany occupies a unique place in the history of design. It is the one American retail institution that has consistently championed beautifully designed objects for dining, wearing, and decorating for more than a century. Charles Tiffany and Louis Comfort Tiffany were two of America's greatest nineteenth-century designers.

Great architects of the Beaux Arts period at the turn of the century, such as Stanford White, collaborated with Tiffany designers. With a few exceptions, however, the books Loring and Jackie did together do not delve much into this history. They concentrate on what was for sale at Tiffany in the 1980s. They are snapshots of the way people spent money in the Reagan decade, when taxes were cut, when the *Dallas* episodes on television had nothing to do with Jackie's moments there, and when Joan Collins in *Dynasty* embodied the era's female zeitgeist. In the books themselves Jackie kept her distance: her name did not appear on the jackets or even in the acknowledgments. Nor was she mentioned in the *New York Times* review of *The New Tiffany Table Settings*. She told Loring that she wanted to do the book because she had worked on table settings at the White House and was proud of her innovations in White House entertaining—for example, she had broken with the old convention of dining stiffly at a long U-shaped table by seating guests at smaller round tables for eight or ten.

In a later Tiffany book, Loring defended the glitzy, over-the-top displays of wealth by saying that the book provided "a unique social document of the times, the end of the Reagan era, and the settings of its celebratory mood, whose buoyant delight in the lavishly, splendidly ephemeral has not been seen since the great balls of eighteenth-century Europe." This was certainly the era of French history to which Jackie gravitated, but Tiffany never produced anything as remarkable in the 1980s as the designers who had been hired by the French court in the 1700s. Neither Paloma Picasso nor Elsa Peretti, both of whom created objects for sale at Tiffany in that era, designed anything to compare with Sèvres porcelain or commodes by Boulle.

Loring wanted to sell good design and make money. Jackie wanted to make beautiful books, and profitability was important to her, too. There was a market for expensive glamour in the Reagan years, and they meant to take advantage of it. They asked people to design table settings partly as a way to show off the chiefs of their two enterprises: for example, they chose Mrs. Walter Hoving at Tiffany and John Sargent at Doubleday. There were tables by decorators like Mario Buatta, whom the Reagans had asked to redo the state guest rooms at Blair House; Sister Parish, from whom Jackie had commissioned interiors; and even Jackie's sister, Lee. There were tables by socialites such as Pat Buckley, C. Z. Guest, and Nan Kempner. There were also eccentric choices: Andy Warhol set up a table for someone spending a night in jail, and Diana Vreeland imagined what Catherine the Great's breakfast table might look like as she read a morning letter from Voltaire. What Jackie and Loring added to Reaganism in these Tiffany books was a sense of humor.

They had trouble on their hands when Henry Platt, who was vice chairman at Tiffany when the project started, insisted on putting his name on the cover of the book. Platt, a descendant of Charles Tiffany and Louis Comfort Tiffany, considered himself a social arbiter and held balls to introduce the young women of the season. When Loring phoned Jackie to tell her that Platt wanted his name on the cover because he believed it would help sell copies, Jackie replied, "Oh, he's going to have to come to Doubleday to tell me that." She set up a large meeting at Doubleday. "We're going to put a spotlight on this behavior," she said. Platt and Loring came to a Doubleday conference room where a large group of senior people from the publisher had gathered. Jackie was not there. It was unusual for her to be late. Finally she came in. "Now, Henry, what is your announcement?" she said as she sat down. Platt began, "For the sake of marketing the book, I will allow my name to go on the cover." Platt meant that he wanted double billing with Loring. "In what order?" Jackie asked. Loring interjected, "Alphabetical!" Laughter came from around the table. Jackie remarked, "It is one of the great tragedies of editors that our names, unlike your own, must go unsung." More laughter. Jackie knew that it was better to be quiet about one's own achievements than to trumpet them aloud. She was not above issuing a public put-down to Platt, who got his name on the cover of the first book but on none of the others. Although she successfully resisted any credits to her in the books, Loring managed to get her to be a little more forthcoming in different ways. As editor, she still remained largely "unsung," but references to her began to crop up in subsequent books.

Tiffany Taste (1986) followed the first book after a gap of five years. In it are more beautifully photographed tables for a variety of meals in splendid locations, indoors and out, designed by socialites, designers, and fashion editors. The first table setting is a plate with caviar and champagne in a Pan Am Boeing 747 airline cabin. Loring had asked Jackie to move this as far forward in the book as possible, as it is clear from the book's acknowledgments that Pan Am had probably flown Tiffany staff for free to many of the book's far-flung locations around the world. She told him, "Pan Am is on page 1 in all its glory," as if to say, "I hope you're happy." Jackie is not mentioned in the *New York Times*'s review, but she did allow a picture of herself at the book party held at Le Cirque to be published in *W*. Carolina Herrera had designed a dress for her with jeweled shoulder pads, which seemed more Las Vegas or Houston than Newport or Middleburg. In the photograph she was promoting not only the book but also Herrera, as one of her chosen designers, and Le Cirque, owned by Sirio Maccioni, who had designed one of the tables in the book and who gestures as if to kiss her hand. In other words, with *Tiffany Taste* she made a number of exceptions to her rule that her name should not be associated with a commercial enterprise. The book has one photo after another of spectacular dinner tables, including one decorated with Chanel perfume bottles and scarlet lipsticks, but Jackie was certainly involved in commercial enterprises beyond the sale of the book.

Tiffany's 150 Years (1987) marked a significant anniversary and examined some of the highlights of the company's production, from jewels produced for the wife of Napoleon III to the silver Super Bowl trophy. One of the book's interesting features is a page on Mary Todd Lincoln, who apparently consoled herself for being poorly received in Washington society by going on "extravagant spending sprees" during her husband's presidency. She bought herself an expensive set of pearls at Tiffany. This recalls a passage in Jackie's televised White House tour in 1962 where she noted—twice—that Abraham Lincoln had criticized his wife in the White House for her extravagance. What no one in the TV audience knew was that

she was privately under fire from JFK for the same thing. Nor would anyone reading this new book on Tiffany's history note that the editor had once publicly declared her sympathy with extravagant first ladies, that she had defended her own extravagance by appealing to a Lincoln precedent, and that the fate that befell Mary Todd Lincoln had also befallen her. The convention for well-bred women in her generation was that it was all right for your name to be in the newspaper on only three occasions: when you were born, when you married, and when you died. Jackie also had a certain native shyness to overcome whenever there was a question of publicity, either for what she did in the White House or for what she did with her books; in addition to that shyness was a repeated attempt to defend her own record by appealing to historical evidence.

For their next book together, *The Tiffany Wedding* (1988), she and Loring looked over the existing guidebooks for planning weddings. They found them far too full of rules and regulations. Jackie particularly objected to Martha Stewart's book on weddings as too prescriptive. "Let's try to liberate the American girl from this nightmare," Jackie told Loring. "Let's tell girls they can do whatever they want." Once again she allowed Loring an unusual liberty. In a section on engagement rings, he superimposed a photo of a sapphire ring on a picture of Hammersmith Farm, the Auchincloss house in Newport where Jackie had held her wedding reception after her marriage to JFK. In a book that mentions her name nowhere at all, this is the one sly reference to her. "It was an in joke," remembered Loring. "We both thought it was kind of cute." By the late 1980s Jackie's mother had been forced to sell the house. Auchincloss finances had taken a turn for the worse, and her mother moved out of the big house into a smaller house on the grounds. A group of investors hoped to remake the big house into a tourist attraction and had renamed it Camelot Gar-

The sapphire runs second after the diamond in popularity as an engagement ring. Shown against the approach to the Auchincloss family's Hammersmith Farm in Newport, this oval sapphire weighs 8.53 carats and is set in platinum with two triangular diamond side stones.

THE TIFFANY WEDDING
100

dens. Jackie told her stepbrother, Yusha Auchincloss, that she thought the name was "tacky." The tourist attraction never came to be, but it is fun to think of America's foremost symbol of taste and style having that word in her vocabulary.

Jackie wrote thank-you notes to Loring that are warmer and friendlier than was necessary for a duty-calls social convention. "You are the nicest kindest most life enhancing person to work with," she wrote in one. In another she said she wanted to get a flagpole for a scarf he had given her "and fly it from my apartment as a banner proclaiming the joy it is to do these beautiful books with you." However, in their next-to-last book together, *Tiffany Parties* (1989), some sort of line was crossed. Loring asked the gossip columnist Aileen Mehle, who wrote under the pen name Suzy Knickerbocker, to write a preface. In this preface, Jackie was referred to as the hostess of an unusual party. Mehle wrote that she had been in Palm Beach "on board Aristotle Onassis's floating palace *Christina* when free-spirited Ari never stopped recounting his Rabelaisian exploits and Jackie, cool in white silk pants and a ruby or two (big ones), charmed lovers of eighteenth-century furniture Jayne and Charles Wrightsman while the famous Mexican society beauty Gloria Guinness wigwagged her kitten hips to the music. I would love to tell you the precious mosaic swimming pool on deck was filled with champagne, but it wasn't. Everyone else was." Jackie didn't mind Mehle, and had once tried to persuade her to write a book of her own on "the world of New York society women. 'Write about them, their lives, their ambitions, their lies. Write how nothing really is the way it seems. How these women who seem to have it all, are really desperate and trapped.'" Mehle thought to herself, "*Et tu,* Jackie?" Mehle never wrote that book, although Jane Hitchcock's *Social Crimes* comes very close to the sort of book Jackie as an editor had imagined.

She allowed Loring to use a picture of her and JFK soon after they were married, arriving for a party in the entrance hall of Marble House in Newport. The picture could not have been more prominently placed. It was opposite Loring's foreword to *Tiffany Parties*. She also allowed her name to be published in the book for "The Literary Lions Dinner," at which famous writers hosted "well-heeled admirers" to benefit the

New York Public Library. People at Doubleday started making fun of it as "the book of empty chairs" or simply "the chair book," as it featured table after table set for grand dinners but without anyone there. Then at the launch party, thrown by three New York socialites, the guests mobbed her. Nearly a hundred of them scrambled to have their picture taken with her by the *W* photographer, one by one. She didn't like it. "Those people have really got my back up," she told Loring. "I can't do it again."

She didn't entirely blame Loring, but no more would she allow references to her to be used. In their last book together, *The Tiffany Gourmet Cookbook* (1992), they still had fun. Loring asked various celebrities to design table settings, this time with recipes for the dishes on the table. Jackie made it clear that she didn't want another chair book. "What it needs is a different beginning, as I have noted on ms., so that we know this is a NEW book about FOOD." In what sounds like a catty remark, probably designed specifically for Loring's consumption, as he would get the joke more than anyone else, she objected to a table set for Thanksgiving by the country music singer Barbara Mandrell. On the table were orange peels stuffed with mashed sweet potato and melted marshmallows. She wanted this out and told him, "You wouldn't want Caroline to think that I would approve of her doing this, would you?" Jackie wasn't a snobbish person, but she knew what would raise a laugh in discussions with the design fraternity. Loring's introduction to the cookbook is surprisingly class-conscious for a person who was already in an influential position at a famous company and with the world's most famous woman as his editor. He tells readers that his mother had a house in Venice, that his brother owned a huge place in Greece, and that when he went to Paris as a young man he was taken up by a grand Parisian family. Even if all these things were true, as no doubt they were, it probably would have been better to pass over them in silence than to exhibit them like a social CV.

Jackie's joke about the mashed sweet potato and marshmallow is in the same vein as one she made to another of her authors. This author telephoned Jackie from Los Angeles, worried that when her book was featured on a game show being filmed there, *To Tell the Truth,* Jackie's name as the editor was being used more prominently than Jackie would have liked. Jackie reassured her, laughing and saying, "Don't worry." Then she whispered, "No one we know watches *To Tell the Truth.*"

Because Jackie loved Loring and wanted to acknowledge all the work they had done together, she nearly paid him the signal favor of speaking to a reporter about him when *The New Yorker* did a profile of him in 1992. He arranged for the magazine's fashion correspondent, Holly Brubach, to meet Jackie at a party at Tiffany & Co. Loring remembered being in a conversational circle when Brubach was introduced to Jackie. He saw Jackie flinch "one-thirty-second of an inch." It was her "I smell a rat" flinch, and though she was polite to Brubach, she later refused to take the interview idea further. In her article, Brubach praised Loring for promoting good design that achieved commercial success, but she also took off her gloves and said that while his Tiffany books claimed to be about taste, they were in fact about cash: "This is the etiquette of consumerism, a course of instruction in the exercise of money." *The Tiffany Gourmet Cookbook*, then on sale, cost fifty dollars, and in 1992 this might have made even a tycoon think twice about buying it. Brubach's *New Yorker* profile of Loring was not quite the unreserved endorsement Jackie and Loring had both hoped for, and this is what Jackie sensed when she turned down the interview with Brubach.

When Jackie grew unwell in 1994 and her cancer was

announced in the papers, many of her friends wrote to her, sensing that her time was near. In reply to a concerned letter Loring wrote to her several weeks before she died, Jackie wrote, "I just loved your letter. I think it is *you* who have given me all these sprees of joy at old Doubleday, and seeing you was always like champagne."

Jackie's family knew how much she was attached to Loring. They asked him to help with some of the arrangements for her memorial service and the reception at 1040 Fifth Avenue after she died. Several years later he was still in touch with Jackie's daughter, Caroline Kennedy. When he published *Magnificent Tiffany Silver* (2001), Loring sent her a copy, along with a memory of her mother. He told Caroline that when he and her mother had been working on *The Tiffany Wedding*, Jackie had noticed a photograph of a thick bunch of wet asparagus tied together with a pink rubber band. "Oh, isn't that beautiful? I just don't know why American brides can't carry bunches of asparagus at their weddings." Pause. "I guess that would be too close to the truth." Loring remembered Jackie as having a genius for the odd, slightly off-kilter remark delivered at an unexpected moment. Thanking Loring for the book, Caroline said she couldn't believe she had escaped the asparagus bouquet at her wedding: "It would have been so like Mummy."

A Debutante's Diary

Louis Auchincloss was twelve years older than Jackie. Via family connections, they met in Washington before she was married to JFK, but they did not see one another at all in the White House and then ran across each other again after Jackie went to New York in the mid-1960s. She regularly invited Auchincloss and his wife to the Christmas parties she threw in the 1970s; they knew lots of people in common during the '70s, '80s, and '90s.

As the chronicler of Manhattan's upper crust, Auchincloss was an expert observer of manners in the social world he and Jackie inhabited. Sitting in his Park Avenue apartment a year before he died, he gave the impression of having observed her and her world very closely indeed. He had the sharp look of an eagle in tortoiseshell glasses.

He recalled first seeing Jackie at a dinner in Washington during the 1950s. "I knew her when she was a girl," he said. He recalled that she had been engaged to John Husted but had broken off that engagement after she began dating JFK. Auchincloss dismissed John Husted as someone who was socially unimportant, then warmed to this theme. Of Lee's first marriage, to the son of one of New York's great publishers, Auchincloss observed, "Michael Canfield was not considered a great match a-*tall*. Cass Canfield had a lot of money but was not going to give it to Michael, an adoptive son rumored to be the bastard son of an English peer. I can't exaggerate how unimportant he was." Why would a Bouvier marry down in the world, to a Husted or a Canfield? Why would Jackie in later life say she felt like an "outsider" in New York society? "Well," said Auchincloss a little impatiently, "the Bouviers weren't important. They were not really 'in' anywhere." He had spent a lifetime examining the descendants of families with big fortunes at the turn of the century. Next to the Vanderbilts, the Bouviers looked like small beer. "Jack Bouvier was a great liability at any party," Auchincloss continued, "because he drank too much. He did come to Lee's wedding reception at Hugh Auchincloss's house in Washington" after Janet had divorced him. "Black Jack whirled Janet around the floor. He looked like a big sexy Negro. He danced Janet around when she didn't want it at all. We thought he'd take Janet away with him."

Auchincloss unwittingly described some of the ways in which Jackie's attitude to social position might have been mixed up with her relationship to difficult parents. There was Black Jack, who was downwardly mobile the whole time she knew him, drinking too much, squandering money borrowed from his father, not doing very well with the funds he invested in the market. Janet always claimed to be descended from southern families that had fought with the Confederate Army, when in fact her relatives were much more recent Irish immigrants. Auchincloss recalled that Janet's temper tantrums were so awful that sometimes "she'd strike Jackie. Then she'd be cooing like a dove a few minutes later. Janet had black moods. She didn't like JFK's girlfriends."

Janet's marriage to Hugh Auchincloss made her the hostess of Hammersmith Farm, but it may not have been easy for either mother or daughter to be rubbing shoulders with blue bloods in Rhode Island's oldest resort for people with Gilded Age fortunes, who would have been examining Janet and Jackie critically, measuring them up. A hint of this comes from Jackie's explanation about why she wanted to publish the Gilded Age diary of Adele Sloane, the grandmother of Louis Auchincloss's wife. The diary repeatedly returns to the question of who is related to whom. Jackie told Auchincloss, "It reminds me of listening to Mrs. Whitehouse and Mummy talking at Bailey's Beach in Newport about what Charlie Whitehouse calls 'tribalism.' I think tribalism is interesting and you might want to discuss it somewhere. How important it was for everyone to know who everyone was."

When Auchincloss submitted his first draft of *Maverick in Mauve: The Diary of a Romantic Age,* Jackie was a little severe with the author. "As it now stands," she told him, "it is a book that should be privately printed. It is a book by one of that world for that world. It lacks interest to the general reader because the gilded world in which the diarist lives is naturally taken for granted by her, so there is not the appraisal and description of it which would interest people who are not of that world." She wanted the analysis and historical context that would make the document more than just a young girl's diary from the 1890s. Auchincloss was happy with the document's antiquarian interest, with the way in which it showed that his wife was directly connected to this turn-of-the-century grandeur. Jackie wanted something bigger: an anatomy and an assessment of where these families fit into the history of the country. He revised the manuscript and resubmitted it to her, but when the book appeared, it still fell short of the broader historical canvas that Jackie had imagined. She persuaded John Kenneth Galbraith to write a short comment for the book to place on its back cover. Even her old friend produced lines that were fairly low-key in their enthusiasm, calling the book "a small but very interesting document."

Author and editor had other disagreements. Auchincloss wanted copious footnotes, and Jackie vetoed them. He wanted to include photographs that were only from the exact years of the diary itself. "Oh, Louis," she said with exasperation, "do we have to be so technical?" He agreed to include some photos of Adele Sloane in her later life. They decided to have the launch party at the Museum of the City of New York, and a small exhibition was specially arranged to coincide with the book's publication. Auchincloss spent $2,000 on the party. "Johnny Sargent added a little so there could be proper glasses," he recalled. "I threatened to have paper cups if he didn't. There was quite an extensive guest list. Everyone accepted. Jackie was to be the hostess." Then, just before the party, "Nancy Tuckerman called to say there would be too many photographers there. 'Jackie can't relax and have fun in such a setting. Therefore, she feels it best not to come.'" Auchincloss was angry but replied coolly that he would consider it to be "an act of nonfriendship" if she didn't come.

In the end, Jackie did attend. She stayed late. However, Auchincloss remembered the occasion as nearly a social slight rather than a successful book party. "She was so used to doing exactly what she wanted. I was outraged that I had been talked into this party and then she proposed at the last minute not to come." He concluded that one had to know how to treat her and not everyone did: "You had to remember that she was the only woman on the planet to whom everyone said yes. Sometimes you had to tell her no."

Auchincloss sold most of his private correspondence with Jackie when her children put up her books and furniture for sale. "If they didn't care, why should I?" he said. He nevertheless brought out a prized letter from Jackie, which he had refused to sell. She had written to say how sorry she was to hear that his wife had died. He kept it carefully preserved in a clear plastic envelope. The letter suggested that his memory of Jackie and her connection to his life had more appeal for him than he was quite willing to admit.

At the end of several hours, when asked to sign a copy of *Maverick in Mauve,* he asked with sparkle, "Shall I sign Louis Auchincloss? Or Florence Adele Sloane?" It was not far off the camp sense of humor Jackie herself used when she asked Loring to remove Barbara Mandrell's Thanksgiving photo. Some part of her personality thrived on her connection to these two men, both of whom enjoyed writing about the American upper classes.

Secrets of the Bedroom

Mary-Sargent Ladd was born into a prominent Boston family that included the descendants of the painter John Singer Sargent. Growing up, she moved in the same debutante circles

that Jackie did and went to Foxcroft, where she and the rest of
the girls were taught to make their beds with military preci-
sion as the hunting horns blew outside their windows. Diana
Vreeland was a friend of her grandmother. She remembered
Vreeland sitting her down in front of a mirror when she was
very young, evaluating her critically, and telling her to stretch
her neck, "like Alice in Wonderland." In the 1950s she had
success as a fashion model. She was photographed by the great
photographers of that era, including Horst, Richard Avedon,
and Lord Snowdon.

In 1960 she married Jean Claude Abreu. They lived in
Paris, where he was the publisher of the art magazine *L'Oeil,*
and in Switzerland. One of the surrealist painters who did
portraits of society women in that era, Jean-Claude Fourneau, painted her picture in a library with a parquet floor and
a bronze leaf in the middle distance. She kept up her contacts
with American magazines after she stopped modeling, writing
articles on interiors and artists for both *Vogue* and *House & Garden.* After the marriage to Abreu ended, she married a French
baron, Bernard d'Anglejan-Chatillon, but she visited New
York regularly, sometimes lunching with Jackie, whom she had
known for decades. Jackie knew of the articles Ladd had been
writing on interiors and told her, "You must do a book." This
was the genesis of *The Frenchwoman's Bedroom,* a big four-color
book with sumptuous photographs of rooms decorated mainly
for titled ladies, which Doubleday published in 1991. It was the
boudoir equivalent of a Tiffany place-setting book.

Ladd said that she did not know Jackie well when they
were growing up, but they saw one another in Newport and
she had been invited to Jackie's wedding to JFK. When she
was young, the Irish—"this is going to sound snobbish"—were
always maids in her parents' house, so she was surprised to find
all these Irish Kennedys so confident at Jackie's wedding. JFK,

"of course," had great charm. This feeling of social miscegenation hung over both of Jackie's marriages. Ladd had spent several weekends with Onassis and recalled that his accent was so thick she could barely understand him. She didn't think he had any charm whatsoever, and she believed that he had married Jackie to prevent the U.S. government from proceeding against his business interests. She thought that Jackie was mostly unhappy in love until she met "her Belgian," Tempelsman, with whom she was very happy indeed.

Her book with Jackie had its origins in a kidney ailment she had had as a child, which had confined her to her bed for long periods of time. In those immediate post–World War II years, she wrote in the preface to her book, "I dreamed of a lost and glamorous past, of coronation bed heads and baldachins, of chintz galore, of French Provincial and of the sunlight slanting through the painted shutters." She didn't realize that this dream would come true and that one day she would sleep in just such French bedrooms herself.

The feeling of exile from lost and fallen grandeur was certainly a theme of Jackie's other books. *The Frenchwoman's Bedroom* includes a long essay on the historical uses of women's bedrooms and their change over time, which would also have appealed to Jackie's historical sense and her continuing interest in the lives of historical women. There are hints of sensuality and eroticism in *The Frenchwoman's Bedroom* that echo Naveen Patnaik's book on the courtly life in India. "The bedrooms included in the present book," wrote Ladd, "are eclectic, dramatic and sensual, from the historical to the trendy. But they all have one thing in common: they intimately reflect the secrets of the women who live in them."

Although Jackie told few of her secrets to Ladd, their book together hints at one significant subterranean theme in Jackie's personality. The only thing Jackie ever really revealed to Ladd—and probably to her because it was a feeling they shared—was insecurity about her expatriate identity. Jackie was as interested as Ladd in French history and decoration, but she was always insistent on her equal interest in American history. Ladd thought this went back to Jackie's time in the White House, when she had been accused, according to Auchincloss, of being "too damned French" at the very moment she wanted to make her mark on American history and culture. Ladd thought Jackie "protested too much" about her interest in American history.

She and Jackie talked of doing another book together before Jackie died. Ladd had seen an article in *House & Garden* on the painter known as Balthus, who produced canvases that were controversial because of their explicit treatment of troubling and eerie girlhood sexuality. He painted many young women with cats, and these works are thematically allied to Manet's *Olympia* and to Vertès's similar image that had been

in Jackie's own collection. The article discussed Balthus and featured the interior of the Swiss chalet where he lived and worked. This gave Ladd the idea to approach Balthus, whom she knew, and pitch the idea of a book about how the interiors depicted in his paintings were closely linked to the interiors of the studios and houses where he had worked. She thought her essay could be accompanied by pictures taken by a French photographer famous for his interiors, Jacques Dirand. Balthus gave her the green light, and Jackie loved the idea too. However, before she could finish the book, Balthus died, and his son protested that he wanted to do a book of his own. Doubleday's lawyers had to get involved, and the project was dropped. Balthus was a painter of international renown, and there's no reason to see any autobiographical interest in either Ladd's or Jackie's fascination with his work. Their willingness to pore over his images and to treat them at book length, however, indicates how Jackie's visual interests encompassed the dark, the weird, and the perverse as well as the beautiful.

In the end Ladd had to set aside her writing career. Although she edited a Christmas issue of *Vogue* in the late 1980s at about the same time Anna Wintour became editor, Wintour didn't like her work and replaced her with André Leon Talley. With Jackie, however, Ladd's relations were always smooth. They agreed when the first design for *The Frenchwoman's Bedroom* came in that the designer would have to be replaced by an excellent Japanese couple, whom Jackie found herself. When Ladd submitted her text to Jackie, she discovered how Jackie worked as an editor: "She encouraged, she didn't criticize." After Jackie's death, Ladd turned her efforts to organizing and fundraising for a museum of Franco-American friendship in Picardie, at a château called Blérancourt. If Jackie's spirit lives on in the books she edited and among authors with whom she liked to work, then a distinctive Jackie ghost also survives in this French castle, looked after in part by a Foxcroft baroness.

The cultural critic Christopher Hitchens has written of the way Americans often think about elegant living with a mixture of envy and disapproval: "The association between luxury and decadence, and the punishment of these by disaster, is an almost automatic one in our culture. Marie Antoinette maintains a sumptuous court while all the while the fires of resentment are being stoked to a white heat. A band plays on the *Titanic* as the gowns and white ties perform their elegant combinations. The nobles of St. Petersburg look down from their brilliantly lit windows and fail to see the snarling hatred that is gathering in the darkness."

Jackie understood that this ambivalence in American attitudes extended to their view of high culture, meaning art and literature, classical ballet and classical music, which many of her contemporaries would have regarded as the exclusive preserve of those with big bank accounts and expensive educations. She also knew that her own life could all too easily be written into Hitchens's framework: Kennedy white ties punished by an early death in Dallas; life on a yacht punished by a lymphoma that came far before a woman's usual time to die. She refused to be so straight-faced and straitlaced about it all. Loring remembered her characteristic attempts to make him laugh just at a moment in a crowded room when laughter would have been most out of place. Her books show her enjoying all the sumptuousness that she could surround herself with in the present and not worrying about the moral disapproval that might follow when she was gone. Even in the 1960s, soon after JFK had died, she had demonstrated a remarkable ability to send up the political idealism that she had learned to share with JFK, along with her own liking for comfort and opulence. For instance, when Dorothy Schiff called on Jackie in her suite in the Carlyle in October 1964, Jackie told her that there had been a lot of requests from magazines but she had barely looked at them. They all wanted her to write about "gracious living or fashion." Then she cried out, *"I am interested in the same things Jack was interested in,"* before she added, "and those things too, of course." The sotto voce self-deprecation is Jackie being endearingly honest.

That she was interested in the same things her first husband had been interested in, that she continued to identify herself with the political themes and personnel of his administration, are shown by a very different group of her books. These books make it clear that however much she might be criticized for it, even by friends like Schlesinger and Galbraith, she insisted that Camelot "shall not be forgot." Despite the image we have of her, with her gentle whisper, she could be surprisingly tough about ensuring that her version of history lasted.

chapter 11

OH, THEY FOUND GUENEVERE WITH HER BOLD CAVALIER . . .
— *Lyrics from the 1960s musical* CAMELOT

It's hard to know precisely what Jackie had in mind when she told the journalist Theodore White on a rainy night in Hyannis, only a week after her husband was murdered, that the idea of Camelot was the best way to remember her husband's presidency after he was gone. Many historians have leapt to the conclusion that Camelot was an overly glorified vision of JFK's presidency, not only because of his serial and compulsive adultery, but also because he actually accomplished so little during his administration of less than three years. They think of Jackie's Camelot idea as at best the understandable idealization of a grieving widow, at worst a public relations spin that covered up much that was wrong with Kennedy's administration.

The much less well known version of how she wanted to remember JFK appeared in her publishing career, when she quietly brought out a series of books either that were written by persons whom she knew from the White House or that recaptured themes of JFK's administration. The matter of Jackie and Camelot was not merely a simple conversation between her and Theodore White late in 1963. It was an ongoing concern.

Jackie confessed in the period immediately following JFK's death that he hadn't liked her to be involved in politics, but after he died she was more forward than she had ever been in the White House about making sure that her view of the Kennedy presidency would be remembered by historians. Jackie might have been a retiring and apparently passive widow on the surface, but underneath she had an iron fist in her white glove and shrewd instincts about when to bring it down hard on the table. Her books show her to be a much more active and knowledgeable figure than she has been supposed to be.

Building a Library

Two important associations with books and libraries formed an important prelude to her life as an editor. She had begun to assemble a library for the White House when she was there, and after JFK died, her chief public activity consisted of assembling the materials necessary to construct his presidential library in Boston. In one of the revealing letters Jackie wrote to Harold Macmillan just after JFK died, she showed how she was ceasing to be a dutiful wife and assuming the role of powerful defender of her husband's legacy. The best way she could remember her love was through history, she thought. She said it was inevitable that inferior presidents and prime ministers would destroy what had been created, but she and Macmillan could still say to one another, "Do you remember those days—how perfect they were? . . . I always keep thinking of Camelot—which is overly sentimental—but I know I am right. For one brief shining moment there was Camelot—and it will never be that way again—And you and Jack were the ones who made it so."

Earlier in the same letter she had conceded that JFK, like many men of his time, did not think she had any role to play in politics. "I have been an observer (not a participant as he did not wish his wife to be that way)," she wrote, "of the political and international scene." With this letter, however, written to one of her husband's most prominent international counterparts, the retired leader of America's most important ally, she showed that she wasn't going to be confined to observing anymore. She would be doing, and making, and building, and forgetting whatever constricted view JFK might have had about women in politics.

The outpouring of feeling following JFK's assassination meant that Jackie and Robert Kennedy were able to collect considerable sums to build JFK's presidential library. Any contribution of a thousand dollars or more got a personal response from Jackie, as the library was her great passion in the period immediately following the assassination. That a bookish woman should have cared about building a library is not so surprising, but her choice of architect and her involvement in allied programs that she was endowing at Harvard also reveal her unique and individual vision of Camelot.

What she did not do is important. She did not choose an imitation Gothic structure appropriate to the era of Camelot, or a Georgian reproduction appropriate to Harvard's main architectural style, for the institution that tourists would visit and historians would turn to for guidance on her husband's archive. She insisted that some of the most prominent architects working in a modernist tradition—Philip Johnson, Louis Kahn, Mies van der Rohe—be invited to advise on the construction of the building. She went to a conference to see their presentations and hear their recommendations. She made trips around the country to visit the latest examples of the work of the most prominent members of this committee of advising architects. In the end she chose the relatively unknown Chinese-born I. M. Pei, who had been educated in the United States and become an American citizen. In a picture of her at the Hyannis conference at which the Kennedys took advice from the assembly of architects, she looks visibly moved by Pei's remarks. Her choice of Pei literally made Pei's career. It led to important commissions to extend the National Gallery in Washington and to build the glass pyramid that has become such a distinctive feature of the Louvre in Paris. She continued to support Pei long after the Kennedy Library was built, going to the party to dedicate

the new National Gallery, traveling to Paris to see his redesign of the Louvre entrance, and going to China for the opening of his Fragrant Hill Hotel in 1982. So one of the lesser-known legacies of Camelot that has to be attributed to her are these striking buildings of glass and steel, both at home and abroad, which Pei might never have been invited to design if she had not first given him her seal of approval.

Jackie was not only a builder. She was also someone who read carefully through the memoirs and histories written by her former husband's staff members as they came out in the 1960s. She made detailed criticisms and asked for changes. Ted Sorensen recalled her comments on his draft of the book that became *Kennedy,* published in 1965: "She wanted me to delete or at least modify virtually every favorable reference I had made to Johnson." Where Sorensen's manuscript said that "JFK 'learned from Lyndon Johnson,' she said emphatically, 'I don't think he learned anything about campaigning from Lyndon Johnson—because Lyndon's style always embarrassed him, especially when he sent him around the world as

Vice-President.' Where my draft mentioned 'a deep mutual respect' between JFK and LBJ, she commented, 'I think you overstate this a bit—from JFK's side. But it doesn't matter.' Then she crossed out that last sentence. It mattered to her," Sorensen concluded.

When Pei's library was finally ready to dedicate, in 1979, she stage-managed the dedication ceremony, saying that she would never invite former president Nixon. She had always thought that President Johnson was absurdly puffed up and proud of his presidential status, but his widow had to be included in the ceremony, Jackie felt. While she and Nancy Tuckerman were in Boston for the library dedication, they traveled quietly in an inconspicuous taxi. By contrast, when a motorcade with motorcycle outriders and a limousine forced their cab to the side of the highway, Jackie looked through the window and observed with her deadpan humor, "Oh look, Nancy, there goes Lady Bird."

Jackie also occasionally put in her oar at Harvard, where funds had been collected to name the school of government after JFK and found the Institute of Politics. The idea was to encourage young people to enter politics with the same kind of youthful idealism that had inspired JFK. When it came to her attention in the later 1960s that Harvard was using the money to bring in retired politicians and sponsor scholarship that she thought was obscure, she wrote a letter of protest, saying that Harvard was abusing the Kennedys' generosity. The institute was becoming a place for retired has-beens, when she had hoped for excellence and originality. Her letter of protest was never sent. Sorensen thought that she was wrong and that Harvard was doing just as it should with the money. Nevertheless, her unsent letter shows the psychology of her continuing wish to establish her version of Camelot. The Harvard institutions, she said, had been created "by the love and grief and sacrifice and effort" of those who had believed most in JFK. Working on the Kennedy Library, she added, had "helped us to overcome grief," but she wasn't content to leave it at that. She wanted to remain actively involved with the foundations she had set in motion and to ensure that they were making themselves felt in the political world.

Maxims of Political Survival and Skulduggery

Once Jackie went to Viking and then to Doubleday, her efforts to be sure the Kennedy era was remembered shifted from bricks to books. One of her first books at Viking was a biography of Chicago's Mayor Daley that vindicated Jack Kennedy's election as president in 1960. She approached Eugene Kennedy with the idea of doing a Daley biography soon after joining Viking in 1975. Jimmy Breslin, a journalist in New York, whom she may well have known via his fellow journalist Pete Hamill, brought Kennedy's work to her attention. She didn't tell Kennedy that she wanted him to investigate the story that Daley's corrupt manipulation of Chicago's ballot boxes had delivered JFK's razor-thin margin of victory over Richard Nixon. She didn't have to.

After Kennedy agreed to write the biography, they decided it might be a good idea if Jackie flew out to Chicago to help him gain Daley's cooperation. He proposed that they meet somewhere nice, quiet, French. "No," she replied, "someplace low-down and dirty"; an ordinary hamburger joint would be fine. Did she need special arrangements to protect her from being accosted? "Oh, no—I never want anything like that! The best thing we can do is just walk fast." Daley defeated them both. He did not turn up, pleading urgent city business at the last minute.

The 1976 Democratic convention was coming up that summer in New York. Kennedy and Jackie figured that they might corner the mayor there. Daley was certain to attend, and he could not turn down a meeting with her if she found him in such a public place. When they finally found Mayor Daley and told him that they wanted to write and publish his biography, with his cooperation, he was not pleased. Eugene Kennedy remembered, "He loved Jackie, but the slight quiver in his jowls meant that he wanted no part of it." Although he was for a moment disconcerted, the wily old politician said, "I'll look into it." He offered no further cooperation, and Kennedy was forced to go ahead and do his research without the mayor's help.

Daley died later that year, while in his twenty-first year as mayor and reigning boss of one of America's oldest political machines. This increased the pressure for Kennedy to finish his work and get his book out as quickly as possible. Jackie helped him. In those early days she was not a line editor. She worked with other editors, such as Viking's Cork Smith, who knew the business better than she did and handled details, but Jackie was a kind of Guenevere who had connections to help authors that other editors didn't have. She helped Kennedy get interviews with former members of JFK's staff, such as Larry O'Brien, and she shared her personal recollections of Daley. She told Kennedy that Daley could have asked for anything in the way of political patronage after the 1960 election, but all he wanted was to spend one night in the White House with Mrs. Daley.

Kennedy and Jackie also discussed the Irish Catholic immigrant background that Mayor Daley shared with JFK's family. She was clear-eyed about the way in which nineteenth-century urban corruption had lasted well into the twentieth century. Kennedy said, "She understood all that. She used to talk about Boss Plunkitt and his maxims of political survival and political skulduggery," referring to a book one of New York's Tammany Hall machine politicians had written. Kennedy's biography of Daley devotes considerable space to showing the legitimacy of Daley's election-night machinations on JFK's behalf. Jackie, however, had no illusions about the sort of foul play that went on in Democratic political machines. Kennedy's book set out in detail how the Cook County vote for Kennedy was legal, but his conversations with Jackie indicated her acknowledgment that skulduggery may also have been in play.

A similar kind of contradiction in her defense of JFK's legacy is evident in subsequent books she commissioned from Eugene Kennedy. JFK had to overcome negative religious stereotypes in order to be elected the first Roman Catholic president, but two of the other books she and Kennedy did together contributed to some of the worst stereotypes possible about Roman Catholic politics. Eugene Kennedy wrote several novels for Jackie after she moved to Doubleday. One of them, *Father's Day* (1981), centers on underhanded political maneuvering in the running of Notre Dame, America's premier Roman Catholic university. The other, *Fixes* (1989), is about dirty politics at work in the Vatican, where angling cardinals, a saint, and the CIA are all involved in getting a new pope elected after the old one dies. In publishing Eugene Kennedy's fiction, Jackie was underscoring negative images still associated with the Roman Catholic Church in the minds of many Americans of other faiths.

Nor was Jackie entirely consistent in her attitude toward biographers. Her editorial colleague Lisa Drew remembered how much she hated to see anything written about her. When John Kenneth Galbraith sent her a copy of his letter refusing to speak to one biographer who wanted to write about her, she thanked him, adding that now she knew "chivalry is not dead." She hoped to control her biography even beyond the grave, and she included in her will a line instructing her children to resist the publication of her letters. Yet she had been willing to try to maneuver Mayor Daley into agreeing to a biography by cornering him at the convention and using her fame to compel him to cooperate. Judith Martin at the *Washington Post,* better known as Miss Manners, pressed Jackie on the question of how she could be the editor of several biographies, some of which were unauthorized by their subjects, when she was legendarily so resistant to having her own biography written. Jackie replied, "When it's past, it becomes history." Martin asked whether she would mind if a historian were someday to publish her unpublished letters. Jackie said disingenuously, "I won't be here to mind." She later made sure that the lawyers writing her will knew that she minded very much.

Jackie also suggested in a casual conversation with her Doubleday colleague Tom Cahill, the religion editor, that he should commission a biography of Cardinal Cushing, a priest whom she knew well and admired. Cushing had officiated at her marriage to JFK, at the inauguration, and at JFK's funeral mass. When Cahill pursued her idea and signed up a biographer to write about Cushing, Jackie had Nancy Tuckerman write a formal letter to Cahill, whose office was adjacent to hers, saying that under no circumstances could this biographer quote from her correspondence with Cushing. It had been Jackie's idea to do the biography of a man whose fame in part rested on his association with her. When Cahill pressed her on this, she told him he wouldn't understand, but as a woman who was under the thumb first of her father, then of her two husbands, she had gotten used to obeying; now that she was free, she was going to do whatever she could to control her words. The tenor of this defense, and her belief in the power of words, sounds very much like Jackie. It's hard to blame the woman for wanting a private life, but because she delighted as a reader in knowing the private lives of the men and women whose biographies she commissioned, it is worth questioning whether she didn't sometimes rather abuse the power she had acquired as Guenevere. Compromising other people's privacy in order to achieve a good biography was one of her editorial priorities. Protecting her privacy and stopping biographies from being written about her own life was among her foremost personal priorities.

In Which Jackie Goes Hiking

Before Stewart Udall died in March 2010, at the age of ninety, he was the last living member of the Kennedy cabinet. He had had a distinguished career, serving as a congressman from Arizona, before joining the administration as interior secretary and adding large acreage to the national parks under both President Kennedy and President Johnson. He also presided over the establishment of the first federally protected national seashores. He was an early voice speaking in favor of the protection of the environment, publicizing the work of Rachel Carson, whose *Silent Spring* alerted readers to the hazards of pesticides, and writing his own *Quiet Crisis* (1963), for which JFK wrote the introduction.

Udall and his wife, Lee, retired from Washington in the 1980s and moved back to Arizona. In his native part of the country and newly aware of the presence of Spanish-speakers in that part of the world, he wondered why Americans paid so little attention to the Spanish dimension of their history. Udall also remembered with shame the social division between whites and Latinos in St. Johns, Arizona, where he had grown up. He wrote a magazine article for *Arizona Highways* in which he and a photographer, Jerry Jacka, traced the trail of the Spanish explorer Francisco Vásquez de Coronado, who had traveled up from Mexico through Arizona, New Mexico, and other parts of what is now the American Southwest in the 1540s. Purely "on impulse," and after a long lapse in their friendship, Udall sent a copy of his magazine article to Jackie in New York and suggested that together they should make a book out of it. Jackie telephoned Udall in Arizona and said, "Let's do it."

Before the contract could be signed or prepared, Udall and his wife invited Jackie and Maurice Tempelsman to visit in Arizona so they could see for themselves a little of the geography Coronado had explored. In June 1984 the four joined photographer Jerry Jacka and his wife to hike part of the trail that Udall had earlier hiked with Jacka. There had been some trepidation about the visitors from New York. Udall characterized himself and his wife as "small-town Mormon kids who grew up on the Colorado plateau." Although the Udalls knew Jackie from the White House years, she had been busy raising small children then. Speaking in a gravelly voice, Udall recollected, "She stood up magnificently in the period after the president's death." He paused, as if to reflect. "Then she married Onassis." Another pregnant silence. "I believe some money was involved." Although he had known her personally in the 1960s, the woman arriving on the plane in the 1980s was almost as much of a stranger to him as she was to millions of other Americans.

Jerry Jacka remembered that Udall had planned "a rather rigorous journey" for the hiking trip. "I had a new 1984 Chevrolet Suburban and we literally broke it in on that trip. We were all in this Suburban, bouncing along, when Lee Udall and Jackie began to share stories from the White

House days." One was about LBJ. The women carried on and laughed. Jacka recalled, "My wife and I are just a couple of country kids and here we were listening to all these revelations about the high life in Washington." Tempelsman, Stewart and Lee Udall, and Jackie, with Jerry and Lois Jacka in front of them, all posed comfortably together, however, for a snapshot on their hike with Canyon de Chelly in the background.

"Stewart wanted to take them into a beautiful canyon," Jacka continued. "We stayed that night at the Thunderbird Lodge, a nice place, but we were out late, and when we got back the café at the Thunderbird was closed. We had to stop at a little dive in Chinle, Arizona, for supper. It was fairly clean. There were just a few tables covered in oilcloth. We had Navajo tacos. Jackie had ice cream to follow, because the tacos were a little hot. A Navajo woman came out, bringing with her a little girl, and said to Jackie, 'Will you shake hands with my daughter?'"

When they stopped for lunch, they each had a plastic cup of wine to celebrate having made it to the other side on a difficult crossing of the Black River. The Jackas went as far as Acoma Pueblo, a historic community believed to have been continuously inhabited since the twelfth century. Jacka remembered that Jackie "was a delightful sport. At Acoma, rather than go up the tourist trail to the pueblo, the tribe gave us permission to go up the old hand-carved stairway in the stone, which probably dated back to the time of Coronado." The Jackas left at Acoma, and a prominent Native American artist, Lloyd Kiva New, and his wife joined the party and took them beyond that to Santa Fe.

It was a spectacular trip for Jackie, and she told the Udalls she had been "absolutely knocked out by the beauty of all that we saw. It affected me much more deeply than going to India." She also confessed that although they had shared the experi-

ence of working together in Washington, she hadn't really known them then. "What made me happiest about this trip was really becoming friends—with so many wonderful things ahead to look forward to." Jackie and the Udalls did become friends. When Stewart and Lee Udall went to New York, they often had supper with Jackie and Tempelsman. This did not stop the editor and the writer from arguing over Udall's book manuscript, however. Perhaps it helped them, as we only really argue with people we like. It also shows the new, more confident woman that Jackie had become.

The trouble centered on the "revisionist essay" on the Coronado trail that Udall wanted in his book. His argument was that compared with the historical record of the others who conquered and settled what would become the United States, the Spanish settlement was "more humane, more compassionate." Jackie objected. She thought to call Spanish colonizers "compassionate" was to ignore the record of the Spanish Inquisition as well as related Spanish crimes in Latin America and elsewhere. "I wish you would rewrite it," she told Udall in a five-page, single-spaced letter with her detailed criticisms. Using a colloquial idiom, she wrote, "You can't brush off the Inquisition in half a sentence, as an unfair rap that has been laid on the Spaniards." She thought his argument would open the book to criticism. She also objected to his writing of the "myth of Spanish cruelty." She pointed out that "they were cruel to some Indians, they love bullfights, the Indian population of Latin America has been decimated today . . . Just stop pushing here." She wanted something more understated, because fundamentally she agreed with him and admired much of the Spanish tradition in the Americas. She even said that she "used to wish the Spanish instead of the Puritans had colonized New England." At the end of this long letter, in which she was as tough with Udall as she was with any of her other authors, she softened her remarks by writing, "Give my love to Lee. Happy Valentine's Day," and drew in a little heart. A year later, when the book was ready to come out, she wrote to ask for a copy of his signature to go on a bag that would be handed out as a promotional gift at a Doubleday sales conference. "Only the Most Important authors go on it," she wrote in teasing capital letters.

Doubleday published *To the Inland Empire: Coronado and Our Spanish Legacy* in 1987. It is a handsome book with spectacular color photographs, dedicated to the wives of Udall and Jacka, Lee and Lois, as well as to Jackie, "the three who made it happen." The book has the marked nostalgic element that is a feature of so many of Jackie's books. In the conclusion, Udall quotes from an Archibald MacLeish poem that imagined the thoughts of the sixteenth-century conquistador Bernal Díaz when he returned to Spain from America, near death, and reflected on the boldness of his expedition to another continent:

> *I: poor as I am: I was young in that country:*
> *These words were my life: these letters written*
> *Cold on the page with the spilt ink and the shunt of the*
> *Stubborn thumb: these marks at my fingers:*
> *These are the shape of my own life . . . .*
> > *and I hunted the*
>
> *Unknown birds in the west with their beautiful wings!*

This was Udall reflecting on the metaphorical birds with their beautiful wings of his own former career as well. His book was the cause for at least one political reunion, as Jackie invited a whole range of Kennedy-era appointees and cabinet members to the book party at Doubleday, and the *Washington Post* ran highlights of the party's guest list. The Spanish government honored Udall by knighting him.

Jackie shared some of Udall's trips down memory lane. But it wasn't JFK's Camelot to which she gave tribute in this book so much as it was her own. Another of her literary themes, the decisive presence of European influence and culture in American history, had attracted her to Udall's story in the first place. What was even more important to her was to have made new friends outside her marriage to her first husband, to have explored new territory with the Udalls, to have met artists like Jerry Jacka and Lloyd Kiva New, and to have produced a book remarkable for its stunning photography. She wrote to the Udalls in 1993, "Please tell Lloyd I still have his red shirt that he gave me—in fact I wore it two days ago." When Jackie's cancer was announced to the press early in 1994, Lee Udall wrote to Jackie to express concern. To reassure Lee that everything was fine and she mustn't worry, Jackie said that she was still wearing Lloyd Kiva New's red denim shirt. She added, "You gave me one of the most heart-stopping experiences of my love [*sic;* she meant "life"] and I love you both for it."

Crossing Swords with Alabama's George Wallace

Jackie could spend hours poring over glossy photographs of vermeil cutlery with John Loring, but she also wanted to publish the history of inequality and racism in America. In two books she preserved not only episodes in the career of JFK but also some of the political ideas of Robert Kennedy, who became especially concerned about race and poverty in his political career after his brother's death. Neither work was merely a tribute to brothers whom she had loved, however. They were also her selections of particular stories and personalities that appealed to her.

Carl Elliott was an eight-term Democratic member of the House of Representatives who served between 1949 and 1965. He spoke on behalf of the poor, especially coal miners in his district, since he himself had made it through the University of Alabama on a special program that allowed poor students to defray their tuition by working. He worked on the National Defense Education Act of 1958, which helped more students enter college via a student loan program. He eventually lost his seat because of redistricting and staked all his savings on running for governor against Lurleen Wallace in the 1960s. She was running as a proxy for her husband, George Wallace, who had already served the maximum number of successive terms under the state's law. The election was hard fought. The pro-segregationist Wallace sent Ku Klux Klan members to appear at Elliott's election rallies, and there were threats of violence. Elliott lost, and later borrowed from his government pension to pay for his election campaign. He then retired into renewed poverty and obscurity, until 1990, when the John F. Kennedy Library, under Jackie's and Caroline Kennedy's auspices, instituted the Profiles in Courage Award. The idea was to memorialize JFK's prizewinning book, *Profiles in Courage,* and recognize the courage of living politicians who had put principle before self-interest. Carl Elliott was the first winner. Though confined to a wheelchair, he went to Boston to accept the award from Jackie, Caroline, and Ted Kennedy.

Elliott decided to use some of the prize money, along with an advance on royalties from Doubleday, to retire what remained of his debt and to write his autobiography. Jackie thought he needed some help, so she contacted Mike D'Orso, who had helped with the writing of *Somerset Homecoming,* and asked him to contribute. D'Orso said of Jackie's request, "The way she approached it was, 'This is a great story,' *not* how

much it meant to JFK." Elliott's wife had died, and he was living alone in a dilapidated house in his coal-mining region of Alabama. Weeds were growing through the windows and the roof leaked. He had sacrificed his political career in a show-down with George Wallace in the 1960s, and now, thirty years later, he had the chance to tell his side of the story.

D'Orso went down to Alabama and lived with Carl Elliott for five months. "It was tough living with him," said D'Orso. "Physically he's a big man. He sat in a wheelchair in his pajamas all day long. When it would rain I'd put pots under the drips. I slept upstairs in his and his wife's bedroom." Elliott was now unable to climb the stairs. "Sometimes I'd make us a sandwich for lunch. We'd sit in the evenings and watch the Gulf War on TV." D'Orso remembered it all as especially depressing because he was going through a divorce himself. Jackie knew this. She would call him up to ask how he was doing. They had several long conversations about D'Orso's relationship with his wife. "To me it felt like I was just talk-ing to a friend. She was a good friend to me." It would only occur to him after he had hung up the phone that he'd just been pouring his heart out to a woman who had been famously involved in difficult marital relations herself.

Afterward she would sometimes invite D'Orso to New York to have lunch together. But he loved what they had on the phone: "I sensed the fragility of it." He didn't want to endanger it and didn't have any stargazing need to do it. He thought going to New York and having lunch with "Jackie O.," in quotation marks, would ruin it. She was the only person who supported him in that season. Even his friends got tired of hearing his story.

When Carl Elliott's *Cost of Courage* came out, in 1992, Jackie sent a copy to every congressman in Washington as well as to all the justices of the Supreme Court. The responses she got were mixed. Some were handwritten thanks mentioning the themes and incidents of the book. Others were recollections of times the correspondent had spent with her in Washington. Phil Gramm, Republican senator from Texas, sent Jackie a form letter saying, "Thank you for your interest in my work." John Seymour, Republican senator from California, wrote, "I am sure this novel will make a fine addition to my personal library." Jackie circled "novel" and put a happy face under it.

The book represented some of the progress Jackie had made in reaching a sense of proportion about JFK's achievement. Whereas she had wanted to micromanage passages by Schlesinger and Sorensen in the 1960s, by the time Elliott's book came to be written, in the 1990s, she could tolerate unflattering references to her former husband. In the midst of generally admiring allusions to Kennedy, Elliott did recall that as a young congressman Kennedy had been capable of making crass remarks about money when he had just been given $2 million by his father. At the same time he opposed legislation to bring libraries to rural poor people. Jackie read this in draft before it was published and did not object.

The following year another book on a crusading and courageous southerner, *Taming the Storm: The Life and Times of Judge Frank M. Johnson Jr. and the South's Fight over Civil Rights,* appeared on Jackie's list. Johnson was a federal judge who made landmark antisegregation rulings in the 1960s, including orders to desegregate the transportation system of Montgomery, Alabama, to allow black people to serve on juries, and to prevent the state from discouraging voter registration among blacks. A Johnson decision also forced Governor George Wallace to allow the last of three famous Selma-to-Montgomery civil rights marches in 1965, led in part by Martin Luther King, Jr. Johnson was a Republican. As a result of his rulings, a cross was burned on the judge's lawn, his mother's house was bombed, and he had to be put under constant protection by a federal marshal.

In 1978, a decade after Robert Kennedy's assassination, his second son published a biography of Johnson. The next year Jackie was in touch with Judge Frank Johnson to see whether he would write his autobiography. He sent her a proposal and completed about a third of his manuscript. Johnson's wife remembered later that Johnson didn't have the time to finish it and Jackie couldn't offer an advance substantial enough to buy him time for it. Ten years later—a long time to carry a torch for a book—Jackie and Johnson were still corresponding about how to get his book into print. At about the same time Jack Bass, a newspaper journalist who had recently left journalism for academia, approached Johnson and told him he'd like to write about him. Judge Johnson had been profiled in Bass's previous book *Unlikely Heroes,* edited by Alice Mayhew at Simon & Schuster. Bass had asked Mayhew whether she would sponsor a full-scale biography of Johnson. She had responded with interest but added that such a biography might be only "a regional book," an editor's way of saying, "Hmmm, this is small potatoes. I'm not thrilled." Bass passed on Mayhew's verdict to Judge Johnson, who told him he should try Jacqueline Onassis instead.

Bass immediately had his proposal for the book sent to Jackie, and within a few days he heard that she was interested and wanted him to sign a contract. Bass's biography traced Johnson's life, beginning with his upbringing in an unusual Alabama county where more men fought with the Union than with the Confederacy in the Civil War. It described the violent showdowns with George Wallace in the 1960s and noted how at the end of Johnson's career, when Wallace sought his forgiveness for the personal attacks Wallace had made on him, Johnson replied that "if he wanted forgiveness, he'd have to get it from the Lord." The book received accolades from former Chief Justice Warren Burger and former president Jimmy Carter. Senator Harris Wofford quoted Martin Luther King, Jr., in his *New York Times* review, saying that the judge's rulings "gave true meaning to the word 'justice.'"

One of Bass's friends had told him that he needed to hire a line editor for detailed revisions of his book, as Doubleday wouldn't provide that sort of thing. "I called Shaye Areheart and asked, 'Who's going to be the line editor?'" he remembered. "Mrs. Onassis," replied Shaye. Bass thought Jackie was a "terrific editor. Certainly the best editor I've ever had." With his previous books he hadn't had much contact with the editor beyond the acquisition stage, but Jackie told him directly where his manuscript needed work. She wanted extensive cuts; about a quarter of the manuscript he had submitted to her had to go. He cut about 17 percent and said that was the most he could do. "In retrospect," he noted, "I should have cut more." Jackie was right.

Bass recalled asking her why she had taken on his book. "She kind of looked at me and said, 'I guess it goes back to the

White House and hearing Jack and Bobby talk about Judge Johnson.'" He felt a little anxious, as his account of Martin Luther King's release from jail, when he had been imprisoned unjustly because of a minor traffic violation in 1960, didn't give the credit to Robert Kennedy, as several other books had. Bass told a more complex story. Both Kennedy brothers were interested in securing King's release because it might help JFK's presidential campaign. King's imprisonment was an injustice that concerned them, but they were also afraid of offending bigoted southern white voters. Bass considered this a different and less flattering story than Sorensen and Schlesinger had told about the episode. "RFK is not the hero," Bass said. "Jackie didn't know until she read my story." She didn't flinch. Instead, she took Bass to lunch upstairs at New York's '21' and said simply, "You are a very good investigative reporter." It was part of Jackie's rewriting of Camelot in the 1990s: if Jack and Bobby didn't always turn out to be quite the heroes they had been made out to be, it was all right with her.

There is an ironic footnote to Jackie's publication of these two books about men who crusaded, at significant personal cost, against the power of George Wallace. After she died, her son, John, chose to publish an article on Wallace in the inaugural issue of his magazine, *George*. The magazine's title referred to George Washington, but its editor flew south to interview another George—Wallace himself. Although late in life Wallace had spoken of his error in supporting segregationist policies, John Kennedy's provocative editorial move was something his mother might not have approved of. Still, John Updike noted after John Kennedy died in an airplane accident in 1999 that the young man had gone through a transition in his life that was a silent tribute to his mother. Although he had started out in law school, grooming himself for a political career modeled on his father's, he ended as an editor, doing work that was modeled on what his mother did at Doubleday.

A Spy Story

It is hard to recapture the way that everyone from the 1950s through the early 1990s worried about nuclear war with the Russians. This war that never happened was a frame for Jackie's life as well. The desk at which JFK had signed the Nuclear Test Ban Treaty in 1963 sat in her apartment at 1040 Fifth Avenue. In her editorial career she published a novel by David Wise, *The Samarkand Dimension* (1987), in which a CIA operative spies on the Soviets, and Jack Valenti's novel about the presidency, in which the cold war is a backdrop. Oddly enough, when it came time to consider *Vogue*'s invitation to join the staff after she won the Prix de Paris in the 1950s, she told the editors that she might have to take a job she was considering at the CIA, which was nearer her home.

When Jackie went with Tom Hoving to Russia for the first time in the 1970s, there was something rather daring about it, as travel behind what was called the Iron Curtain was not common then. It was even more daring for her and Vreeland to sponsor works at the Costume Institute that celebrated the era of the tsars and the Russian aristocracy at a time when American politics revolved around trying to set up careful, nonconfrontational exchanges with a regime that defined itself as the people's antithesis to royal Romanov rule. Jackie also became friends with Leonid Tarassuk, a former curator of Arms and Armor from the Hermitage who ran afoul of the Soviet system. When he was a young man, his apartment was bugged, possibly as a result of survival supplies he and his cousin had hidden away in a cave in the Crimea. Remarks critical of the government were recorded, and Tarassuk spent time in a Soviet prison. After his release he was allowed to rejoin the staff of the Hermitage in a diminished position. Tarassuk and his family were Jewish, and when he applied to emigrate to Israel in the 1970s, the Soviet government fired him from his job at the Hermitage, as the application alone was considered "anti-Soviet." His plight came to the attention of Americans, along with that of some other prominent Soviet Jews, including the dancer Valery Panov and his wife, who were also harassed by the Soviets. With the help of American sponsors, the Tarassuks left Russia in 1973, spent some time in Israel, and then came to New York in 1975. Tarassuk later joined the staff of the Metropolitan Museum as an expert in the Arms and Armor department. Jackie's friend Karl Katz introduced her to Tarassuk, and Tarassuk helped her write captions and introductory remarks for *In the Russian Style*. When the book received a hostile review in the *New York Review of Books,* Tarassuk leapt to Jackie's defense. Tarassuk's daughter, Irina, remembered Jackie coming to visit them at their New York apartment. She was stunning not only in her appearance—she always had her dark glasses on—but also in her demeanor. As a joke, Irina's father once framed one of the cigarette butts this elegant woman had left behind.

Tarassuk and his wife died in an automobile accident while they were on vacation in France in 1990. Jackie sent a large bouquet of flowers to their memorial service and contributed to a fund organized to support the Tarassuks' children. Then, on New Year's Eve 1991, a man—a stranger to her—faxed an odd story about Tarassuk to Jackie's assistant at Doubleday. Philip Myers was an attorney from Santa Barbara who had business in the high-tech industry. His work had taken him to the Soviet Union in the summer of 1991, and there a colleague had told him that Leonid Tarassuk had been part of a small band of spies who volunteered to work on behalf of the United States, with the goal of alerting America if the Soviets tried to launch a nuclear first strike. Tarassuk, Myers learned, had also collaborated with Jacqueline Onassis on one of her first books at Viking.

Myers thought this story would make a great book, maybe a film, so he faxed a summary of what he had discovered to Jackie. He didn't expect to hear back from her right away, if at all. He was shocked when he found a message from her on his answering machine a few days later, asking him to call her back at Doubleday. "I'm fascinated by what you sent me," she said, sounding less like her whispery-voiced White House self than a polite but busy editor, talking fast with a New York accent. "Holy smokes!" Myers thought to himself when he played her message. He called her back, expecting to deal with someone aloof and reserved. When she came on the phone, he found himself talking to what he described as "the most funny, unguarded, candid person imaginable." She was intrigued by the idea that her friend had been an undercover spy, but she found Myers's story about Tarassuk convoluted. There were parts Myers wasn't willing to disclose, even to her, for fear of endangering his Russian contacts. When Myers shared some of his cloak-and-dagger concerns with her, she replied, "You're going to end up squished in a trash can somewhere." She began taking Myers's story around to her contacts. She ran it by Steve Rubin at Doubleday. She also approached Bob Silvers at the *New York Review of Books,* who encouraged her to believe that the periodical might run an article on Tarassuk and other cold war spies. She also went to Mort Janklow, one of New York's most prominent literary agents, and asked him whether Myers's story might work for Hollywood. She mentioned Jann Wenner and Mike Nichols as people she thought might be interested. Myers's head was spinning. One minute Jackie was an impossibly distant figure; the next she was working the phones and trying to sell his idea to the most powerful people in the media business.

Rubin rejected the idea. With the end of the cold war, he told Jackie, they had too many Russian books in the pipeline. Janklow said the story was still too confusing for him to be able to sell it to the film business, although he asked to be kept informed if she did turn it into a book. Myers and Jackie decided to go it alone, with Jackie helping him outline what further research he would need to do to make his story viable. This wasn't something she was being paid for; her interest in the story was what drove her. She also told Myers she considered Tarassuk to be a hero of the cold war. She reported to Myers a conversation she had had with Karl Katz in which he had speculated that maybe the Tarassuks' car crash hadn't been an accident; maybe it was some sort of Soviet revenge for Tarassuk's having worked for the Americans. This surprised Myers, because it hadn't come up in his discussion with his Russian contacts. Myers was also shocked because "for someone who was supposed to crave privacy and stand above the fray, it seemed like a pretty dicey thing to pass along to me, a comparative stranger."

Myers began the research program he and Jackie had discussed, requesting Tarassuk's files from the American intelligence services under the Freedom of Information Act. When the file arrived, 90 percent of it was blacked out. Clearly there was something to hide. The high level of welcome the Tarassuks had received from American officials when they arrived in the 1970s indicated this, too. Their daughter, Irina, remembered that her father had met with both Henry Kissinger and President Nixon—pretty good for someone who was supposed to be simply a museum curator who knew about historic guns.

The first time Myers met with Jackie in her office at Doubleday, she once again surprised him. She appeared at the end of a corridor, striding toward the reception area to meet him and looking like an athlete in her thirties rather than a former first lady in her sixties. Her office was also "a big shock." Myers had imagined "something grand, with parquet floors and museum-quality paintings." Instead it was tiny, dominated by what looked like an army-issue Formica-topped desk. The floor was linoleum. In this strange room, the story deepened, for here Jackie recalled Tarassuk as "a refined Old World gentleman." D'Artagnan from Alexandre Dumas's *Three Musketeers* had been his hero. He and Jackie had spoken French together. "I loved the man," said Jackie. She said it in a restrained, detached way, as if she were speaking about a work of art rather than a man, but the honesty of it still surprised Myers.

When Myers told her that he had been in touch with Nixon's former chief of staff, H. R. Haldeman, who had been convicted for his role in the Watergate scandal, Jackie wasn't pleased. She said Haldeman was "a felon," but she did ask with curiosity if he "still had his short funny hair," gesturing with a chopping motion over the top of her head to indicate Haldeman's famous crew cut. Nevertheless, Haldeman had furnished Myers with a key piece of the puzzle that the Tarassuk story had become. He said that art museums like the Metropolitan, the Getty, and the National Gallery were all routinely used as covers by CIA operatives. It lent credibility to the idea that Tarassuk had been working for the intelligence services under the cover of his curatorial work for the Met. Myers believed that some lines about Jackie and Tarassuk in Tom Hoving's memoir, *Making the Mummies Dance,* that didn't align with what his Russian sources had told him or what the newspapers had reported, were the result of intentional obfuscation on Hoving's part, spreading disinformation to cover up the spying activity that was going on at the Metropolitan.

When Myers proposed interviewing former president Nixon, Jackie "recoiled in horror" and was adamantly opposed to Myers's idea. Nevertheless, she was still on board with the project. She ended the meeting by putting on a full-length black leather coat as she prepared to walk out with him and go to lunch. She struck him as free, unafraid, and determined to follow the story wherever it led.

Myers began receiving some odd telephone calls that seemed to be timed just in advance of his meetings with Jackie. In one there had been no voice, just a recording of Gregorian chants. This led Myers to wonder whether there was some Vatican connection to the Tarassuk story. Tarassuk had been imprisoned in the Soviet Union with Cardinal Slipyj, a figure in both the Eastern Orthodox and Roman Catholic churches whose freedom in 1963 had been won partially through lobbying by both Pope John XXIII and President Kennedy. Still, Jackie was not afraid, and according to Myers "was clearly delighted with the whole effort, and was enjoying robustly the adventure of it all." She even agreed to meet with Myers's prime Russian contact, who came to New York in the fall of 1992. She met with both men in her apartment, and she gave a copy of *Profiles in Courage* to Myers's Russian friend, signing it not "Jacqueline Onassis," but "Jacqueline Kennedy." She had slipped back into her role as the heroine of Camelot.

Jackie died before Myers could finish the research for his story, though she had Nancy Tuckerman write to him and acknowledge one of his letters in the week before she died. Even though the Tarassuk story was becoming more bizarre and approaching dimensions of her life in the White House that he thought she would never consider, she was still giving Myers her encouragement. After her death, the Tarassuk story

opened up on stranger avenues still. She had believed that it was about a courageous group of pro-American spies who had risked their lives to warn the Americans about Soviet nuclear plans. After her death, Myers believed that he had uncovered information that Tarassuk was working on behalf of the American government when he was at the Met to acquire guns for covert American operations. He was also mixed up with a shady character, well known among gun collectors and prominent in the effort to get the Tarassuks out of Russia, called Larry Wilson, who later served time in a federal prison. Myers had a creased picture of Tarassuk in this era, standing before a cache of weapons, holding a gun with a price tag. It doesn't look like it's a museum-quality piece.

Irina Tarassuk posed for *Playboy*. She moved to Atlanta, married, and opened a catering business. She became a Rottweiler fancier and started rescue work to save endangered Rottweiler puppies. She recalled that Jackie had reassured her about Myers when he first approached her and her brother out of the blue. Jackie had faxed her a three-page letter saying that Myers was "naïve," with an off-putting manner, and "very American," but she also said she thought Irina could trust him. Jackie told Myers that helping the Tarassuk children was one of the prime reasons why she was still involved.

There the story still stands, intriguingly and mysteriously half finished. In the spy-following fraternity, belief in high-level conspiracies is common. One would have expected Jackie, who had to endure a lifetime of speculation about whether there had been a Soviet or other high-level conspiracy to murder JFK, to have steered well clear of such a tale. Here she was, however, countenancing Philip Myers as he connected the dots between the Soviet Union, the CIA, the Vatican, and the Kennedy presidency, although we do not know if she believed it all.

Nancy Tuckerman remembered how courageous Jackie could be, even to the extent of foolhardiness. She would go out to jog around the reservoir in Central Park on the edge of evening in the face of sensational newspaper reports about how women were being attacked there. Jackie was a fighter, a crusader, a woman determined to be her own historian and to endorse her own stories about what she and Jack and Bobby Kennedy cared about. She was dedicated to remembering the country's Spanish heritage as much as her husband's Irish ancestry, and she memorialized the sacrifices of those who fought George Wallace at home and Soviet power abroad. That multidimensional, multifaceted part of her personality also helped make her what she is now: America's most powerful myth.

chapter 12

THE POWER OF MYTH

— The book Jackie edited of which she was proudest

•

In September 1995, looking like a cross between JFK and Black Jack Bouvier, John Kennedy, Jr., stood before the press in a dark suit and tie, with a white handkerchief rakishly tucked into his breast pocket. It was the year after his mother died and he was launching his magazine. *George,* he told the assembled reporters, would investigate the connections between celebrity and politics. "The marriage of publishing and politics," he explained, "simply weaves together two strands of my family's business." He might have said three strands, because ever since the 1920s, when Joseph Kennedy, Sr., started making Hollywood films, celebrity had been a strand of the family enterprise, too.

John made the rounds of the television talk shows to promote his magazine. His pitch was that the magazine would be an irreverent, insider's look at politics. Larry King briefly disarmed him by saying that his mother had been a success in publishing at Doubleday and asking what she would think of this new publishing venture. Laughing, John remembered that when he had first mentioned his idea to her, she had asked him, "Well, John, you're not going to do the *MAD* magazine of politics, are you?" It was a typical Jackie move: wrap a criticism in an unexpected joke. Her son defended himself by saying to King, "I think she would have appreciated the fact that people always said that you can't do a fun magazine about politics, that combines the serious along with the playful." *George* would look at personalities, "because that's what public life is all about." In an interview with CBS News, John said the magazine would acknowledge that celebrities attract attention, which is an important dimension of how modern American politics works.

John was owning up to a dimension of his own appeal, his own celebrity, in a way that his mother never had. Jackie seemed forever camera-shy. She had disliked walking in the grounds at the White House because tourists could look through the shrubbery and she hated the idea of "starring in everybody's home movies." She would even refuse to show up at a party to launch one of her books if she thought too many cameras would be there. Perhaps the most intriguing thing about her work as an editor, then, was that she, too, like her son, although more covertly than he, explored the phenomenon of celebrity, of fame, even of what it meant when an ordinary person was transformed into a myth. In public she remained hidden behind her dark glasses, but at Doubleday she acknowledged to her colleagues that one of her special roles was sometimes to bring celebrity projects to the publisher. Her books on John Lennon and Michael Jackson show her behind the scenes, asking for answers to problems she had spent a lifetime dealing with herself. Further, Bill Moyers's PBS interviews with Joseph Campbell, *The Power of Myth,* delved into how the small and transient features of celebrity might be transformed into the large and eternal stories dealt with in mythology. She had seen the programs and she saw the potential for a book.

Across the Park from Jackie's Apartment

Annie Leibovitz was one of the last to see John Lennon alive, and the morning of his assassination she had taken one of her most iconic photographs of him. She captured Yoko Ono clothed and lying on the floor while the naked Lennon curled around her like a baby in a fetal position. The photo was to accompany a *Rolling Stone* interview by Jonathan Cott, scheduled to run in an upcoming issue. That morning Lennon had insisted that he and Yoko Ono be photographed together, although no one at the magazine thought it was a good idea. They wanted him alone. He was the real star.

Shortly after five that same December afternoon, Lennon and Ono left their apartment at the Dakota on Seventy-second Street, south of and on the other side of the park from Jackie at 1040 Fifth Avenue. They were on their way to a recording studio to mix a song on an album Ono was making. Before getting into their car, Lennon stopped to sign autographs. A crowd was nearly always assembled to see him come and go, and he frequently obliged fans by writing his name on the albums they'd brought. On December 8, 1980, one of the autograph seekers was Mark David Chapman, a twenty-five-year-old security guard from Hawaii. Lennon signed a copy of the album Chapman presented to him, *Double Fantasy,* which had been released only three weeks previously, and asked him, "Is that all you want?" Chapman didn't ask for anything more.

Six hours later, Lennon and Ono returned to Central Park West from the recording studio. It was nearly eleven at night. Ono went into the Dakota ahead of Lennon. As Lennon followed her into the building, Chapman stepped from the shadows of an interior archway and shot him four times in the back. One of the gunshots severed Lennon's aorta. Two policemen laid him on the back seat of their squad car to take him for help, but doctors pronounced him dead on arrival at New York's Roosevelt Hospital. Chapman sat quietly on the curb and waited to be arrested.

Ono declared that there would be no funeral, but memorial services were held around the world a week later, when fans observed ten minutes of silence, at Ono's request. More than 225,000 people went to the memorial service in Central Park alone. In the aftermath, at least two of Lennon's fans committed suicide. In the twentieth century, Lennon's assassination ranked with those of JFK, Martin Luther King, and Bobby Kennedy for the magnitude of the shock waves that spread around the country and the world. Though Lennon was not a politician or a clergyman, his songs embraced some of the same political idealism associated with the two Kennedys and King. For many, there was the same collective sense of disbelief and loss.

That sense was particularly poignant at *Rolling Stone*, which had followed Lennon's career almost from the beginning and to which Lennon had granted a number of privileged and searching interviews. Jann Wenner felt Lennon's death as a strong blow, but it did not blunt his publisher's instincts. Wenner backed an idea to convert the January 1981 issue of the magazine, which was already scheduled to carry Cott's interview with Lennon, into a special issue of the magazine memorializing the artist, and then to assemble all the different pieces the magazine had run on Lennon over the years, together with some new material, and publish them as a book. The magazine decided to have an auction for it among competing publishers. Wenner already had an offer of $25,000 before they began. In the competition, Doubleday bid $200,000, an enormous sum in the early 1980s, and won the deal. Jackie, as a friend of Wenner's, agreed to be the editor of the project. She was not in charge of the auction, if she was involved at all, but she did know that the book on Lennon was something that Doubleday had paid a huge amount for in advance and that a lot was riding on whether she could make it a success.

The book, a collaborative venture between *Rolling Stone* and Doubleday, appeared in 1982 as *The Ballad of John and Yoko*. "We thought *John and Yoko* would be a commercial project," remembered Wenner. "Jackie was always interested in taking commercial projects as well as the arcane stuff she liked." The book's appearance so soon after Lennon's death was not entirely an opportunistic commercial venture, however. Wenner had the contract written so that some of the profits would benefit the Foundation on Violence in America. This organization, founded by Wenner after Lennon's death, was a nonprofit dedicated to reducing handgun violence in America. In order to help him obtain support for his foundation in Washington, D.C., Jackie introduced Wenner to Sargent Shriver, who was married to JFK's sister Eunice and then a prominent lawyer in the capital. Wenner admitted that for Jackie, Lennon's death must have had an "unpleasant association, which she could have avoided and walked away from, but she didn't." She didn't want to be too prominently in the fore on gun control advocacy, but, Wenner pointed out, she was also "the principal sponsor of this book."

Jackie's friendship with Wenner had begun on sunnier slopes. He had been introduced to her by Dick Goodwin, a lawyer and speechwriter who assisted JFK, Lyndon Johnson, and Bobby Kennedy. Goodwin also wrote on politics for *Rolling Stone*. In the early days, Wenner and the magazine were out in California, but when they moved to New York, Jackie took Wenner and his wife under her wing, inviting them to parties and introducing them to her friends. She even went to the opening party for *Rolling Stone*'s new offices in New York and allowed herself to be photographed by Annie Leibovitz as she sat with Wenner, although her body language conveys distinct discomfort with having Leibovitz circling her in the room. She thought of Wenner as a bridge between her generation and the generation of her children. For his part, Wenner was one of the few who weren't afraid of her, and the two developed a teasing relationship. Scott Moyers remembered that when Wenner called Jackie at the office, he could tell that they "knew each other *very* well. Jann was a bad boy, who was very irreverent, very cheeky to Jackie. They had this kind of badinage. She really enjoyed him, actually."

Jackie asked Wenner to write an introduction to *John and Yoko*, which he did. In October 1981, Jackie told him that she thought it needed work. She was trying to improve a piece of writing and also to help him deal with what she knew was causing the problem with the piece's detachment and emotional distance: his grief. Speaking directly from personal experience, she told Wenner, "It helps people who mourn to be able to do something for the cause of the fallen, not to have let them die in vain. Even though you may feel a deep weariness and despair, you mustn't abdicate a leadership that has

meant a great deal to mankind." In her letter to him, even the unconventional way Jackie spaced her final four suggestions for revision on the page suggest that she was using her own appreciation for style to make her writer come up with a more moving piece. She thought Wenner could make his text better by saying why he loved Lennon's music, or his unique point of view, or what he was fighting for, or by referring to their friendship. In subtle ways, unknown to the Lennon fans who would buy the book, Jackie was putting her imprint on the book's contents. Her line about helping people who mourn was important enough to Wenner that he reproduced it twice in the book without attributing it to Jackie (and she may specifically have asked him not to attribute it to her).

The book's authors acknowledged the importance of Jackie's faith and sponsorship in completing the project. Many people who worked with Jackie remember her reading the entire text of a manuscript closely, even when she was not required to comment or chose not to. She certainly would have noticed a passage from Jonathan Cott's last interview with Lennon, days before he was killed, in which Lennon talked about his fame. Lennon remarked that fans don't like letting famous people break out of their pigeonholes. They hadn't liked it when the Beatles ceased to be. They hadn't liked it when he had married Yoko Ono. Those actions didn't fit with the image they had formed of him. "But that's the same as living up to your parents' expectations, or to society's expectations, or to so-called critics," said Lennon. You shouldn't do it, and you just have to cope with the fans' wrath when you choose to be a different person. Lennon mentioned that Bruce Springsteen's fame was then growing. He's popular now, Lennon remarked, but "when he gets down to facing his own success and growing older and having to produce it again and again, they'll turn on him, and I hope he survives it." It's hard to know whether the changes in Lennon's identity are the reason why Chapman killed him, but they certainly infuriated some of Lennon's fans. Jackie had experienced precisely that violent turning away from her, and the same swift condemnation, when she had married Onassis. Jackie, however, had somehow learned to separate herself from all that. In the old-fashioned Newport tradition, she certainly wasn't going to complain about her lot—and that's why she had a hard time getting along with Michael Jackson.

Moontalk

"They both actually talked the same," remembered Wenner. Michael Jackson talked "in that same breathy voice" Jackie sometimes used. Nevertheless, it wasn't Jackson's idea to approach Jackie about editing his autobiography, which became *Moonwalk* in 1988. Nor was it the sort of project Jackie would have proposed to do on her own. Bill Barry remembered of the Jackson autobiography that Jackie "took one for the home team"; the book for her was "an exercise in pure for-profit responsibility" and one that he "suspected she came to regret." The journalist Hillel Italie described the book as the "classic celebrity project," because it wasn't written or conceived by Jackson himself. Rather, it was an idea that originated at Doubleday, and Jackie agreed to sponsor it. One of the unspoken expectations at Doubleday was that the publisher might support the more speculative books that she was passionate about if every once in a while she agreed to go after a commercial book that might generate significant profit.

In the mid-1980s, Jackie and Shaye Areheart flew out to Encino, California, in order to meet Jackson, something she rarely did for her authors. Those who weren't already based in New York usually flew there to meet her. Areheart tells one version of this meeting and the subsequent writing of Jackson's book in the new edition of *Moonwalk,* rushed out in 2009 after Jackson's unexpected death.

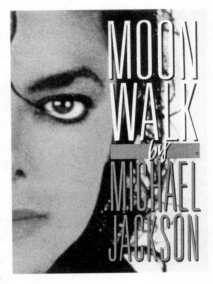

According to Areheart, Jackie and Jackson got along well. Jackie was present at the initial meeting with Jackson in Encino in 1983, but it was Areheart who had to follow up when the project got messy. At the first meeting Jackson took Areheart and Jackie to his trailer adjacent to the studio where he was making the music video for his song "Thriller," and there they talked about what the book might look like. Jackson proposed a kind of picture book with text, and both Doubleday editors were willing to entertain that as an idea. It was in his trailer that Jackson asked Jackie to write the foreword and she agreed. She also wanted something unusual from him, though: to reveal something important about a life lived in the spotlight. Areheart noticed that he was enthusiastic about setting the record straight when so many false things had been written about him but that he also felt some conflict. Some things he wanted to stay private.

Areheart found that writing the book was less interesting to him than making music, and that delayed the book's appearance. When the first writer who was assigned to the project didn't work out, Areheart got more actively involved. She flew to California with a tape recorder to record Jackson's responses to her questions about his life and career. She had a full-time job in New York, however, and eventually handed off her material to a second writer, Stephen Davis, who had written books on Bob Marley and Led Zeppelin. He took the recorded material and shaped it into a narrative. At this point Jackson was on tour in Asia and Areheart had to fly to Australia to get his approval of the text. He didn't want to read it, so she read it to him, line by line, for two weeks in 1987, making notes of his changes. They could work only on the nights when he wasn't performing, and they would sit on his bed, Areheart in a pair of jeans and Jackson in red silk pajamas, going over the manuscript.

When they were finished, and after Areheart had flown to Los Angeles so Jackson could approve Doubleday's plans for promotion, Jackson decided that he didn't want the book published after all. After all the expense of time and production—the book was ready at that point to go to the printer—the people at Doubleday were shocked. Areheart thought this about-face happened because Jackson suddenly felt "terribly exposed," in a way he had never done before. Eventually, after some high-level persuading, he relented, and *Moonwalk* immediately went to first place on the *New York Times* bestseller list, as well as elsewhere around the world.

Jackie's colleagues remembered different dimensions of the story. Areheart herself told one literary agent that dealing with Jackson was "a huge nightmare, just a lot of *sturm und drang.*" J. C. Suarès, the designer hired from outside Doubleday to work on the book, was present at Jackie and Areheart's second meeting with Jackson in California, when they showed Jackson some layout ideas. Even before Jackie went to California, Suarès's answering machine recorded a fragment of her dismay at being involved in the project. "How the hell did I get [to be] doing a book on Michael Jackson? I'm still trying to think of why," her voice says on the tape. "Someone must have told me to go and do it." Suarès remembered the Encino meeting as a bizarre occasion. He, Jackie, and Areheart had arrived at Jackson's house and been seated at a long table. Jackie was at one end. At the other was an empty spot for Jackson. He was late. It was not enough that Jackie had flown out to meet him; he had to show his superior star power by being the last to arrive. On the plane back to New York, Jackie asked Suarès, "Do you think he likes girls?" and she went back to the subject several times while they were working together. The star's studied ambiguity on the question made them curious.

Jackie told Edward Kasinec, whom she sometimes met over a sandwich and a can of V8 juice when she went to work quietly at the New York Public Library on days when the library wasn't open to the public, "Michael Jackson is driving me mad with his phone calls." Jackson would make lengthy calls to her house on Martha's Vineyard to complain about something he was sure she would understand: the burdens of fame. She didn't want to talk about that. Few of her authors remember her ever being willing to discuss it, except by mistake or in passing. She refused to entertain it as a topic of discussion, although she listened politely to the singer's complaints.

When a first draft of the book arrived, it was much shorter than everyone had anticipated. Nancy Tuckerman recalled experimenting with the old college-student trick of double- or triple-spacing it so it would come out at a respectable length. Suarès described it as "all puff and no substance." Jackie called Jann Wenner and asked him what she should do. "The book she thought she was getting," said Wenner, "was an autobiography. Michael was not going to provide anything like that. He was not going to write it, let alone speak it. He wanted to provide a photo book of how wonderful he was. His idea of a good photograph book was him receiving this award or that award. It wouldn't even have been a good photo book, because it was going to be his personal achievement scrapbook."

After thinking long and hard about it, Jackie decided to reject Jackson's manuscript. "But she didn't want to upset Michael," recalled Suarès. "She gave him an ultimatum in a calm, firm voice. She instructed him to open up and give the reader a sincere show of feeling—about growing up black in show business, for example." She finished by telling him that if the book was only public relations or promotional material, "we'd all be made fools of." Suarès said that Jackie's performance was vintage Bette Davis. Jackie loved that, but it wasn't the end of the troubles for the book.

Alberto Vitale, who was then the CEO of the holding company, Bantam Doubleday Dell, into which Doubleday had been merged, reported that it was nearly impossible to pin down Jackson when Jackson needed to give final approval to his manuscript. "He was like a moving target," and that's why Vitale approved spending the money to fly Areheart out to see Jackson in Australia. When Jackson wanted to back out of his contract with Doubleday, Vitale and the head of Doubleday, Nancy Evans, had to meet with him in New York in order to persuade him to stay in. It was a civilized meeting, but Vitale thought the people surrounding Jackson were not necessarily helpful. Jackson ultimately abided by his contract, but Vitale remembered publishing the book as an exasperating experience. The fact that no paperback followed the hardback was a testament to the bad blood between Jackson and the publisher.

Jackson discussed his fame in several lines of his finished

manuscript. He said that he had tried to "shun personal publicity and keep a low profile as much as possible." This was the only way he could survive, he said. "The price of fame can be a heavy one," he continued. "Is the price you pay worth it?" He admitted to being obsessed with privacy. He said that the dark glasses and the surgical mask he often wore were his ways of taking a break from having everyone look at him. In the final version, he wrote, "My dating and relationships with girls have not had the happy endings I've been looking for. Something always seems to get in the way." Reading this, a music critic for the *New York Times* observed that *Moonwalk* was "eccentric, contradictory and helplessly revealing." Jackson was "a master of deadpan banality" who had given out "significant information between the lines of psychobabble."

Ultimately, what Jackie disliked about celebrity was the cheapness of it, its transience, the fact that it so often lacked substance, that she could be lumped into a category with Michael Jackson on the basis of fame alone. What gave her greater satisfaction was to think about the way something small and light and impermanent, like a singer's fame or her own, could be transformed into something bigger, heavier, and riper with potential significance. That was the subject that Bill Moyers investigated with Joseph Campbell in *The Power of Myth,* which came out in the same year as *Moonwalk*. It was a bestseller too, and understandably gave her a lot more pride than the Jackson book.

Follow Your Bliss

Joseph Campbell was a writer and lecturer whose success in the 1960s came from popularizing academic research in comparative mythology and religion as well as from distilling these common themes into simple rules to live by. In one of the masterpieces of nineteenth-century fiction, George Eliot's *Middlemarch,* the character of Edward Casaubon is a little like Campbell. Casaubon is a clergyman toiling away at a work that he conceives will provide the "key to all mythologies," the underlying truth and meaning that hold all the different world religions of the past together. Casaubon never finished his work and died in obscurity. Joseph Campbell, on the other hand, went on public television with Bill Moyers and recorded a series of interviews about the meaning of mythology. Campbell was a beacon for millions of people who were tired of conventional religion and wanted an alternative path to spiritual revelation. When once asked how human beings should live their lives, Campbell said, "Follow your bliss, and doors will open for you that you didn't even know were there."

Jackie found something like bliss working with Moyers on the Campbell interviews. The project encompassed her past, present, and future. Campbell had a link to one of her other authors, because he had first come to the attention of Moyers when Campbell and Eugene Kennedy published a collaborative article in the *New York Times*. Further, Campbell repeatedly cited Jackie's performance at JFK's funeral as the only modern example he knew of in which a myth—a story to live by—was made. He himself had participated in this large communal rite, when an entire diverse nation was united as one, rapt in its attention for those few moments. Jackie was the behind-the-scenes genius of President Kennedy's funeral. She had begun planning it on Air Force One, flying back from Texas. It was she who insisted that the precedents from Abraham Lincoln's funeral be looked up at the Library of Congress. The riderless horse with reversed boots in the funeral procession was included at her insistence, as was the eternal flame at

Arlington. What Jackie may have found moving about Campbell was that he was one of the few who could write a sensitive appreciation of all she had done. The funeral, wrote Campbell, had been a ritual that was of the utmost importance and necessity. It compensated for the shock and grief people felt. It was a restatement of American dignity before the world. It reestablished national solidarity. It helped Americans begin to heal after the wounding sense of disorder and disbelief that had followed the tragedy. That terrible need for a meaningful ceremony was the challenge to which Jackie had risen, and her specific choices, thought Campbell, made the ritual a piece of compelling, sacred theater.

Campbell's name continued to crop up after Jackie commissioned *The Power of Myth*. Martha Graham, whose autobiography had yet to be conceived, later testified to the overwhelming influence of Campbell on her choreography. Jonathan Cott also relied on Campbell's work in trying to describe the significance of the Egyptian mythology of Isis and Osiris in a book he later wrote for Jackie. These were not coincidences but part of the network of attraction Jackie felt for Campbell's work.

The Power of Myth was also the beginning of a fruitful partnership between Jackie and Moyers, who collaborated on several other books—books that could be marketed through Moyers's television programs, thus usually ensuring healthy sales. Jackie's contribution to *The Power of Myth* was to put an emphasis on art rather than publishing the text of the interviews alone. The book, just over 200 pages long, includes ninety-seven different images. Jackie went out of her way to try to make the book equal the visual impact of the television series. The color insert included excerpts from some of her favorite cultural traditions: representations of the Hindu gods

Krishna and Vishnu, a Navajo sand painting, and a stained glass window from Chartres Cathedral. Judith Moyers recalled Jackie saying, "There will be some people who don't care about mythology, but when they see this marvelous art, they will buy the book and read it." Working with Jackie, Judith Moyers discovered that "her sensibilities had been honed to a very fine point not just by tragedy but by the lyrical, beautiful parts of life as well."

Several passages in *The Power of Myth* go to the heart of why fame and celebrity, though burdensome to the person who is famous, can be of use to society at large. Campbell had told Moyers, "We're so engaged in doing things to achieve purposes of outer value that we forget that the inner value, the rapture that is associated with being alive, is what it's all about." He explained that the power of myth is to take us out of the realm of getting and spending. It leads us into a world of intense appreciation by manifesting themes from our everyday lives in stories of the eternal. Campbell had told Moyers that it was natural to focus on personalities, on modern, accessible versions of godlike figures, in order to reach that higher plane of consciousness. "I imagine some kings and queens are the most stupid, absurd, banal people you could run into, probably interested only in horses and women, you know. But you're not responding to them as personalities, you're responding to them in their mythological roles. When someone becomes a judge, or President of the United States, the man is no longer that man, he's the representative of an eternal office; he has to sacrifice his personal desires and even life possibilities to the role that he now signifies." Bill Moyers pressed Campbell on the subject of an ordinary mortal's becoming a legend, a myth. "What happens when people become legends? Can you say, for example, that John Wayne has become a myth?" How could you possibly say that a tough-talking Hollywood cowboy had become a sacred figure? "When a person becomes a model for other people's lives," replied Campbell, "he has moved into the sphere of being mythologized." If people chose to pattern themselves after him, he had to be seen as occupying a quasi-divine status. Moreover, knowing the stages of such a Hollywood actor's life was a way of becoming accustomed to the difficult stages in one's own life. Calmly preparing for death is one of life's great challenges, but myths help us accustom ourselves to it. "One of the great challenges of life is to say 'yea' to that person or that act or that condition which in your mind is most abominable," noted Campbell. *The Power of Myth* might well have helped Jackie say "yea" to Michael Jackson and to the way her own fame seemed no more than tinsel, by showing how that fame could be of use to other people in living their lives.

She Will Go on Eternally

The last of several books on the subject of fame that Jackie brought out in 1988 was David Stenn's biography of Clara Bow. Stenn's book discussed how Bow had been "catapulted to oppressive fame" in the 1920s. Did the author have the impression that his editor had experienced something similar? Stenn thought not. Jackie saw a difference between Hollywood stars, who were famous for their acting careers, and her own fame, which had come from being married to JFK. Bow, said Jackie, "was famous." Of herself, she would say only, "I'm well known." Stenn explained, "She drew a distinction between the two. She accepted her celebrity as a byproduct of someone whom she was once married to. It didn't have anything to do with her, in terms of anything she had done."

This came up again in connection with Stenn's biography of Jean Harlow, *Bombshell* (1993). According to Stenn, Harlow also suffered from "a professional imprisonment by her public image." He did not see Jackie as someone who was imprisoned. He saw her as someone who had gone through a period of imprisonment and then freed herself. She was doing what she loved and had created a life for herself. So whether she identified with some of the tribulations of David Stenn's two Hollywood stars or not, he saw her as "controlling everything." One additional piece of evidence of Jackie's success in controlling the use of her image came when Stenn went to look for a video clip of Jackie, which he intended to use in his documentary on Patricia Douglas, *Girl 27*. Jackie had encouraged him at the start of the project and he wanted to use her image, but he couldn't find anything available for purchase from any of the ordinary news or film outlets. Video cameras were less ubiquitous then than they are now, and Jackie had carefully limited the occasions on which she appeared in moving images.

Stenn also recalled a conversation he had with Jackie about Marilyn Monroe, a topic that he had avoided touching upon. That's why he was surprised when she brought it up. Jackie didn't mention Monroe in the context of JFK but rather as part of a continuum with Jean Harlow: both of them were blondes who made their sexual appeal the center of their screen personalities. As with Vreeland, Jackie was willing to discuss Monroe with Stenn in a completely dispassionate, even admiring way.

Jackie's colleagues saw something similar when Jackie was sometimes forced to deal with her own fame at work. Tom Cahill remembered the difficulty of traveling in the elevator with her when people were going to floors of the building that Doubleday didn't occupy. "She would get on the elevator. No matter how many people were on it, she would manage to get on, move to the back, and put her head down. That's how she traveled the elevator," he said. "There were plenty of people who had some sense of decorum, but then there were plenty of people who didn't. Almost inevitably, there would be somebody in the elevator who would say, 'My God! You're Jackie Kennedy!' I remember one day a woman said this when I was on the elevator with Jackie and she replied"—here Cahill imitated the Jackie O. whisper—"'No, I'm not.'"

Doubleday's art director, Peter Kruzan, said that under certain circumstances, Jackie would allow herself to be teased about her fame. She once said to him of Princess Diana, "I don't know how anyone can withstand that kind of media attention." Kruzan said, "You sometimes had to call her on these things. I looked at her and said, 'Jackie, you have *got* to be kidding me!' She giggled. That's how she handled it when you called her on something." On another occasion they visited the office of an important magazine publisher. When she was asked to sign the visitors' book, she avoided the question. They kept insisting. "All *right*," she said. She signed and they left. Kruzan wanted to kid her a little about this: "Well, they finally got you to sign the book." "Yes," she said, "but I only gave them 'Jacqueline Onassis,' not 'Jacqueline *Kennedy* Onassis.'"

The best jokes have a kernel of truth in them. She acknowledged that the Kennedy part of her legend was more admired and more valuable than the Onassis part. She even told some of her post-Onassis boyfriends, like Pete Hamill, how much she had loved the senator from Massachusetts, and this was long after the extent of his serial infidelity was well known to her and the outside world. Choosing to be buried at Arlington next to JFK rather than on Skorpios next to Onassis was certainly a statement about how she wanted to be remembered. But her books speak more warmly of who she was than a grave next to an eternal flame does.

She was a woman who transformed her maternal pride into successful children's books with Carly Simon and who recognized the talent of Peter Sís before he was ever considered for a MacArthur "genius" grant. Although she had been the wife of a president and a billionaire, her books championed a black slave who bore children to Thomas Jefferson and a newlywed who walked out on Sam Houston to spend the rest of her life fiercely guarding her privacy. Her books were often written by strong-minded women like Dorothy West and Dorothy Spruill Redford, Martha Graham and Judith Jamison, who made their own unusual careers in the twentieth century; or they examined the lives of eighteenth-century Frenchwomen who had had unprecedented influence on the politics and high culture of their time. She was the subject of some of the last century's most famous photography, and as an editor she made photography one of her specialties and looked hard, as Vreeland taught her, to find art even in the work of the paparazzi. She was sometimes accused of being too regal for American public life, and indeed a dozen of her books examined and defended regal traditions in different international contexts. She was a tastemaker whose Tiffany coffee-table books linked her as undeniably with a luxury goods store as the movie made from Truman Capote's novella had done with Audrey Hepburn. Camelot was not only a metaphor but also a library she built, an award she helped endow, and a series of books she edited about Kennedy-era ideals, doings, and personalities. She flew to California to commission Michael Jackson's book and stood behind Joseph Campbell to say what it might mean in a mythological context to be the king of pop or America's queen. Her books were inextricably bound up with who she was, how she reflected on her past, and who she aspired to be. They are prism-like reflections of the persistent passions of a woman with a beautiful mind.

If Jackie was a more imperious figure than we had known before, American twentieth-century history has yet to acknowledge that she was also a more intellectual, better-read, and better-informed woman than we had known before. To have worked on about a hundred books in a career she came to only late in life certainly raises her stature not only among American first ladies but also among all people in American public life. Who else in the public life of the twentieth century could come close to her personal elegance combined with her knowledge of European and American history, manners and fashion, dance and photography, civil rights and children's books, historic architecture and historic preservation, women's history and women's fiction, as well as the art and archaeology of India and Egypt?

Through it all she remained someone who appreciated the absurd and the ridiculous. That was an enduring trait that appeared throughout the many stages in her career as well as in the different facets of her personality. It's the part of her that redeems her from her commercial and imperial moments. It's the part that humanizes her in her mythological moments.

The White House senior usher during the 1960s, who was the official in charge of keeping all the servants and ceremonies in order, was J. B. West. He and Jackie became friends. One of West's anecdotes about dealing with Jackie holds the key to how she experienced her own role as a legend, as well as to why her legend remains fresh and attractive for us. When she was first lady, West enjoyed what he called her "breezy, mock-autocratic" instructions written to him on lined yellow paper. After the assassination, she moved briefly to Georgetown before deciding that it wasn't private enough and she would live in New York instead. We have a chilling image of her behind the black silk veil in that era, but when she invited West to dinner in Georgetown, he found elements of the old

Jackie still alive and well. When he came inside, she greeted him at the door, and he kissed her. "Oh, Mr. West, you never kissed me when I lived at the White House," she said. She then narrowed "her eyes wickedly. 'Did you ever kiss Mamie?'" "All the time," West answered. They stood back and looked at one another and laughed.

epilogue

In the last twelve months of Jackie's life, from about June 1993 through May 1994, more than a dozen projects crossed her desk. They were in all different stages of development, from rudimentary proposals to imminent publication as books. They give a final glimpse of her not only as a woman who was continuing to draw on the familiar authors and the well-established themes of her list, but also as someone breaking new ground and exploring new territory. She was over sixty, but her mind was still curious and she was continuing to grow.

Two of her last books addressed the subject of healing. She edited Bill Moyers's *Healing and the Mind* (1993) and Naveen Patnaik's *Garden of Life: An Introduction to the Healing Plants of India* (1993). She had worked with both authors before, but the subject of unconventional medicine improving the lives of those who were ill was new. The Moyers book was based on a five-part television series which first aired on PBS early in 1993. It examined the difference between "healing" and "curing." Conventional medicine aimed at curing diseases, but in the early 1990s there was a movement that aimed at healing, in some cases where a cure wasn't possible, by paying attention to the spiritual and emotional dimensions of disease. At the end of the series, one director of a California retreat for cancer patients said that a cancer diagnosis is like "being pushed out of an airplane with a parachute into a jungle, into a guerrilla war, with no training and no weapons and the expectation you'll survive." He wanted to give cancer patients some of the training and the weapons that traditional doctors would deny them.

Judith Moyers and Bill Barry both recalled one of Jackie's signal contributions to this book. At her urging, Doubleday used an image from a Georgia O'Keeffe painting for the cover. This was unusual, because the owners of the rights to O'Keeffe's work had never before allowed the painter's art to be reproduced as jacket art. The painting showed a nautilus shell's internal spiral, which to Jackie suggested eternity or infinity. What *Healing and the Mind* conveyed, both the book and its cover, was that some spiritual part of our selves is independent of and may live on beyond the lives of our physical bodies.

Jackie's book with Naveen Patnaik on the healing plants of India was also about a kind of medicine that cannot be found in an American pharmacy. It explored *ayurveda,* an Indian system of medicine complementary and alternative to traditional medical practice. Ayurvedic therapies use herbs, massage, and yoga to return people to health. The book explores the medicinal properties of herbs and other plants, such as ginger, plantain, and mango. Jackie and the author commissioned unusual artwork to illustrate it. One of the artists they employed, Bannu, was from the family of the hereditary court painters to the maharajahs of Jaipur. Sarah Giles remembered going to the launch party for this book, where Jackie remarked of enormous plants in brass containers distributed around the room, "My, will you look at all these brass pots!" Giles thought this was Jackie's trademark whimsicality. It was the most exotic and glamorous party in New York that night. Indian artists circulated, painting the guests' hands with henna. The author, who was a very social man, had invited every personality he knew. There was Jackie, taking no notice of all the social buzz and remarking on the planters instead. Although she could not have known what was coming, Jackie had forearmed herself with these books. In the lead-up to her own illness, she had learned about some of the resources, as well as some of the limits, of alternative medicine. She also knew about how healing might work for cancer patients when curing would not. Her sense of humor was another alternative therapy at her command.

In the last months of her life, Jackie worked on two novels by Ruth Prawer Jhabvala, *Poet and Dancer* (1993) and *Shards of Memory* (1995). Jhabvala was a novelist whose reputation was already established and who had recently acquired renown through her screenwriting collaboration with the film producers Ismail Merchant and James Ivory. There was some fiction of which Jackie was very proud, Mahfouz's work foremost, but fiction hadn't been as marked a specialty for her as dance and photography. To acquire Jhabvala was to branch out into something new, and to do so with a writer of distinction. When one of Jackie's Doubleday colleagues congratulated her on signing Jhabvala, Jackie replied, "Every once in a while you have to do something for the soul."

If the soul is nourished by where we've been as well as by our hopes for the future, some part of Jackie's soul continued to live in Paris while she worked in New York. She had published a dozen books that touched upon the Paris of the eighteenth and nineteenth centuries. Soon after she arrived at Doubleday, in 1978, she worked on acquiring a project with Ray Roberts about the women of Montparnasse, one of the most intellectual and bohemian neighborhoods of twentieth-century Paris. When her friend John Russell sent her his book on Paris in 1983, she told him, "I am drowning in it, in a sweet agony of wishing I were back there, wishing I could live another passage of my life there." It is not surprising, then, that in the last year of her life she was working on a new book on Paris. This was a controversial project, because it dealt with the bloodletting, rough justice, and score-settling that followed the Germans' departure from Paris in 1944. Antony Beevor and Artemis Cooper's *Paris After the Liberation 1944–1949* (1994) examined the ways in which collaborators with the Nazis and members of the French resistance battled with one another in the French capital in the years immediately following the Second World War. Jackie had arrived to study in Paris just after the time examined in the book, and she had met some of the people it discussed. Antony Beevor recalled the book's interest for her: "Her time in France had been such an impressionable one that she was attracted to the idea of our book." She had known his wife's grandparents, the postwar British ambassador, Duff Cooper, and his wife, Diana, as well as a number of other characters in the story through parties given by the writer Louise de Vilmorin at Verrières. One mark of Jackie's personal investment in the book was the way she resisted Beevor's suggestion for the jacket cover. "Over here," she told Beevor, who was writing the book in Britain, "the choice of a book's cover is akin to a Japanese tea ceremony." Doubleday would certainly look at anything he would like to propose, but she wouldn't let him dictate. It was her book, too, and she was passionate about getting the jacket art right.

Several books from her last months also indicate Jackie's love of history. *Isis and Osiris: Exploring the Goddess Myth* (1994) tells the story of the ancient Egyptian goddess Isis, who married her brother Osiris. Osiris died in a violent fight with his brother Set, who cut Osiris to pieces. Isis and her sister went all around Egypt, from the Nile Delta to Nubia, collecting the pieces of Osiris in order to put him together for a proper burial. As Jonathan Cott tells the story, they were "re-membering Osiris, as they remembered him in their hearts, for to remember is to heal." In putting him back together, in burying him properly, they also resurrected Osiris. They rendered his spirit eternal.

The Temple of Dendur had originally been dedicated to the worship of Isis. Although Jackie had worked hard to have the temple saved, she was not initially happy about bringing it to New York. When Tom Hoving phoned her in the 1960s to see if she would support the Met's application to acquire it, she told him she did not want it in the museum. She wanted to keep to the original plan of rebuilding it in Washington as a memorial to JFK. When the Met won the competition to get the temple and it was reconstructed within view of her apartment, she complained about reflections from the floodlights at night shining into her bedroom.

By the time that Jackie was working with Cott on *Isis and Osiris*, she had forgotten all about that. She ended up rather liking the temple. It enhanced the view. She remained interested in anything ancient or modern that had to do with Egypt. Cott's book is both, because it explores how ancient Egyptian gods are still worshipped today in places as far away as a castle in Ireland and the suburbs of Edmonton, Alberta. Cott believed that this movement back and forth between ancient and modern was one of the features that attracted Jackie. "She was really enamored of the Isis and Osiris myth," he said. "We used to talk about that a lot. That's what gave me the idea for a book about Isis and Osiris: how those particular gods—god and goddess—were worshipped and are worshipped still by people all over the world. Jackie was very, very attached to that story. It's about the dead husband who is restored and remembered, so to speak, by his wife and given eternal, immortal life by her. She didn't say that to me, but I assume she maybe had an identification with that story." It is no great stretch of the imagination to say that Jackie, like Isis, spent a part of her life picking up the pieces of JFK and trying to re-member or immortalize him.

Some of the most surprising of Jackie's last books were also unconventional histories. Through Karl Katz she had been introduced to Larry Gonick, once a student of mathematics at Harvard, now a cartoonist. He had written *The Cartoon History of the Universe 1, Volumes 1–7, From the Big Bang to Alexander the Great* (1990), which had been a surprise success and was totally unlike anything that had ever been on Jackie's list before. It was a comic retelling of all of recorded history from the beginning of the universe to the end of classical Greece. It may have been aimed at children, but it had humor that appealed to adults, too. Jackie and Gonick got into trouble with Ann Landers, the pen name of Eppie Lederer, whom Jackie persuaded to promote the book in her column. Gonick's cartoons take a highly literal but also irreverent view of history, so since the Old Testament related that David presented the foreskins of two hundred Philistines to King Saul, Gonick designed an image based on the biblical text. Christian readers objected that this was not suitable for children, and Jackie had the Doubleday religion editor write a letter for Landers to send to her angry readers about how there was nothing in Gonick's book that wasn't also in the Bible. Jackie wasn't at all put off by the angry reaction to Ann Landers's column, and in her last months she commissioned a new book from Gonick, *The Cartoon History of the Universe 2, Volumes 8–13, From the Springtime of China to the Fall of Rome, India Too!* (1994). The distinguished historian of China Jonathan Spence wrote in his review that Gonick's books were a "curious hybrid, at once flippant and scholarly, witty and politically correct, zany and traditionalist." Spence believed that Gonick had answered the question "Why study history?" with "Because it is interesting and because it is fun."

Gonick too has an account of Isis and Osiris, colored with the author's comic view of religion and mythology. Gonick emphasizes that the only part of Osiris that Isis couldn't find after Set cut him to pieces was his penis, which had been eaten by a fish. Nevertheless, in burying him, Isis successfully resurrected Osiris, and he became a judge of the dead. As in many sacred stories, Isis also defied common sense by conceiving a child, Horus, even though her husband had apparently lost the organ to effect this. After his resurrection, Osiris judged good souls at death and sent them to labor in his fields, while he condemned bad souls to be eaten by a demon, which Gonick drew as a fat crocodile sitting at the feet of a mummified pharaoh on a throne.

It wasn't just other people's religions and other cultural traditions that Jackie allowed to be spoofed. Tom Cahill remembered Jackie's reaction when an American cardinal condemned a Doubleday book about women in the Catholic Church and thereby won some welcome additional publicity for the book. As Cahill and Bill Barry conferred about the cardinal's statement in the morning paper, they walked

past Jackie's office and heard her call out to them, "You two *bad* Catholic boys!" Cahill also recalled Jackie's telling him, "We're all relaxed Catholics here," playing, possibly it was unintentional, on the similarity between "lapsed" and "relaxed." She did remain interested in Catholic history, however. Cahill ceased to be an editor and wrote a book, the first volume in a successful series called The Hinges of History, entitled *How the Irish Saved Civilization: The Untold Story of Ireland's Heroic Role from the Fall of Rome to the Rise of Medieval Europe* (1995). When Jackie heard of this, and learned that it would be edited by one of her colleagues, she asked Cahill with pretend exasperation, "Why didn't you give that book to *me?*"

Two of her final books were about recluses who chose communing with nature over socializing with other human beings. Her last book with Jonathan Cott was a specially illustrated collection of Emily Dickinson's verse, *Skies in Blossom: The Nature Poetry of Emily Dickinson* (1995). Dickinson rarely left her room and preferred guarding her privacy to the varied social life of Amherst, Massachusetts. She turned her private hours to account through the composition of lines about intensely observed natural phenomena.

At roughly the same time Jackie plucked a book from the Paris bestseller list about a Russian family who, owing to a religious schism, journeyed to a remote part of Siberia and cut themselves off from civilization for forty years. This was Vasily Peskov's *Lost in the Taiga: One Russian Family's Fifty-Year Struggle for Survival and Religious Freedom in the Siberian Wilderness* (1994). When Russian scientists doing research in the area happened to come across them, they found the family living in a handmade hut, wearing shoes made from bark. The daughter of the family, who had been born there and knew no other world, used handwriting reminiscent of Old Church

Slavonic print. The family stayed away from the geologists and intensely disliked being photographed, but their daughter was willing to speak to Peskov and tell him their story. This book was not about gorgeous interiors or beautifully laid tables. It was not about court ritual or dance. It was not about the Kennedy administration or the power of myth. But it was a story that Jackie wanted to read, and she bet that others would, too. It's the best evidence there is that in her last year she continued to look forward to learning something new.

. . .

Most of Jackie's colleagues' favorite memories about her are those in which she ceased to be Jackie the myth and was clearly an ordinary mortal, an editor, a coworker, one of them. Jackie usually had a simple lunch of foil-wrapped celery and carrot sticks at her desk. Very occasionally she ventured downstairs to the company cafeteria. Nancy Tuckerman took her down the first time. Jackie selected different dishes from both the hot and the cold counters. Then she walked by the three islands with cash registers and sat down at a table. When Nancy joined her at the table and asked her, "Did you pay, Jackie?" Jackie said with surprise, "Oh. Do you have to pay?" Nancy went back and paid for her: "I could just see the stories in the papers if I didn't."

On another trip to the cafeteria, one fellow editor remembered Jackie encountering the big Irish cook who routinely stood behind the counter where hot dishes were served. When Jackie took her tray and came to the counter, the smiling cook said in an Irish brogue, as if she saw her there every day, "All right, Jackie! Whaddya want?" After Jackie finished her lunch and went with a friend to drop off her tray, she looked with amazement into the kitchen, where the dishes were being washed, and said, "Gosh, it looks like a dry cleaner's in there."

Another of her colleagues has an indelible image of her. Young Paul Golob, sitting at an internal desk that stood outside the offices with windows, heard a commotion down at one end of the hall. He heard footsteps running down the corridor. He looked up and there was "Jacqueline Onassis in stocking feet running. She wasn't wearing any shoes and she was tearing down the hall as if she were still a schoolgirl. She was in her sixties then. Did I just see that?" Golob asked himself. "Did it really happen? It humanized her. She was one of us. She was on deadline. It was something any of us would have done." Reading Jackie was also running Jackie, and for the most authentic vision of that woman, intent on getting one of her titles into print, turn now not to a picture of her but to the pages of one of her books.

Acknowledgments

My previous books have been on nineteenth-century British politics and biographies of people at the court of Queen Victoria. One of Jackie's specialties as an editor was the history of European court life. Nevertheless, I could not have moved between Victorian England and Jackie's more recent history without the help of two books and the backing of four people. The Metropolitan Museum of Art in New York staged an exhibition of Jacqueline Kennedy's clothes from her White House years in 2001. The essays in the book that accompanied the exhibition commented on the way Jackie's considerable intellect contributed to her sense of style. A few years earlier, Wayne Koestenbaum's *Jackie Under My Skin* (1995) touched on the biographical parallel between Jackie's publishing work on the Russian royal family and her reputation as a regal figure in American history. Both books drew me in and compelled me to reevaluate the woman I thought I knew from having looked at her pictures and read some of her biographies. Two literary agents, Zoë Waldie in London and David Kuhn (no relation) in New York, took my original idea of exploring Jackie's editorial career and helped make it into something very much more than it had been. Nor would the book have gotten off the ground without Steve Rubin and Nan Talese at Doubleday. These are the ideas and the people who brought this book to life.

At Carthage College, where I taught for fifteen years and where the initial stages of the research for this book took place, I had the support of generous colleagues: F. Gregory Campbell, Kurt Piepenburg, Judith Schaumberg, David Steege, and Christian von Dehsen. Paul Ulrich and Mimi Yang chaired a committee that funded early trips to the archives. Thanks go also to members of the History Department who encouraged me and took on my classes while I was away: John Leazer, Stephanie Mitchell, John Neuenschwander, Eric Pullin, and Steve Udry. A number of students assisted, too, but most of all I want to thank Claire Rogoski, the sort of bright young person who makes a teaching career fun. The staff at the college's library who provided information technology support were also essential.

A number of readers gave me detailed suggestions about how to make a first draft better. I'd like to thank not only my father, Albert J. Kuhn, but also Pamela Kuras and Tom Noer. Ronit Feldman and the rest of the team at Nan A. Talese/Doubleday were instrumental here, too, and I could not have done it without them.

The book was written at libraries and with the assistance of librarians whose expertise was greater than mine. I'd like to thank the staffs of the Boston Athenaeum, the Boston Public Library, the Harvard University Libraries, the Northwestern University Library, the Newberry Library, the Chicago Public Library, the Library of Columbia College in Chicago, the London Library, and the British Library.

I also received expert assistance from archivists who guided me through the manuscript collections of the John F. Kennedy Library in Boston; the Bodleian Library in Oxford; the Library of St. John's College, Cambridge; the Harry Ransom Center at the University of Texas, Austin; the New York Public Library; the Library of the University of Arizona, Tucson; the National First Ladies' Library in Canton, Ohio; and the Library of Wesleyan University.

A number of people allowed me to see papers in their own collections; among them I would like to thank Robert Alderman, Ruth Ansel, Irina Clow, Elizabeth Crook, William

Dalrymple, Lynn Franklin, John Loring, Philip Myers, Edna O'Brien, and Jann Wenner.

I had help with photographs from a number of people who are credited elsewhere, but I am particularly grateful for the research and assistance of Catherine Talese. Robert Nedelkoff was also a helpful resource in conducting research, especially into U.S. government records.

The people who agreed to be interviewed for this book, mainly Jackie's colleagues and authors, also made it possible. I have listed their names in a separate section, but I would like to record here what a thoughtful group of people they were and what a pleasure it was to learn through them about what it was like to work with Jackie.

Writing a book is a reminder of how important friends are in keeping the show on the road. Warm thanks, then, last of all, to Nimish Adhia, Greg Baer, Mary Bishop, Pauline Bieringa and Wyger Velema, Carol Birnbaum and Adam Manacher, Jane Bond, Bradford Brown and Maribeth Gettinger, Ric Camacho, Carrie Clark, Richard Davenport-Hines, George Dickson, Gregory and Cristina Gaymont, David Gelber, Lisa Jane Graham and David Sedley, Michael Holland, Nigel Hubbard, Fritz Kuhn, Rajiv Laroia, Julia MacKenzie, Sheila Markham, David Parrott, Christopher Phipps, Marla Polley, Laura Ponsonby, Nabeel Razzaq, John Martin Robinson, Ian and Catherine Russell, John Silva, Mark Studer, and Paul Wolfson.

Books Edited by Jacqueline Kennedy Onassis

1976

De Pauw, Linda Grant, and Conover Hunt. *Remember the Ladies: Women in America, 1750–1815.* With the assistance of Miriam Schneir. New York: Viking/Pilgrim Society.

Onassis, Jacqueline, ed. *In the Russian Style.* With the cooperation of the Metropolitan Museum of Art. Introduction by Audrey Kennett, designed by Bryan Holme. New York: Viking.

1978

Kennedy, Eugene C. *Himself! The Life and Times of Mayor Richard J. Daley.* New York: Viking.

Zvorykin, Boris. *The Firebird and Other Russian Fairy Tales.* Edited and with an introduction by Jacqueline Onassis. New York: Viking.

1979

Adams, William Howard. *Atget's Gardens: A Selection of Eugène Atget's Garden Photographs.* Introduction by Jacqueline Onassis. Exhibition sponsored by Royal Institute of British Architects, London; International Center of Photography, New York; International Exhibitions Foundation, Washington. Garden City, N.Y.: Doubleday.

Appelbaum, Stephen A. *Out in Inner Space: A Psychoanalyst Explores the New Therapies.* Garden City, N.Y.: Anchor /Doubleday.

Chase-Riboud, Barbara. *Sally Hemings: A Novel.* New York: Viking.

Zaroulis, N. L. *Call the Darkness Light.* Garden City, N.Y.: Doubleday.

1980

Grace, Princess of Monaco, with Gwen Robyns. *My Book of Flowers*. Garden City, N.Y.: Doubleday.

Vreeland, Diana. *Allure*. With Christopher Hemphill. Garden City, N.Y.: Doubleday.

Weller, Edwin. *A Civil War Courtship: The Letters of Edwin Weller from Antietam to Atlanta*. Edited by William Walton. Garden City, N.Y.: Doubleday.

1981

Bernier, Olivier. *The Eighteenth-Century Woman*. Garden City, N.Y.: Doubleday/Metropolitan Museum of Art.

Cook, Don. *Ten Men and History*. Garden City, N.Y.: Doubleday.

Kennedy, Eugene C. *Father's Day: A Novel*. Garden City, N.Y.: Doubleday.

Loring, John, and Henry B. Platt. *The New Tiffany Table Settings*. Garden City, N.Y.: Doubleday.

Ramati, Raquel. *How to Save Your Own Street*. In collaboration with the Urban Design Group of the Department of City Planning, New York. Garden City, N.Y.: Dolphin Books [Doubleday].

Turbeville, Deborah. *Unseen Versailles*. Introduction by Louis Auchincloss. Garden City, N.Y.: Doubleday.

1982

Cott, Jonathan, and Christine Doudna. *The Ballad of John and Yoko*. Garden City, N.Y.: Dolphin Books [Doubleday] / Rolling Stone Press.

Kennedy, Eugene C. *Queen Bee*. Garden City, N.Y.: Doubleday.

1983

De Combray, Richard. *Goodbye Europe: A Novel in Six Parts*. Garden City, N.Y.: Doubleday.

Sloane, Florence Adele. *Maverick in Mauve: The Diary of a Roman-*

tic Age. With commentary by Louis Auchincloss. Garden City, N.Y.: Doubleday.

1984

Auchincloss, Louis. *False Dawn: Women in the Age of the Sun King.* Garden City, N.Y.: Anchor/Doubleday.

Bernier, Olivier. *Louis the Beloved: The Life of Louis XV.* Garden City, N.Y.: Doubleday.

Plimpton, George. *Fireworks.* Garden City, N.Y.: Doubleday.

1985

Bernier, Olivier. *Secrets of Marie Antoinette: By Marie Antoinette, Queen Consort of Louis XVI, King of France.* Garden City, N.Y.: Doubleday.

Patnaik, Naveen. *A Second Paradise: Indian Courtly Life, 1590–1947.* Introduction by Stuart Cary Welch, illustrations by Bannu. Garden City, N.Y.: Doubleday.

1986

Kirkland, Gelsey. *Dancing on My Grave: An Autobiography.* With Greg Lawrence. Garden City, N.Y.: Doubleday.

Loring, John. *Tiffany Taste.* Garden City, N.Y.: Doubleday.

1987

Bernier, Olivier. *Louis XIV: A Royal Life.* Garden City, N.Y.: Doubleday.

Cott, Jonathan. *The Search for Omm Sety: A Story of Eternal Love.* In collaboration with Hanny El Zeini. Garden City, N.Y.: Doubleday.

Loring, John. *Tiffany's 150 Years.* Garden City, N.Y.: Doubleday.

Udall, Stewart L. *To the Inland Empire: Coronado and Our Spanish Legacy.* Photographs by Jerry Jacka. Garden City, N.Y.: Doubleday.

Wise, David. *The Samarkand Dimension.* Garden City, N.Y.: Doubleday.

1988

Campbell, Joseph. *The Power of Myth*. With Bill Moyers. Edited by Betty Sue Flowers. New York: Doubleday.

Giles, Sarah. *Fred Astaire: His Friends Talk*. New York: Doubleday.

Jackson, Michael. *Moonwalk*. New York: Doubleday.

Loring, John. *The Tiffany Wedding*. New York: Doubleday.

Redford, Dorothy Spruill, with Michael D'Orso. *Somerset Homecoming*. New York: Doubleday.

Stenn, David. *Clara Bow: Runnin' Wild*. New York: Doubleday.

1989

Bernier, Olivier. *At the Court of Napoleon: Memoirs of the Duchesse d'Abrantès*. New York: Doubleday.

Custine, Astolphe, Marquis de. *Empire of the Czar: A Journey through Eternal Russia*. Foreword by Daniel J. Boorstin, introduction by George F. Kennan. A translation of *La Russie en 1839*. New York: Doubleday.

Eggleston, William. *The Democratic Forest*. Introduction by Eudora Welty. New York: Doubleday.

Kennedy, Eugene C. *Fixes*. New York: Doubleday.

Loring, John. *Tiffany Parties*. Preface by Aileen Mehle, introduction by Jane Lane. New York: Doubleday.

Moyers, Bill D. *A World of Ideas: Conversations with Thoughtful Men and Women About American Life Today and the Ideas Shaping Our Future*. With Betty Sue Flowers. New York: Doubleday.

Pushkin, Alexander. *The Golden Cockerel and Other Fairy Tales*. Illustrated by Boris Zvorykin, translated from the French by Jessie Wood, introduction by Rudolf Nureyev. New York: Doubleday, 1990.

Simon, Carly. *Amy the Dancing Bear*. Illustrated by Margot Datz. New York: Doubleday.

Steinke, Darcey. *Up Through the Water*. New York: Doubleday.

Zamoyska-Panek, Christine, with Fred Benton Holmberg. *Have You Forgotten? A Memoir of Poland, 1939–1945*. New York: Doubleday.

1990

Gonick, Larry. *The Cartoon History of the Universe 1, Volumes 1–7, From the Big Bang to Alexander the Great.* New York: Doubleday.

Kirkland, Gelsey. *The Shape of Love.* With Greg Lawrence. New York: Doubleday.

Mahfouz, Naguib. *The Cairo Trilogy: Palace Walk, Palace of Desire, Sugar Street.* New York: Doubleday, 1990, 1991, 1992.

Moyers, Bill D. *A World of Ideas II: Public Opinions from Private Citizens.* With Andie Tucher. New York: Doubleday.

Riboud, Marc. *Capital of Heaven.* New York: Doubleday.

Simon, Carly. *The Boy of the Bells.* Illustrated by Margot Datz. New York: Doubleday.

1991

Crook, Elizabeth. *The Raven's Bride.* New York: Doubleday.

Graham, Martha. *Blood Memory.* New York: Doubleday.

Ladd, Mary-Sargent. *The Frenchwoman's Bedroom.* New York: Doubleday.

Larsen, Stephen, and Robin Larsen. *A Fire in the Mind: The Life of Joseph Campbell.* New York: Doubleday.

Linscott, Jody. *Once Upon A to Z: An Alphabet Odyssey.* Illustrations by Claudia Porges Holland. New York: Doubleday.

Mason, Francis. *I Remember Balanchine: Recollections of the Ballet Master by Those Who Knew Him.* New York: Doubleday.

Pope-Hennessy, John. *Learning to Look.* New York: Doubleday.

Previn, André. *No Minor Chords: My Days in Hollywood.* New York: Doubleday.

Rothschild, Miriam. *Butterfly Cooing Like a Dove.* New York: Doubleday.

Simon, Carly. *The Fisherman's Song.* Illustrated by Margot Datz. New York: Doubleday.

Simon, Paul. *At the Zoo.* Illustrated by Valérie Michaut. New York: Doubleday.

Walter, Jakob. *The Diary of a Napoleonic Foot Soldier.* Edited and with an introduction by Marc Raeff. New York: Doubleday.

1992

Elliott, Carl, Sr., and Michael D'Orso. *The Cost of Courage: The Journey of an American Congressman.* New York: Doubleday.

Hampton, Mark. Legendary Decorators of the Twentieth Century. New York: Doubleday.

Loring, John. *The Tiffany Gourmet Cookbook.* New York: Doubleday.

Lowe, David Garrard. *Stanford White's New York.* New York: Doubleday.

Lyons, Robert. *Egyptian Time.* Photographs by Robert Lyons. With a short story by Naguib Mahfouz, translated by Peter Theroux, introduction by Charlie Pye-Smith. New York: Doubleday.

Radzinsky, Edvard. *The Last Tsar: The Life and Death of Nicholas II.* Translated by Marian Schwartz. New York: Doubleday.

Valenti, Jack. Protect and Defend. New York: Doubleday.

1993

Bass, Jack. *Taming the Storm: The Life and Times of Judge Frank M. Johnson, Jr., and the South's Fight over Civil Rights.* New York: Doubleday.

Jamison, Judith, with Howard Kaplan. *Dancing Spirit: An Autobiography.* New York: Doubleday.

Jhabvala, Ruth Prawer. *Poet and Dancer.* New York: Doubleday.

Kirkland, Gelsey. *The Little Ballerina and Her Dancing Horse.* With Greg Lawrence. Illustrated by Jacqueline Rogers. New York: Doubleday.

Linscott, Jody. *The Worthy Wonders Lost at Sea: A Whimsical Word Search Adventure.* Illustrations by Claudia Porges Holland. New York: Doubleday.

Love, Robert, ed. *The Best of Rolling Stone: 25 Years of Journalism on the Edge.* New York: Doubleday.

Moyers, Bill D. *Healing and the Mind.* With Betty S. Flowers and David Grubin. New York: Doubleday.

Patnaik, Naveen. *The Garden of Life: An Introduction to the Healing Plants of India.* New York: Doubleday.

Simon, Carly. *The Nighttime Chauffeur.* Illustrated by Margot Datz. New York: Doubleday.

Stenn, David. *Bombshell: The Life and Death of Jean Harlow.* New York: Doubleday.

1994

Beevor, Antony, and Artemis Cooper. *Paris After the Liberation, 1944–1949.* New York: Doubleday.

Cott, Jonathan. *Isis and Osiris: Exploring the Goddess Myth.* New York: Doubleday.

Crook, Elizabeth. *Promised Lands: A Novel of the Texas Rebellion.* New York: Doubleday.

Frissell, Toni. *Photographs, 1933–1967.* Introduction by George Plimpton, foreword by Sidney Frissell Stafford. New York: Doubleday/Library of Congress, Prints and Photographs Division.

Gonick, Larry. *The Cartoon History of the Universe 2, Volumes 8–13, From the Springtime of China to the Fall of Rome, India Too!* New York: Doubleday.

Peskov, Vasily. *Lost in the Taiga: One Russian Family's Fifty-Year Struggle for Survival and Religious Freedom in the Siberian Wilderness.* Translated by Marian Schwartz. New York: Doubleday.

Sís, Peter. *The Three Golden Keys.* New York: Doubleday.

1995

Dickinson, Emily. *Skies in Blossom: The Nature Poetry of Emily Dickinson.* Edited by Jonathan Cott, illustrations by Mary Frank. New York: Doubleday.

Jhabvala, Ruth Prawer. *Shards of Memory.* New York: Doubleday.

Moyers, Bill D. *The Language of Life: A Festival of Poets.* With James Haba and David Grubin. New York: Doubleday.

West, Dorothy. *The Wedding.* New York: Doubleday.

1996

Radzinsky, Edvard. *Stalin: The First In-Depth Biography Based on Explosive New Documents from Russia's Secret Archives.* New York: Doubleday.

Jacqueline Kennedy Onassis as an Author

(In Chronological Order)

Onassis, Jacqueline. "Randolph." In *The Grand Original: Portraits of Randolph Churchill by His Friends,* edited by Kay Halle. Boston: Houghton Mifflin, 1971.

Bouvier, Jacqueline, and Lee Bouvier. *One Special Summer.* New York: Delacorte, 1974.

Onassis, Jacqueline. "The Talk of the Town: Being Present." *The New Yorker,* January 13, 1975.

Onassis, Jacqueline Bouvier. Afterword to *Longing for Darkness: Kamante's Tales from Out of Africa with Original Photographs (January 1914–July 1931) and Quotations from Isak Dinesen (Karen Blixen),* by Peter Beard. New York: Harcourt Brace Jovanovich, 1975; San Francisco: Chronicle Books, 1990.

Onassis, Jacqueline, ed. *In the Russian Style.* With the cooperation of the Metropolitan Museum of Art. Introduction by Audrey Kennett, designed by Bryan Holme. New York: Viking, 1976.

Onassis, Jacqueline Kennedy. "A Visit to the High Priestess of Vanity Fair." In *Vanity Fair,* with essays by Jacqueline Kennedy Onassis, Polaire Weissman, and Stella Blum. New York: Metropolitan Museum of Art, 1977.

Zvorykin, Boris. *The Firebird and Other Russian Fairy Tales.* Edited and with an introduction by Jacqueline Onassis. New York: Viking, 1978.

Adams, William Howard. *Atget's Gardens: A Selection of Eugène Atget's Garden Photographs.* Introduction by Jacqueline Onassis. Garden City, N.Y.: Doubleday, 1979.

Nevins, Deborah, ed. *Grand Central Terminal: City Within the City.* With a foreword by Jacqueline Kennedy Onassis. New York: Municipal Art Society of New York, 1982.

Young, James L. *A Field of Horses: The World of Marshall P. Hawkins.* With a foreword by Jacqueline Kennedy Onassis. Dallas: Taylor, 1988.

Jackson, Michael. *Moonwalk.* With a foreword by Jacqueline Kennedy Onassis. New York: Doubleday, 1988.

Sources

Interviews

Interviewees are identified by their occupation at the time they were dealing with Jackie.

Alderman, Robert—partner of Mark Zebrowski, consulted for book on Indian art

Ansel, Ruth—art director, *New York Times Magazine*

Auchincloss, Hugh D., III—stepbrother

Auchincloss, Louis (d. 2010)—author

Barry, Bill—colleague

Bass, Jack—author

Beevor, Antony—author

Bernier, Olivier—author

Bernier, Rosamond—friend

Beyer (formerly Porges Holland), Claudia—illustrator

Bradford, Sarah—biographer

Bryson, Bill—author

Cabot (formerly Brandon), Mabel—author

Cahill, Thomas—colleague

Chase-Riboud, Barbara—author

Clow, Irina—daughter of Leonid Tarassuk, consulted for books on Russian art

Cookman, Whitney—colleague

Cott, Jonathan—author

Crook, Elizabeth—author

D'Anglejan-Chatillon (formerly Ladd), Mary-Sargent—author

Dawnay, Caroline—literary agent

De Combray, Richard—author

De Pauw, Linda Grant—author

D'Orso, Mike—author

Ewing, William—curator at International Center of
   Photography, consulted for books on photography

Feibleman, Peter—neighbor on Martha's Vineyard

Fitzgerald, Jim—colleague

Franklin, Lynn—literary agent

Fraser, Lady Antonia (Lady Antonia Pinter)—friend

Gere, Richard—author

Gernert, David—colleague

Giles, Sarah—author

Gollob, Herman—colleague

Golob, Paul—colleague

Gonick, Larry—author

Haslam, Nicky—acquaintance

Haykel, Navina—curator, colleague of Stuart Cary Welch,
   consulted for book on Indian art

Hitchcock, Jane—friend

Hoving, Thomas (d. 2009)—director, Metropolitan Museum
   of Art

Hunt, Conover—author

Jacka, Jerry—photographer

Jong, Erica—acquaintance

Kaplan, Howard—colleague

Kasinec, Edward—librarian, New York Public Library,
   consulted for books on Russia

Katz, Karl—director of film, television division of
   Metropolitan Museum of Art, friend

Kennedy, Eugene C.—author

Kornbluth, Jesse—author

Kruzan, Peter—colleague

Kuhn, David—arts editor, *Vanity Fair,* consulted about serial
   rights

Lawrence, Greg—author

Lazin, Sarah—book packager at *Rolling Stone*, later literary agent

Levin, Martha—colleague

Linscott, Jody—author

Linz, Mark—director, American University in Cairo Press, colleague

Loring, John—author

Lyons, Robert—photographer, author

Mansel, Philip—author

Mason, Francis (d. 2009)—author

Moyers, Judith—executive producer of Bill Moyers's TV interviews

Moyers, Scott—colleague

Myers, Philip—author

O'Brien, Edna—friend

Porizkova, Paulina—author

Quinn, Marysarah—colleague

Radzinsky, Edvard—author

Ramati, Raquel—author

Riboud, Marc   photographer, author

Rossetti, Chip—editor, American University in Cairo Press, colleague

Rubin, Stephen—colleague

Rusoff, Marly—colleague

Schwartz, Marian—translator

Simon, Carly—author

Sís, Peter—author

Stafford, Sidney Frissell—author

Stenn, David—author

Swan, Bill—photo editor, *Town & Country*, consulted about serial rights

Talese, Nan—colleague

Tarassuk, Ilya—son of Leonid Tarassuk, consulted about
  books on Russian art
Tracy, Bruce—colleague
Trewin, Ion—editor, Hodder & Stoughton, colleague
Tuckerman, Nancy—friend, assistant, colleague
Udall, Stewart (d. 2010)—author
Vickers, Hugo—author
Vitale, Alberto—colleague
Wasserman, Stephen—colleague
Welch, Edith—contributor to book on India, wife of author
  Stuart Cary Welch
Wenner, Jann—friend, collaborator on several book projects
Zaroulis, Nancy—author

Archives and Manuscripts

Ansel, Ruth: Courtesy of Ruth Ansel
Auchincloss, Hugh D., III: John F. Kennedy Library, Boston
Beaton, Cecil: St. John's College, Cambridge, U.K.
Crook, Elizabeth: Courtesy of Elizabeth Crook
Doubleday Papers: Courtesy of Doubleday, New York
Franklin, Lynn: Courtesy of Lynn Franklin
Galbraith, John Kenneth: John F. Kennedy Library, Boston
Macmillan, Harold, Lord Stockton: Bodleian Library, Oxford, U.K.
Myers, Philip: Courtesy of Philip Myers
O'Brien, Edna: Courtesy of Edna O'Brien
Oral histories: John F. Kennedy Library, Boston
Pinter, Harold: British Library, London, U.K.
Roberts, Ray: Harry Ransom Center, University of Texas, Austin
Salinger, Pierre: John F. Kennedy Library, Boston
Schiff, Dorothy: New York Public Library
Schlesinger, Arthur M., Jr.: John F. Kennedy Library, Boston
Udall, Stewart L.: University of Arizona, Tucson

Notes

Abbreviations

JBK   Jacqueline Bouvier Kennedy

JKO   Jacqueline Kennedy Onassis

JFK   John F. Kennedy

JFKL   John F. Kennedy Library

NYPL New York Public Library

Prologue

1 *flu symptoms:* K. L. Kelleher, *Jackie: Beyond the Myth of Camelot* ([Philadelphia]: Xlibris, 2000), p. 199.

1 *a famous paint:* Author interview with Peter Sís, June 10, 2009.

1 *non-Hodgkin's lymphoma:* Robert D. McFadden, "Jacqueline Kennedy Onassis Has Lymphoma," *New York Times*, February 11, 1994.

1 *She told Arthur Schlesinger:* Sarah Bradford, *America's Queen: The Life of Jacqueline Kennedy Onassis* (New York: Penguin, 2001), p. 437; Arthur M. Schlesinger, Jr., *Journals: 1952–2000*, ed. Andrew Schlesinger and Stephen Schlesinger (New York: Penguin, 2007), pp. 761–62.

2 *"Nancy, what's a sabbatical?":* Author interviews with Nancy Tuckerman.

2 *former president Nixon:* Schlesinger, *Journals,* p. 472.

4 *three of her favorite books:* Kelleher, *Jackie,* p. 199.

4 *one of the Kennedy sisters:* Marie Brenner, *Great Dames: What I Learned from Older Women* (New York: Crown, 2000), p. 108.

5 *She was "surrounded":* Janny Scott, "Onassis Burial to Be Monday at Arlington," *New York Times*, May 21, 1994.

5 *"I drop everything for a book on ballet":* *Vogue*, Prix de Paris application form, JFKL.

7 *wiped the soles of her bare feet:* Ibid.

7 *Mary Barelli Gallagher:* Mary Barelli Gallagher, *My Life with Jacqueline Kennedy*, ed. Frances Spatz Leighton (London: Michael Joseph, 1970), p. 154.

7 *Antony Beevor:* Author interview with Antony Beevor, January 29, 2008.

7 *"a brain":* Nancy Tuckerman, "A Personal Reminiscence," *The Estate of Jacqueline Kennedy Onassis*, auction, April 23–26, 1996 (New York: Sotheby's, 1996), p. 17.

8 *"There was an unwritten law": A Tribute to Jacqueline Kennedy Onassis* (New York: Doubleday, 1995), p. 1.

9 *"You have the power"*: JKO to Edna O'Brien, May 5 [1991], courtesy of Edna O'Brien.

9 *"The books of somebody who reads"*: Nancy Mitford, *Madame de Pompadour* (New York: Harper & Row, 1968), p. 181.

9 *a group of midwestern ladies*: Carl Sferrazza Anthony, *As We Remember Her: Jacqueline Kennedy Onassis in the Words of Her Family and Friends* (New York: HarperCollins, 1997), p. 134.

9 *"regarded books as his 'friends' "*: Thomas Wright, *Oscar's Books* (London: Chatto & Windus, 2008), pp. 4, 5.

10 *"I think it's too bad"*: Author interview with Jane Hitchcock, February 23, 2008.

Chapter 1

15 *"never be a ballet dancer"*: Mary Van Rensselaer Thayer, *Jacqueline Bouvier Kennedy: A Warm, Personal Story of the First Lady Illustrated with Family Pictures* (Garden City, N.Y.: Doubleday, 1961), p. 39.

16 *"Rhett Butler reminded her"*: Hugh D. Auchincloss III, "Growing Up with Jackie, My Memories, 1941–1953," originally published in *Groton School Quarterly* 60, no. 2 (May 1998): 27; in Papers of Hugh D. Auchincloss III, JFKL.

17 *"edged into her teens"*: Thayer, *Jacqueline Bouvier Kennedy,* p. 39.

17 *"some funny-looking 'gink' "*: Ibid., p. 74.

18 *The biggest framed photo:* Philip Myers, "Squished," unpublished manuscript; author interviews with Philip Myers, September 1 and 3 and December 21, 2009.

18 *British prime minister Lord Melbourne:* Barbara Leaming, *Mrs. Kennedy: The Missing History of the Kennedy Years* (New York: Free Press, 2001), pp. 9–10.

19 *She asked the academic editors:* Press release about White House library, June 21, 1962, Salinger Papers, Box 101, JFKL.

19 *"a library is dead"*: JBK to Arthur Schlesinger, undated [1963?], Schlesinger Papers, Box P-6, JFKL.

20 *Denis Diderot, Benjamin Franklin, and Thomas Jefferson:* Carl Sferrazza Anthony, "The Substance Behind the Style," *Town & Country,* July 1994, p. 59.

21 *"The Greek way"*: JBK to Harold Macmillan, September 14, 1965, Papers of Harold Macmillan, Lord Stockton, Bodleian Library, Oxford, MS. Macmillan dep. C. 563, folios 54–59; see also Alistair Horne, *Harold Macmillan, Volume II, 1957–1986* (New York: Viking, 1989), p. 294.

22 *"Lyndon Johnson is really the Roman"*: JBK to Arthur Schlesinger, May 28, 1965, Schlesinger Papers, Writings, *A Thousand Days,* Background Material, JFKL.

22 *Kazantzakis led her:* See also her comments on Kazantzakis in John F.

Baker, "Editors at Work: Star Behind the Scenes," *Publishers Weekly*, April 19, 1993, p. 20.

22 *"half Tarzan, half Byron"*: Christopher Andersen, *Jackie After Jack: Portrait of the Lady* (New York: William Morrow, 1998), p. 248.

23 *Aristotle Onassis complained:* Donald Spoto, *Jacqueline Bouvier Kennedy Onassis: A Life* (New York: St. Martin's Press, 2000), p. 254.

23 *Schiff's note of what she recalled:* Dorothy Schiff memorandum on lunch with JBK at her apartment, 1040 Fifth Ave., April 16, 1968, dated April 19, 1968, Dorothy Schiff Papers, New York Public Library, Box 45, Editorial Files, Onassis, Jacqueline, December 13, 1960, to August 31, 1970.

23 *Greta's chief complaint:* Ibid., article translated from *Oggi*.

23 *lounging on a sofa reading a book: The Estate of Jacqueline Kennedy Onassis,* auction, April 23–26, 1996 (New York: Sotheby's, 1996), 76; see image at p. 557, lot 1175.

24 *Boucher painting of Pompadour with a book:* Princess Grace of Monaco, with Gwen Robyns, *My Book of Flowers* (Garden City, N.Y.: Doubleday, 1980), p. 103.

25 *he would not let her:* Author interviews with Nancy Tuckerman.

25 *wearing a blouse that was unbuttoned:* Dorothy Schiff memorandum on lunch with JKO, November 7, 1975, Schiff Papers, NYPL, Box 45, Editorial Files, Onassis, Jacqueline, 1971–77.

26 *shared a mistress with President Kennedy:* Sally Bedell Smith, *Grace and Power: The Private World of the Kennedy White House* (New York: Random House, 2004), pp. 172–73.

27 *last person she allowed in:* Eleanor Dwight, *Diana Vreeland* (New York: HarperCollins, 2002), p. 285.

28 *"out of the middle classes":* Diana Vreeland, *Allure*, with Christopher Hemphill (Garden City, N.Y.: Doubleday, 1980), p. 116.

29 *"I have a holy attitude":* Martha Graham, *Blood Memory* (New York: Doubleday, 1991), p. 274.

30 *The second of two authors:* Author interviews with Judith Moyers, May 26, June 11 and 12, 2009.

30 *"one sure path into the world":* Joseph Campbell, *The Power of Myth*, with Bill Moyers, ed. Betty Sue Flowers (New York: Doubleday, 1988), p. xv.

Chapter 2

32 *"I keep thinking":* Gerald Clarke, *Capote: A Biography* (New York: Simon & Schuster, 1988), p. 272.

32 *"temperament and talent of a writer":* Carl Sferrazza Anthony, *As We Remember Her: Jacqueline Kennedy Onassis in the Words of Her Family and Friends* (New York: HarperCollins, 1997), p. 19.

32 *"could write like a million":* Ibid., p. 49.

32 *"by writing a book":* Mary Van Rensselaer Thayer, *Jacqueline Bouvier Kennedy: A Warm, Personal Story of the First Lady Illustrated with Family Pictures* (Garden City, N.Y.: Doubleday, 1961), p. 36.

32 *clearly a writer:* Mary E. Campbell to Carol Phillips, *Vogue* Prix de Paris file, JFKL.

33 *"Jackie and my mother":* Author interview with Carly Simon, June 7, 2009.

34 *"pronounced enough": Vogue*, Prix de Paris file, JFKL.

36 *short story she submitted:* The story is reproduced in full in Anthony, *As We Remember Her,* pp. 49–51.

37 *envious of Pamela Harriman:* Author interview with Sarah Bradford, January 28, 2008.

37 *among the first presidential wives:* "First Ladies and College Degrees," at firstladies.org, the Web site of the National First Ladies' Library.

39 *"John is always taking one out":* Jacqueline Onassis, "Randolph," in Kay Halle, ed., *The Grand Original: Portraits of Randolph Churchill by His Friends* (Boston: Houghton Mifflin, 1971), pp. 283–85.

39 One Special Summer: Jacqueline Bouvier and Lee Bouvier, *One Special Summer* (New York: Delacorte, 1974).

42 *"Lovely it is":* "Being Present," *The New Yorker*, January 13, 1975, pp. 26–29.

43 *freeing her at last to take up a career:* Author interviews with Nancy Tuckerman.

44 *"A huge man":* Jacqueline Kennedy Onassis, ed., *In the Russian Style* (New York: Viking, 1976), p. 29.

44 *Catherine the Great:* Ibid.

44 *$60,000 for a snuffbox:* C. David Heymann, *American Legacy: The Story of John and Caroline Kennedy* (New York: Atria, 2007), p. 148.

44 *Nabokov said that her book:* Nicolas Nabokov, "Under the Cranberry Tree," *New York Review of Books*, March 3, 1977.

45 *her friend Leonid Tarassuk:* Leonid Tarassuk, "Cranberry Sauce," Letters to the Editor, *New York Review of Books*, November 24, 1977, and "Cranberry Jello," March 23, 1978; both of the foregoing with replies from Nicolas Nabokov.

45 *The exhibition, entitled Vanity Fair:* Jacqueline Kennedy Onassis, "A Visit to the High Priestess of Vanity Fair," in *Vanity Fair* (New York: Metropolitan Museum of Art, 1977).

46 *"many summer mornings when":* C. P. Cavafy, "Ithaka," read by Maurice Tempelsman, quoted in *In Memoriam Jacqueline Bouvier Kennedy Onassis, 1929–1994* (New York: Doubleday, 1995), pp. 20–22.

48 *"a gift of gratitude":* Jacqueline Onassis, ed., *The Firebird and Other Russian Fairy Tales* (New York: Viking, 1978), p. 6.

48 *"The royal vision lingers":* William Howard Adams, *Atget's Gardens* (London: Gordon Fraser Gallery, 1979), pp. 6–7.

51 *"Let us now praise Grand Central Station":* Deborah Nevins, ed., *Grand Central Terminal: City Within the City* (New York: Municipal Art Society of New York, 1982), p. 8.

52 *"The inexorable press":* James L. Young, M.F.H., *A Field of Horses: The World of Marshall P. Hawkins* (Dallas: Taylor, 1988), p. 9.

52 *pressed her to write a foreword:* Mark Shanahan and Meredith Gold-

stein, "Names: Remembering Michael," interview with Stephen Davis, *Boston Globe*, June 27, 2009.

52 *"What can one say about Michael Jackson?"*: Michael Jackson, *Moonwalk* (New York: Doubleday, 1988).

53 *"The secret is not so much"*: Jane Stanton Hitchcock, *Social Crimes* (New York: Hyperion, 2003), pp. 29, 202; author interview with Jane Hitchcock, February 23, 2008.

53 *She said it was "agony"*: Dorothy Schiff memorandum, April 19, 1968, Dorothy Schiff Papers, NYPL, Box 45, Editorial Files, Onassis, Jacqueline, December 13, 1960, to August 31, 1970.

53 *"His conquest of us"*: Adams, *Atget's Gardens,* p. 6.

Chapter 3

54 *"literally abasing herself"*: Author interview with Scott Moyers, November 18, 2008.

54 *"Oy vey"*: Author interview with Howard Kaplan, April 1, 2009.

55 *"aren't we lucky"*: Author interview with Mabel Cabot, March 26, 2009.

56 *"The only way to exist happily"*: Carl Sferrazza Anthony, *As We Remember Her: Jacqueline Kennedy Onassis in the Words of Her Family and Friends* (New York: HarperCollins, 1997), p. 58.

56 *"always lived through men"*: Donald Spoto, *Jacqueline Bouvier Kennedy Onassis: A Life* (New York: St. Martin's Press, 2000), p. 264.

56 *only three days a week:* "Jackie Onassis Lunch," Dorothy Schiff memorandum, November 7, 1975, p. 3, Dorothy Schiff Papers, NYPL, Box 45, Editorial Files, Onassis, Jacqueline, 1971–77.

57 *"some language conundrum"*: William Noonan, *Forever Young: My Friendship with John F. Kennedy, Jr.* (New York: Viking, 2006), p. 31.

58 *"you only work part-time"*: Author interview with anonymous source.

59 *new contact with writers:* Author interviews with David Stenn, May 8, 2008, March 26, 2009.

59 *$10,000 a year:* Spoto, *Jacqueline Bouvier Kennedy Onassis,* p. 265.

60 *Lisa Drew had told Jackie:* Ibid., pp. 281–82; Anthony, *As We Remember Her,* pp. 283–85.

61 *"still upsetting to her"*: John F. Baker, "Editors at Work: Star Behind the Scenes," *Publishers Weekly*, April 19, 1993, p. 19.

61 *"dealing with the Kennedys wasn't easy"*: Author interview with Olivier Bernier, April 11, 2008.

61 *"she had never been so happy"*: "Lunch with Jackie Onassis, Le Madrigal, Wednesday, April 20, 1977," Dorothy Schiff memorandum, April 21, 1977, Box 45, NYPL, p. 12.

62 *"a kid straight out of college"*: Christopher Andersen, *Jackie After Jack: Portrait of a Lady* (New York: William Morrow, 1998), p. 307.

62 *found her more interesting:* "Jackie Onassis Lunch," Schiff memorandum, November 7, 1975, p. 4.

62 *Mason was "shocked"*: Author interview with Francis Mason, November 18, 2008.

62 *middlebrow readership:* Jason Epstein, *Book Business: Publishing Past, Present, and Future* (New York: Norton, 2001), pp. 39–40, 70.

62 *"I sell books, I don't read them":* Al Silverman, *The Time of Their Lives: The Golden Age of Great American Book Publishers, Their Editors and Authors* (New York: Truman Talley/Macmillan, 2008), pp. 190–91.

62 *"rubber stamped on newspaper":* Author interview with Marysarah Quinn, May 28, 2009.

63 *Sargent asked Tuckerman:* Author interviews with Nancy Tuckerman.

64 *"a sense of complicity":* Author interview with Scott Moyers, November 18, 2008.

64 *"another guardian of Camelot":* Elizabeth Crook, "Editor Jackie: A Guiding Hand Through the Forest," *Austin American-Statesman*, May 27, 1994.

64 *Jackie had a slow start:* See the chronological list of her books, pp. 292–97.

64 *not accomplishing very much:* C. David Heymann, *A Woman Named Jackie* (London: Heinemann, 1989), p. 583.

64 *lacked business smarts:* Author interview with Herman Gollob, April 1, 2009.

65 *"things of a scholarly nature":* Author interviews with Nancy Tuckerman.

66 *"These are the books I most love to do":* JKO to Robert Banker, June 3, 1980, Ray Roberts Papers, Ransom Center, University of Texas, Austin.

67 *he was "amazed":* Author interview with Ion Trewin, June 16, 2009.

68 *"she hated to lose money":* Author interview with Steve Rubin, November 17, 2008.

68 *sometimes filtered the proposals:* Author interviews with Bruce Tracy, September 15, 2008, March 23, 2009.

68 *"high culture and famous friends":* Author interview with David Gernert, February 19, 2009.

68 *exotic bird in a gilded cage:* Author interview with Steve Wasserman, May 13, 2009.

69 *"look as beautiful as possible":* Baker, "Editors at Work," p. 20.

70 *watched the designer "melt":* Author interview with Olivier Bernier, April 11, 2008.

70 *"a little too fanciful":* Author interview with Peter Kruzan, May 13, 2009.

70 *"lope on down":* Author interview with Whitney Cookman, May 13, 2009.

71 *"I was only twenty-five":* Author interview with Marysarah Quinn, May 28, 2009.

72 *"if you need some hand holding":* Crook, "Editor Jackie."

72 *"I want to be the kind":* C. Romano, "Doubleday's Editor of Distinction," *Philadelphia Inquirer*, May 22, 1994.

72 *an offer to Jackie's friend:* Author interview with Herman Gollob, April 1, 2009.

73 *Barry, for example, was the person:* Author interview with Lynn Franklin, February 20, 2009.

73 *"Jackie Onassis would like to edit this book":* Author interview with Jack Bass, April 6, 2009.

73 *expected to be the hunter:* Author interviews with Nan Talese.

73 *the names that got away:* Correspondence with JKO in Doubleday papers.

75 *Arthur Gold and Robert Fizdale:* JKO correspondence offered for sale via lionheartinc.com, Lion Heart Autographs.

75 *had to tell Cathy Rindner Tempelsman:* Correspondence with JKO in Doubleday papers.

75 *Bill Barry worked for many years:* Author interview with Bill Barry, February 20, 2009.

76 *"I did everything she told me to do":* "Charlie Rose: 20 May 1994," via YouTube.com.

79 *an autobiography or a book on Eastern spirituality:* E-mail exchange with Jonathan Cott, March 31, 2009.

79 *about whom she felt especially protective:* Author interview with Marly Rusoff, March 23, 2009.

Chapter 4

83 *One of the times she called:* Author interview with Mike D'Orso, May 15, 2009.

84 *encouraging Barbara Chase-Riboud:* "Chase-Riboud, Barbara," in Sara Pendergast, Tom Pendergast, *Contemporary Black Biography* (Detroit: Thomson Gale, 2005).

85 *"Nancy, can you come now?":* Author interviews with Nancy Tuckerman.

85 *on the beach with Jackie:* Author interview with Barbara Chase-Riboud, March 16, 2009.

86 *the historian Fawn Brodie:* Fawn McKay Brodie, *Thomas Jefferson: An Intimate History* (New York: Norton, 1974).

87 *her step-uncle, Wilmarth Lewis:* Carl Sferrazza Anthony, "The Substance Behind the Style," *Town & Country*, July 1994, p. 59.

87 *two of Jefferson's chairs: The Estate of Jacqueline Kennedy Onassis,* auction, April 23–26, 1996 (New York: Sotheby's, 1996), 56–57, lot 40.

87 *"Thomas Jefferson's way":* JKO to Dorothy Schiff [on Viking letterhead], April 4, 1977, Dorothy Schiff Papers, NYPL, Box 45, Editorial Files.

88 *Annette Gordon-Reed has written:* Annette Gordon-Reed, *Thomas Jefferson and Sally Hemings: An American Controversy* (Charlottesville: University Press of Virginia, 1997), pp. 4, 181, 183.

88 *Echo of Lions:* Author interview with Barbara Chase-Riboud, March 16, 2009.

90 *a man who didn't want to be married:* Mary Van Rensselaer Thayer, *Jacqueline Bouvier Kennedy: A Warm, Personal Story of the First Lady*

Illustrated with Family Pictures (Garden City, N.Y.: Doubleday, 1961), p. 95.

90 *people would think he was "queer":* David Pitts, *Jack and Lem: John F. Kennedy and Lem Billings: The Untold Story of an Extraordinary Friendship* (New York: Carroll & Graf, 2007), p. 138.

91 *find some pretty girl:* Arthur M. Schlesinger, Jr., *Journals: 1952–2000*, ed. Andrew Schlesinger and Stephen Schlesinger (New York: Penguin, 2007), p. 167.

91 *"Her silent acceptance":* Donald Spoto, *Jacqueline Bouvier Kennedy Onassis: A Life* (New York: St. Martin's Press, 2000), p. 159.

92 *Grace and Rainier often lived:* Robert Lacey, *Grace* (New York: Putnam, 1994), pp. 332–33.

93 *a tribute to Josephine Baker:* JKO to Dorothy Schiff, [1976], Schiff Papers, NYPL, Box 45, Editorial Files.

94 *"how magnificent the flowers were":* Princess Grace with Gwen Robyns, *My Book of Flowers* (Garden City, N.Y.: Doubleday, 1980), p. 8.

95 *The one that would have mortified:* Kiki Feroudi Moutsatsos, *The Onassis Women: An Eyewitness Account* (New York: Putnam, 1998), pp. 239–40.

96 *"I wanted to go away":* Pete Hamill, "A Private Life Defined by Wit, Compassion," *Newsday*, May 22, 1994.

96 *marriage to Onassis as "a mistake":* Author interviews with Nancy Tuckerman.

97 *"I think this is where":* William Sylvester Noonan, *Forever Young: My Friendship with John F. Kennedy, Jr.* (New York: Viking, 2006), p. 41.

97 *"Allure holds you":* Diana Vreeland, *Allure* (Garden City, N.Y.: Doubleday, 1980), p. 11.

97 *letter of introduction:* JKO to Whom It May Concern, November 28, 1978, Diana Vreeland Papers, NYPL, Mss. Coll. 5980, Box 10, folder 10.6.

99 *"She was a geisha":* Vreeland, *Allure,* p. 142.

99 *"this tremendous charm":* Sarah Bradford, *America's Queen* (New York: Penguin, 2001), p. 37.

99 *"Marilyn Monroe!!!":* JKO to Ray Roberts, May 14, 1980, Ray Roberts Papers, Ransom Center, University of Texas, Austin. The book was eventually published as Bert Stern and Annie Gottlieb, *The Last Sitting* (New York: Morrow, 1982).

100 *"If eyes were bullets":* Vreeland, *Allure,* p. 8.

101 *"She was as common as mud":* Ibid., p. 24.

102 *because of its similarity to her own story:* Author interviews with Judith Moyers, May 26 and June 11 and 12, 2009.

103 *The novel's author:* Author interview with Elizabeth Crook, May 22, 2009.

103 *"to write about a woman":* Bob Tutt, " 'Bride' Explores Sam Houston's 2-Month Marriage," *Houston Chronicle*, February 21, 1991.

103 *"an old married couple":* JKO to Elizabeth Crook, August 10, 1990, courtesy of Elizabeth Crook.

104 *"was insane for Elizabeth Crook"*: Author interview with Steve Rubin, November 17, 2008.

104 *"People go to California"*: JKO to Judith Moyers, February 7, 1991, courtesy of Elizabeth Crook.

105 *"listening to an HOUR-long"*: Karen Karbo, "The Accidental Breadwinner," *New York Times*, December 14, 2008; e-mail exchange with Karen Karbo, December 27 and 28, 2008.

107 *a respected literary agent*: Author interviews with Scott Moyers, November 18, 2008, October 19, 2009.

108 *"I was as unique to her"*: *A Tribute to Jacqueline Kennedy Onassis* (New York: Doubleday, 1995), p. 33.

108 *"This sounds like a white person"*: Author interview with anonymous source.

109 *"Josephine boarded the train"*: Dorothy West, *The Wedding* (New York: Doubleday, 1995), p. 43.

109 *"romantic love"*: Ibid., p. 200.

110 *"all men are unfaithful"*: Marie Brenner, "The Unforgettable Jackie," *Vogue*, August 1994, p. 301; reprinted in Brenner, *Great Dames: What I Learned from Older Women* (New York: Crown, 2000).

110 *"Marriage is not a simple love affair"*: Joseph Campbell, *The Power of Myth* (New York: Doubleday, 1988), p. 7.

110 *dropping a memory of Jack*: Brenner, *Great Dames*, p. 104; Carl Sferrazza Anthony, *As We Remember Her: Jacqueline Kennedy Onassis in the Words of Her Family and Friends* (New York: HarperCollins, 1997), p. 348.

111 *"May I speak with Mr. Onassis, please?"*: Author interview with Bill Barry, February 20, 2009.

111 *"my Greek alabaster head"*: "Last Will and Testament of Jacqueline K. Onassis," at livingtrustnetwork.com.

Chapter 5

112 *"she loved her children"*: Pete Hamill, "A Private Life Defined by Wit, Compassion," *Newsday*, May 22, 1994.

113 *"Probably I will be too intense"*: JBK to Harold Macmillan, May 17, 1965, Macmillan Papers, Bodleian Library, MS. Macmillan deposit C. 553, folios 38–40.

113 *"if they grow up to be all right"*: JBK to Harold Macmillan, September 14, 1965, in ibid., folios 54–59.

113 *John curtsied, too*: Arthur M. Schlesinger, Jr., *Journals: 1952–2000*, ed. Andrew Schlesinger and Stephen Schlesinger (New York: Penguin, 2007), p. 200.

115 *Caroline, published a book*: Caroline Kennedy, *The Best-Loved Poems of Jacqueline Kennedy Onassis* (New York: Hyperion, 2001).

115 *"My strongest image"*: *Property from Kennedy Family Homes: Hyannis Port, Martha's Vineyard, New Jersey, New York, Virginia* (New York: Sotheby's, 2005), p. 9.

115 *he had the feeling:* J. B. West with Mary Lynn Kotz, *Upstairs at the White House: My Life with the First Ladies* (New York: Coward, McCann & Geoghegan, 1973), p. 217.

116 *"in public she had a 'face' ":* Author interview with Bill Barry, February 20, 2009.

117 *" 'books for children of all ages' ":* Author interview with Steve Rubin, November 17, 2008.

117 *Herman Gollob is now retired:* Author interview with Herman Gollob, April 1, 2009.

118 *Carly Simon's recollections:* Author interview with Carly Simon, June 7, 2009.

121 *stumbled onto a new genre:* Author interview with Steve Rubin, November 17, 2008.

121 *Plácido Domingo:* Sheila Weller, *Girls Like Us: Carole King, Joni Mitchell, Carly Simon—and the Journey of a Generation* (New York: Atria, 2008), p. 473.

122 *one-time publisher Joe Armstrong:* Ibid., p. 472.

123 *his friendship with Jackie worked:* Author interview with Jann Wenner, April 8, 2009.

124 *"I used to work for Joe":* Author interview with Claudia Beyer, May 28, 2009.

128 *"Who's going to refuse a phone call":* Author interview with Peter Kruzan, May 13, 2009.

129 *"would make a suggestion":* Author interview with Jody Linscott, February 10, 2009.

130 *Czech artist Peter Sís:* Author interview with Peter Sís, June 10, 2009; K. L. Kelleher, *Jackie: Beyond the Myth of Camelot* ([Philadelphia]: Xlibris, 2000), pp. 186, 191.

135 *journey into something she didn't know before:* John F. Baker, "Editors at Work: Star Behind the Scenes," *Publishers Weekly,* April 19, 1993, p. 19.

135 *recounting of the Czech "Velvet Revolution":* Author interview with Marly Rusoff, March 23, 2009.

136 *In the 1990s, when Jackie:* Author interview with Elizabeth Crook, May 22, 2009; Elizabeth Crook, "Editor Jackie: A Guiding Hand Through the Forest," *Austin American-Statesman,* May 27, 1994.

137 *"CUT" and "DELETE":* Crook, "Editor Jackie."

138 *He was a young man:* Author interviews with David Stenn, May 8, 2008, March 26, 2009.

138 *"things I'd told her":* Author interview with Scott Moyers, November 18, 2008.

139 *increasing the assistant's pay:* Bill Barry e-mail to author, August 16, 2010.

139 *When he worked briefly:* Author interview with Paul Golob, April 1, 2009.

Chapter 6

144 *a hardback book to accompany the exhibition:* Mabel Brandon quoted by Judith Martin in "Behind Every Good Colonial," *Washington Post*, May 28, 1976. See also Judy Klemesrud, "Mrs. Ford Helps 'Remember the Ladies' of Revolutionary Era," *New York Times*, June 30, 1976. Additional background information from author interview with Mabel Cabot [formerly Brandon], March 26, 2009.

145 *An article in* Ms. *magazine:* Miriam Schneir, the exhibition's research assistant, was commissioned to write about it in *Ms.*, July 1976, pp. 82–83.

145 *well informed about Abigail Adams:* Author interview with Olivier Bernier, April 11, 2008.

145 *"like a state prisoner":* Quoted in Klemesrud, "Mrs. Ford Helps 'Remember the Ladies.'"

145 *inveterate and extravagant shopper:* Linda Grant De Pauw and Conover Hunt, *Remember the Ladies: Women in America 1750–1815* (New York: Viking/Pilgrim Society), p. 149.

146 *"few mothers who did not bury at least one child":* Ibid., p. 40.

146 *printing and newspaper publishing:* Ibid., p. 62.

146 *"Among the sponsors":* Author interview with Conover Hunt, November 14, 2008.

148 *"Tom Guinzburg did her a very great service":* Author interview with Mabel Cabot, March 26, 2009.

148 *This book, about Muffie's mother:* Mabel H. Cabot, *Vanished Kingdoms: A Woman Explorer in Tibet, China, and Mongolia 1921–1925* (New York: Aperture, 2003).

149 *"wild role-playing parties":* Hahn's granddaughter's tribute to her grandmother is quoted in "Emily Hahn," en.wikipedia.org (accessed May 6, 2010).

149 *William and Roslyn Targ:* Leonore Fleischer, "Letter from New York: Socializing," *Washington Post*, August 12, 1979; "William Targ," en.wikipedia.org (accessed May 6, 2010).

150 *significant commercial success:* Frederick M. Winship, "Jackie's Publishing Coup," *Washington Post*, July 15, 1979.

151 *"Why Does This Woman Work?":* Gloria Steinem, "On Jacqueline Kennedy Onassis," *Ms.*, March 1979, p. 50.

152 *kept a framed copy of the* Ms. *issue: The Estate of Jacqueline Kennedy Onassis,* auction, April 23–26, 1996 (New York: Sotheby's, 1996), 477, lot 895.

152 *"a closet feminist":* Frank Rich, "Journal: The Jackie Mystery," *New York Times*, May 26, 1994.

152 *far too much influence:* Author interview with Linda Grant De Pauw, November 13, 2008; C. David Heymann, *A Woman Named Jackie* (London: Heinemann, 1989), p. 574.

152 *to benefit a library:* Lee Lescaze, "Radcliffe Revisionism," *Washington Post*, June 13, 1979.

152 *turnout for the Zaroulis book:* Author interview with Steve Rubin, November 17, 2008.

153 *the crowd broke and ran toward her:* Leonore Fleischer, "Letter from New York," *Washington Post*, August 12, 1979.

153 *"I didn't know Mrs. Onassis":* Nancy Zaroulis to author, May 20, 2009.

153 *connection between Zaroulis's examination:* Winship, "Jackie's Publishing Coup."

153 *road toward female emancipation:* Beverly Stephen, "Novel Is Center of Attention Thanks to Its Editor—Jackie O.," *Chicago Tribune*, September 2, 1979.

153 *"I was born in 1946":* Author interview with Conover Hunt, November 14, 2008.

155 *"very much Jackie's dish":* Author interviews with Louis Auchincloss, November 19, 2008, March 24, 2009.

156 *"an eighteenth-century woman":* Dorothy Schiff memorandum, dated January 27, 1967, of a meeting with JBK at the Carlyle November 19, 1964, Schiff Papers, NYPL, Box 45, Editorial Files, Onassis, Jacqueline, December 13, 1960, to August 31, 1970.

156 *arranged in brief chapters:* Olivier Bernier, *The Eighteenth-Century Woman* (Garden City, N.Y.: Doubleday/ Metropolitan Museum of Art, 1981).

156 *Jong believed that she was invited:* Author interview with Erica Jong, May 29, 2009.

157 *dinner after the seminar:* Author interview with Olivier Bernier, April 11, 2008.

157 *commissioned a subsequent book:* Olivier Bernier, *At the Court of Napoleon: Memoirs of the Duchesse d'Abrantès* (New York: Doubleday, 1989).

158 *entirely Jackie's idea:* Author interview with Olivier Bernier, April 11, 2008.

159 *"Being an Edith Wharton fan":* K. L. Kelleher, *Jackie: Beyond the Myth of Camelot* ([Philadelphia]: Xlibris, 2000), p. 197.

160 *"real-life Edith Wharton heroine":* Advertisement for *Maverick in Mauve*, *New York Times*, November 13, 1983.

161 *"no trace of the baby-doll voice":* Marie Brenner, "The Unforgettable Jackie," *Vogue*, August 1994, p. 301; reprinted in Brenner, *Great Dames: What I Learned from Older Women* (New York: Crown, 2000).

162 *"What one can see today":* Louis Auchincloss, *False Dawn* (Garden City, N.Y.: Anchor/Doubleday, 1984), p. 5.

162 *"strides toward emancipation":* Advertisement for *False Dawn*, *New York Times*, August 30, 1984.

162 *"despite the age's chauvinism":* Karen Ray, [untitled book review], *New York Times*, September 16, 1984.

162 *"laid an egg":* Author interviews with Louis Auchincloss, November 19, 2008, March 24, 2009.

163 *"Just think, Nancy":* Author interviews with Nancy Tuckerman.

164 *he should write a book about Byrne:* Author interview with Eugene C. Kennedy, January 14, 2009.

164 *"all the innocence of a cobra":* Anne Chamberlin, "The Power and the Glory," *Washington Post*, December 3, 1982.

164 *whether he'd have to leave town:* John Blades, "Writing Around the Loop," *Washington Post*, September 5, 1982.

165 *"No woman would react":* Quoted in Donald Spoto, *Jacqueline Bouvier Kennedy Onassis: A Life* (New York: St. Martin's Press, 2000), p. 277.

166 *D'Orso remembers:* Author interview with Mike D'Orso, May 15, 2009.

167 *"a remarkable woman":* Carl Senna, [untitled book review], *New York Times*, November 13, 1988.

168 *"When are you going to come back?":* Author interviews with David Stenn, May 8, 2008, March 26, 2009.

168 *one of cinema's feminist pioneers:* Mick Lasalle, quoted in "Norma Shearer," en.wikipedia.org (accessed May 17, 2010).

170 *He remembered the table:* Author interview with Steve Wasserman, May 13, 2009.

170 *"her feats of personal courage":* Steve Wasserman, "How Remarkable . . . to Have Lived Such a Life," *Los Angeles Times*, May 23, 1994.

Chapter 7

171 *"wanted to convey her beliefs":* Grace Glueck, "The Nation; The World Through Her Eyes," *New York Times*, May 22, 1994; thanks to Peter Kruzan.

172 *"I preferred to be on the other side of the camera":* "The Kennedys: An American Family," DVD (New York: A&E Television Networks, 2009).

173 *"a dress of barbed wire":* JBK to Diana Vreeland, February 2, 1961, Diana Vreeland Papers, NYPL, Mss. Coll. 5980, Box 18, folder 18.27.

173 *ugly child:* Henry Allen, "Diana Vreeland's Vision of Allure," *Washington Post*, November 28, 1980.

174 *"San Simeon must have been":* Diana Vreeland, *D.V.*, eds. George Plimpton and Christopher Hemphill, with a new foreword by Mary Louise Wilson (1984; New York: DaCapo Press, 1997), p. 189.

174 *"paltry sum":* Diary of Hugo Vickers, November 8, 1990, courtesy of Hugo Vickers.

174 *fashion luminary André Leon Talley:* André Leon Talley, *A.L.T.: A Memoir* (New York: Villard, 2003), p. 186.

174 *"no pictures of poverty":* Diana Vreeland, *Allure* (Garden City, N.Y.: Doubleday, 1980), p. 19.

175 *"She shrank to half":* Author interview with William Ewing, April 19, 2010.

175 *"fashion is an authentic art form":* Eleanor Dwight, *Diana Vreeland* (New York: HarperCollins, 2002), p. 89.

175 *"exaggerate and embellish":* Ibid., p. 129.

175 *"They have their dreary vices":* Oscar Wilde, "The Decay of Lying," in *The Soul of Man Under Socialism and Selected Critical Prose,* ed. Linda Dowling (London: Penguin, 2001), p. 169; thanks to Maria Carrig.

176 *"an original"*: Lynn Langway with Lisa Whitman, "High Priestess of 'Allure,'" *Newsweek*, September 22, 1980, p. 51.

177 *"hands on her hips"*: Allen, "Diana Vreeland's Vision."

177 *"from the corner of her mouth"*: Ibid.

177 *"She sees like Diaghilev"*: Langway with Whitman, "High Priestess."

177 *"a contemporary theory of beauty"*: Diana Loercher, "Feminine Beauty: Defining an Enigma," *Christian Science Monitor*, January 13, 1981.

177 *"the revelation of character"*: Francesca Stanfill, "A Vision of Style," *New York Times Magazine*, September 14, 1980.

178 *Vickers discovered Jackie:* Author interviews with Hugo Vickers, January 24, 2008, January 29, 2009.

179 *"stuffy and pompous"*: Diary of Hugo Vickers, November 8, 1990, courtesy of Hugo Vickers.

180 *"ghost stories"*: Brian Dillon, "Deborah Turbeville," *Frieze Magazine*, no. 103 (November–December 2006), at frieze.com.

181 *"we wanted to match"*: "Editor's Note," in Deborah Turbeville, *Unseen Versailles* (Garden City, N.Y.: Doubleday, 1981), p. 18.

181 *"soft-focus style"*: Vicki Goldberg, "The Hidden Versailles," *New York Times Magazine*, September 20, 1981.

181 *"These worn-out girls at $1,000 a day"*: Stanfill, "A Vision of Style."

182 *"Jacqueline felt that she was a kind of Madame de Pompadour"*: K. L. Kelleher, *Jackie: Beyond the Myth of Camelot* ([Philadelphia]: Xlibris, 2000), p. 142.

182 *a great feeling for buildings:* Goldberg, "Hidden Versailles."

182 *"On the back stairs"*: Quoted in ibid.

183 *editorial colleague Jim Fitzgerald:* Author interview with Jim Fitzgerald, November 18, 2008.

185 *"Looking every lanky inch"*: Malcolm Jones, Jr., "Translating Ideas into Color," *Newsweek*, January 1, 1990, p. 59.

186 *"like bullies"*: Eudora Welty, "Introduction," *The Democratic Forest* (New York: Doubleday, 1989), p. 12.

187 *"She had a sense of humor"*: Author interview with Jim Fitzgerald, November 18, 2008.

187 *"The First Lady shot"*: Letitia Baldrige, *In the Kennedy Style: Magical Evenings in the Kennedy White House* (New York: Doubleday, 1998), p. 103.

188 *promised her the loan:* Margaret Leslie Davis, *"Mona Lisa" in Camelot* (New York: Da Capo, 2008).

188 *Angkor Wat:* Carl Sferrazza Anthony, *As We Remember Her: Jacqueline Kennedy Onassis in the Words of Her Family and Friends* (New York: HarperCollins, 1997), p. 232.

188 *French photojournalist Marc Riboud:* Author interview with Marc Riboud, June 11, 2009.

188 *strangely sexy:* Author interview with anonymous source.

189 *"first to believe that those misty snapshots"*: Marc Riboud, *Capital of Heaven* (New York: Doubleday, 1990), p. 4.

190 *"We remained long silent"*: François Cheng, "Introduction," in ibid., p. 18.

191 *"For Jackie": The Estate of Jacqueline Kennedy Onassis*, auction, April 23–26, 1996 (New York: Sotheby's, 1996), p. 523, lot 1032.

191 *Alberto Vitale:* Author interview with Alberto Vitale, April 20, 2009.

191 *David Morse, a prominent New Yorker:* David Streitfeld, "Book Report," *Washington Post*, February 16, 1992.

192 *She told her Doubleday colleague:* Author interview with Martha Levin, May 12, 2009.

193 *"No daughter of mine":* Naguib Mahfouz, *Palace Walk*, trans. William M. Hutchins and Olive E. Kenny (New York: Doubleday, 1990), p. 157.

193 *young photographer Robert Lyons:* Author interview with Robert Lyons, June 3, 2009.

194 *"Life's first love":* Naguib Mahfouz, "The Cradle," trans. Peter Theroux, in Robert Lyons, *Egyptian Time* (New York: Doubleday, 1992), p. 9.

194 *"Why don't I do a book?":* Author interview with Sidney Frissell Stafford, May 26, 2009.

195 *"When we give a dinner party":* Toni Frissell, *Photographs: 1933–1967* (New York: Doubleday/Library of Congress, 1994), p. xii.

195 *Tuskegee Airmen:* Martin W. Sandler, *America Through the Lens: Photographers Who Changed the Nation* (New York: Henry Holt, 2005), p. 149ff.

198 *"We had gone through":* Author interview with Peter Kruzan, May 13, 2009.

198 *"It was kind of uncomfortable":* Author interview with Sidney Frissell Stafford, May 26, 2009.

199 *"not your typical coffee-table photography book":* Marjorie Kaufman, "Photographer 'Plucked from Oblivion,'" *New York Times*, August 28, 1994.

200 *"I was sitting in a chair":* Pamela Fiori, "Jacqueline Bouvier Kennedy Onassis 1929–1994," *Town & Country*, July 1994, p. 48.

201 *"Now, scamper in":* Author interview with Bill Swan, October 6, 2008.

201 *"I don't think my mother":* Kaufman, "Photographer 'Plucked from Oblivion.'"

202 *"but works of art":* John Pope-Hennessy, *Learning to Look* (New York: Doubleday, 1991), p. 3.

202 *"surnaturel":* Author interview with Marc Riboud, June 11, 2009.

Chapter 8

203 *"It was eviscerated":* Author interviews with David Stenn, May 8, 2008, March 26, 2009.

205 *"one of the rankest places":* Gelsey Kirkland with Greg Lawrence, *Dancing on My Grave: An Autobiography* (Garden City, N.Y.: Doubleday, 1986), p. 272.

205 *She accused Lawrence of manipulating her:* Ibid., p. 276.

206 *men in Kirkland's life:* Ibid., p. 284.

206 *"I developed the habit":* Ibid., p. 50.

206 *she lost her confidence:* Ibid., p. 20.

207 *twisting the femur:* Ibid., p. 34.

207 *"was a mixture of convent and harem":* Ibid., p. 40.

207 *had silicone injected:* Ibid., p. 108.

207 *radio in her hotel room:* Ibid., pp. 89–90.

208 *"After groping with buttons":* Ibid., p. 127.

208 *"so intense and panicky":* Deborah Jowitt, "Through the Flames on Thin Soles," *New York Times*, October 19, 1986.

208 *"one of the saddest stories":* Jennifer Dunning, "Out of Pain," *New York Times*, November 15, 1986.

208 *"crudely sensationalist":* Alan M. Kriegsman, "Dance of Death; Gelsey Kirkland's Harrowing Story," *Washington Post*, December 14, 1986.

208 *"the Judy Garland of ballet":* Harris Green, "The Judy Garland of Ballet," *Ballet Review* 14 (Winter 1987): 77–80.

208 *caused trouble for her there:* Gelsey Kirkland and Greg Lawrence, in *A Tribute to Jacqueline Kennedy Onassis* (New York: Doubleday, 1995), p. 13.

209 *"She's a little nuts":* Author interview with Steve Rubin, November 17, 2008.

209 *"high-maintenance":* Author interviews with Bruce Tracy, September 15, 2008, March 23, 2009.

209 *"There wasn't much of a direct relationship there":* Author interview with Scott Moyers, November 18, 2008.

209 *book-signing tour:* Author interview with Herman Gollob, April 1, 2009.

210 *"diet food":* Marta Sgubin and Nancy Nicholas, *Cooking for Madam: Recipes and Reminiscences from the Home of Jacqueline Kennedy Onassis* (New York: Scribner, 1998), p. 22.

210 *"Edna! I've always been thin":* Edna O'Brien, contribution to "Jacqueline Kennedy Onassis: The White House Years," JFKL Forum, February 3, 2002.

210 *tear at her hands:* Author interviews with Karl Katz, March 25 and May 27, 2009.

210 *flossy underclothes:* See Sarah Bradford's interviews with Puffin D'Oench in *America's Queen: The Life of Jacqueline Kennedy Onassis* (New York: Penguin, 2001), p. 204.

211 *"I picked it up":* Author interview with Sarah Giles, January 30, 2009.

213 *hostile review:* Jules Feiffer, "Without Top Hat," *New York Times*, December 18, 1988.

214 *Astaire's shyness and his elegance:* Sarah Giles, *Fred Astaire: His Friends Talk* (New York: Doubleday, 1988), p. 44.

214 *"graceful movement of the horses":* Ibid., p. 180.

214 *"I first saw him":* Quoted in Julie Kavanagh, *Nureyev: The Life* (New York: Pantheon, 2007), p. 281: John Lombardi, "Nureyev's Fight Against Time," *New York Times*, December 13, 1981. See also Diane Solway, *Nureyev: His Life* (New York: Morrow, 1998), pp. 275, 454.

215 *dressing room backstage:* Carolyn Soutar, *The Real Nureyev: An Intimate Memoir of Ballet's Greatest Hero* (Edinburgh: Mainstream, 2004), p. 83; Solway, *Nureyev,* p. 338.

216 *dance critic Francis Mason:* Author interview with Francis Mason, November 18, 2008.

216 *Edward Kasinec:* Author interview with Edward Kasinec, May 13, 2009.

216 *house on St. Bart's:* Solway, *Nureyev,* p. 523.

216 *She asked Ted Kennedy:* Ibid., p. 483; Kavanagh, *Nureyev*, p. 618.

217 *history of homosexuality: The Estate of Jacqueline Kennedy Onassis*, auction, April 23–26, 1996 (New York: Sotheby's, 1996), p. 125, lot 182. A. L. Rowse, *Homosexuals in History: A Study of Ambivalence in Society, Literature and the Arts* (New York: Macmillan, 1977), was considered important enough by Sotheby's to be sold as a lot by itself, that is, separate from other books: "The rear fly-leaves and free endpaper are filled with brief autograph notes by Mrs. Onassis about various authors and artists discussed in the text. Many page corners in the volume have been turned down for quick reference." Sold for more than $5,000.

217 *"She gave some money":* Author interview with Francis Mason, November 18, 2008.

218 *"Martha gave him the world":* Felicia R. Lee, "Graham Legacy, On the Stage Again," *New York Times*, September 29, 2004. Agnes de Mille also takes a hostile view of Protas in her biography, *Martha: The Life and Work of Martha Graham* (New York: Random House, 1956, 1991), pp. 382–83ff.

218 *"I brought Jackie backstage":* Quoted in Gayle Feldman, "Martha Graham 'Revealing a Life' in a Fall Autobiography from Doubleday," *Publishers Weekly*, April 26, 1991, p. 38.

219 Blood Memory: For an explanation of this term, see Martha Graham, *Blood Memory* (New York: Doubleday, 1991), p. 9.

219 *"Always I have resisted":* Ibid., p. 17.

220 *"doom eager":* Ibid., p. 118.

220 *"'She never would have been":* Ibid., pp. 211–12.

221 *"I could eat you up":* Ibid., p. 184.

222 *"I went to Jackie":* Author interview with Francis Mason, November 18, 2008; Francis Mason, "Jacqueline Bouvier Kennedy Onassis, 1929–1994," *Ballet Review* 23 (Spring 1995): 4.

222 *"Blame it on me":* Ibid., p. 6.

223 *thirty-fifth anniversary:* Carolyn M. Mulac, [review of Jamison, *Dancing Spirit*], *Library Journal*, November 1, 1993, p. 95.

223 *Kaplan recalled an adventure:* Author interview with Howard Kaplan, April 1, 2009.

224 *"I just come from a legacy":* K. L. Kelleher, *Jackie: Beyond the Myth of Camelot* ([Philadelphia]: Xlibris, 2000), p. 124.

224 *"blood memories":* Judith Jamison with Howard Kaplan, *Dancing Spirit: An Autobiography* (New York: Doubleday, 1993), pp. 186, 72.

224 *"she was having trouble in those days":* Ibid., p. 171.

224 *a dancer is at her most moving:* Ibid., p. 208.

224 *"carelessly edited and produced":* Doris Hering, "Dancing Spirit," *Dance Magazine,* July 1994, p. 78.

224 *Ailey and other dancers, such as Nureyev, had died of AIDS:* Deirdre Kelly, "Can't Separate the Dancer from the Dance," *Toronto Star,* December 4, 1993.

225 *"Her physical manners":* Marie Brenner, *Great Dames: What I Learned from Older Women* (New York: Crown, 2000), p. 113.

226 *"The rules of classroom decorum":* Kirkland, *Dancing on My Grave,* p. 31.

Chapter 9

227 *"meretricious charm":* Marietta Tree, Oral History, second interview, JFKL, p. 24.

228 *"tomboy and dream princess":* C. David Heymann, *A Woman Named Jackie* (London: Heinemann, 1989), p. 30; Mary Van Rensselaer Thayer, *Jacqueline Bouvier Kennedy: A Warm, Personal Story of the First Lady Illustrated with Family Pictures* (Garden City, N.Y.: Doubleday, 1961), p. 36.

228 *"could strike with severity":* Hugh D. Auchincloss III, "Growing Up with Jackie, My Memories, 1941–1953," originally published in *Groton School Quarterly* 60, no. 2 (May 1998): 2; in Papers of Hugh D. Auchincloss III, JFKL.

229 *"undemocratic to wear a tiara":* JBK to Diana Vreeland, September 7, 1960, Vreeland Papers, NYPL, Mss. Coll. 5980, Box 18, Folder 18.27.

230 *"The Queen had her revenge":* Sarah Bradford, *America's Queen: The Life of Jacqueline Kennedy Onassis* (New York: Penguin, 2001), p. 269.

230 *what notable manners she had:* Author interviews with Philip Mansel, February 4, 2009, and Lady Antonia Fraser, February 7, 2009.

231 *"must be acceptable to me":* Jan Pottker, *Janet and Jackie: The Story of a Mother and Her Daughter, Jacqueline Kennedy Onassis* (New York: St. Martin's Press, 2001), pp. 238–39.

231 *curt with William Manchester:* William Manchester, *Controversy and Other Essays in Journalism, 1950–1975* (Boston: Little, Brown, 1976), pp. 39, 59.

232 *Sorensen wrote:* Ted Sorensen, *Counselor: A Life at the Edge of History* (New York: HarperCollins, 2008), pp. 248-49, 267.

232 *"How dare you use my name?":* Author interview with Tom Cahill, February 19, 2009.

232 *Jackie's assistant Judy Sandman:* Author interview with Herman Gollob, April 1, 2009.

234 *"vulgarly out of hand":* Oleg Cassini, *A Thousand Days of Magic: Dressing Jacqueline Kennedy for the White House* (New York: Rizzoli, 1995), pp. 29–30.

234 *"a gentleman never tells whom he's sleeping with":* Author interview with Howard Kaplan, April 1, 2009.

235 *"We were obsessed!"*: Author interview with Jane Hitchcock, February 23, 2008.

235 *box that had once belonged to Marie Antoinette: The Estate of Jacqueline Kennedy Onassis*, auction, April 23–26, 1996 (New York: Sotheby's, 1996), p. 200, lot 309.

236 *New York was more like the French court:* Jane Stanton Hitchcock, *Social Crimes* (New York: Hyperion, 2003), p. 244.

237 *commissioned work from Jacqueline Duhême:* Jacqueline Duhême, *Mrs. Kennedy Goes Abroad,* introduction by John Kenneth Galbraith, text by Vighuti Pavel (New York: Artisan/Callaway, 1998), p. 26.

237 *the French painter Marcel Vertès: Property from Kennedy Family Homes: Hyannis Port, Martha's Vineyard, New Jersey, New York, Virginia* (New York: Sotheby's, 2005), p. 340, lot 633. Sotheby's 1996 sale showed that Jackie also owned a volume by Francis Carco: *Vertès,* lot 699, p. 419.

238 *"What a cruel fate!"*: K. L. Kelleher, *Jackie: Beyond the Myth of Camelot* ([Philadelphia]: Xlibris, 2000), p. 62.

238 *something Josephine might have worn:* Cassini, *A Thousand Days of Magic,* p. 181.

238 *exhibition at the Costume Institute: The Age of Napoleon: Costume from Revolution to Empire, 1789–1815*, ed. Katell Le Bourhis (New York: Metropolitan Museum of Art/Abrams, 1989).

238 très Princesse de Réthy: Cassini, *A Thousand Days of Magic,* pp. 29–30.

241 "Amriki Rani": "Delhi Gives Rousing Welcome to the 'Amriki Rani,'" *Blitz Newsmagazine*, March 17, 1962; thanks to Eric Pullin.

241 *"a fraud"*: Galbraith, "Introduction," in Duhême, *Mrs. Kennedy Goes Abroad,* pp. 6–9.

241 *the arrival of Girlfriend:* John Kenneth Galbraith to Jim Wagner, June 1, 1998, Galbraith Papers, JFKL, Series 3, Box 211, file "Kennedy Library 1993–99."

241 *"Don't you think she's old enough?"*: Kelleher, *Jackie,* p. 172; Duhême, *Mrs. Kennedy Goes Abroad,* p. 7.

242 *among the most sensuous men she had ever met:* Lee Radziwill, afterword, in Jacqueline Bouvier and Lee Bouvier, *One Special Summer* (New York: Rizzoli, 2006).

243 *"original inspiration"*: Naveen Patnaik, *A Second Paradise: Indian Courtly Life, 1590–1947* (Garden City, N.Y.: Doubleday, 1985), p. 5.

243 *"she literally had two pairs"*: Dominick Dunne, "Forever Jackie," *Vanity Fair,* July 1994, p. 137.

243 *"pages of research material"*: Quoted in Edward Klein, "The Other Jackie O.," *Vanity Fair*, August 1989, p. 100.

244 *"caressed [it] lovingly"*: John F. Baker, "Editors at Work: Star Behind the Scenes," *Publishers Weekly*, April 19, 1993, p. 20.

244 *"erotic spells"*: Patnaik, *A Second Paradise,* p. 103.

244 *"The beautiful courtesan"*: Ibid., p. 132.

244 *"They're like the Folies Bergères"*: Author interviews with Edith Welch, April 19 and May 18, 2009.

245 *"he talked to me frequently"*: Author interview with Navina Haykel, May 14, 2009.

245 *She approached Mark Zebrowski*: Author interview with Robert Alderman (partner of Zebrowski), March 21, 2009; JKO to Zebrowski, partly quoted in William Dalrymple, "The Lost World," *Guardian*, December 8, 2007; unquoted portions of JKO to Mark Zebrowski courtesy of Robert Alderman and with thanks to William Dalrymple.

247 *"very much in Jackie's style"*: Author interview with Jann Wenner, April 8, 2009.

247 *live in a mud hut*: Author interview with Jonathan Cott, February 23, 2008.

247 *"I remember the ancient garden was here"*: John Anthony West, "She Had Her Life to Live Over," *New York Times*, July 26, 1987.

248 *she had seen the same paragraph*: Rosemary L. Bray, "Astral Trysts and Egyptology," *New York Times*, July 26, 1987.

248 *particularly proud of the Blue Room*: Carl Sferrazza Anthony, *As We Remember Her: Jacqueline Kennedy Onassis in the Words of Her Family and Friends* (New York: HarperCollins, 1997), p. 141.

248 *limited-edition book: Estate of Jacqueline Kennedy Onassis,* 1996, p. 526, lot 1056; see also André Malraux, "Préface," in André Parrot, *Sumer* (Paris: Librairie Gallimard, 1960), illustration XIV B, *"Fécondité."*

248 *"It's one of the most precious things"*: Author interview with Jonathan Cott, February 23, 2008.

249 *Noblecourt had also acted as their guide*: Kelleher, *Jackie,* p. 131.

249 *"Perhaps these passionate affairs"*: West, "Her Life to Live Over."

250 *"the glamour, the glory"*: Francis Mason, "Beautiful, Wild and of Another World," *New York Times*, September 8, 1991.

250 *"intrigued by the Russian Revolution"*: Author interview with Jane Hitchcock, February 23, 2008.

252 *During this visit with Hoving*: Thomas Hoving, *Making the Mummies Dance: Inside the Metropolitan Museum of Art* (New York: Simon & Schuster, 1993), pp. 390–95.

252 *"she was a tsarina"*: Author interview with Edvard Radzinsky, May 3, 2009; *A Tribute to Jacqueline Kennedy Onassis* (New York: Doubleday, 1995), pp. 23–25.

252 *DNA testing*: Thomas H. Maugh II, "DNA Testing Ends Mystery Surrounding Czar Nicholas II Children," *Los Angeles Times*, March 11, 2009; Mike Eckel, "DNA Tests May Confirm IDs of Russian Tsar's Children," *National Geographic News*, April 30, 2008.

252 *literary agent Lynn Franklin*: Author interviews with Lynn Franklin, February 20 and May 28, 2009.

253 *" 'No cuts' ": A Tribute to Jacqueline Kennedy Onassis,* p. 24.

253 *the translator, Marian Schwartz*: Author interview with Marian Schwartz, May 5, 2009.

254 *"They sipped unsweetened tea"*: Edvard Radzinsky, *The Last Tsar: The Life and Death of Nicholas II*, trans. Marian Schwartz (New York: Doubleday, 1992), p. 8.

254 *"the Archive of Blood"*: Ibid., p. 10.
254 *"was the woman who had had the same tragedy"*: Author interview with Edvard Radzinsky, May 3, 2009.
256 *He remembered meeting her*: Author interview with Ion Trewin, June 16, 2009.
257 *"our nightly conversations"*: Radzinsky, *Last Tsar*, pp. 8, 26.
257 *"I just couldn't look at that"*: Diane Solway, *Nureyev: His Life* (New York: Morrow, 1998), p. 456.
257 *jumped several feet out of her seat*: Hugo Vickers, *Cecil Beaton: The Authorized Biography* (London: Weidenfeld and Nicolson, 1985), p. 520.
257 *"It was a terrible mistake"*: Author interviews with Karl Katz, March 25 and May 27, 2009.
259 *purchased a harlequin design*: JBK to Cecil Beaton, June 3, 1968, Cecil Beaton Papers, St. John's College, Cambridge.

Chapter 10

261 *"the artistic sensibilities"*: JBK to Arthur M. Schlesinger, Jr., undated [1962?], Arthur M. Schlesinger, Jr., Papers, JFKL, Writings, *A Thousand Days*—Background Material, JBK correspondence 1961–65.
261 *"But I love her"*: Arthur M. Schlesinger, Jr., *Journals: 1952–2000*, eds. Andrew Schlesinger and Stephen Schlesinger (New York: Penguin, 2007), p. 155.
262 *"too much status and not enough quo"*: Kitty Kelley, *Jackie Oh!* (Secaucus, N.J.: Lyle Stuart, 1978), p. 49.
262 *drab and compassionate*: John Kenneth Galbraith to Edward M. Kennedy, June 9, 1971, Galbraith Papers, JFKL, Series 3, Box 211, correspondence files, "Edward Kennedy 1970–77."
263 *John Loring used to lunch*: Author interview with John Loring, May 14, 2009.
263 *"she liked him"*: Author interviews with Nancy Tuckerman.
263 Tiffany Table Settings: *Tiffany Table Settings* (New York: Crowell/Bramhall House, 1960).
265 *famous hostesses and decorators*: Marilyn Bethany, "Design: Tales of Tables at Tiffany's," *New York Times*, August 30, 1981.
265 *top sellers on Jackie's list*: Sales figures courtesy of Doubleday.
267 *"a unique social document"*: John Loring, *Tiffany Parties* (New York: Doubleday, 1989), p. 20.
269 *it is clear from the book's acknowledgments*: John Loring, *Tiffany Taste* (Garden City, N.Y.: Doubleday, 1986), p. 224.
269 *"Pan Am is on page 1"*: JKO to John Loring, undated, courtesy of John Loring.
269 *book party held at Le Cirque*: Carol Vogel, "Home Design: Travels with Tiffany," *New York Times*, August 31, 1986; "Toasting Tiffany," *W*, October 20–27, 1986.

271 *"Let's try to liberate the American girl"*: Edward Klein, *Just Jackie: Her Private Years* (New York: Ballantine, 1998), p. 322.

273 *"tacky"*: Hugh D. Auchincloss III, "Growing Up with Jackie, My Memories, 1941–1953," originally published in *Groton School Quarterly* 60, no. 2 (May 1998): 6; in Papers of Hugh D. Auchincloss III, JFKL.

273 *"nicest kindest most life enhancing person to work with"*: JKO to John Loring, undated, courtesy of John Loring.

273 *"floating palace Christina"*: Quoted in John Loring, *Tiffany Parties* (New York: Doubleday, 1989), p. 10.

273 *"the world of New York society women"*: Carl Sferrazza Anthony, *As We Remember Her: Jacqueline Kennedy Onassis in the Words of Her Family and Friends* (New York: HarperCollins, 1997), p. 261.

274 *Marble House in Newport:* Loring, *Tiffany Parties,* p. 19.

274 *"The Literary Lions Dinner"*: Ibid., p. 176.

275 *"Those people have really got my back up"*: Author interview with John Loring, May 14, 2010.

275 *"What it needs is a different beginning"*: JKO to John Loring, February 4, [1992?], courtesy of John Loring.

276 *"Don't worry"*: Author interview with Elizabeth Crook, May 22, 2009.

276 *"etiquette of consumerism"*: Holly Brubach, "Profiles: Giving Good Value," *The New Yorker*, August 10, 1992, p. 35.

277 *"I just loved your letter"*: JKO to John Loring, undated [1994?], courtesy of John Loring.

277 Magnificent Tiffany Silver: John Loring, *Magnificent Tiffany Silver* (New York: Abrams, 2001).

277 *"so like Mummy"*: Caroline Kennedy to John Loring, postmarked November 28, 2001, courtesy of John Loring.

278 *"I knew her when she was a girl"*: Author interviews with Louis Auchincloss, November 19, 2008, March 24, 2009.

279 *recent Irish immigrants:* Sarah Bradford, *America's Queen* (New York: Penguin, 2001), p. 7.

279 *"It reminds me of listening"*: Quoted in K. L. Kelleher, *Jackie: Beyond the Myth of Camelot* ([Philadelphia]: Xlibris, 2000), p. 196.

279 *"As it now stands"*: Ibid.

280 *"a small but very interesting document"*: John Kenneth Galbraith, quoted on back cover of Florence Adele Sloane, *Maverick in Mauve,* with commentary by Louis Auchincloss (Garden City, N.Y.: Doubleday, 1983).

282 *"like Alice in Wonderland"*: Author interview with Mary-Sargent d'Anglejan-Chatillon, November 17, 2009.

283 *"I dreamed of a lost and glamorous past"*: Preface to Mary-Sargent Ladd, *The Frenchwoman's Bedroom* (New York: Doubleday, 1991).

284 *an article in* House & Garden: See Jean Leymarie and Jacques Dirand, "Chalet Balthus," *House & Garden*, December 1987, pp. 108–10.

286 *"The association between"*: Christopher Hitchens, "Divine Decadence," in Graydon Carter and the Editors of *Vanity Fair, Vanity Fair: The Portraits, A Century of Iconic Images* (New York: Abrams, 2008), p. 7.

287 *"gracious living or fashion"*: Dorothy Schiff memorandum, October 14, 1964, Dorothy Schiff Papers, NYPL, Box 45, Onassis 1960–70 file.

Chapter 11

289 *she told the journalist Theodore White*: See Joyce Hoffmann, "How 'Camelot' Lived Happily Ever After: The Rainy Evening When Jackie Kennedy Invented Our National Myth," *Washington Post*, May 21, 1995 [photocopy], and White's notes in Theodore White Papers, JFKL, Series 11, Camelot Documents.

290 *"Do you remember those days"*: JBK to Harold Macmillan, January 31, 1964, Papers of Harold Macmillan, Lord Stockton, Bodleian Library, Oxford, MS. Macmillan deposit C. 553, folios 1–4.

291 *Any contribution of a thousand dollars or more*: Oral history of Pamela Turnure and Nancy Tuckerman, JFKL, p. 48.

292 *"She wanted me to delete"*: Ted Sorensen, *Counselor: A Life at the Edge of History* (New York: HarperCollins, 2008), 148–49.

293 *she stage-managed the dedication ceremony*: Arthur M. Schlesinger, Jr., *Journals: 1952–2000*, eds. Andrew Schlesinger and Stephen Schlesinger (New York: Penguin, 2007), p. 472.

293 *"there goes Lady Bird"*: Author interviews with Nancy Tuckerman.

293 *wrote a letter of protest*: Draft letter JBK to Richard Neustadt, head of Kennedy Institute of Politics, August 1968, marked "not sent," in Galbraith Papers, JFKL, Box 212, "Kennedy Library."

294 *She approached Eugene Kennedy*: Donald Spoto, *Jacqueline Bouvier Kennedy Onassis: A Life* (New York: St. Martin's Press, 2000), pp. 275–76; also author interview with Eugene C. Kennedy, January 14, 2009.

296 *Daley's election-night machinations*: Eugene C. Kennedy, *Himself! The Life and Times of Mayor Richard J. Daley* (New York: Viking, 1978), pp. 184–86.

296 *Her editorial colleague*: Lisa Drew e-mail to author, December 3, 2008.

297 *"chivalry is not dead"*: JKO to John Kenneth Galbraith, undated [1993?], Galbraith papers, JFKL, Box 430, file "Onassis, Jacqueline Kennedy, 1991–1994."

297 *"When it's past"*: Carl Sferrazza Anthony, *As We Remember Her: Jacqueline Kennedy Onassis in the Words of Her Family and Friends* (New York: HarperCollins, 1997), p. 334.

297 *When Cahill pursued her idea*: Author interview with Tom Cahill, February 19, 2009.

298 *social division between whites and Latinos*: Stewart L. Udall, *To the Inland Empire: Coronado and Our Spanish Legacy*, photographs by Jerry Jacka (Garden City, N.Y.: Doubleday, 1987), p. 8.

299 *"Let's do it"*: Author interviews with Stewart Udall, March 26 and April 28 and 29, 2009; author interviews with Jerry Jacka, May 23, June 7, and August 26, 2009; also L. Boyd Finch, *Legacies of Camelot: Stewart and Lee Udall, American Culture, and the Arts* (Norman: University of Oklahoma Press, 2008), p. 129.

300 *"absolutely knocked out":* JKO to Lee and Stewart Udall, June 11, 1984, Stewart L. Udall Papers, University of Arizona, Tucson.

302 *"more humane":* Stewart Udall, "A Concept Outline—The Coronado Book for Doubleday," April 23, 1984, in ibid.; also in JFKL, Miscellaneous Accessions, Stewart Udall, 2009–007.

302 *"I wish you would rewrite it":* JKO to Udall, February 11, 1986, in Udall Papers, University of Arizona.

303 *"Only the Most Important authors":* JKO to Udall, February 26, 1987, JFKL, Miscellaneous Accessions, Stewart Udall, 2009-007.

303 "I: poor as I am": Quoted in Udall, *Inland Empire*, p. 215.

303 *book party at Doubleday:* "Personalities," *Washington Post*, October 21, 1987.

303 *Spanish government honored Udall:* Udall to JKO, March 14, 1989, Udall Papers, University of Arizona.

304 *"Please tell Lloyd":* JKO to Udall, August 22, 1993, in ibid.

304 *"one of the most heart-stopping experiences":* JKO to Lee Udall, March 9, 1994, in ibid.

305 *" 'This is a great story' ":* Author interview with Mike D'Orso, May 15, 2009.

307 *"I am sure this novel":* John Seymour to JKO, March 26, 1992, and other thank-you notes for *The Cost of Courage,* Doubleday papers.

307 *crass remarks about money:* Carl Elliott, Sr., and Michael D'Orso, *The Cost of Courage: The Journey of an American Congressman* (New York: Doubleday, 1992), pp. 129–30, 136.

308 *his second son published:* Robert Francis Kennedy, *Judge Frank M. Johnson, Jr.: A Biography* (New York: Putnam, 1978).

308 *a third of his manuscript:* Frank M. Johnson, Jr., to JKO, November 26, 1979, Doubleday papers.

308 *how to get his book into print:* Frank M. Johnson, Jr., to JKO, September 13, 1989, Doubleday papers.

308 *Jack Bass, a newspaper journalist:* Author interview with Jack Bass, April 6, 2009; Jack Bass, *Unlikely Heroes: The Dramatic Story of the Southern Judges of the Fifth Circuit Who Translated the Supreme Court's Brown Decision into a Revolution for Equality* (New York: Simon & Schuster, 1981); Jack Bass, "Onassis the Editor: A Professional," *Atlanta Journal and Constitution,* May 23, 1994.

309 *"if he wanted forgiveness":* Quoted in Harris Wofford, "A Righteous Alabamian," *New York Times*, February 7, 1993.

309 *"gave true meaning to the word 'justice' ":* Ibid.

310 *afraid of offending bigoted southern white voters:* Jack Bass, *Taming the Storm: The Life and Times of Judge Frank M. Johnson, Jr., and the South's Fight over Civil Rights* (New York: Doubleday, 1993), pp. 169–72.

311 *he ended as an editor:* John Updike, "The Talk of the Town: Comment," *The New Yorker,* August 2, 1999, p. 23. For John Kennedy, Jr.'s interview with George Wallace, see the inaugural issue of *George,* October-November 1995.

311 *a job she was considering at the CIA:* Prix de Paris application file, *Vogue,* JFKL.

311 *friends with Leonid Tarassuk:* "Soviet Museum Said to Oust Aide Seeking Visa to Israel," *New York Times*, July 13, 1972; Lionel Leventhal, "And Another Thing: Working with the Soviets," *Logos* 13, no. 2 (2002): 117–18.

312 *the dancer Valery Panov:* "Soviet Withholds Exit Visa from Panov, Kirov Dancer," *New York Times*, September 11, 1973.

312 *Tarassuk's daughter, Irina:* Author interview with Irina Clow, October 12, 2009.

312 *died in an automobile accident:* "Obituaries: Museum Researcher and His Wife Die in a Crash in France," *New York Times*, September 16, 1990.

312 *Philip Myers was an attorney:* Philip Myers, "Squished," unpublished manuscript, courtesy of Philip Myers; author interviews with Philip Myers, September 1 and 3 and December 21, 2009.

313 *She also went to Mort Janklow:* Morton L. Janklow to JKO, February 4, 1992, courtesy of Philip Myers.

314 *hadn't been an accident:* Author interviews with Karl Katz, March 25 and May 27, 2009.

315 *intentional obfuscation:* Thomas Hoving, *Making the Mummies Dance: Inside the Metropolitan Museum of Art* (New York: Simon & Schuster, 1993), p. 393.

318 *Jackie had faxed her a three-page letter:* JKO to Irina Clow, undated [April 4, 1992?], courtesy of Philip Myers.

318 *jog around the reservoir in Central Park:* Nancy Tuckerman, "A Personal Reminiscence," *The Estate of Jacqueline Kennedy Onassis*, auction, April 23–26, 1996 (New York: Sotheby's, 1996), p. 26.

Chapter 12

319 *"The marriage of publishing and politics":* "The Kennedys: An American Family," DVD, 2 discs (New York: A & E Television Networks, 2009); "JFK Jr George Magazine," YouTube.com (accessed April 24, 2010).

320 *"starring in everybody's home movies":* The Eloquent Jacqueline Kennedy Onassis: A Portrait in Her Own Words*, ed. Bill Adler (New York: HarperCollins, 2004), p. 112.

320 *She had seen the programs:* John F. Baker, "Editors at Work: Star Behind the Scenes," *Publishers Weekly*, April 19, 1993, p. 21.

320 *Annie Leibovitz was one of the last:* "Assassination of John Lennon," en.wikipedia.org (accessed April 24, 2010).

322 *Doubleday bid $200,000:* Author interview with Sarah Lazin, February 19, 2009.

323 *a collaborative venture: The Ballad of John and Yoko,* ed. The Editors of *Rolling Stone*, Jonathan Cott, and Christine Doudna (Garden City, N.Y.: Doubleday/Rolling Stone, 1982).

323 *"We thought* John and Yoko": Author interview with Jann Wenner, April 8, 2009.

323 *Foundation on Violence in America: Ballad of John and Yoko,* p. 306.

324 *"knew each other very well":* Author interview with Scott Moyers, November 18, 2008.

324 *"It helps people who mourn":* JKO to Jann Wenner, October 29, 1981, courtesy of Jann Wenner; quoted in *Ballad of John and Yoko,* pp. xiii, 305.

325 *acknowledged the importance of Jackie's faith: Ballad of John and Yoko,* p. ix.

325 *"But that's the same":* Ibid., p. 188.

325 *"when he gets down":* Ibid., p. 191.

326 *"They both actually talked the same":* Author interview with Jann Wenner, April 8, 2009.

326 *"took one for the home team":* Author interview with Bill Barry, February 20, 2009.

326 *"classic celebrity project":* Hillel Italie, "Making of a Memoir: Jackson, Jackie and 'Moonwalk,'" news.yahoo.com, July 28, 2009 (accessed July 28, 2009).

327 *Areheart tells one version:* Shaye Areheart, "New Afterword to the 2009 Reissued Edition," *Moonwalk* (New York: Harmony, 2009), p. 291ff.

328 *"a huge nightmare":* Author interview with literary agent.

329 *"How the hell":* "The Michael Jackson–Jackie Kennedy Onassis Collaboration," *Inside Edition,* original airdate July 8, 2009, CBS Studios Inc., at insideedition.com (accessed May 4, 2010).

329 *superior star power:* Author interview with Jim Fitzgerald, November 18, 2008.

329 *"Do you think he likes girls?":* Jean-Claude Suarès and J. Spencer Beck, *Uncommon Grace: Reminiscences and Photographs of Jacqueline Bouvier Kennedy Onassis* (Charlottesville, Va.: Thomasson-Grant, 1994), p. 8.

329 *"Michael Jackson is driving me mad":* Author interview with Edward Kasinec, May 13, 2009.

329 *lengthy calls to her house:* Author interview with Bill Barry, February 20, 2009.

329 *old college-student trick:* Author interviews with Nancy Tuckerman.

329 *"all puff and no substance":* Suarès and Beck, *Uncommon Grace,* p. 8.

329 *"The book she thought she was getting":* Author interview with Jann Wenner, April 8, 2009.

330 *"But she didn't want to upset Michael":* Suarès and Beck, *Uncommon Grace,* pp. 8–9.

330 *"He was like a moving target":* Author interview with Alberto Vitale, April 20, 2009.

331 *"shun personal publicity":* Michael Jackson, *Moonwalk* (New York: Doubleday, 1988), pp. 270–72.

331 *"eccentric, contradictory and helplessly revealing":* Quoted in Italie, "Making of a Memoir."

332 *"Follow your bliss":* Jacket copy for Stephen Larsen and Robin Larsen,

A Fire in the Mind: The Life of Joseph Campbell (New York: Doubleday, 1991).

332 *a collaborative article:* Ibid., pp. 3, 502.

332 *repeatedly cited Jackie's performance:* Ibid., pp. 454, 494.

333 *The color insert included:* Joseph Campbell, *The Power of Myth,* with Bill Moyers, ed. Betty Sue Flowers (New York: Doubleday, 1988), pp. 3, 4, 6, 7.

334 *"There will be some people":* Author interviews with Judith Moyers, May 26 and June 11 and 12, 2009.

334 *"We're so engaged":* Campbell, *Power of Myth*, p. 6.

334 *"I imagine some kings":* Ibid., p. 12.

334 *"What happens when people":* Ibid., p. 15.

335 *"One of the great challenges":* Ibid., p. 66.

335 *"She drew a distinction":* Author interviews with David Stenn, May 8, 2008, March 26, 2009.

336 *"She would get on the elevator":* Author interview with Tom Cahill, February 19, 2009.

337 *"I don't know how anyone can withstand":* Author interview with Peter Kruzan, May 13, 2009.

337 *like Pete Hamill:* Pete Hamill, "A Private Life Defined by Wit, Compassion," *Newsday*, May 22, 1994.

339 *"breezy, mock-autocratic":* J. B. West, *Upstairs at the White House: My Life with the First Ladies,* with Mary Lynn Kotz (New York: Coward, McCann & Geoghegan, 1973), p. 282.

Epilogue

341 *"being pushed out of an airplane":* Sandy Rovner, " 'Healing' vs. 'Curing': A Look at New Age Treatments," *Washington Post*, February 16, 1993; see also Eric Cassell, "Healing and the Mind," *New York Times*, May 23, 1993.

342 *Judith Moyers and Bill Barry both recalled:* Author interviews with Judith Moyers, May 26 and June 11 and 12, 2009; author interview with Bill Barry, February 20, 2009.

342 *One of the artists they employed:* Lavina Melwani, "Art and Ayurveda Showcased in Book on Healing Plants of India," *Hinduism Today*, June 1994, online at hinduismtoday.com.

342 *"My, will you look":* Author interview with Sarah Giles, January 30, 2009.

343 *"Every once in a while you have to do something for the soul":* Author interview with Doubleday colleague, November 17, 2008.

343 *women of Montparnasse:* JKO to Ray Roberts, March 1, 1978, Ray Roberts Papers, Ransom Center, University of Texas, Austin.

343 *"I am drowning in it":* JKO to John Russell, "Sunday" [1983?], Ray Roberts Papers, Ransom Center, University of Texas, Austin.

344 *"Her time in France":* Author interview with Antony Beevor, January 29, 2008; see also, David Coward, "France at War with Herself," *New York Times*, September 11, 1994.

344 *"re-membering Osiris":* Jonathan Cott, *Isis and Osiris: Exploring the God-dess Myth* (New York: Doubleday, 1994), p. 16.

345 *She wanted to keep to the original plan:* Thomas Hoving, *Making the Mummies Dance: Inside the Metropolitan Museum of Art* (New York: Simon & Schuster, 1993), p. 60.

346 *"curious hybrid":* Jonathan Spence, "Then Came the Fall of Rome (Splat!)," *New York Times,* December 18, 1994.

347 *he condemned bad souls:* Larry Gonick, *The Cartoon History of the Universe 1: Volumes 1–7, From the Big Bang to Alexander the Great* (New York: Broadway Books, 2001), p. 142.

348 *"You two bad Catholic boys!":* Author interview with Tom Cahill, February 19, 2009.

348 *plucked a book from the Paris bestseller list:* Author interview with Marian Schwartz, May 5, 2009.

349 *"Did you pay, Jackie?":* Author interviews with Nancy Tuckerman.

349 *"All right, Jackie! Whaddya want?":* Author interview with Martha Levin, May 12, 2009.

350 *"Jacqueline Onassis in stocking feet":* Author interview with Paul Golob, April 1, 2009.

Selected Bibliography

Adler, Bill, ed. *The Eloquent Jacqueline Kennedy Onassis: A Portrait in Her Own Words*. New York: William Morrow, 2004.

Andersen, Christopher. *Jackie After Jack: Portrait of the Lady*. New York: William Morrow, 1998.

Anthony, Carl Sferrazza. *As We Remember Her: Jacqueline Kennedy Onassis in the Words of Her Family and Friends*. New York: HarperCollins, 1997.

————. "The Substance Behind the Style." *Town & Country*, July 1994.

Aronson, Steven M. L. "The Missing Years [interview with Peter Beard]." *Town & Country*, July 1994.

Baker, John F. "Editors at Work: Star Behind the Scenes [interview with Jacqueline Kennedy Onassis]." *Publishers Weekly*, April 19, 1993.

Baldrige, Letitia. "The Essence of Style." *Town & Country*, July 1994.

————. *In the Kennedy Style: Magical Evenings in the Kennedy White House*. With menus and recipes by White House chef René Verdon. New York: Doubleday, 1998.

Bowles, Hamish. *Jacqueline Kennedy: The White House Years, Selections from the John F. Kennedy Library and Museum*, with essays by Arthur M. Schlesinger Jr., Rachel Lambert Mellon, and Hamish Bowles. New York: Metropolitan Museum of Art; Boston: Bullfinch /Little, Brown, 2001.

Bradford, Sarah. *America's Queen: The Life of Jacqueline Kennedy Onassis*. New York: Penguin, 2001.

Bradlee, Benjamin C. *Conversations with Kennedy*. New York: Norton, 1975.

————. *A Good Life: Newspapering and Other Adventures*. New York: Simon & Schuster, 1995.

Brenner, Marie. *Great Dames: What I Learned from Older Women*. New York: Crown, 2000.

Brodie, Fawn McKay. *Thomas Jefferson: An Intimate History*. New York: Norton, 1974.

Brubach, Holly. "Profiles: Giving Good Value [profile of John Loring]." *The New Yorker*, August 10, 1992.

Campbell, Joseph. *Myths to Live By*. Foreword by Johnson E. Fairchild. New York: Viking, 1972.

Cannell, Michael. *I. M. Pei: Mandarin of Modernism*. New York: Carol Southern Books, 1995.

Cassini, Oleg. *A Thousand Days of Magic: Dressing Jacqueline Kennedy for the White House*. New York: Rizzoli, 1995.

Colette. *Short Novels of Colette*. Introduction by Glenway Wescott, translated by Janet Flanner. New York: Dial, 1951.

David, Lester. *Jacqueline Kennedy Onassis: A Portrait of Her Private Years*. New York: Birch Lane, 1994.

Davis, Margaret Leslie. *"Mona Lisa" in Camelot*. New York: Da Capo, 2008.

———. "The Two First Ladies." *Vanity Fair*, November 2008.

Dinesen, Isak. *Out of Africa*. Introduction by Bernardine Kielty. New York: Random House/Modern Library, 1952.

Duhême, Jacqueline. *Mrs. Kennedy Goes Abroad*. Introduction by John Kenneth Galbraith, text by Vibhuti Patel. New York: Artisan/Callaway, 1998.

Dunne, Dominick. "Forever Jackie." *Vanity Fair*, July 1994.

Dwight, Eleanor. *Diana Vreeland*. New York: HarperCollins, 2002.

Epstein, Jason. *Book Business: Publishing Past, Present, and Future*. New York: Norton, 2001.

Evans, Peter. *Ari: The Life and Times of Aristotle Socrates Onassis*. London: Jonathan Cape, 1986.

———. *Nemesis: The True Story of Aristotle Onassis, Jackie O, and the Love Triangle That Brought Down the Kennedys*. New York: Regan Books/HarperCollins, 2004.

Fenn, Dan H., Jr. "Launching the John F. Kennedy Library." *American Archivist* 42, no. 4 (October 1979): 429–42.

Finch, L. Boyd. *Legacies of Camelot: Stewart and Lee Udall, American Culture, and the Arts*. Foreword by Tom Udall. Norman: University of Oklahoma Press, 2008.

Fiori, Pamela. "Jacqueline Bouvier Kennedy Onassis 1929–1994." *Town & Country*, July 1994.

Gallagher, Mary Barelli. *My Life with Jacqueline Kennedy*. Edited by Frances Spatz Leighton. London: Michael Joseph, 1970.

Gordon-Reed, Annette. *Thomas Jefferson and Sally Hemings: An American Controversy*. Charlottesville: University Press of Virginia, 1997.

Heymann, C. David. *American Legacy: The Story of John and Caroline Kennedy*. New York: Atria, 2007.

———. *A Woman Named Jackie*. London: Heinemann, 1989.

Hitchcock, Jane Stanton. *Social Crimes*. New York: Hyperion, 2003.

Hitchens, Christopher. "Divine Decadence." In *Vanity Fair, The Portraits: A Century of Iconic Images*. Foreword by Graydon Carter. New York: Abrams, 2008.

Hoving, Thomas. *Making the Mummies Dance: Inside the Metropolitan Museum of Art*. New York: Simon & Schuster, 1993.

In Memoriam: Jacqueline Bouvier Kennedy Onassis 1929–1994. New York: Doubleday, 1995.

Kavanagh, Julie. *Nureyev: The Life*. New York: Pantheon, 2007.

Kelleher, K. L. *Jackie: Beyond the Myth of Camelot*. [Philadelphia]: Xlibris, 2000.

Kelley, Kitty. *Jackie Oh!* With photographs by Ron Galella. Secaucus, N.J.: Lyle Stuart, 1978.

Klein, Edward. *Just Jackie: Her Private Years*. New York: Ballantine, 1998.

———. "The Other Jackie O." *Vanity Fair*, August 1989.

Koestenbaum, Wayne. *Jackie Under My Skin: Interpreting an Icon*. New York: Farrar, Straus, and Giroux, 1998.

———. *The Queen's Throat: Opera, Homosexuality and the Mystery of Desire*. New York: Poseidon, 1993.

Lacey, Robert. *Grace*. New York: Putnam, 1994.

Leaming, Barbara. *Mrs. Kennedy: The Missing History of the Kennedy Years*. New York: Free Press, 2001.

Littell, Robert T. *The Men We Became: My Friendship with John F. Kennedy, Jr*. New York: St. Martin's Press, 2004.

Lydon, Kate. "Straight from the Heart: Gelsey Kirkland Looks Back . . . and Ahead." *Dance Magazine*, September 2005; dancemagazine.com.

Manchester, William. *Controversy and Other Essays in Journalism, 1950–1975*. Boston: Little, Brown, 1976.

Manguel, Alberto. *The Library at Night*. Toronto: Knopf Canada, 2006.

Martin, Richard, and Harold Koda. *Diana Vreeland: Immoderate Style*. New York: Metropolitan Museum of Art, 1993.

Moon, Vicky. *The Private Passion of Jackie Kennedy Onassis: Portrait of a Rider*. New York: Regan Books/HarperCollins, 2005.

Moutsatsos, Kiki Feroudi. *The Onassis Women: An Eyewitness Account*. New York: Putnam, 1998.

Noonan, William. *Forever Young: My Friendship with John F. Kennedy, Jr*. With Robert Huber. New York: Viking, 2006.

Pitts, David. *Jack and Lem: John F. Kennedy and Lem Billings: The Untold Story of an Extraordinary Friendship*. New York: Carroll & Graf, 2007.

Pottker, Jan. *Janet and Jackie: The Story of a Mother and Her Daughter, Jacqueline Kennedy Onassis*. New York: St. Martin's Press, 2001.

Rigg, Frank. "The John F. Kennedy Library." *Government Information Quarterly* 12, no. 1 (1995): 71–81.

Said, Edward W. "The Cruelty of Memory [review of novels by Naguib Mahfouz]." *New York Review of Books*, November 30, 2000.

Schiffrin, André. *The Business of Books: How International Conglomerates Took Over Publishing and Changed the Way We Read*. London: Verso, 2000.

Schlesinger, Arthur M., Jr. "Jacqueline Kennedy in the White House." In Hamish Bowles, *Jacqueline Kennedy: The White House Years, Selections from the John F. Kennedy Library and Museum*. New York: Metropolitan Museum of Art; Boston: Bullfinch/Little, Brown, 2001.
———. *Journals: 1952–2000*. Edited by Andrew Schlesinger and Stephen Schlesinger. New York: Penguin, 2007.

Sgubin, Marta, and Nancy Nicholas. *Cooking for Madam: Recipes and Reminiscences from the Home of Jacqueline Kennedy Onassis*. New York: Scribner, 1998.

Silverman, Al. *The Time of Their Lives: The Golden Age of Great American Book Publishers, Their Editors and Authors*. New York: Truman Talley, 2008.

Smith, Sally Bedell. *Grace and Power: The Private World of the Kennedy White House*. New York: Random House, 2004.

Sorensen, Ted. *Counselor: A Life at the Edge of History*. New York: HarperCollins, 2008.

Sotheby's. *The Estate of Jacqueline Kennedy Onassis*. Auction, April 23–26, 1996. New York: Sotheby's, 1996.
———. *Property from Kennedy Family Homes: Hyannis Port, Martha's Vineyard, New Jersey, New York, Virginia*. Auction, February 15–17, 2005. New York: Sotheby's, 2005.

Spoto, Donald. *Jacqueline Bouvier Kennedy Onassis: A Life*. New York: St. Martin's Press, 2000.

Steinem, Gloria. "On Jacqueline Kennedy Onassis." *Ms.*, March 1979.

Suarès, Jean-Claude, and J. Spencer Beck. *Uncommon Grace: Reminiscences and Photographs of Jacqueline Bouvier Kennedy Onassis*. Introduction by Nina Auchincloss Straight. Charlottesville, Va.: Thomasson-Grant, 1994.

Talley, André Leon. *A.L.T.: A Memoir*. New York: Villard, 2003.

Thayer, Mary Van Rensselaer. *Jacqueline Bouvier Kennedy: A Warm,*

Personal Story of the First Lady Illustrated with Family Pictures. Garden City, N.Y.: Doubleday, 1961.

A Tribute to Jacqueline Kennedy Onassis. New York: Doubleday, 1995.

Tuckerman, Nancy. "A Personal Reminiscence." In *The Estate of Jacqueline Kennedy Onassis*. Auction, April 23–26, 1996. New York: Sotheby's, 1996.

Van Gelder, Lawrence. *The Untold Story: Why the Kennedys Lost the Book Battle*. New York: Award Books, 1967.

Vreeland, Diana. *D.V.* Edited by George Plimpton and Christopher Hemphill, foreword by Mary Louise Wilson. New York: Da Capo, 1997.

Weller, Sheila. *Girls Like Us: Carole King, Joni Mitchell, Carly Simon— and the Journey of a Generation*. New York: Atria, 2008.

West, J. B. *Upstairs at the White House: My Life with the First Ladies*. With Mary Lynn Kotz. New York: Coward, McCann & Geoghegan, 1973.

Wiseman, Carter. *I. M. Pei: A Profile in American Architecture*. New York: Abrams, 2001.

Wright, Thomas. *Oscar's Books*. London: Chatto & Windus, 2008.

Illustration Credits

Grateful acknowledgment is given to the following
for permission to reprint:

Interior

i	Paul Adao/New York News Service ©
24	(left) © Aaron Shikler
24	(right) Bildarchiv Preussicher Kulturbesitz/Art Resource, NY
27	© Horst P. Horst/Art + Commerce
41	Courtesy of the International Center of Photography
58	Alfred Eisenstaedt /Getty Images
100	Courtesy of The Dallas Opera, 1958
105	Mario Suriani/Special to the *Dallas Morning News*
114	Wesley/Getty Images
115	© Aaron Shikler
176	Courtesy of the International Center of Photography
178	(right and left) © Hugo Vickers, 2010
184	Alan Ulmer Photographe © '90
190	Marc Riboud
196	(top and bottom) Toni Frissell/Sidney Frissell Stafford
197	Toni Frissell/Sidney Frissell Stafford
198	Toni Frissell/Sidney Frissell Stafford
199	Toni Frissell/ Sidney Frissell Stafford
215	Robin Platzer/Getty Images
221	© Barbara Morgan/The Barbara Morgan Archive
229	Popperfoto/Getty Images
239	(top) Erich Lessing/Art Resource, NY
239	(middle) Courtesy of Jacqueline Duhême
239	(bottom) Photograph Courtesy of Sotheby's, Inc. © 2005
242	Kulwant Roy collection © Aditya Arya Archive
249	Cover of *The Search for Omm Sety* by Jonathan Cott, Doubleday. Used by permission of The Knopf Doubleday Publishing Group, a division of Random House, Inc.
251	Estate of Thomas Hoving

258   Ron Frehm/Associated Press

264   John F. Kennedy Presidential Library and Museum, Boston

265   Photo by Marina Garnier

266   Courtesy of Tiffany & Co.

270   Courtesy of Le Cirque

272   Page from *The Tiffany Wedding* by John Loring, Doubleday. Used by permission of The Knopf Doubleday Publishing Group, a division of Random House, Inc.

274   Ralph Morse/Getty Images

283   *Mary-Sargent Abreu*, by Jean-Claude Fourneau, oil on canvas, 1961. Courtesy of J.C. Fourneau's family.

285   Image copyright © The Metropolitan Museum of Art/Art Resource, NY and © 2010 Artists Rights Society (ARS), New York/ADAGP, Paris

292   John F. Kennedy Presidential Library and Museum, Boston

301   (right, left, and bottom) Jerry Jacka Photography

306   (right and left) John F. Kennedy Presidential Library and Museum, Boston

317   Courtesy of Irina Tarassuk Clow

324   Photograph by Annie Leibovitz, © Jann S. Wenner

327   Cover of *Moonwalk* by Michael Jackson, Doubleday. Used by permission of The Knopf Doubleday Publishing Group, a division of Random House, Inc.

347   © Larry Gonick. All rights reserved

Insert

1   © Yousuf Karsh

2   (top and bottom) © Bettmann/CORBIS

3   Image, Library of Congress Duplication Service. *The Firebird and Other Russian Fairy Tales*; The Metropolitan Museum of Art, Gift of Thomas H. Guinzburg, The Viking Press, 1979 (1979.537.11)

4   (top) Art Rickerby/Getty Images; (bottom) Tom Wargacki/Getty Images

5   Courtesy of the International Center of Photography

6   Building Design

7   (top) Robin Platzer/Twin Images; (bottom) UPI Photo Files

8   Bert Stern/Courtesy Staley-Wise Gallery

9   (top) Cover of *How to Save Your Own Street* by Raquel Ramati, Dou-

bleday. Used by permission of The Knopf Doubleday Publishing Group, a division of Random House, Inc.; (bottom) Title page of *To the Inland Empire* by Stewart Udall and Jerry Jacka, Doubleday. Used by permission of The Knopf Doubleday Publishing Group, a division of Random House, Inc.

10   Robin Platzer/Getty Images

11   (top) Courtesy of Eugene C. Kennedy; (bottom) Robin Platzer/Getty Images

12   Peter Simon

13   © Chris Steele-Perkins/Magnum Photos

14   (top) Robin Platzer/Getty Images; (bottom) Cover of *Healing and the Mind* by Bill Moyers, Doubleday. Used by permission of The Knopf Doubleday Publishing Group, a division of Random House, Inc.

Index

(Italic page numbers indicate illustrations)